The British Library Studies in Medieval

Women and the Book

Dr Jane H.M. Taylor is a Fellow and Tutor in French at St Hilda's College, Oxford.

Dr Lesley Smith is a Fellow and Tutor in Politics at Harris Manchester College, Oxford. They are the co-editors of *Women, the Book and the Godly* (Woodbridge, 1995) and *Women, the Book and the Worldly* (Woodbridge, 1995).

WOMEN AND THE BOOK

Assessing the Visual Evidence

Edited by
Lesley Smith
and
Jane H.M. Taylor

THE BRITISH LIBRARY
AND
UNIVERSITY OF TORONTO PRESS
1996

© 1997 The Contributors

First published 1997 by
The British Library
Great Russell Street
London WC1B 3DG

British Library Cataloguing in Publication Data
A catalogue record for this title is available from the British Library

ISBN **0 7123 0498 3**

Published in North America in 1997 by
University of Toronto Press Incorporated
Toronto and Buffalo

Canadian Cataloguing in Publications Data
is available from University of Toronto Press

ISBN **0-8020-4216-3** (cloth)
ISBN **0-8020-8069-3** (paper)

Designed and Typeset by
A.H. Jolly (Editorial) Ltd.
Yelvertoft. Northants.

Printed in Great Britain

CONTENTS

List of Illustrations 7

Preface 11

Abbreviations 12

Introduction 13

Part One

Images of Women

CHAPTER 1
Scriba, Femina: Medieval Depictions of Women Writing
Lesley Smith, *Harris Manchester College, Oxford*
Page 21

CHAPTER 2
Æsop's Cock and Marie's Hen: Gendered Authorship in Text and Image
in Manuscripts of Marie de France's *Fables*
Sandra Hindman, *Northwestern University, Evanston*
Page 45

CHAPTER 3
Interpreting Images of Women with Books in Misericords
Wendy Armstead, *Aberystwyth*
Page 57

CHAPTER 4
Mirrors of a Collective Past: Reconsidering Images of Medieval Women
Martha W. Driver, *Pace University*
Page 75

Part Two

Images and Books by Women

CHAPTER 5
Two Twelfth-Century Women and their Books
Thérèse McGuire, *Chestnut Hill College, Philadelphia*
Page 97

CHAPTER 6
Worship of the Word: Some Gothic *Nonnenbücher* in their Devotional Context
Judith Oliver, *Colgate University*
Page 106

CHAPTER 7
A Library Collected by and for the Use of Nuns: St Catherine's Convent, Nuremberg
MARIE-LUISE EHRENSCHWENDTNER, *Munich*
Page 123

CHAPTER 8
Women's Work at the Benedictine Convent of Le Murate in Florence:
Suora Battista Carducci's Roman Missal of 1509
KATE LOWE, *Goldsmith's College, London*
Page 133

PART THREE

Images and Books for Women

CHAPTER 9
The Gospels of Margaret of Scotland and the Literacy of an Eleventh-Century Queen
RICHARD GAMESON, *University of Kent, Canterbury*
Page 149

CHAPTER 10
From Eve to Bathsheba and Beyond: Motherhood in the Queen Mary Psalter
ANNE RUDLOFF STANTON, *University of Missouri, Columbia*
Page 172

CHAPTER 11
Fables for the Court: Illustrations of Marie de France's *Fables* in Paris, BN, MS Arsenal 3142
SUSAN L. WARD, *Rhode Island School of Design*
Page 190

CHAPTER 12
The Wound in Christ's Side and the Instruments of the Passion:
Gendered Experience and Response
FLORA LEWIS, *Southampton*
Page 204

CHAPTER 13
The Cult of Angels in Late Fifteenth-Century England:
An Hours of the Guardian Angel presented to Queen Elizabeth Woodville
ANNE F. SUTTON, *Mercers' Company, London,* and LIVIA VISSER-FUCHS, *Baarn, The Netherlands*
Page 230

CHAPTER 14
Women and Books of Hours
SANDRA PENKETH, *Walker Art Gallery, Liverpool*
Page 266

Index of Manuscripts Cited   282

Index   284

LIST OF ILLUSTRATIONS

Colour Plates

1. Nativity. Codex Gisle. Osnabrück, Gymnasium Carolinum und Bischöfliches Generalvikariat, MS p.25.
2. Easter Day chants: Noli me tangere, Throne of Grace, Pelican in its piety, and Eagle. Codex Gisle. Osnabrück, Gymnasium Carolinum und Bischöfliches Generalvikariat, MS p.140.
3. Matthew. Oxford, Bodleian Library, Lat. liturg. fol. 5, fols 3v+4r.
4. John. Oxford, Bodleian Library, Lat. liturg. fol. 5, fols 30v–31r.
5. Abraham and Hagar. Queen Mary Psalter. London, BL, MS Royal 2 B. VII, fol. 9v.
6. Hannah presents Samuel. Queen Mary Psalter. London, BL, MS Royal 2 B. VII, fol. 48v.
7. Christ in the Temple. Queen Mary Psalter. London, BL, MS Royal 2 B. VII, fols 150v–51r.
8. *Image du Monde*, Paris, BN, MS fr. 547, fol. 140r.
9. Presentation miniature and first page of text of Hours of the Guardian Angel. The scroll between the donor and the queen reads 'with everlasting joy', more or less a quotation from the hymn to the Guardian Angel which is part of the text of the Hours. Liverpool, University Library, Liverpool Cathedral MS Radcliffe 6, fols 5v–6r.

Figures

1. Dame Justice and Christine welcome the Virgin Mary, Paris, BN, MS fr. 607, fol. 67v.
2. Rohan hours. Mary with Jesus cradled in book. Paris, BN, MS lat. 9471, fol. 133r.
3. Bridget of Sweden. New York, Pierpont Morgan, MS 498, fol. 8r.
4. Bridget of Sweden. Stockholm, Ericsberg Castle, MS *Liber celestis*, fol. 85v.
5. Bridget of Sweden. Stockholm, Ericsberg Castle, MS *Liber celestis*, fol. 94v.
6. The nun Guda. Frankfurt, MS Barth. 42, fol. 110v.
7. The nun Adelhaid. Munich, Bay. Staatsbibl., MS 23046, fol. 144r.
8. Baudonivia. Poitiers, Bib. mun., MS 250, fol. 21v.
9. Fortunatus. Poitiers, Bib. mun., MS 250, fol. 43v.
10. Anonymous woman writing. Cambridge, Trinity Coll., MS B. 11. 22, fol. 100r.
11. Cistercian nun. Aachen, private collection.
12. Amalthea. Paris, BN, MS fr. 12420, fol. 36r.
13. Io directing a scriptorium. Paris, BN, MS fr. 606, fol. 15r.
14. Above: Initial 'C' with clerk. Below: The rooster and the gem. Paris, BN, MS fr. 2173, fol. 58r.
15. Above: The woman and the hen. Below: Marie de France with open book. Paris, BN, MS fr. 2173, fol. 93r.
16. Marie de France reading. Paris, BN, MS Arsenal 3142, fol. 273r.
17. The lion and the peasant. Paris, BN, MS Arsenal 3142, fol. 262v.
18. The preacher and the wolf. Paris, BN, MS Arsenal 3142, fol. 269v.
19. Alart de Cambrai writing at his lectern. Paris, BN, MS Arsenal 3142, fol. 141r.

WOMEN AND THE BOOK

20   Aristotle with scroll. Paris, BN, MS Arsenal 3142, fol. 155v.
21   *Le Chevalier au lion*, Yvain on horseback. Paris, BN, MS fr. 1433, fol. 61r.
22   *Le Chevalier de la charrette*, Marie de Champagne. Paris, BN, MS fr. 794, fol. 27r.
23   Solomon with Dares and Dictys, Benoît de Saint-Maure, *Roman de Troie*. Paris, BN, MS fr. 1610, fol. 1r.
24   Supporter (detail). Ely Cathedral.
25   Centrepiece (detail). Ely Cathedral.
26   The demon Tutivillus. Ely Cathedral.
27   Woman with package of books. Winchester Cathedral.
28   St Mary. Whalley.
29   Woman reading a book. Parish Church of St Mary, Nantwich.
30   Seated woman. Worcester Cathedral.
31   Supporter (detail). Worcester Cathedral.
32   The Merode altarpiece. Robert Campin (Master of Flemalle). New York, Metropolitan Museum of Art, Cloisters Coll.
33   Princess Claude learning to read. Primer of Claude de France. Cambridge, Fitzwilliam Mus., MS 159, fol. 14r.
34   Untitled. Cindy Sherman.
35   Reader. Giovanni Boccaccio, *Le Livre des Cleres et Nobles Femmes*. Paris, BN, MS fr. 599, fol. 22r.
36   Dairy scene. *The Da Costa Hours*. New York, Pierpont Morgan, MS 399, fol. 5v.
37   Sweeping. Barthélémy l'Anglais, *Livre des Propriétés des Choses*. Paris, BN, MS fr. 9140, fol. 107r.
38   Woman in labour (detail). *Bible Historiale de Guiars des Moulins*. Geneva, Bibliothèque publique et universitaire, MS FR/T.1, fol. 22r.
39   Dame Nature at the forge. Guillaume de Lorris, Jean de Meun, *Roman de la Rose*. Paris, Bibliothèque Sainte-Geneviève, MS 1126, fol. 115r.
40   Miner. Montferrant, *Les Douze Dames de Rhetorique*. Paris, BN, MS fr. 1174, fol. 29r.
41   Women Builders. *Roman des Girart von Roussillon*. Vienna, ON, MS 2549, fol. 167v.
42   Bath-house. Valerius Maximus, *Des Faits des Romains*. Paris, BN, MS Arsenal 5196, fol. 372r.
43   Bath maidens washing hair. Wenceslaus Bible. Vienna, ON, MS 2759, fol. 174v.
44   St Barbara. Breviary, Roman office for Franciscan use. New York, Pierpont Morgan, MS 52, fol. 558v.
45   Madonna and child with saints. Robert Campin (Master of Flemalle) and assistant. Washington, DC, Nat. Gallery of Art, S. Kress Coll.
46   Deathbed scene. *The Hours of Catherine of Cleves*, Use of the Augustinian Canons. New York, Pierpont Morgan, MS 917, fol. 180r.
47   Anne of Brittany with her book. Jean Bourdichon, the *Grandes Heures*, Use of Rome, France, Tours or Paris, Paris, BN, MS lat.9474, fol. 3r.
48   The money-lender and his wife. Quentin Massys. Paris, Louvre Mus.
49   God the Father capturing Leviathan. Herrad of Landsberg, *Hortus deliciarum*, fol. 84r.
50   The woman clothed with the sun. Herrad of Landsberg, *Hortus deliciarum*, fol. 261v.
51   Synagogue. Hildegard of Bingen. *Scivias* (Rupertsberg), i, vision 5.
52   Tree of Jesse and Annunciation with Old Testament prophets in roundels. Liège Psalter. London, BL Add. MS 21114, fol. 8v.
53   Easter Antiphon. Nazareth Antiphonal. Bornem, Abdij Sint Bernardus, MS 1, fol. 46v.

LIST OF ILLUSTRATIONS

54 Coronation of the Virgin. Rhenish Psalter. London, BL, Add. MS 60629, fol. 56v.

55 Adoration of the Magi. Antiphonal of Loppa de Speculo. Stockholm, KB, MS A. 172, fol. 84v.

56 Memorial inscription. Codex Gisle. Osnabrück, Gymnasium Carolinum und Bischöfliches Generalvikariat, MS p.004.

57 Resurrection. Codex Gisle. Osnabrück, Gymnasium Carolinum und Bischöfliches Generalvikariat, MS p.139.

58 Resurrection with kneeling nuns. Westphalian Homilary. Baltimore, Walters Art Gallery, MS 148, fol. 2v.

59 Virgin and Child. Westphalian Homilary. Baltimore, Walters Art Gallery, MS 148, fol. 23r.

60 Psalm 2 with Christ Child. Rhenish Psalter. London, BL, Add. MS 60629, fol. 7v.

61 Virgin kneels before Christ Child. Codex Gisle. Osnabrück, Gymnasium Carolinum und Bischöfliches Generalvikariat, MS p.19.

62 Nativity. Embroidery from Wienhausen.

63 The end of the Office of the Feast of SS. Fabian and Sebastian (20 Jan.), and the beginning of the Office of the Feast of St Agnes (21 Jan.). Roman missal of 1509 written by Suora Battista Carducci and illuminated by Attavante Attavanti. Paris, BN, MS lat. 17323, fol. 250r.

64 Lesson for the Office of the Feast of the Birth of the Virgin (8 Sept.). Paris, BN, MS lat. 17323, fol. 385r.

65 Part of the blessing of candles at the Easter Vigil (Holy Saturday). Paris, BN, MS lat. 17323, fol. 147r.

66 Part of the Order of Mass for the first Sunday of Advent, with the arms of Pope Leo X. Paris, BN, MS lat. 17323, fol. 13r.

67 Full-page illumination of the Crucifixion. Paris, BN, MS lat. 17323, fol. 177v.

68 Part of the canon of the Mass, with an illuminated initial of Christ and the instruments of the Passion. Paris, BN, MS lat. 17323, fol. 178r.

69 Verse inscription. Oxford, Bodleian Library, Lat. liturg. fol. 5, fol.2r.

70 Mark. Oxford, Bodleian Library, Lat. liturg. fol. 5, fols 13v–14r.

71 Luke. Oxford, Bodleian Library, Lat. liturg. fol. 5, fols 21v–22r.

72 Pericopes from Luke. Oxford, Bodleian Library, Lat. liturg. fol. 5, fol. 24r.

73 Expulsion from Paradise. Queen Mary Psalter. London, BL, MS Royal 2 B. VII, fol. 4r.

74 Abraham and Sarah. Queen Mary Psalter. London, BL, MS Royal 2 B. VII, fol. 8v.

75 Deception of Isaac. Queen Mary Psalter. London, BL, MS Royal 2 B. VII, fol. 13v.

76 Jacob, Joseph, and Rachel. Queen Mary Psalter. London, BL, MS Royal 2 B. VII, fol. 20r.

77 Birth of Samuel. Queen Mary Psalter. London, BL, MS Royal 2 B. VII, fol. 48r.

78 Bathsheba and David. Queen Mary Psalter. London, BL, MS Royal 2 B. VII, fol. 57r.

79 Bathsheba reminds David of Solomon. Queen Mary Psalter. London, BL, MS Royal 2 B. VII, fol. 63v.

80 Genealogical charts. Queen Mary Psalter. London, BL, MS Royal 2 B. VI, fols 67v–68r.

81 Birth of Nicholas of Myra. Queen Mary Psalter. London, BL, MS Royal 2 B. VII, fol. 314v.

82 Birth of Thomas Becket. Queen Mary Psalter. London, BL, MS Royal 2 B. VII, fol. 290r.

83 Marie de France's *Fables*, frontispiece. Paris, BN, MS Arsenal 3142, fol. 256r.

84 Letter C (detail). Paris, BN, MS Arsenal 3142, fol. 266v.

85 Marginalia showing a Battle of Rabbits (detail). Cambridge, Fitzwilliam Mus., MS 298, fol. 41r.

86 Marie de France (detail). Paris, BN, MS Arsenal 3142, fol. 256r.
87 Marie de France (detail). Paris, BN, MS Arsenal 3142, fol. 273r.
88 Frontispiece. Paris, BN, MS Arsenal 3142, fol. 1r.
89 Villers Miscellany. Brussels, Bib. Roy., MS 4459–70, fol. 150r.
90 Psalter of Bonne of Luxembourg. New York, Cloisters Museum, MS 69.86, fol. 331r.
91 Psalter of Bonne of Luxembourg. New York, Cloisters Museum, MS 69, 86, fol. 329r.
92 Passional of Abbess Kunigunde. Prague, National and University Library, MS XIV A 17, fol. 7v.
93 Rothschild Canticles, New Haven, Beinecke Rare Book and Manuscript Library, MS 404, fols 18v–19r.
94 The ladder of virtues. Herrad of Hohenbourg. *Hortus Deliciarum*, fol. 215v.
95 *Speculum humanae salvationis*. Chicago, Newberry Library, MS 40, fol. 30v.
96 Dedicatory poem to her 'lady sovereyn princes'. The beginning and end of the acrostic ELISABETH are clearly marked by the additional decoration of the first and last letters (all 5 pages of the text are shown). Liverpool, University Library, Liverpool Cathedral MS Radcliffe 6, fols 2r–4r.
97 Mary of Burgundy reading her book of hours. Hours of Mary of Burgundy. Vienna, ON, MS 1857, fol. 14v.
98 Mary Magdalene reading. Rogier van der Weyden. London, National Gallery, 654.
99 a and b: A female worshipper is encouraged in her devotions by the Angel Gabriel; opposite, the Annunciation. Buves Hours. Baltimore, Walters Art Gallery, MS 267, fols 13v, 14r.
100 Virgin and Child and female worshipper before vernacular prayer. Book of Hours. Oxford, Bodleian Library, MS Buchanan e 3. fol. 74r.
101 Annunciation. In the borders are two symbolic representations of lust; top left 2 monkeys display a man's genitals, lower a siren admires herself in a mirror. Book of Hours. Rouen. Liverpool, Walker Art Gallery, MS Mayer 12024, p.151.
102 St Agatha. Book of Hours. Blackburn, Museum and Art Gallery, Hart Coll. MS 20844, fol. 202v.
103 Crucifixion. In the border a dog captures a stag. Hours of Anne of Bohemia. Oxford, Bodleian Library, MS Lat. liturg. fol. 3, fol. 71r.

PREFACE

THE PAPERS published in this volume consist in part of papers read at the St Hilda's Conference on Women and the Book in the Middle Ages, held in 1993, and in part of papers independently commissioned. The book has been so long in the making that our first debt is to the contributors, both for their papers – original in both senses of the word – and for their forbearance and exemplary patience: we hope that they will agree that the wait has been worth it. We should thank David Way of the British Library, and the readers – Janet Backhouse, Scott McKendrick, and Andrew Prescott – whose comments have served to sharpen arguments and define analyses; similarly, we thank the anonymous reviewers for the University of Toronto Press. The Oxford Modern Languages Faculty has provided help throughout. Finally, once again, we owe a debt of gratitude to Christina Malkowski Zaba, who has followed the *Women and the Book* project from the outset, meticulously proof-read all the contributions, and ensured that they are, as far as is humanly possible, error free.

Medieval scribes occasionally allowed themselves the luxury of personalizing a dry colophon or *explicit* with phrases like: 'Thank God that's finished, give me a glass of wine'.[1] We have lived with this project – cheerfully, irritatedly, excitedly – for some three years: a glass of wine, a celebration is due, we feel, to all of us, contributors, editors, publishers, proof-readers ... and even readers!

Jane H.M. Taylor
Lesley Smith

---

1 *See* Marc Drogin, *Anathema!* (Totowa, NJ, 1983).

ABBREVIATIONS

Paris, BN	*Paris, Bibliothèque Nationale*
Paris, BA	*Paris, Bibliothèque de l'Arsenal*
Lucca, Bib. Stat.	*Lucca, Biblioteca Statale*
Palermo, Bib. Naz.	*Palermo, Biblioteca Nazionale*
NY, Pierpont Morgan	*New York, Pierpont Morgan Library*
London, BL	*London, British Library*
Brussels, Bib. Roy.	*Brussels, Bibliothèque Royale*
Munich, Bay. Staatsbibl.	*Munich, Bayerische Staatsbibliothek*
Poitiers, Bib. mun.	*Poitiers, Bibliothèque municipale*
Vienna, ON	*Vienna, Österreichische Nationalbibliothek*
Stockholm, KB	*Stockholm, Kungliga Bibliotekt*
EETS	*Early English Text Society* (o.s. = original series)
VCH	*Victoria County History*
RS	*Rolls Series*
PMLA	*Publications of the Modern Languages Association of America*

INTRODUCTION

NE OF THE magnificently illuminated manuscripts of Christine de Pizan's *Cité des Dames*, Paris, Bibliothèque Nationale, français 607, introduces the third and final book of the treatise with an interesting miniature (fol. 67v; FIG. 1). In the background, its towers a gleaming and pristine white, is the city completed. In the foreground, in the great gateway of the city, stand Dame Justice and Christine herself with the ranks of famous women behind them, welcoming the Virgin Mary and the company of women saints and martyrs into the city that has been built for them. And in her left hand, the Virgin Mary carries a book.

Now, there is nothing particularly unusual in this: as Lesley Smith shows in her essay in this volume, the Virgin Mary is frequently shown holding or reading a book. But what, in Christine's miniature, does the book signify? Nothing in Christine's allegory calls for the Virgin Mary to carry a book – Christine's portrait is a moral, not a physical one. No doubt commentators assume the unobtrusive little volume to be a Bible, metonymically encapsulating the role Christine gives to the Virgin as Vessel of the Trinity:

FIG. 1 Dame Justice and Christine welcome the Virgin Mary, Paris, BN, fr. 607, fol. 67v.

> Heavenly Queen, Temple of God, Cell and Cloister of the Holy Spirit, Vessel of the Trinity, Joy of the Angels, Star and Guide to those who have gone astray, Hope of true believers.[1]

Exploiting the multiple meanings of the verb – in French as in English – Mary, uncomplicatedly, bears the Book as She bore the Saviour.

But can we be confident in interpreting the image so simply – so glibly? Christine's *Livre de la Cité des Dames* is, after all, a book about the reading of books and the making of

---

[1] 'Royne celeste, temple de Dieu, celle et cloistre du Saint Esperit, habitacle de la Trinité, joye des anges, estoille et radrece des desvoyez, esperance des vrays creans.' We use M.Curnow's edition of the *Cité*. Ph.D. (Vanderbilt Univ., 1975), p.976. The translation is that of E. J. Richards (London, 1982), p.218 (slightly emended).

books.² It opens with a generic reading scene: Christine sitting alone in her study surrounded by books, idly picking up a viciously misogynist treatise by Matheolus and cast into a despair from which she is rescued by the three Virtues, Raison, Droitture and Justice.³ Christine, they say, is to write: with 'the trowel of her pen' (*la truelle de [sa] plume*), she is to 'build' a textual city of women on the Field of Letters, a city of which every stone, every brick, every tower is an exemplary remarkable woman – and thus manuscript 607, which the reader is holding in his or her hand, *is* the City of Ladies in a material, a textual, and a metaphorical sense. Might the closed book which Mary carries as she enters the city, therefore – by a process of iconic *mise en abyme* – be, metaphorically speaking, the city itself, Christine's completed book? Or might the closedness of the book signify rather the completion of Christine's designated task: that her textual enterprise, the vanquishing of the ranks of misogynist writers, Matheolus, Jean de Meun, the philosophers and poets and orators, is complete, and, as it were, the book may be closed on them?

But even this does not exhaust the possibilities. Christine, of course, was profoundly involved in the preparation of presentation copies of her own work.⁴ It is probable, indeed, that MS fr. 607 is one of them:⁵ the fifth and final part of what is known as the Duke's Manuscript, that is, a copy planned for the Duc d'Orléans and presented, after his assassination in 1407, to the Duc de Berry. Christine – it is reasonable to suggest – may have played a considerable part in the planning and execution of the miniatures.⁶ It can be no more than hypothesis, of course – *did* Christine indeed suggest the motif?⁷ – but is the Virgin's book this very volume, français 607, encapsulated in these most prestigious of hands? Is the very

---

2 On Christine's textuality, *see* M.Quilligan, 'Allegory and the Textual Body: Female Authority in Christine de Pizan's *Livre de la Cité des Dames*', *Romanic Review*, 79 (1988), pp.222–48.

3 *See* Curnow, *Cité des Dames*, pp.616–19, and transl. Richards, pp.3–6.

4 On Christine's scribal activities, *see* particularly G.Ouy and C.M.Reno, 'Identification des autographes de Christine de Pizan', *Scriptorium*, 34 (1980), pp.221–238, and on Christine's role as 'publisher' of collected editions of her own works, *see* most recently and most fully J.C.Laidlaw, 'Christine de Pizan: A Publisher's Progress', *Modern Language Review*, 82 (1987), pp.35–75, and S.L.Hindman, *Christine de Pizan's 'Epistre Othéa': Painting and Politics at the Court of Charles VI* (Toronto, 1986).

5 Curnow, *Cité*, pp.353–71, 590–2, would certainly argue that this is so, and cf. Laidlaw, 'Christine de Pizan', p.58–59, in agreement.

6 It is true, as S.Hindman points out, that exaggerated claims may have been made for Christine's supervision of the miniatures in her manuscripts ('*Epistre Othéa*', pp.61–63). However, as she also points out, the absence of direct evidence for Christine as deviser of programmes of miniatures does not invalidate the claim that she was active in such matters: it was not unusual – on the contrary – for writers or patrons to produce such programmes.

7 It is interesting that in another manuscript, London, British Library, MS Harley 4431, which is universally recognized as prepared under Christine's supervision (the Queen's Manuscript, prepared for Isabeau de Bavière in 1410/11), the equivalent miniature on fol. 361r shows the Virgin Mary and another, unidentifiable, woman saint carrying a book; is it legitimate to wonder if the latter is Saint Christine, the only one of Christine's saints for whom Christine mentions an individual Vita (*see* Curnow, *Cité*, p.1009: 'Et un sien parent que elle avoit converti ensevli le saint corps et escript sa glorieuse legende.' 'One of her relatives whom she had converted buried her body and wrote out her glorious legend'. transl. Richards, p.240). On the Queen's MS, *see* S.L.Hindman, 'The Composition of the Manuscript of Christine de Pizan's Collected Works in the British Library: A Reassessment', *British Library Journal*, 9 (1983), pp.93–123.

INTRODUCTION

material object of parchment and leather that we read from mirrored in this last, triumphant allegorical moment? And a possibility more audacious still. Maureen Quilligan has argued,[8] convincingly, that there are typological similarities between the appearance of the three Virtues to Christine, and the Annunciation. The sudden ray of sunlight which falls on Christine's lap, the very phrases with which she is called to a great allegorical destiny, are irresistably reminiscent of the phraseologies of the Gospels. Could the book in the Virgin Mary's hand signify, then, a *shared* enterprise? Is Christine's gestation and bearing of the book, which signifies the building of the city, equated at some metaphorical level with that greater gestation which brought forth the Saviour?[9]

The fact that we are unable to anchor the Virgin Mary and Her book to one simple signification, the fact that all or any of the readings that we propose could be substantiated, explains in part the genesis of this volume of essays. At its core are papers read at a conference on *Women and the Book in the Middle Ages* held at St Hilda's College, Oxford, in the summer of 1993,[10] to which we have added certain invited contributions: all the essays testify to just such a luxuriant – and contentious – iconographic universe. The written texts of the Middle Ages have long been debated and discussed, and have called forth many variant and contradictory opinions; they nevertheless possess a long history of interpretation and scholarship which agrees on the need for exegesis and on the fundamentally worthwhile and fruitful outcome of close study. We agree that medieval written texts can tell us something valuable about the culture in which they were produced. It may well be that we are simply habituated to thinking this way about written works, but the fact remains that we consider written texts to be both helpful and important in our desire to make sense of the medieval past.

With pictures, this statement cannot be made so flatly; their virtues are much less clear, and the lines of interpretation much less clearly drawn. Until relatively recently, the general, if tacit, understanding was that images were univocal and, as it were, photographic in intent. But there is a new scepticism about such an interpretation, one which is reflected in the papers collected here. Whereas semioticians long ago – as far back as Saint Augustine – realized that the value of the word as sign was ambivalent and ambiguous, the visual image as sign has only latterly been subjected to the same exegetical processes. Using pictures as historical evidence is far more likely to raise heated debate. The problem is not so much that images should be considered at all; that at least is conceded. What remains problematic, however, is just *how* visual images can be understood and explained, and to what extent they can be relied upon, rather than simply used as prompts, to shed further light on the complexity of the medieval mind.

8 *The Allegory of Authority: Christine de Pizan's Cité des Dames* (Ithaca/London, 1991), pp.54–55.

9 Another manuscript, Paris, Bibliothèque Nationale, MS français 1171, fol. 95v – not this time prepared under Christine's supervision – substitutes a child for the book: *see* Fig. 8 in Quilligan, 'Allegory and the Textual Body', p.246, and briefly p.235.

10 *See* the two volumes of proceedings previously edited by L.Smith and J.H.M.Taylor: *Women, the Book and the Holy* and *Women, the Book and the Worldly* (Woodbridge, 1995).

15

Historians know that images, as much as sentences and paragraphs, are texts to be read. And just as sentences are not always (if indeed they can ever be said to be so) straightforward accounts of an object or person or event which would be identically worded or put together by any equivalent writer, but which take a specific viewpoint or focus in order to construct a particular literary picture of the world, so an image can never be a 'simple record' of the artist's world. We are too knowing ever to use a term like *cinéma vérité* without an edge of irony or self-regard. Images, too, are constructions, whether conscious or not, of the artists who made them; and in turn they may be construct*ors* of the worlds they profess to record.

This dual role of image as construction and as constructor must be particularly borne in mind when the images are of a largely disempowered group such as medieval women. In such cases, crucial questions spring instantly to mind: were the images made *by* men or by women? Were the images made *for* men or for women? were the images *about* men or about women? It is not enough to look at an image of, say, a woman reading a book, without knowing who made the image, and why, and for whom, and for what reason. A book of hours containing a picture of a woman reading a book of hours when commissioned by a woman for herself might well be a self-designation of piety and goodness. The same image commissioned by a man for his daughter might rather express his desire that she conform to a pious model, than any aspiration of her own. A picture of a woman as a miner, made by a woman, might be expressive of woman's ability to undertake any task; when made by a man it might be a satirical joke about women in unsuitable positions; or, in both cases, it might be an allegory of mining the jewels of religious knowledge; or it might be a simple representation of women mining (both plausible as Martha Driver argues in her essay here).

Another problem arises, of course, from the very choice and nature of images appearing in books owned by or designed for women. Anne Rudloff Stanton, in the present volume, detects in the Queen Mary Psalter a choice and an orientation of the images which suggest a particular emphasis on female authority and in particular an interest in the strong mother; is this additional evidence for its having been prepared for Isabella, queen of Edward II? Conversely, how far are we entitled to draw conclusions about an individual woman's literacy and reading-patterns in general, as Richard Gameson finds he can from the design of a particular volume incontrovertibly owned by a woman? And how about the writing woman – a woman like Marie de France? Sandra Hindman finds in the illustrations of her *Fables* confirmation that the workshops which designed and the artists who illuminated her manuscripts understood and exploited Marie's own sense of literary mission: how do we interpret the juxtaposition – the equation – of the woman writer and the clerkly male authority, Æsop?

In all cases, the image itself cannot resolve the controversy. Visual evidence must be used along with the texts it supports or illustrates, as well as with the fruits of other disciplines, economic, political, or theological. The essays by Lowe, McGuire, Smith, and Sutton and Visser-Fuchs are examples of such scholarship. Equally illuminating may be the mobilization of challenging new approaches: Flora Lewis's careful collation of matters of gender

THE PLATES

PLATE 1 Nativity. Codex Gisle. Osnabrück,
Gymnasium Carolinum und Bischöfliches Generalvikariat,
MS p.25.

PLATE 2 Easter Day chants: Noli me tangere, Throne of Grace, Pelican in its piety, and Eagle. Codex Gisle. Osnabrück, Gymnasium Carolinum und Bischöfliches Generalvikariat, MS p.140.

PLATE 3 Matthew. Oxford, Bodleian Library, Lat. liturg. fol. 5, fols 3v+4r.

PLATE 4 John. Oxford, Bodleian Library, Lat. liturg. fol. 5, fols 30v+31r.

PLATE 5 Abraham and Hagar. Queen Mary Psalter. London, BL, MS Royal 2 B. VII, fol. 9v.

PLATE 6 Hannah presents Samuel. Queen Mary Psalter. London, BL, MS Royal 2 B. VII, fol. 48v.

WOMEN AND THE BOOK

PLATE 7 Christ in the Temple. Queen Mary Psalter. London, BL, MS Royal 2 B. VII, fols 150v and 151r.

PLATE 8 *Image du Monde,* Paris, BN, MS fr. 547, fol. 140r.

WOMEN AND THE BOOK

PLATE 9 Presentation miniature and first page of text of Hours of the Guardian Angel.
The scroll between the donor and the queen reads 'with everlasting joy',
more or less a quotation from the hymn to the Guardian Angel
which is part of the text of the Hours.
Liverpool, University Library,
Liverpool Cathedral MS Radcliffe 6,
fols 5v–6r.

with the *arma Christi*, or Martha Driver's wide-ranging discussion of medieval specularity, are cases in point. In this collection we have attempted to include many areas of women's relationships with the visual aspects of books. These are not simply pictures of women, but images made for and commissioned by women, and texts that were about women. The scarcity of images by and for women, noted by Smith and Lowe, may seem disheartening to some or confirmatory to others; but the careful scholarship represented by these papers also has another function, to act as a record. As we seek to make generalizations about medieval women, it is hard not to be struck by the lack of evidence, for and against, which can be pinned down to actual women in actual situations. Even truisms such as 'most books of hours were made for female owners' would be hard to substantiate, if one needed quantitative evidence. And further, given that we knew the ownership of such books, we could not honestly say whether they were commissioned by women for themselves or their female relatives, or by men who wanted to think of their women as delighting in, and satisfied by, such religious trinkets. To this end, Penketh, Lowe, Visser-Fuchs and Sutton, and Gameson investigate the ownership of actual books by individuals, and Oliver, Ehrenschwendtner and McGuire look in detail at how communities of women provided for themselves.

Our original conference, and this volume growing out of it, show clearly both how much interest there is in the topic of literate women and medieval imagery (the art historical-codicological sessions were the best-attended of all those at the conference) and how little hard evidence there is yet to rely on when attempting to make generalizations. Is the scarcity of women artists and commissioners caused by a lack of women to find, or a lack of looking? Kate Lowe's essay, with its unlocking of the identity of Suora Battista Carducci, is emblematic of the difficulty of identifying a woman in an 'unusual' place. And of course this difficulty makes for circularity, generally leading us to *assume* that image-makers will be men. Yet reality can be different, as the painstaking uncovering of Jeanne de Montbaston by Richard and Mary Rouse, and the tantalizing glimpse of Anastasia afforded us – once again – by Christine de Pizan, reveal:

> I know a woman today, named Anastasia, who is so learned and skilled in painting manuscript borders and miniature backgrounds that one cannot find an artist in all the city of Paris – where the best in the world are found – who can surpass her, not who can paint flowers and details so delicately as she does, nor whose work is more highly esteemed.[11]

What *did* she paint? Which of Christine's treatises did she illustrate? If only we knew![12]

Does our gender investigation naturally involve a limitation of class as well? Most women so far known to be associated with books are from the aristocracy. Can we move out of the

---

11 'Je congnois aujourd'uy une femme que on appelle Anastaise qui tant est experte a faire vigneteures d'enlumineure en livres et champaignes d'istoires qu'il n'est mencion d'ouvrier en la ville de Paris, ou sont les souverains du monde, qui point l'en passe, ne qui aussi doulcement face fleureteure et menu ouvraige qu'elle fait, ne de qui on ait plus chiere la besongne.' Curnow, *Cité*, p.760; transl.Richards, p.85.

12 For some hypotheses, however, *see* P.M.De Winter, 'Christine de Pizan, ses enlumineurs et ses rapports avec le milieu bourguignon', in *Actes du 104e. Congrès National des Sociétés Savantes, Bordeaux 1979 (Section d'Archéologie et d'Histoire de l'Art)* (Paris, 1982), pp.335–76; *see* however the reservations expressed by Hindman, '*Epistre Othéa*', pp.68–70.

noble classes, as Sutton and Visser-Fuchs do, to find the nouveaux riches or even the lower classes with some interest in writings, and especially, perhaps, pictures? Is there a distinction of class or gender to be made between owners of sacred texts, like books of hours, and the owners of vernacular literature and romance? Was there, more fundamentally, a difference between books, even prayer books, designed for men and those made for women? The list of questions could easily be extended. One small volume cannot hope to answer, even in part, these larger issues, but it can, we hope, show the way forward and show just how interesting the questions are.

Lesley Smith
Jane H. M. Taylor

Part One
IMAGES OF WOMEN

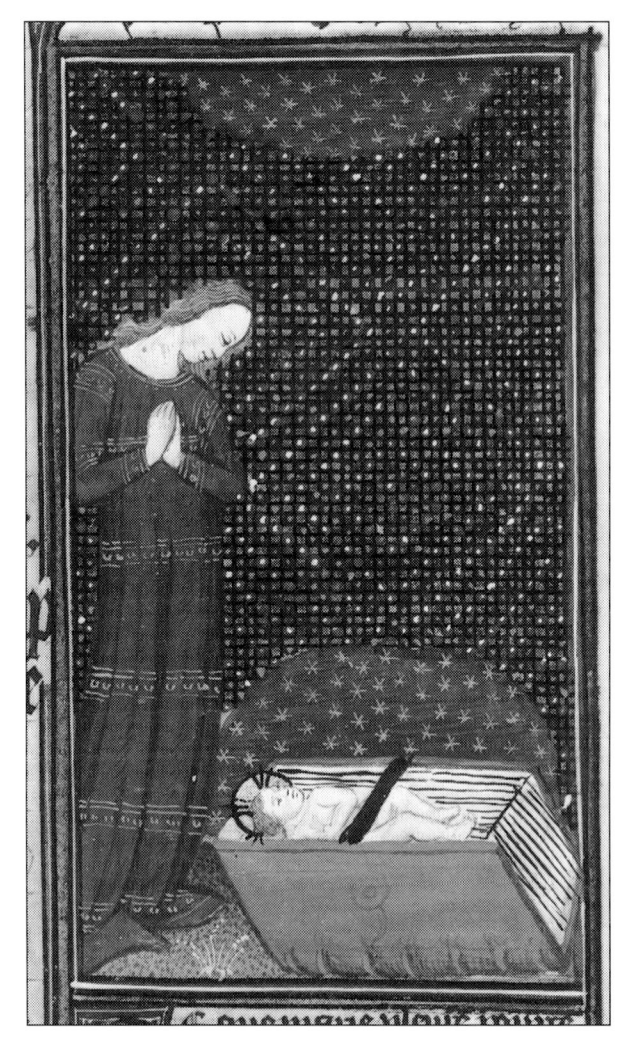

FIG. 2 Rohan hours. Mary with Jesus cradled in book.
Paris, BN, MS lat. 9471, fol. 133r.

CHAPTER ONE

Scriba, Femina:
Medieval Depictions of Women Writing

LESLEY SMITH

MY INTEREST IN writing women began by being one. More specifically, this study began when I was asked by a colleague working on depictions of male scribes if I would contribute a short codicil on women. We hoped to compare the sorts of writing posture, instruments shown, and general setting of the scribe, male or female. We even thought to distinguish between Eastern and Western depictions of women, as he had begun to do for men.[1] The results of my digging surprised us by their paucity. I had thought there would be many depictions of women writing that had simply been overlooked. I was aware that discovering Eastern women scribes was unlikely, but surely, since there were Western women writers, there must be pictures of Western women writing. There are very few. One of my aims, then, in publishing this piece, is to encourage the development of a virtually complete conspectus of images. I limit my time framework to medieval images before *c*.1400. After this date, many more writing women appear, especially in vernacular and secular texts. In addition, I shall discuss only images found in manuscripts; I am not competent to address images on seals, statues, or misericords, although this would be a fascinating addendum.[2] My final exclusion is of female personifications and mythological figures. There are a few images of women as Rhetoric, Grammar, or as sibyls holding writing instruments.[3] I set these aside for another occasion, since at present they seem to raise less interesting issues than depictions of actual women as writers.

To begin with the conclusion: there are very few depictions of women writing in the Middle Ages. Of course, there are very few depictions of women as blacksmiths in the Middle Ages either; but that argument begs the question. Writing would seem to be a task inherently suited to women's participation, requiring no great physical hardship (*pace* disgruntled scribes' complaints), but rather care, neatness, manual dexterity, and concentration. Just as nowadays women workers are preferred to men in factories assembling printed electronic circuits, so one might imagine that these same skills of hand-eye co-ordination and application would lend themselves to copying manuscripts. And indeed, we know that women, especially nuns, did write and copy books, often to very high standards. If women do not appear as scribes in representations of writing, we must ask ourselves why. In seeking to interpret this scarcity of depictions, what began as a hopeful quest to make some sense of female scribes has become, *force majeure*, a rather more generalized expedition into the land of reading and writing, and women's place in it.

We must begin by making a distinction between women writing and women reading. Depictions of women with books and of women reading are relatively common. For example, books form a recurrent theme in images of the Virgin Mary, who is regularly shown reading in a number of episodes throughout her life. One series of depictions is of the delightful, but non-biblical, theme of St Anne teaching her daughter to read, which occurs with frequency from the early fourteenth century. Whilst I would not wish to take medieval illustration naïvely to illuminate actual practice (a point to which we will return), this image seems to be frequent and straightforward enough to suggest that it was usual practice for a mother to teach her daughter her letters.[4]

Another scene from the various medieval lives of Mary[5] shows the Virgin and other young girls being educated in the Temple, again with books, following along where a teacher reads. In probably the most famous Marian scene of all, the Annunciation, it is customary for Mary to be shown reading whilst Gabriel appears to announce the will of God. A dove, baby, crucifix, or some other small token of the infant Jesus or the Holy Spirit flies in to complete the conception.[6] Mary is described as occupying herself in the Office, holy reading, or prayer – emphasizing her goodness of character and devotion. Paul Saenger, in an article on the use of Books of Hours,[7] suggests that the inclusion of a book in such scenes signifies prayer, probably spoken or murmured out loud, rather than simply reading. But I would argue that the presence of the book has another symbolism: it represents the Christ that Gabriel is sent to announce. Lest we think that Christ did not exist before the birth of Jesus, this already-present book reminds us of the doctrine of the eternity of the Word. The Word made flesh (so graphically evident in the parchment pages of a manuscript book) in Mary's book is symbolically present at the very moment of his conception. This confluence of the meanings of the Word of God is startlingly clear in an image of the Annunciation from a manuscript in Ferrara where a book flies into the room in place of the dove.[8]

In a further group of images, of the Visitation, the now-pregnant Mary meets her cousin Elizabeth, who is pregnant with the future John the Baptist. In these pictures, Mary commonly holds a book over the foetal Christ: she is with book as well as with child. In some nativity scenes, she kneels before an open book as well as the babe, again illustrating the identity of the eternal Word with the Word made flesh.[9] The insoluble link between the tiny child and the scripture is nowhere more marvellously depicted than in an image from the Rohan hours, where the infant is cradled in a clasped book (Fig. 2).[10]

The final scene where Mary is shown with a book is at Pentecost. Traditionally, Mary is included amongst the apostolic gathering, in an attitude of prayer, kneeling at a desk, hands clasped, but with a book open in front of her. Again, the open book (which often only Mary possesses) testifies to the presence of Christ in the assembly, and confirms and heightens Mary's authority amongst the waiting apostles. Holding the book, she reminds viewers of her role as *theotokos* (God-bearer), and the authority of the book-as-Christ rebounds onto her.[11]

So much for Mary as reader, if not writer.[12] I have spent some time on her both to point up the distinction between woman reading and woman writing, and to illustrate, in brief, the role of the book as a symbol of authority, appearing in crucial scenes in the Marian story, reminding us of the Christ to come, and enhancing the authority of the Mother-to-be of God.

We will revisit both of these points when we turn to women depicted writing. For the moment, though, we must ask whether, in life as in art, we can legitimately make a distinction between reading and writing in the Middle Ages. For us, reading and writing go hand-in-hand; our own learning to write goes along with learning to write *our own spoken language*. Our culture is such that the inability to write is a severe handicap, and one of our measures of the 'development' of other countries is that of rates of literacy. But recent scholarship points out that what 'literacy' means is difficult to define, let alone measure.[13] 'Literate', in medieval society, meant the ability to read Latin, the language of the Church, the law, and the government. Michael Clanchy has shown how the initially separate distinctions between 'cleric' and 'layman', and between 'literate' and 'illiterate', converged until lay people who could read Latin to a fairly narrow extent were called 'clerics'.[14]

Educated daughters of wealthier families appear to have been taught reading and a little Latin in just the same way as sons.[15] Even if they knew no Latin, the inability to actually understand or compose in a language would not preclude women from acting as scribes. Manuscripts show us that some male scribes had little or no idea what they were copying (as we can see from the mistakes they make); moreover, copying by an ignorant scribe may be just as good as by a knowledgeable one because he will reproduce what he sees faithfully, rather than trying to amend to what he thinks ought to be there.

Perhaps women did not need books and writing? Not at all. In a variety of circumstances, women as much as men had to read and write. Just like men, women in trade needed to keep accounts, take stock, and record transactions. For this they were likely to use tally sticks, which rarely survive, but also account books, wax tablets, and registers. Women could be members of guilds and might take over businesses originally owned by father or husband.[16] Any streetwise businesswoman would be able to count, read, write, and record debts just as ably as her male counterpart. The canny housewife, too, must have had some skills. From the early thirteenth century, didactic works on manners and morals were addressed to women. The famous book of the Goodman of Paris (*c.*1393) was *written* for his wife to read. One of the instructions in the section on 'Medicine to cure the bite of a dog or other wild beast' runs, 'Take a crust of bread and write what follows'. Clearly, women could write what they needed for everyday affairs.[17]

Women in the religious life needed books. Like men, they followed the Rule of St Benedict, which presupposes that monks will have books for liturgy, for devotional reading, and for study. They made many of these themselves. We know that some convents had libraries of considerable size.[18] Some nuns certainly acted as scribes, and probably made at least some of their own service and library books.[19] But here we hit a dearth of information. Little work has been done on convent libraries or nuns' books in general,[20] and service books are not the sorts of manuscripts likely to survive the introduction of cheaper printed editions and standardized liturgy.

For comparison, let us turn from invisible writing women to writing men. Male scribal depictions can be divided loosely into four types: author portraits, scribal portraits (often self-portraits), marginal illustrations of an anonymous, generalized sort of character, and portraits of saints. The great majority of author portraits are those of the evangelists, usually preceding their respective gospels, writing their text, accompanied by their symbolic creatures, and almost always including some symbol of divine authority – the hand or head of God or a dictating bird are the most common.

We have become so inured to these evangelists' portraits that we may forget to ask why they are there; and yet no modern illustrated bible would be likely to show such a moment. We have become thorough sceptics about the two kinds of authorship and authority that such a frontispiece declares, that is, the human authorship of the evangelist, and the direct, divine authorship of God. Linking the two is the evangelist's symbol, the man, the lion, the ox, and the eagle: the four living creatures of Revelation 4: 6-7. A portrait of an evangelist as scribe stresses the continuity between God's revelation and the written word in front of the reader. The actual process of writing, the tools employed and the position assumed, need only be recognizable in schematic or symbolic form: what we are meant to see is the direct line from the hand of God to the hand of the author *cum* scribe and the pages of the text. The writing evangelist fulfils the function of guarantee, a seal of authenticity for the text.

It is instructive at this point to turn to perhaps the most famous medieval woman author/scribe portrait of a religious nature, Hildegard of Bingen. In the glorious illustrations from the *Scivias* and the *Book of Divine Works*,[21] Hildegard appears both outside the main frame of a number of the illustrations, as a tiny writing figure observing and recording the scene, and also in a more usual author portrait. Her appearance outside the frame is often overlooked in reproductions of the pictures of her visions, but it is an important sign of her control and influence. In the author portrait Hildegard is dictating to her scribe, Volmar. They occupy separate rooms, although Volmar leans, curious and slightly in awe, into Hildegard's space. The rays of the Holy Spirit beam downward onto her head – and onto hers alone; Volmar is definitely excluded from this divine inspiration. She writes on wax tablets, making notes of the visions as, or shortly after, they come to her, and she dictates the text from these to Volmar, who holds a book and, sometimes, a pen. In the tiny out-of-frame portraits we see Hildegard alone, with the same wax tablets, linking the visions as they happen to the subsequent dictation and vice versa. The direct line between the Holy Spirit and the text in front of the reader is expressed and emphasized in every illustration.

What we have here is an almost direct parallel between Hildegard's author portrait and that of an evangelist, with the iconographical emphasis in each case on the direct recording of a revelation of God. In both cases, the human author acts in the manner merely of a corporeal channel through which the spiritual message can flow. But Hildegard was an extraordinary woman, as we come increasingly to appreciate, not only in the quality and range of her mind and religious experience, but also in her temporal power. Brought up in the religious life, she was a woman of strength in a situation sufficiently isolated to amplify her position; she bears out Caroline Bynum's suggestion that women whose lives had been confined to the cloister had absorbed fewer of the outside world's expectations that women should adopt the attitudes and behaviour of inferiors.[22]

But the remarkable symbolism of the Hildegard illustrations only serves to point up the dearth of anything similar elsewhere at this time. Anglo-Saxon women seem to have been freer to write and compose than women who came later. Eadburg, abbess of Thanet, wrote the Epistles of Peter in letters of gold for Boniface; Bucga, the abbess of Withington in Kent, exchanged books with him; Lioba, educated at Wimbourne, and later abbess of Bischofsheim, sent him her Latin verses. Boniface, at least, did not think it wrong for women to write.[23] A manuscript from the nunnery at Winchester written around 1100 is signed by a *scriptrix*.[24] Sally Thompson has suggested that this 'may reflect the higher degree of literary activity in those nunneries founded before the Conquest'[25] – perhaps itself reflecting the high status women enjoyed in Anglo-Saxon society. But Eileen Power was not optimistic about learning in English nunneries:

> The Anglo-Saxon period seems, however, to have been the only one during which English nuns were at all conspicuous for learning. There is indeed very scant material for writing their history between the Norman Conquest and the last years of the thirteenth century, when Bishops' Registers begin. It is never safe to argue from silence and some nuns may still have busied themselves over books; but two facts are significant: we have no trace of women occupying themselves with the copying and illumination of manuscripts and no nunnery produced a chronicle .... They recorded nothing. The whole trend of medieval thought was against learned women and even in Benedictine nunneries, for which a period of study was enjoined by the rule, it was evidently considered altogether outside the scope of women to concern themselves with writing. While the monks composed chronicles, the nuns embroidered copes; and those who sought the gift of a manuscript from the monasteries, sought only the gift of needlework from the nunneries.[26]

The thirteenth century produced a flowering of women's mystical writing, especially from the convent of Helfta under the 40-year rule of abbess Gertrude of Hackeborn. I have yet to find a depiction of one of them writing. Whereas at Chelles, perhaps the best-known convent of writing nuns, whose script Bischoff designates 'nuns' minuscule',[27] the women seem to have acted mainly as copyists (signing their work, but not drawing their portraits), at Helfta the writing was original. The Helfta example is instructive. Gertrude became abbess there at the age of 19, a career nun, dedicated to female community life and education. The sisters were taught not only the seven liberal arts, but also engaged in theological, spiritual, and devotional studies. It seems likely that they were guided by Dominican friars who serviced the sacramental life of the community. Although they were learned, it seems that the Helfta nuns did not turn to writing themselves until the Beguine, Mechthild of Magdeburg, came to live with them in 1270, when she was around 60 years old. At this point Gertrude had been abbess for 19 years, and within the community were the two other sisters who were to follow Mechthild's example, Gertrude the Great and Mechthild of Hackeborn.[28]

It must be true that an important factor in the literary output of Helfta is what we can term the 'permission' or role model for writing that the presence of Mechthild of Magdeburg, already a writer of some repute and authority, brought with her. Mechthild's confidence to write down her experience built confidence in the others. But a crucial question in women's writing must be publication, in the widest sense of simply getting the work to any audience outside their own restricted circle. This issue is interestingly reflected in the portraits of St Bridget of Sweden, the only female saint I have found who is consistently depicted writing.

Bridget was born in 1302. By divine revelation she received a rule of religious life and was bidden, by the vision, to have it confirmed by the Pope, Urban V. He agreed to her founding two monasteries, but stipulated that they must follow the Rule of St Augustine, not the Rule she had received. In her life Bridget was served by a series of four male secretary-confessors who took down her *Liber celestis revelationum* and translated it into Latin;[29] and in three of her revelations she was commanded to place the editorship of her 'writings' in the hands of her then-confessor, Alphonso de Vadaterra (who was later to become a bishop). Bridget died in 1373. In 1378 her daughter, St Catherine, managed to have her Bridgettine Rule confirmed by the new Pope, Urban VI. Alphonso, the confessor, was a fierce promoter of Bridget's cause and of her *Liber celestis*. He appears to have had a number of de luxe illustrated copies of her work made, very soon after her death, in order to provide evidence – indeed the chief evidence – for her canonization. He succeeded: she was made a saint in 1391.

The *Liber celestis* manuscripts contain almost-identical cycles of pictures, 'the purpose of which is not so much to illustrate the text as to substantiate its divine inspiration'.[30] The rightness of this judgement is clear in images from the Palermo, Pierpont Morgan, and Ericsberg Castle copies of the text.[31] In one set of images we see Bridget at a desk, writing (or poised to write), receiving her revelations from heaven (FIG. 3). Even more strikingly, the cycles contain what I term *traditio* images, which depict the genesis and probity of her work (FIG. 4).[32] Bridget receives her book from heaven with her left hand and passes it on to a cleric (probably Alphonso or another of the secretaries) with her right; he in turn hands it to a messenger who hands it to a king. In one of the images of her receiving her revelations[33] we notice the writing desk, empty but pregnant, at the side of the scene (FIG. 5). Once again, the direct link between Bridget's written text and heavenly inspiration is heavily played up. But in contrast to the Hildegard pictures, the impetus for the making of these books and the direction of their images came from a man, Alphonso. In no religious example would a woman or female community be able to circulate a piece of work without male ecclesiastical approval.[34]

For author portraits where the woman herself was instrumental in deciding the image projected, we must compare Hildegard to another famous woman writer who closely supervised the production of her own works, Christine de Pizan. Her story, of widowhood and a subsequent career in her own writing and publishing business, are well-known. Forced into the trade to support herself and her family, she was a hands-on boss: Ouy and Reno

FIG. 3 Above: Bridget of Sweden. New York, Pierpont Morgan, MS 498, fol. 8r.

FIG. 4 Right: Bridget of Sweden. Stockholm, Ericsberg Castle, MS *Liber celestis*, fol. 85v.

calculate that fifty-five autograph or part-autograph books are extant.[35] The same image of her writing is found in a number of her books, and this reinforces the notion of an iconographical model of a scribe. The depictions of her are almost exactly alike. Christine, alone in her room, is seated at the left side of the picture, facing right, writing in a ruled codex at a cloth-covered table or desk, with a pen, knife, and open penbox. She wears the same (or very similar) dress and hat. A little dog often sits at her feet. She is right-handed.[36] This flush of depictions of a woman writing appears to be unique. It forcibly reminds us of four points: first, that Christine is writing secular works, not religious ones; secondly, that she oversaw the work and the illustrations herself (and indeed, we know that, for some work, she employed a woman illustrator[37]); thirdly, that she may have realized the oddity value of such books written by a woman and advertised as such (she may have thought to use it as a point of uniqueness for her productions); and finally, that being secure enough in her career and place in society, she was proud enough to proclaim her status and herself.[38]

Christine tells us that she came to enjoy her work and her independence; but we should be cautious in thinking of her writing career as a kind of romantic success story. Far from being of high standing, writers – those who physically wrote – were servants to those who wanted books. Christine, in her widowhood, was *reduced* to writing for a living.

It is easy to fall into a modern misconception about the place of writing – the actual act – for medieval people. Modern studies of literacy stress that it is intimately linked with, and leads to, power. Robert Pattison makes much of the clerical abrogation of literacy to itself in the early Middle Ages.[39] The ability to read and write was important in medieval life, as it is today. However, we should not make the mistake of thinking that this meant that anyone had to do either themselves. All that mattered was to have people to do it for you.

27

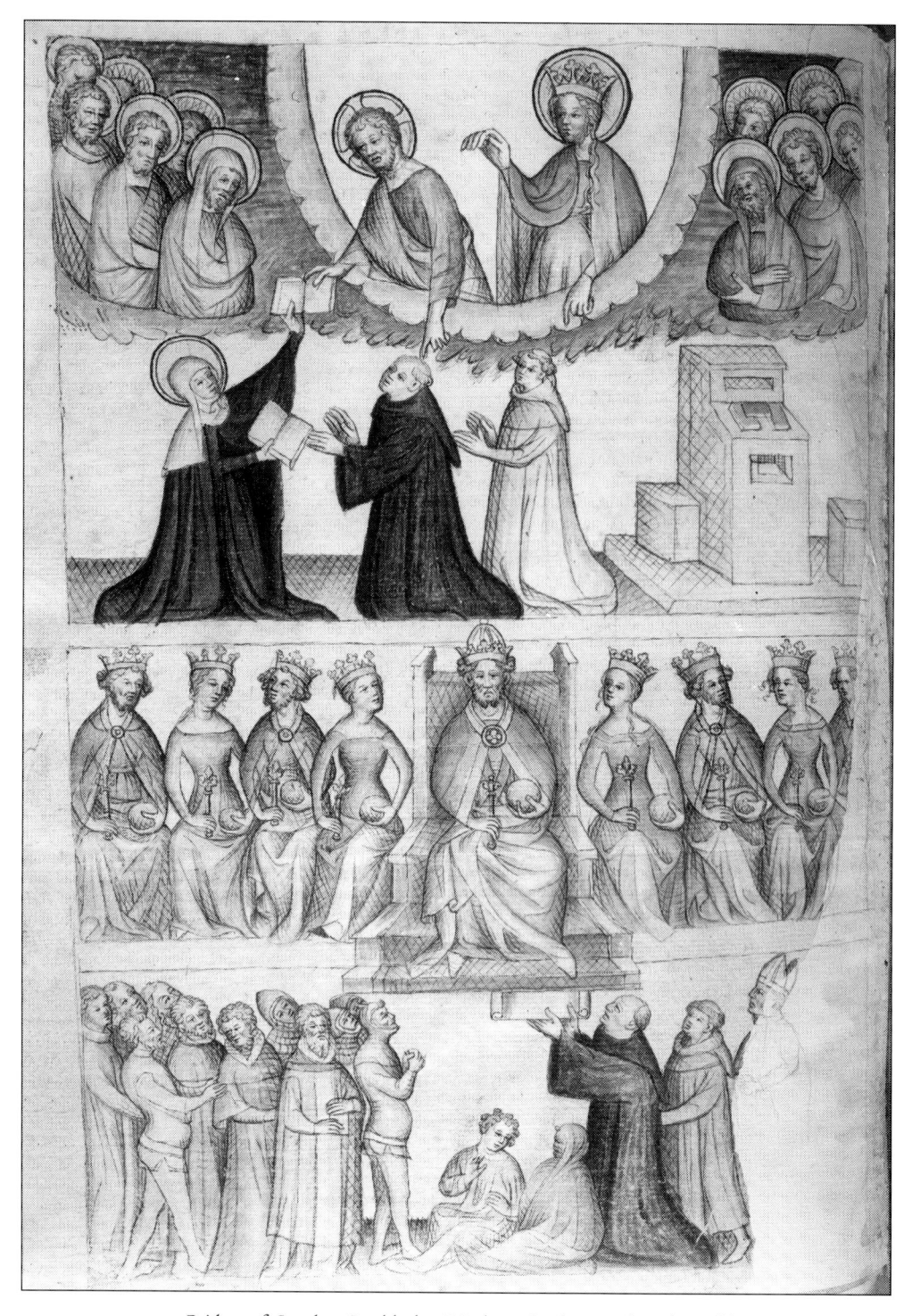

FIG. 5 Bridget of Sweden. Stockholm, Ericsberg Castle, MS *Liber celestis*, fol. 94v.

FIG. 6 The nun Guda. Frankfurt, MS Barth. 42, fol. 110v.

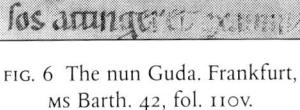

FIG. 7 The nun Adelhaid. Munich, Bay. Staatsbibl., MS 23046, fol. 144r.

To 'write' a book or document was unlikely to mean actually penning it oneself. You might make notes or do a rough draft on wax tablets, as we see Hildegard doing, but the final writing out might be a menial's work. Writing was often dictation.[40] Parenthetically, one might compare this with today, when writing is once again a menial's work – but secretaries are generally women. Peter the Venerable notes that writing is a work of the hand, but composing is the work of the heart. Alcuin says that sacred authors wrote 'to God's dictation'.[41] Few Church Fathers wrote their own works: they dictated, except as an act of mortification.[42] Writing was manual labour, not something indulged in by a gentleman. How much less, as Barbara Cartland reminds us, might a gentlewoman wish to do it.[43]

This division of writing into composition and copying reminds us that when we see Christian male authors portrayed as scribes we are really seeing a shorthand representation of the process of composition and publication, rather than the visual truth. Again, the issue is authority: nothing stands between the writer's inspiration and the words in front of the reader. Historians of scribal practice would do well to bear this in mind. The image presented may not be intended as a perfect representation of what the spectator would see; the depiction has a symbolic function instead of, or at least as well as, simply showing a quasi-photographic scene.

If this is true for male scribal portraits, it is even more the case for female ones, for, even putting evangelists' portraits aside, the fact remains that we have many more depictions of male scribes than female. Even where we know women wrote, they seem neither to be depicted writing nor to depict themselves. I have not found any small portraits of writing nuns in initials, or self-portraits pictured writing, after the fashion of Eadwine, Hildebertus, or Hugo *pictor*.[44] If we compare Hugo's self-portrait from his manuscript of Jerome's commentary on Isaiah, we can see that it is virtually identical to his portrait of Jerome, apart from Hugo's left-handedness. This may provide an insight into why men rather than women scribes draw themselves into manuscripts. I am anxious to avoid any amateur psychology about the likelihood of each sex to advertise itself, even given Hugo's smug look, and

FIG. 8 Above: Baudonivia. Poitiers, Bib. mun., MS 250, fol. 21v.

FIG. 9 Right: Fortunatus. Poitiers, Bib. mun., MS 250, fol. 43v.

Eadwine's famous 'I am the prince of scribes'. Indeed, there are *some* female scribal self-portraits, such as the two nuns, Guda and Adelhaid, in manuscripts now in Frankfurt and Munich (FIGS 6 and 7);[45] but they are *not* depicted writing. Contrast, too, Eadwine's 'I am the prince of scribes' with 'Guda, a sinner, a woman, wrote and decorated this book'. Both these women appear to be German; nuns in Germany have left more evidence of their literacy than elsewhere.[46]

The talents of scribe and artist are not identical. The Chelles nuns signed their work, but did not draw their portraits. In a small community, where the women scribes's work was for in-house consumption, they may have felt it unnecessary or inappropriate to leave their images. Where they were writing for an outside patron or on request, they may have felt too timid or modest to advertize themselves, especially if the book were for a male ecclesiastical superior, as seems to have been often the case.[47]

But the similarity of Hugo's self-portrait to his portraits of Isaiah or Jerome suggests how easily male scribes had available models, and how they and their readers were simply used to seeing men depicted writing. They could recognize their situation as that of the evangelists and doctors. Women had literally no such models. A manuscript of the prose *Tristan* shows Yseult dictating a letter to Tristan to a scribe although the text specifically mentions her writing the letter with her own hand.[48] Could the illustrator not conceive of a queen writing for herself? Was it not the sort of thing that a queen should do?

There *are* learned women in this period, and a number of female saints, such as Catherine of Siena, Mary Magdalene, or St Scholastica, are traditionally associated with learning; but it is rare to find them depicted writing rather than simply holding a book. St Bridget is the exception. Even holy or religious women specifically associated with writing, such as Héloise, are rarely so depicted. In one modern book about Héloise which pictures a women writing as illustration on its front cover the woman turns out to be Baudonivia, writer of the life of St Radegund.[49]

Radegund was a sixth-century nun of Ste Croix in Poitiers. Two *Lives* of her were circulated, one by her friend, the hymnodist Venantius Fortunatus, written shortly after her death, the other written in the early seventh century by Baudonivia, a nun of the same house. It seems possible that Baudonivia's *Life* was composed after a revolt in the convent (over washing!), to remind the sisters of their saintly predecessor and restore convent routine. The two *Lives* were often found together, although in the late-eleventh-century Poitiers manuscript from which Baudonivia's portrait comes the text of Baudonivia's *Life* is lost, and only the author portrait remains.

Baudonivia and Fortunatus are interesting with regard to the question of scribal models (FIGS 8 and 9).[50] They are striking for their similarity of general posture, especially in the position of the right hand. The same basic model has been used for both author-scribes. The author portraits of people who knew her, or came near to knowing her, connect the living Radegund with the text in front of the reader in a direct, physical way. The antiquity of both Fortunatus and Baudonivia is suggested by their writing on wax tablets, rather than in codices. This manuscript seems to have been made for, and possibly by, the nuns of Ste Croix, who did not possess the body of their foundress, Radegund. It was important, then, for them to preserve and identify the link between her actual life, the texts of her *Life*, and themselves the readers.

Finally, in this context of women writers drawn from male models, we must consider Marie de France. She is depicted twice in a French manuscript containing a number of vernacular poetic works amongst which Marie is the only woman author.[51] At the beginning of the text of her *Fables* she is shown writing in a large codex with a pen and a knife (see FIG. 83); at the end, she sits in an initial E ('El finement de cest escrit...marie....de france') reading the same codex. Beside her is a table with other books. The manuscript is illustrated at almost every turn, and the male authors are treated in the same way as Marie. At ff.73r and 141r, for instance, male authors are writing at desks with codices, pens, and knives, exactly as she is. No man is depicted reading his codex quite as Marie does, but they do appear in initials, holding scrolls. Others appear in court scenes with books. Adding Marie's picture is just a female variation on the same theme, for which male models already exist, and so in this context it is easy for the illustrator to do.

The small male portraits in this Arsenal manuscript take us to the next group of male scribal depictions, that of casual portrayals of men, usually monks, writing – the kind of

FIG. 10 Above: Anonymous woman writing. Cambridge, Trinity Coll., MS B. 11. 22, fol. 100r.

FIG. 11 Left: Cistercian nun. Aachen, private collection.

depictions one finds in initials or margins. Lilian Randall lists only two women writing in her index of manuscript marginal illustration[52] and one of these has turned out, on inspection, to be St Athanasius with long hair. The second, now in Cambridge,[53] is in a late-thirteenth-century, probably Flemish, manuscript, which has a mass of marginal illustration. It shows a woman, apparently not a nun, writing on a scroll of parchment which descends from her lectern like computer paper (FIG. 10). The rest of the manuscript is full of figures, of everyday animals and scenes, 'ordinary' saints and angels, and fantastic reversals such as a horse playing a fiddle (fol. 185v), or a sheep with a dog in its mouth (fol. 37r). Although M. R. James thinks this book of hours was written for a woman with Franciscan connections there is no other evidence to connect this little writing figure with the production of the book itself, or its intended owner. Enough tiny women are running around the manuscript to confuse the issue. No conclusions are evident from this unusual writing female – except her unusualness.[54]

A second, somewhat smarter laywoman is writing in a famous book, the Heidelberg *Codex Manesse*.[55] The poet Reinmar von Zweter is dictating, and his words are taken down by a young man with wax tablets and a golden-haired girl with a scroll and pen. The girl is anonymous, balancing the anonymous boy, and both are types that appear elsewhere in the manuscript. Although unexpected, the German origin of the manuscript, the secular text, and a dating *c.*1320 make it the least surprising combination of circumstances in which to find a writing woman.

One other supposed writing woman, a nun in a British Library Royal manuscript, a rather lovely early-fourteenth-century illuminated Bible with historiated initials, causes me some puzzlement. The figure is in an initial F(rater Ambrosius) at the beginning of Jerome's prologue to the scripture – the usual spot for a miniature of a generic writing monk meant to represent Jerome. The Royal manuscript catalogue of 1921 says, 'a nun in the act of writing, which may have reference to the scribe of this manuscript'.[56] And yet I think she must be a man. There is curly hair and a pretty face, but the habit and cowl must belong to a Benedictine monk, not to a nun. The real question here is why the cataloguers took the extraordinary line, in this context, of assuming he was female.

Finally, a Cisterican nun from the early fourteenth century. She lives in a private collection in Aachen, and so I can only say that she is found in a *Liber usualis*, and is standing next to what might be a tree with a seat behind her, writing in an open codex, and holding a large pen and knife (FIG. 11).[57] She is my solitary example of an anonymous writing woman religious, for whom so many male counterparts exist. Her very singularity leads me to expect that she cannot really be anonymous. I expect closer inspection of the manuscript to reveal her as a named saint, that is, a specific individual rather than a generic female.

When I first began to work on writing women I expected to find that depictions of woman writing had simply been ignored, that they existed but had been overlooked. In fact, there have been many fewer depictions than I imagined. This must lead us to ask whether writing was ever prohibited to women. Jewish tradition, surprisingly, allowed women to write Torah scrolls, but not the Talmud.[58] Considering the sacred status of the scrolls this is an extraordinary situation. However, the Talmud is about disputation and questioning, and it seems to be this that was considered unsuitable for women, whereas writing the holy word was perfectly fitting. As always, there were certain exceptions: the great Rabbi Rashi's daughter acted as his amanuensis.

But Jewish communities in Europe had something of a reputation for learning, even amongst their women. Did Christian women have the same chances? The famous Pauline passages on female authority and deportment mention only women *speaking* in a congregation. Clearly, Paul would have been equally horrified to see a woman writing; he simply thought in terms of the oral culture of the early church. But this literary prohibition of women speaking in church finds its way into medieval illustration. The Oxford version of the *Bible moralisée*,[59] a French manuscript from the mid-thirteenth century, transforms the text in Deuteronomy on men dressing in women's clothes and women in men's (Deut. 22: 5) into an admonition against women preaching. The Bible has no such prohibitions on women writing, as the orthodox Jewish practice shows us.

In the Patristic period Jerome, Ambrose, and Augustine wrote to and for women, Jerome in particular carrying on a long correspondence with Eustochium and Paula, presumably in answer to letters that they also wrote to him.[60] A fifth-century manuscript of Jerome on Ecclesiastes belonged to a late-seventh-century Anglo-Saxon abbess, Cuthswith[61]. We have seen Anglo-Saxon women writing to Boniface, and the Goodman of Paris assuming his wife will read and write. But Eileen Power points out that Philip of Navarre and the author of the *Knight of the Tour Landry* both specifically forbid women from writing, and allow them to read only to glean the good of the Scriptures.[62] By the thirteenth century, too much frivolous literature was available for women; reading was no longer necessarily 'improving'. When we picture groups of men and women being read to in courtly garden scenes, we know they are not reading the Bible![63]

The early thirteenth century marks the beginning of university learning, superseding the somewhat passé (as it seemed) scholarship of the cloister. This was true for men as well as women. But whereas women could participate (if they so wished) in study in the convent, they were not allowed into the new universities, which were exclusively male clerical institutions. As well as isolating women from higher learning, this isolated the higher learners from women. Academics were most likely to have dealings with women servants and prostitutes: not, perhaps, the contacts likely to produce the best impression on those writing and developing theological ideas about women.

We can see a hardening of attitudes towards women and authority over time pointed up in the *Glossa Ordinaria*. On the text of Judges which tells of Deborah[64], the only woman ruler of Israel of whom we hear, the main, twelfth-century text cites Origen, Theodoret, and Ambrose. They give quite a lot of space to Deborah, explaining that her inclusion is meant as a consolation to women. With the aid of grace, women can overcome the effects of the Fall, prophesy legitimately, and be the equal, and even the support (*subsidio*) of men[65]. But by the early fourteenth century Nicholas of Lyra's gloss is notable for its silence.

After a short note on *Debora prophetes*, explaining that she is allowed to rule the people because the spirit of prophecy which has been given to her mitigates (*relevaret*) the weakness of her sex, Nicholas turns all his attention to Lapidoth, her husband, trying to determine who he might be. In the spiritual exposition of the text (the *moraliter* section of the Gloss) he concentrates on the allegorical meaning of *apis*, a bee, the meaning of Deborah's name. In the glosses on 1 Cor. 14 and 1 Tim. 2: 11-12[66] Nicholas again takes a harder line than the older gloss. Both these passages are prohibitions of women speaking in church and teaching. The twelfth-century gloss makes the distinction between women acting *in public* and their role in private: 'A woman ought not to teach in public, but can help others towards salvation if, by daily instruction of her children about God, she brings them to new spiritual birth, so that they remain in faith and love.'[67] Nicholas has a somewhat jaundiced view: women cannot teach because to teach is a work of wisdom, which women do not commonly possess.[68] And on women maintaining silence and obeying their husbands, one senses the sharpness of personal experience: 'and they should not contradict him, but honestly and lawfully obey him!'[69] Gratian's *Decretum* codifies the silence women must maintain in church and legal affairs.[70] The re-emergence of Aristotle in the early thirteenth century, and Peter Lombard's copious use of Augustine in the *Sentences* which were the main theological textbook of the thirteenth century, solidified the theological view of women as inferior.

Must we then conclude that the men of the period knew that words were a way of ordering and subduing the world; that, in some sense, written words *make* the world in their own image; and that it was too dangerous for this power to fall into unauthorized and uncontrollable hands? Are there mitigating circumstances? Might women not wish to write? 'Did not' does not necessarily imply 'could not'. Women had other things to do with their time, both work and leisure. Writing is an essentially solitary pursuit: even if done in company with others, it is done best in silence and concentration. But needlework, making vestments, and tapestry are much more social and cooperative activities: one thinks of knitting circles or sewing bees. One might have a reading party – but not a writing soirée. Perhaps the more laterally orientated and networking nature of women makes them prefer more social work, so that even women who do write or compose tend to do so in groups wherein they can discuss experience, build confidence, and receive support.

So what other wider implications might we draw from this apparent lack of female participation in writing, or certainly in being depicted writing? The question points up a number of lacunae in our knowledge. We know little about women's education – not much more than Eileen Power lays out in the 1920s. We know little about convent libraries and their use[71]. We know little about the provision of monastic service books for either women or men. We know little about the application of the Benedictine rule to women, in practice. We know little, in fact, about the general education of ordinary monks. We know little about the 'publication' of works in the Middle Ages, about the fortuitous process of copying and circulation. How much did women rely on male approval and patronage? As Bynum notes, the female mystics whose writings we know tend to support basic church structures and positions, not be subversive of them. What of the writings of the subversives; have

FIG. 12 Amalthea. Paris, BN, MS fr. 12420, fol. 36r.

they survived? Up until quite recently we thought there was little extant women's writing from the Middle Ages. Now we have much mystical writing, autobiographical in a way that male writing often is not, and deeply personal. But can we say that no women were interested in systematic and doctrinal theology? Clearly some, like Hildegard, were. What expression was this given? How many of the anonymous works of the Middle Ages are attributable to women?

Recent work raises the question of whether there is a distinctive woman's voice or woman's hand. Nordenfalk, writing in 1961 about women artists in the Middle Ages, thought there was:

> It is a matter of discussion whether it is at all possible to talk about a feminine style .... There are many women who paint or draw in a way that does not visibly differ from that of their male colleagues. Yet I think there is a style or a tendency which deserves to be called typically feminine, and I might cite as good examples of it the paintings of Berthe Morisot ... or of Marie Laurencin .... The history of medieval illumination also contains several cases of manuscripts decorated by typically feminine hands. They are generally characterized by a certain lack of plastic structure, a design layout which carries one's thoughts to the art of embroidery .... [This miniature] displays all the looseness of a typically feminine design. Even more 'thread like' is the design in the *Revelations* of Marienboem. Here the feminine style appears almost pushed towards caricature. There is no inscription saying that the miniatures and initials in these books were executed by nuns, but I believe that most people would agree with me in thinking that this is the simplest explanation for their peculiar style.[72]

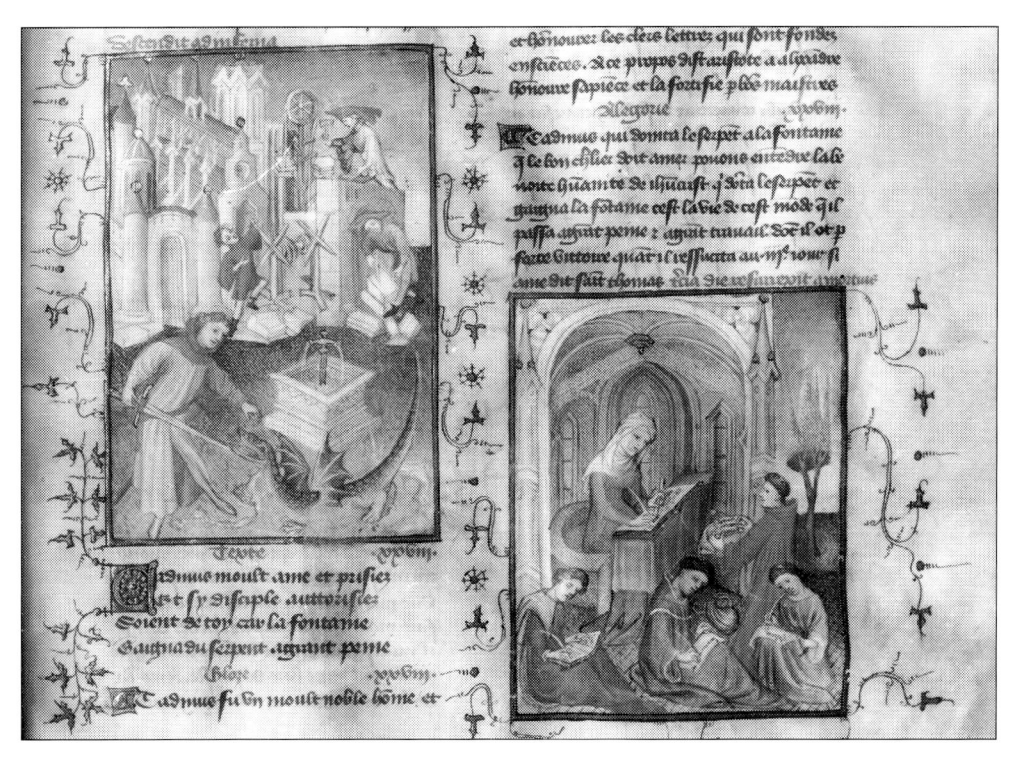

FIG. 13 Io directing a scriptorium. Paris, BN, MS fr. 606, fol. 15r.

Few, I hope, would want to make that simple judgement today. But this distinction between men and women reminds us that, in fact, we do not know much about the scriptoria of men either. Modern work has begun on some scriptoria,[73] but we do not know much about who was recruited, whether, for example, every monk was expected to write, regardless of aptitude (and everyone has seen writing by men who clearly were unsuited for the job), and about questions like length of service and rotation of jobs. Apart from monasteries, we need to know about university and professional book services,[74] and royal scriptoria. It is they who must have trained and employed the women scribes and illuminators who suddenly begin to appear in the late fourteenth and fifteenth centuries, and which may have given Christine de Pizan her start. [75]

I end, then, at the point where I had hoped to begin – a writing woman shown with writing tools (FIG. 12).[76] In this depiction of Amalthea, the scribe has more writing equipment than any other writing woman I have seen so far. Seated at an elaborate copyist's desk, surrounded by books and scrolls, she works with a pen, knife, inkpot, and compasses.[77] Despite the realistic instruments, the depiction is fanciful in that the parchment position and writing posture are hugely ungainly. This is not because she is a woman, but is rather another reminder that we should never – as historians of male scribal practice have tended to do – *look* at a medieval image without *reading* it. These portraits are not *cinema verité* images of how scribes worked. The question that gave rise to this work on women originally was why Western evangelist-scribes are so often depicted with many fewer, and more schematic, writing instruments than Byzantine scribes. The answer is clearly not a simple matter of comparative hardware.

This Amalthea's provenance will be recognisable when I name some of her sisters – Erithraea, Sappho, Tamar, Irene, Marcia, and Proba.[78] All are from Boccaccio's *Book of Famous Women*. These women are becoming famous once more, reproduced on 'medieval women's' calendars, day books, and address books where, as Sandra Boynton says of the Renaissance, any turkey can do anything at all. Such propaganda misses the point: these women are exceptions, included by Boccaccio because of their extraordinary lives and legends, not because they are typical women of the day. (They are also, of course, pagan.) Boccaccio wrote this work in 1375, when Christine de Pizan was 11 years old; it was translated into French in 1401 when she was 37. The de luxe versions of the text, with their rich illustrations of women, were made by 1404 in exactly the milieu in which she was working. As Millard Meiss has said:

> Christine's own literary life was certainly facilitated by Boccaccio's treatise. Among the career women included in it were the Sibyls and several writers, including Sappho, lucky in poetry, according to Boccaccio, but unlucky in love. Their example sanctioned Christine's unprecedented career. We will not underestimate the novelty of her life and her work if we recall that in 1521 Pepwell, the English translator of her *Cité des Dames*, said in his prologue that he liked the book but he hesitated to print it because of its unconventional estimates of women.[79]

Only in Christine's *Epistre d'Othéa* can we see a woman, Io, directing a scriptorium of men (FIG. 13).[80] Christine's own life provided her with the model.

This work is only a beginning; but it is a beginning that takes us to a road with many forks, for the ways forward involve study not only of manuscript illustration and iconography, but also of theological questions of the *logos* and the active-passive roles of receivers of divine inspiration, of distinctions between sacred and secular scribes and authors, of pen-portraits of scribes and self-portraits of writers in vernacular works, and of status differences between scribes in sacred and secular writing. There can be no single answer to why portraits of writing women are so few, because what is crucial about the images of women writing that I have found so far is their peculiarity. By this I mean that, unlike those of writing men, they are not a constant, repeated illustration of the text in many manuscripts at expected points, for example, where women were known writers or scholars, but one-offs – very much the unusual. With the three small exceptions of Aachen, Cambridge, and Heidelberg, we can name every writing woman depicted, and relate something about her. I hope we might find more writing women than these, but when we do they will appear as unexpected straying visitors, not as women in their own element.

Inventory of Women Depicted Writing

Hildegard of Bingen
Wiesbaden, Hessische Landesbib., MS 1: *Liber Scivias* (c.1165) [colour pictures from Eibingen, Bibl. der Abtei Skt. Hildegard, *s.n.*, made 1927-33]; Lucca, Bib. Stat., MS lat. 1942: *Liber divinorum operum = De operatione Dei* (second half of 13th cent.).

St Bridget of Sweden
New York, Pierpont Morgan, MS 498; Palermo, Bibl. Naz., MS IV.G.2; Stockholm, Ericsberg Castle, MS *Liber celestis*; Tübingen, Universitätsbib., formerly Berlin, Preussische Staatsbibl., MS Theol. Lat.

Baudonivia (Life of St Radegund)
Poitiers, Bib. mun., MS 250.

Christine de Pizan (*Book of the City of Ladies*)
London, BL, MS Harley 4431; Paris, BN, MS fr. 1176, MS fr. 836, MS fr. 603, MS fr. 835; MS Arsenal fr. 2681; Brussels, Bib. Roy., MS 9508, MS 10309, MS 10366; Munich, Bay. Staatsbibl., MS gall. 11, abb. 158; The Hague, Koninklijke Bibl., MS 78 D 42.

Io (Christine de Pizan, *Epistre d'Othéa*)
Paris, BN, MS fr. 606.

Marie de France
Paris, BN, MS Arsenal 3142: Æsop's *Fables*.

Amalthea (Boccaccio, *Book of Famous Women*)
Paris, BN, MS fr. 12420, MS fr. 598; New York, Public Library, Spencer Collection, MS 33.

Eurythrea (Boccaccio, *Book of Famous Women*)
Paris, BN, MS fr. 12420, MS fr. 598; New York, Public Library, Spencer Collection, MS 33.

Sibyls, Muses, and Allegoricals
Montecassino, Monastery, MS 132: Rabanus Maurus *De universo*; Stuttgart, Landesbib., MS Hist. fol. 411: Eckehard of Aura *World Chronicles*; Florence, Laurenziana, MS S. Marco 190: *Grammatica*, Martianus Capella *De nuptiis Mercurii et philologiae*; Herrad of Hohenbourg, *Hortus deliciarum*, ed. R.Green, M.Evans, C.Bischoff, and M.Curschman, 2 vols. (London/Leiden, 1979), fol. 32r.

Miscellaneous
Aachen, Private coll., Liber usualis, fol. 2r: Cistercian nun; Cambridge, Trinity College, MS B. 11. 22, fol. 100r; Heidelberg, Universitätsbib., MS Germ. 848: Reinmar von Zweter.

Notes to Chapter One

1 I would like to thank Randall Rosenfeld for setting me along this path. Jane Taylor and the members of the *Text and Image* seminar, Oxford, were a marvellously eclectic audience for the second stage. Michael Gullick, Adelaide Bennett, and Jenny Sheppard generously shared information with me. My gratitude also goes to the British Academy for a post-doctoral fellowship which funded me during this research.

2 For some of these sources *see Medieval Women and the Sources of Medieval History*, ed. J.Rosenthal (Georgia, 1990), and W.Armstead's chapter in this volume.

3 For example, *Rhetorica* in Herrad of Hohenbourg, *Hortus deliciarum*, ed. R.Green, M.Evans, C.Bischoff, M.Curschman, 2 vols (London/Leiden, 1979), fol. 32r = ii, plate 18 (second half of 12th cent.); *Grammatica* in Martianus Capella, *De nuptiis*, Florence, Bibl. Medicea-Laurenziana, MS S. Marco, 190, fol. 15v (French, c.1100); Sibyls in Rabanus Maurus, *De universo*, Montecassino, Monastery Library, MS 132, p.377 (c.1023), and Eckehard of Aura, *World Chronicles*, Stuttgart, Landesbib., MS Hist. fol. 411, fol. IV (first half of 12th cent.). The writing implements are not always book and pen. *Rhetorica* holds the wax tablets and stylus of composition rather than fair copy, and sibyls often write on scrolls, symbolizing speech.

4 For St Anne teaching Mary to read, see C.Norton, D.Park, P.Binski, *Dominican Painting in East Anglia. The Thornham Parva Retable and the Musée de Cluny Frontal* (Woodbridge, 1987), pp.51–53, with good bibliography. A small number of images depict Mary attending to Jesus' schooling: e.g., National Museums and Galleries on Merseyside, MS M. 12004, p.13, with Mary (as *Grammatica*) threatening Jesus with a beating on his way to school. More pacifically, she sees Jesus off to school with his packed lunch and wax tablets in Aarau, Kantonsbib., MS Wett. Fol. 1 (MS 7), fol. 260r, reproduced in H.Wentzel, 'Das Jesuskind an der Hand Mariae auf dem Siegel des Burkard von Winon', in *Festschrift Hans R. Hahnloser zum 60. Gerburtstag*, ed. E.Beer, P.Hofer, and L.Mojon (Basel, 1961), pp.251–70. St Antoninus disapproved of artists who depicted Jesus with wax tablets at school, since he could have learned nothing from humans, see R.H. and M.A.Rouse, 'St Antoninus on Manuscript Production', in *Litterae medii aevi. Festschrift für Johanne Autenrieth*, ed. M.Borgolte and H.Spilling (Sigmaringen, 1988), pp.260–61; id., 'Wax tablets', *Language and Communication*, 9 (1989), pp.175–91.

5 Examples of lives of Mary may be found in *Bibliotheca Hagiographica Latina* (Brussels, 1898–99), i, p.791 *et seq*.

6 For a discussion of the iconography of the Annunciation (largely ignoring, however, the presence of books) *see* G.Schiller, *Iconography of Christian Art*, transl. J. Seligman, 2 vols. (London, 1971), i, pp.33–53.

7 P.Saenger, 'Books of Hours and Reading Habits of the Later Middle Ages', in R.Chartier, *The Culture of Print* (Princeton, 1989), pp.152–53.

8 Ferrara, Statuti MS 47, no page number; reproduced in P.D'Ancona and E.Aeschlimann, *Dictionnaire des Miniaturistes du Moyen Age et de la Renaissance* (Milan, 1949), plate 46. Mary's folded cloak forms a lozenge shape at the place of her womb. The ray on which the book travels is directed exactly at this spot.

9 e.g., Paris, Musée Jacquemart-André, MS 2, fol. 73v.

10 Paris, BN, MS lat. 9471, fol. 133r; Rohan Hours. The image is of Moses and Miriam as an allegory of Jesus and Mary.

11 *Compare also* Byzantine depictions of Mary as the throne of wisdom, with the Christ-child on her lap, and depictions of the enthroned Gospel book. R.Gilchrist, *Gender and Material Culture* (London and New York, 1994), notes that by far the majority of surviving nunnery seals in medieval England portray the throne of Wisdom (pp.144–46).

12 I have found one very tiny (c.1 x 1.5cm) depiction of Mary writing, sitting face-on at a desk with a very large feather pen, in Oxford, Keble College, MS 40, fol. 29r. The image is in the border of an Annunciation, from a late-fifteenth-century French book of hours.

13 *See* e.g., R.Pattison, *On Literacy* (Oxford, 1982), H.Graff, *Legacies of Literacy* (Bloomington, 1987), P.Freire, *Literacy: Reading the Word and the World* (London, 1987), C.Cipolla, *Literacy and Development* (Harmondsworth, 1969). And compare M.-D.Chenu, 'Auctor, Actor, Autor', *Bulletin du Cange*, 3 (1927), pp.81–86.

14 M.T.Clanchy, *From Memory to Written Record: England 1066–1307* (London, 1979), pp.177–85, 201.

15 E.Power, *Medieval Women*, ed. M.Postan (Cambridge, 1975), pp.76–88.

16 On women in guilds *see* E.Power, *Medieval Women*, pp.55–68; S.Shahar, *The Fourth Estate* (London and New York, 1983), pp.189–203; D.Herlihy, *Opera Muliebra* (New York, 1990), pp.95–97, 142–50, 161–62, etc. Etienne Boileau's *Book of Crafts* (second half of the 13th cent.) lists the 100 crafts of Paris. Six were reserved solely for women, and only 14 barred to them completely.

17 The good wife was to write, ' + Bestera + bestie + nay + brigonay + dictera +sagragan + es + domina + fiat + fiat + fiat': *Le Ménagier de Paris*, transl. E.Power, *The Goodman of Paris* (London, 1928), p.305. Some medical treatises on women's diseases were translated into English so that women could act as physicians to one another, avoiding the potential embarrassment of consulting a male doctor: E.Power, *Medieval Women*, p.86.

18 J.Sheppard (Lucy Cavendish College, Cambridge) has found 50 extant books from Buildwas Abbey. The titles themselves are very much as one would find in a house of monks: service books, the Fathers, commentaries, sermon collections, and devotional texts. See, for other convent libraries, N.R.Ker, *Medieval Libraries of Great Britain* (London, 1964) and its *Supplement* by A.G.Watson (London, 1987), and R.H. and M.A.Rouse and R.A.B.Mynors, *Registrum Anglie De Libris Doctorum et Auctorum Veterum* (London, 1991), pp.247–324.

19 *See* E.Power, *Medieval English Nunneries* (Cambridge, 1922), pp.237–38. It seems to me more usual to see nuns singing and praying from individual books, as opposed to monks gathered around one large volume. Nuns had to get their books from somewhere, and not all could have been left by donors. It is surely most likely that they produced the books themselves, just as convents today often produce their own liturgical books, incorporating their own preferences for pointing and chants. *See also* L.Eckenstein, *Woman Under Monasticism* (Cambridge, 1896), *passim*.

20 J.Sheppard is preparing a study of the books of Buildwas Abbey. S.Thompson, *Women Religious: The Founding of English Nunneries after the Norman Conquest* (Oxford, 1991), notes that the scarcity of sources is a fundamental problem in the study of women's convents founded in the twelfth and early thirteenth centuries (p.15).

21 The illustrated Hildegard *Scivias* manuscript was Wiesbaden, Hessische Landesbibliothek, 1, but this manuscript has been lost since 1945. All reproduced colour images are actually pictures of Eibingen, Bib. der Abtei St Hildegard, MS *s.n.*, a handmade, parchment copy from 1927–33. It has been edited, with colour plates, by A.Führkötter in *Corpus Christianorum Continuatio Medievalis*, 43 and 43A (Turnhout, 1978). The *Book of Divine Works* is Lucca, Bib. Stat. MS lat. 1942.

22 C.W.Bynum, *Jesus as Mother* (Berkeley, 1982), p.185.

23 E.Power, *Medieval English Nunneries*, p.237; L.Eckenstein, *Woman Under Monasticism*, pp.118–34.

24 Oxford, Bodleian Library, MS Bodl. 451, fol. 199v. The MS, of monastic moral treatises and sermons, is written in a regular, clear, practised hand.

25 S.Thompson, *Women Religious*, suggests it 'may reflect the higher degree of literary activity in those nunneries founded before the Conquest' (p.14).

26 E.Power, *Medieval English Nunneries*, pp.237–38.

27 *See* B.Bischoff, 'Die Kölner Nonnenhandschriften und das Skriptorium von Chelles', in *Mittelalterliche Studien* (Stuttgart, 1966–67), i, pp.16–34. Chelles was presided over by Charlemagne's sister, Gisela. In Oxford, Queen's College, MS 305, a fifteenth century French kalendar, St Bertille of Chelles (the first, seventh-century, abbess) and her sisters are shown carrying books, but not writing.

28 E.A.Petroff, *Medieval Women's Visionary Literature* (Oxford, 1986), p.211. In general for Helfta *see* Bynum, *Jesus as Mother*, ch.5, 'Women Mystics in the Thirteenth Century: The Case of the Nuns of Helfta', pp.170–262; L.Eckenstein, *Woman Under Monasticism*, pp.328–53.

29 Note that Bridget could not translate the work herself: she composed in the vernacular.

30 C.Nordenfalk, 'St Bridget of Sweden as Represented in Illuminated Manuscripts', in *De artibus XL opuscula: Essays in Honor of Erwin Panofsky*, ed. M.Meiss (New York, 1961), p.376.

31 *See* especially Palermo, Bib. Naz., MS IV. g. 2; NY, Pierpont Morgan, MS 498; Stockholm, Ericsberg Castle,

MS *Liber celestis* (no number); Tübingen, Universitätsbib., formerly Berlin, Preussische Staatsbib., MS Theol. Lat. Nordenfalk, in 'St Bridget' reproduces a good selection of images from these manuscripts and others.

32 *See* e.g., NY, Pierpont Morgan, MS 498, fol. 328r; Stockholm, Ericsberg Castle, MS *Liber celestis*, fol. 85v; Tübingen, Universitätsbib., formerly Berlin, Preussische Staatsbib., MS Theol. Lat., fol. 33r.

33 For example, NY, Pierpont Morgan, MS 498, fol. 343v; Stockholm, Ericsberg Castle, MS *Liber celestis*, fol. 94v.

34 The importance of models and tradition in pictorial representation and illustration is pointed up by later woodcuts of Bridget who is still depicted in her cell, surrounded by books and writing equipment, or actually writing. Once the image had 'set', it continued easily; but no other female saints were treated similarly. *See* the editions of B.Ghotan (Lübeck, 1492) and A.Köberger (Nürnberg, 1500).

35 G.Ouy and C.Reno, 'Identification des autographes de Christine de Pizan', *Scriptorium*, 34 (1980), pp.221–38.

36 *See* L.Schaefer, *Die Illustrationen zu den Handschriften der Christine de Pizan* (Sonderdruck aus dem Marburger Jahrbuch für Kunstwissenschaft, 10, n.d. [1939?]). Schaefer refers to (and reproduces) portraits of Christine from London, BL, MS Harley 4431, fol. 4r; Paris, BN, MS fr. 1176, fol. 1r; MS fr. 836, fol. 42r; MS fr. 603, fol. 81v; MS fr. 835, fol. 1r; MS Arsenal fr. 2681, fol. 4r; Brussels, Bib. Roy., MS 9508, fol. 2r; MS 10309, fol. 1r; MS 10366, fol. 3r; Munich, Bay. Staatsbibl., MS gall. 11, abb. 158, fol. 2r. Only in one manuscript is she facing left: The Hague, Koninklijke Bibl. MS 78 D 42, fol. 1r: she is still right-handed. Although right- and left-handedness can be symbolic in the Middle Ages, the overwhelming evidence here would seem to be on the side of representation.

37 *See* C.C.Willard, *Christine de Pisan. Her Life and Works*, (New York, 1984). 'In *The Book of the City of Ladies*, Christine speaks of having paid a high price for the services of a certain woman artist' (p.45). This woman, whose name was Anastasia, is praised in the highest terms by Christine. By the early fifteenth century (*The Book of the City of Ladies* and *The Book of Three Virtues* were both written in 1405) writing was a type of work open to honest women: 'In her writings, Christine often refers to aspects of book production. In her biography of Charles V, for instance, she speaks of the scribes who were constantly at work copying manuscripts in the royal library. Although she is never referred to specifically as one of these scribes, that this is a sort of work that would have been available to women is confirmed by records of that time of women working as both copyists and illustrators' (p. 45). Willard thinks that working as a scribe would have given Christine both professional training and a source of income in the years before she set up on her own and became successful.

38 Willard cites her as being peculiarly and unusually outspoken in favour of women and against the attitude of men, *Christine de Pisan*, p.73 *et seq.*

39 Note 11 above; and *see* S.Noakes, *Timely Reading: Between Exegesis and Interpretation* (Cornell, 1988); B.Stock, *The Implications of Literacy* (Princeton, 1983); and id., *Listening for the Text* (Johns Hopkins, 1990).

40 M.Carruthers, *The Book of Memory* (Cambridge, 1990) has an interesting short section on writing, dictation, autograph, and recension (pp.195–208). Prodigious writers like Thomas Aquinas dictated to more than one scribe simultaneously. According to the testimony at his canonization, 'all declared' that he dictated to three, and sometimes four, at once. K.Foster, *The Life of St. Thomas Aquinas: Biographical Documents* (London and Baltimore, 1959), no. 32, p.51.

41 Alcuin, *Carmina*, nos.66 line 4, 69 line 15, *MGH. Poetae latini aevi Carolini*, ed. E.Dümmler, i, pp.285, 288: 'dictante deo'.

42 *The Letters of Peter the Venerable*, ed. G.Constable (Harvard, 1967), no.26, i, p.48; E.Dekkers in 'Les autographes des Pères latins', in *Colligere Fragmenta: Festschrift Alban Dold* (Beuron, 1952), p.131, emphasizes that few of the Fathers physically wrote their works, rather than dictating, except as a penance. M.Drogin, *Anathema!* (New Jersey, 1983) has many examples of scribes who thought their own work was drudgery.

43 Barbara Cartland, an upper-class British romantic novelist with some hundreds of books to her credit, writes her novels lying on a couch, surrounded by goodies, dictating to her secretary.

44 Oxford, Bodleian Library, MS Bodl. 717 (Hugo; *Jerome on Isaiah*; first half of the 12th cent.); Cambridge, Trinity College, MS R. 17. 1 (987) (Eadwine; *Canterbury Psalter*; c.1147); Prague, Universitätsbib., MS Kap. A XXI (Hildebertus and Erewinus; Augustine, *De civitate Dei*; 12th cent.).

45 Guda: Frankfurt, MS Barth. 42, fol. 110v (sermon collection; second half of the 12th cent.); Adelhaid: MS Munich, Bayer. Staatsbib., MS Clm 23046, fol. 144r (antiphoner; 14th cent.).

46 *See* e.g., H.Grundmann, 'Die Frauen und die Literatur im Mittelalter: Ein Beitrag zur Frage nach der Entstehung des Schrifttums in der Volksprache', *Archiv für Kulturgeschichte*, 26 (1936), pp.129–61; N.Palmer, *German Literary Culture in the Twelfth and Thirteenth Centuries. An Inaugural Lecture ... 4 March* 1993 (Oxford, 1993), with bibliography; and the chapters by M.L.Ehrenschwendtner and J. Oliver in this volume.

47 E.Power, *Medieval English Nunneries*, pp.240–47.

48 Aberystwyth, National Library of Wales, MS 5667, fol. 288v: prose *Tristan*, 14th cent.

49 See M.Carrasco, 'Spirituality in Context: The Romanesque Illustrated Life of St. Radegund of Poitiers (Poitiers, Bibl. mun., MS 250)', *The Art Bulletin*, 82 (1990), pp.414–35 and plates; E.Ginot, 'Le Manuscrit de Ste Radegonde de Poitiers et ses peintures du XIe siècle', *Bulletin de la Société Française de Reproduction de Manuscrits à Peintures*, 4 (1914–20), pp.9–80; L.Eckenstein, *Woman Under Monasticism*, pp.51–65.

50 Poitiers, Bib. mun., MS 250, fol. 21v (Fortunatus) and fol. 43v (Baudonivia).

51 Paris, BN, MS Arsenal 3142, fol. 256r (writing) and fol. 273r (reading).

52 L.Randall, *Images in the Margins of Gothic Manuscripts* (Berkeley, 1966), p.213: 'Scribe-saint, female'.

53 Cambridge, Trinity College, MS B. 11. 22, fol. 100r. My thanks go to Prof. Norman Zacour for examining this MS for me. For a description of the manuscript *see* M.R.James, *The Western Manuscripts in the Library of Trinity College Cambridge: A Descriptive Catalogue* (Cambridge, 1900), i, pp.364–73.

54 It is possible that an ironic point is being made here as a 'fantastic reversal' for, just as there is a cow milking a woman (fol. 118v) or a sheep chasing a dog (fol. 37r), the folio with the small writing woman in the bottom right hand corner has a writing man at the top left.

55 Heidelberg, Universitätsbib., MS Germ. 848: *Codex Manesse*, portrait of Reinmar of Zweter (c.1320). *See Codex Manesse. Katalog zur Ausstellung Universitätsbibliothek Heidelberg*, ed. E.Mittler and W.Werner (Heidelberg, 1988), Fig.8, p.182.

56 London, BL, MS Royal 1 E. IV, fol. 1r. G.F.Warner and J.P.Gilson, *Catalogue of Royal and King's Manuscripts in the British Museum*, (London, 1921), i, p.19.

57 *See Die Zisterzienser: Ordensleben zwischen Ideal und Wirklichkeit* (Cologne, 1981), p.451. Note that the catalogue entry should read *usuum*, not *ussum*, and the initials 'H. M. W.'. I am most grateful to the owner of the manuscript for the photograph and for permission to publish it here.

58 I owe this information, with gratitude, to Prof. Malachi Beth-Ariye, formerly of the National Library, Jerusalem, and to Prof. Ora Limor, Open University, Jerusalem.

59 Oxford, Bodleian Library, MS Bodl. 270b, fol. 88r.

60 E.Matter, *The Voice of My Beloved: The Song of Songs in Western Medieval Christianity* (Philadelphia, 1990), notes that the treatise *Cogitis me* claims it is by Jerome, and was written for Paula and Eustochium. Actually it was written by Paschasius Radbertus for his friends Theodrada and Irma (p.152).

61 P.Hunter Blair *The World of Bede* (Cambridge, 1990), p.219: Wurzburg, Univ. Bibl., MS M. P. Th. Q. 2.

62 E.Power, *Medieval Women*, p.79.

63 The chronicler Froissart attended a mixed school in Valenciennes. He tells how he fell in love with a girl he saw there reading under a tree. *Les Chroniques de J. Froissart*, ed. J.Buchon (Paris, 1835), iii, pp.479, 482.

64 Judges 4: 4 *et seq*.

65 Origen: 'Praestat hoc consolationem muliebri sexui, ne pro infirmitate desperet se prophetiam posse suscipere: sed credat, quia confert hanc gratiam mentis puritas, non sexus diversitas.' Theodoret: 'Mulier prophetizat, quia virorum ac mulierum eadem est natura .... In Christo Iesu non est masculus, aut femina. Quemadmodum Moses propheta fuit, ita et Maria prophetissa.' Ambrose: 'Debora docuit non solum viri auxilio viduas non egere, verum etiam viris posse esse subsidio.' All from *Biblia Sacra cum Glossa Ordinaria* (Lyons, 1589) on Judges 4.

66 1 Cor. 14: 34–35; 1 Tim. 2: 11–14.

67 'In ecclesia non debet mulier docere, sed in augmentum salutis habet si filios quotidie instruendo generat

68 'quia docere est opus sapientis. Sapientia vero non viget in mulieribus in communis cursu', *ibid.*

69 'ei non contradicendo, sed in licitis et honestis ei obediendo', *ibid.*

70 *Decretum* d.23, c.29, *Mulier quamvis*; *De consecr.* d.4, c.20; II, c.33, q.5, c.17, *Mulierem constat.*

71 Although eventually the *Corpus of British Medieval Library Catalogues* series will go far towards making up this gap.

72 C.Nordenfalk, 'St Bridget', p.385.

73 For instance, M.T.J.Webber, *Scribes and Scholars at Salisbury Cathedral* (Oxford, 1992); D.Ganz, *Corbie in the Carolingian Renaissance* (Sigmaringen, 1990); M.B.Parkes, *The Scriptorium of Wearmouth-Jarrow* (Jarrow Lecture, 1982).

74 The work of the Rouses has done much to open up this field. *See* especially their 'The Book Trade at the University of Paris, ca. 1250 – ca. 1350', in *La production du livre universitaire au moyen âge: exemplar et pecia*, ed. L.Bataillon, B.Guyot, and R.Rouse (Paris, 1988), and the forthcoming publication of their 1993 Lyell lectures (Oxford).

75 *See* C.Willard, *Christine de Pisan*, p.45 *et seq.*

76 Paris, BN, MS fr. 12420, fol. 36r: Amalthea.

77 In the language of scribal tools compasses = *punctorium*, knife = *cultellus*, pen = *penna*, inkstand = *atramentarium*.

78 Paris, BN, MS fr. 12420, ff.30r, 71v, 86r, 92v, 101v, 147r. We may compare their portraits in other manuscripts of *De claribus mulieribus*, e.g., Paris, BN, MS fr. 598, ff.31r, (37r: Amalthea), 71v, 86r, 92r, 100v, 143v. Both manuscripts written at Paris 1403/4.

79 M.Meiss, *French Painting in the Time of Jean de Berry: The Limbourgs and Their Contemporaries* (London, 1974), p.15.

80 Paris, BN, MS fr. 606, fol. 15r.

Chapter Two

Æsop's Cock and Marie's Hen: Gendered Authorship in Text and Image in Manuscripts of Marie de France's Fables

Sandra Hindman

'My name's Marie, I am from France.' ('Marie ai num, si sui de France.') So concludes Marie de France in line 4 of the Epilogue of her *Fables*.[1] She continues in lines 12 to 15 of the same Epilogue, reiterating remarks made in her earlier Prologue, and pointing out that, just as she translated the fables from English to Romance at the behest of Count William, so Æsop translated them from Greek into Latin for his master, the Emperor Romulus. In this way she makes a direct analogy between herself and Æsop. Even briefly summarized, these well-known lines confirm in Marie's poetics the importance of the idea of a *translatio studii*, a sort of patriarchical lineage extending from ancient Greece to modern-day France, coupled with a focus on the search for literary authenticity, especially for a female author. Through the proliferation of first-person verbs, they also call attention to the personalized character of Marie's enterprise, 'narrating a chapter in her own life', as Foulet and Uitti put it with regard to the *Lais*.[2]

In fact, a good deal has been written on Marie's poetics especially as reflected in this 'double' prologue of the *Lais* (for example, by Spitzer, Robertson, Pickens, Foulet and Uitti, Freeman, Leupin, Sankovitch, and others).[3] Whereas there is some difference of opinion as to exactly how Marie understands her project of writing, there is near consensus concerning her self-consciousness as a female author and her resulting desire to carve out a place for herself in the literary establishment through the use of the strategy of a *translatio studii* in the *Lais*.[4] Surprisingly, especially considering the content of the Prologue and Epilogue of the *Fables* as summarized above, virtually no-one has carefully studied these complementary texts to determine how they might contribute to, refine, or recast our idea of Marie's poetics.[5] In fact, scholars often casually dismiss the *Fables* as derivative translations, at best adaptations of an original; they are popularly considered to be either remnants of oral, primitive societies or commonplace instructions to children. Just as no-one has taken seriously the Prologues and Epilogues of the *Fables*, no-one has systematically examined the manuscripts of the *Fables* to determine whether the concerns voiced in the text, especially in the Prologue and the Epilogue, might also be expressed in the illustrations that accompany them.[6] My brief remarks here are part of a much larger project on the medieval reception of Marie de France based on a study of the manuscripts of her writings.

I will argue that, at least in two illuminated manuscripts of the *Fables* produced in France and in Italy in the century after Marie wrote, the pictures take up ideas found in her poetics, which they visually reinforce; and I will specifically show how the manuscripts give visual form in an unprecedented way to the concept of a *translatio studii* while simultaneously calling attention to her gendered authorship. My argument hinges on an interpretation of paired miniatures at the beginning and end of the *Fables*. These miniatures represent the authors Æsop and Marie (or, in one of the instances, Marie and Marie), and the first and last fables, the 'Cock and the Pearl' and the 'Woman and her Hen' respectively. Conspicuously framing the work in manuscript form, these paired miniatures force us to reconsider the *Fables* in the light of Marie's overall project, her poetics, as well as her particular use of the fable genre. I will also show how text and pictures in certain other fables, when read with the framing paired miniatures, offer further clarification of her use of the genre. My analysis leads us to reread the text of the *Fables* in interesting ways, with consequences not just for our understanding of Marie's poetics and their reception by her readers in both the *Lais* and the *Fables*, but also for the status of manuscripts of her writings in the changing milieu of oral and written cultures in the thirteenth century.

We might begin by considering some background information on the manuscripts in question in the context of Marie's work. As is the case with most twelfth-century vernacular authors, there are no extant manuscripts of her writings that date before the thirteenth century.[7] Marie's works – the *Lais* and the *Fables* (I am not treating the *Livre de l'Espurgatoire*) – survive in four manuscripts of the *Lais*, none of which is illustrated, and twenty-three manuscripts of the *Fables*, of which four are illustrated. I will focus on two illuminated manuscripts of the *Fables*; the third illustrated manuscript is fragmentary, incomplete at the beginning and the end, and the fourth is a fifteenth-century copy of one of the thirteenth-century exemplars. My first manuscript, probably made in Italy, perhaps in Venice, between about 1250 and 1275, includes, in addition to Marie's work, Gautier de Metz's *Image du Monde* and five *fabliaux* (Paris, BN, MS fr. 2173).[8] One hundred and four small paintings, charmingly executed in gouache, thinly painted directly on the parchment and within the columns of text *à l'antique*, illustrate this manuscript. Nothing is known about its original owner, but it was in the hands of a Parisian merchant, Guillaume Joubert, in the fifteenth century. My second manuscript, certainly made in France – most likely in Paris – around 1285, includes, in addition to Marie's *Fables*, some twenty-nine other works, romances, *chansons de geste*, moralizing poetry, and prayers, all in verse (Paris, BN, MS Arsenal 3142).[9] It is illustrated with literally hundreds of miniatures, 18 large miniatures, and 103 historiated initials for the *Fables*, as well as with numerous other historiated initials for the remaining texts. Sparkling with highly burnished gold leaf and precious lapis lazuli, this manuscript is a de luxe presentation copy made for Marie of Brabant, Queen of France and second wife of King Philip III.

The earlier of the two manuscripts opens with a historiated initial *C* ('Cil ki sevent de letreüre') showing a clerk dressed in an orange mantle over a blue robe and wearing the

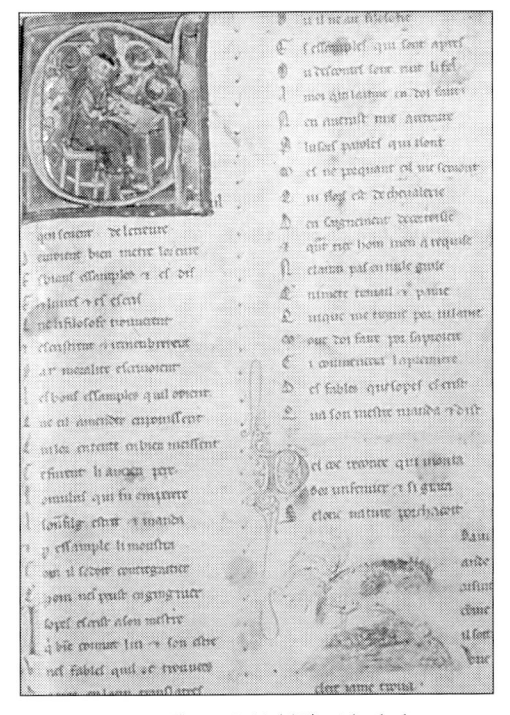

FIG. 14 Above: Initial 'C' with clerk.
Below: The rooster and the gem.
Paris, BN, MS fr. 2173, fol. 58r.

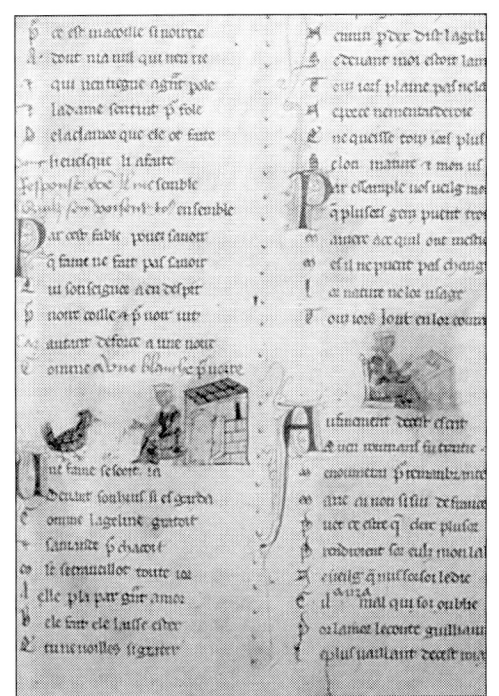

FIG. 15 Above: The woman and the hen.
Below: Marie de France with open book.
Paris, BN, MS fr. 2173, fol. 93r.

bonnet or cap typically worn by teachers (FIG. 14). Portraying him as one of the 'ancient fathers' or 'philosophers' referred to in the opening text of the prologue (*le ancien pere* or *li philosophe*), this figure is unquestionably meant to represent Æsop:

> Those persons, all, who are well-read,/Should study and pay careful heed/To fine accounts in worthy tomes,/To models and to axioms:/That which philosophers did find/And wrote about and kept in mind./The sayings which they heard, they wrote,/So that the morals we would note;/Thus those who wish to mend their ways/Can think about what wisdom says./The ancient fathers did just this.[10]

Continuing, the Prologue situates Æsop as one of the 'ancient fathers' or 'philosophers' through the line 'Thus Æsop to his master wrote' ('Esopes escrist a sun mestre'). Standing out on a burnished gold ground – one of only two uses of burnished gold in the manuscript – Æsop follows the conventional model of an author portrait, derived from evangelist portraits (and ultimately from images of classical writers), a seated figure writing at his lectern.[11] The Paris manuscript of Marie's collected writings thus conveys pictorially that Æsop authored the version of the fables on which Marie's reworking depends.

This manuscript ends with a second author-portrait introducing the opening lines of the Epilogue (FIG. 15): 'To end these tales I've here narrated/And into Romance tongue translated,/I'll give my name, for memory:/I am from France, my name's Marie.'[12] Marie sits at her desk, writing instruments in hand, composing her work, like Æsop at the start of the book, the visual analogy between them as authors pursuing comparable activities reinforcing the idea of a feminine *translatio studii* already implicit in the text. But the analogy cuts both ways when read with the text; for, in the Epilogue, Marie declares that 'it may hap that many a clerk/Will claim as his what is my work./But such pronouncements I want not!/It's folly to become forgot!'[13] Through his portrayal as a clerk, Æsop is not only Marie's ancient antecedent in the line of important transmitters of the fables stretching back to classical times, but is also likened to the clerks who claim her work for their own. Thus, as Marie is like Æsop, she is also, by her gender – as well as by her professional activity as a female writer – distinguished from him. Pictorial forms refocus ideas in the text to fashion a uniquely female version of the concept of *translatio studii*: Æsop may have initially authored the fables, but Marie has the last word, in an unforgettable image in which she appears as a full-fledged author rather than as a mere translator.

The prominent juxtaposition of the first and last fables with the two author-portraits, through layout and, in the case of the last pair, also through costume and composition, invites further scrutiny (Figs 14 and 15), the fables themselves providing further glosses on the activities of writing that frame them both visually and verbally.[14] The first fable, 'The Cock and the Pearl', tells the story of a rooster who, in search of food, uncovers instead a precious stone, which he disdains. Marie uses this fable to comment on the person who doesn't know a good thing when he sees it, specifically on 'men and women ... /The worst they seize; the best, despise'. Scholars have rightly pointed out that in the Greek and Latin Æsopic traditions this fable served immediately after the Prologue as an authorial address, or even challenge, to the reader, who does not understand the work.[15] It came to be transformed in the Middle Ages, in the Latin branch of Æsop known as the *Romulus Nilantii* that Marie adapted, to apply to those generally lacking in wisdom.[16] Marie has used it in its former sense, challenging her audience to take to heart the moralities of the fables. In redefining this audience, however, she apparently made one important change to the text of the *Romulus* that she adapted. None of the Latin versions I have traced specifies both men and women in the accompanying moral.[17] Thus, just as she calls attention to her own gender as an author, she welcomes an audience composed of women as well as men. Whatever her changes in wording, however, in her pairing of the first fable with the Prologue Marie shows herself through the order of the fables to be a faithful transmitter of the Æsopic tradition, since 'The Cock and the Pearl' invariably comes first in collections of both the Phaedrus and the *Romulus*.

This is not the case with Marie's last fable, 'The Woman and her Hen'. This fable occurs relatively infrequently and only in certain collections of the *Romulus*, and it never comes last.[18] Like the cock, the hen, scratching in the ground, searches for food, which, when the woman generously offers it, the hen nonetheless disdains, preferring its own ceaseless pursuit. Juxtaposed with the image of Marie writing and related to the author-portrait/fable-pair at the beginning of the work, the illustration of the woman and her hen invites further reflection on Marie's initiative with respect to both her authorship and her audience. Here, it would seem, she repeats her challenge to the reader.[19] According to Marie, in the end,

FIG. 16 Marie de France reading. Paris, BN, MS Arsenal 3142, fol. 273r.

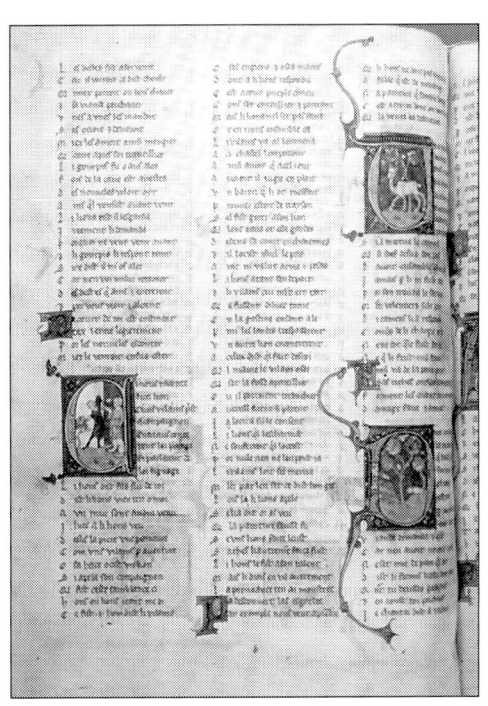

FIG. 17 The lion and the peasant. Paris, BN, MS Arsenal 3142, fol. 262v.

even as the world abides as it is, the significance of fable for her readers' lives comes from the act of searching for meaning. For the conclusion of her work, Marie went out of her way to find a fable that completed her neat textual pairing, an uncommon fable in which a woman offers sustenance to the hen, just as Marie proposes morals to her readers. Layout, composition, and costume reinforce the textual link between the woman in the fable and Marie by implying that the women are mirror images of each other. The shift in gender from the cock to the hen strengthens our understanding of Marie's consciousness that her audience encompasses both men and women.

In the Arsenal manuscript the illustrations impart a new twist to the ideas about writing and reading communicated by the inventively paired vignettes framing the manuscript at the beginning and end. The Arsenal manuscript suppresses altogether the author-portrait of Æsop, substituting a miniature of Marie writing before her lectern (FIG. 87). The manuscript then ends with a second image of Marie, likewise seated in front of a lectern, but this time depicted as a reader instead of a writer, perhaps a reader looking over her finished product (FIG. 16). Other books – her sources, testimonies to her learning, her writings? – lie in a chest before her. In and of themselves, the two miniatures are apparently less concerned with the authority acquired through origins than with the question of Marie's identity. They forcefully underscore this identity through the placement of the second author-portrait within the text directly before the verse 'Marie ai num, si sui de France'. Read with its text, the miniature thus becomes a kind of 'stand-in' for Marie.

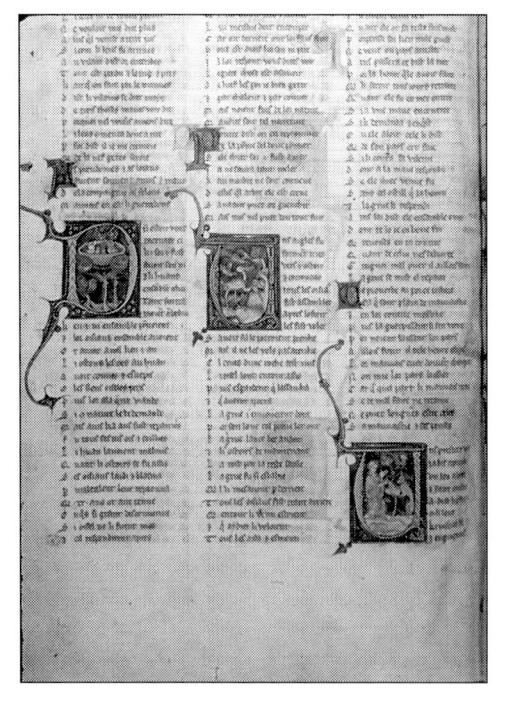

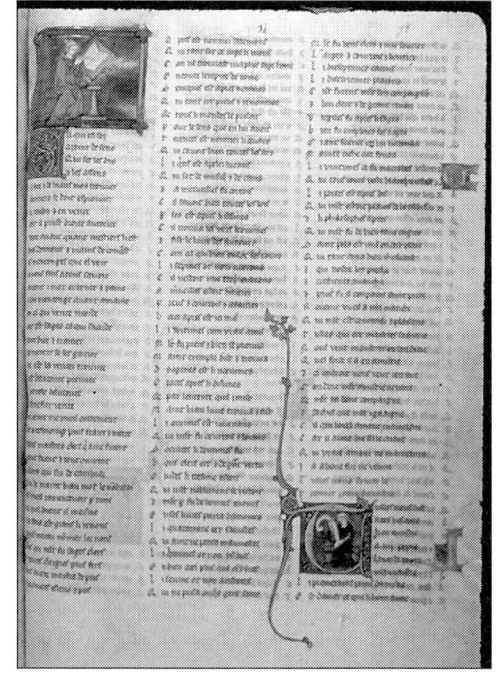

FIG. 18 The preacher and the wolf.
Paris, BN, MS Arsenal 3142, fol. 269v.

FIG. 19 Alart de Cambrai writing at his lectern.
Paris, BN, MS Arsenal 3142, fol. 141r.

Pictures and text in two additional fables contained in the manuscript offer clarification of Marie's beliefs in the moral efficacy of fables. Fable 37, 'The Lion and the Peasant', recounts the tale of a peasant who shows a lion a painting of a man killing a lion with an axe (FIG. 17). The lion asks who painted it. The peasant affirms, 'The work is man's'. The lion then leads the peasant before an emperor, who convicts a baron of treason and throws him to the lions as punishment. The lion smugly tells the peasant that whereas the painting is but 'upon a stone', the real-life example 'is far more true:/It's what you see in front of you'. Marie moralizes: 'Not to accept that something's so/From fables which are but false seeming/Or paintings similar to dreaming./Believe only in what you see:/The truth revealed openly.'[20]

What signals the importance of this fable is, first, the moral, which explicitly comments in a universal way on how to learn from the fables. Most of the morals refer instead to the feudal hierarchy and comment on the behaviours of the different individuals in it: kings, barons, knights, merchants, and so forth. Second, the pictorial treatment, executed in gold leaf, sets it apart from the other illustrations. It would seem thus that fables perform a didactic function for those who can learn to apply their lessons to life (*gloser la lettre*, as the Prologue of the *Lais* states).

The distinction between the mere signs that make up words and the meaning constituted by those words – or, we might say between literacy and cognition – is the subject of Fable 81, 'The Preacher and the Wolf,' or 'The Wolf Goes to School' (FIG. 18). As the tale goes, a

FIG. 20 Aristotle with scroll.
Paris, BN, MS Arsenal 3142, fol. 155v.

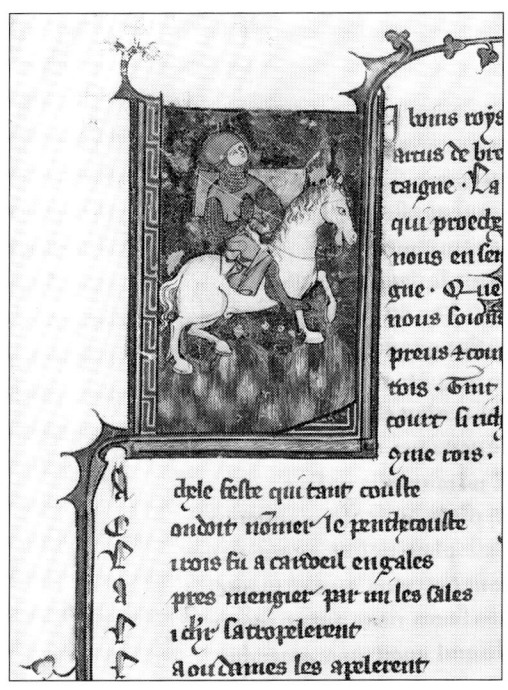

FIG. 21 *Le Chevalier au lion*, Yvain on horseback.
Paris, BN, MS fr. 1433, fol. 61r.

priest tries to teach a wolf the alphabet, which he urges him to repeat after him, alternately refraining A, A, B, B, C, C. At the end of this refrain, he coaxes the wolf to recite the alphabet alone, and the wolf, momentarily hesitating, suddenly cries out 'Aignel?' ('Lamb?'). Marie's moral is that 'The mouth exposes what one thinks/Though it would speak of other things.'[21]

I have written elsewhere about how manuscript compilation functioned for Old French romances to reinforce or to shift meanings of a particular text when it is grouped in a larger compendium.[22] In the Arsenal manuscript the inclusion of other texts and pictures reinforces Marie's credentials as a writer owing to her classical lineage. Her author-portrait is visually linked with that of a male writer, Alart de Cambrai, which appears earlier in the Arsenal manuscript (FIG. 19). A thirteenth-century author roughly contemporary with Marie, Alart de Cambrai used the erudite work of the twelfth-century Chartrian grammarian William of Conches, the *Moralium Dogma*, as the basis for his vernacular *Moralités des philosophes*, composed between about 1260 and 1268.[23] Alart's novel contribution was to present in a systematic manner authors of antiquity as though they were wise contemporary clerks. Thus, just as Alart de Cambrai transmits the moral sayings attributed to philosophers, including such august classical authorities as Solomon, Seneca, Cicero, Boethius, Socrates, and Aristotle, among others, so Marie – his equivalent, the pictures imply – hands down the ancient fables with her own morals appended to them (FIG. 20).

Whereas the illustration of Alart de Cambrai's work places Marie in a *translatio studii*, the

51

frontispiece of the entire manuscript helps focus attention on female agency (FIG. 88). In this celebrated miniature, prefacing Adenet le Roi's romance *Cleomadés*, Marie de Brabant (c.1260–1321) reclines on a *lit de parade*, beside which stand Blanche, the daughter of Louis IX, sister of King Philip III, and widow of Ferdinand of Castile, and Jean II, the young Duke of Brabant and nephew of Marie. At the foot of the bed appears Adenet, holding a musical instrument. The miniature illustrates the prologue, where Adenet praises 'two ladies in whom remains the flower of good sense, of beauty, and of merit',[24] who requested that he tell the story. Concealing their identity in the prologue, he promises to disclose their names only at the end of the work, where they appear in an acrostic (vv.18541–18579): 'La Reine de France Marie Madame Blanche Ann'. As the women gesture toward the minstrel he begins, the picture suggests, to sing his romance. Appearing a second time below the large miniature, Adenet occupies a historiated initial, where he writes the romance down on wax tablets – that is, in book form, on the support often used for a writer's first draft. Read together, this pair of miniatures underscores female agency in the composition of a literary work, the theme to which the miniatures of Marie placed later in the manuscript of the *Fables* return. Simultaneously, read as a double author-portrait, the prefatory miniatures situate literary creation between the acts of telling and writing.

Here we have before us an impressive visualization of the ambiguous world of oral and written culture in the thirteenth century. The multiple author-portraits designed to convey pictorially a *translatio studii* and the particular emphasis on a certain kind of learning in Marie's work both emphasize the pedagogical function of the *Fables*.[25] With the manuscripts of the *Fables* of Marie de France we find ourselves located in clerical culture, close to Latin culture. This can be seen by comparing their frontispieces with those in other Old French texts contemporary with Marie's. No one has previously observed that the author-portraits in Marie de France's *Fables* are virtually unprecedented in vernacular verse. For example, surprisingly, in works by Chrétien de Troyes, the poet usually regarded as Marie's closest counterpart, there exists not a single author-portrait.[26] Chrétien's romances usually open with a depiction of a riding knight, the *chevalier*, the protagonist, who is himself the teller of the tale, as in a miniature from a copy of *Yvain* (FIG. 21). Or they occasionally open with another scene of storytelling, such as in the Princeton manuscript of *Yvain*, which begins with Calogrenant recounting the story before Guinevere at Arthur's court.[27] Exceptionally, they begin, like the 'Guiot' manuscript, with a miniature of the patron, in this case Marie de Champagne, commanding Chrétien to tell the story of Lancelot (FIG. 22). In all such instances, they thus inscribe orality into the pictures. The same holds true for other Arthurian verse romances, such as the *Atre perilleux* and the *Chevalier as deus espees*, two other examples both prefaced by the ubiquitous riding knight.[28] Manuscripts of Chrétien, I argue, were used in a milieu that still privileged oral or performative culture. How different their images are from those of the author writing, even sometimes surrounded by books, in manuscripts of Marie's works.

Comparable examples to the author portraits in Marie's manuscripts occur in the thirteenth century in two sorts of vernacular texts: the antique romances and the prose ro-

FIG. 22 *Le Chevalier de la charrette*,
Marie de Champagne.
Paris, BN, MS fr. 794, fol. 27r.

FIG. 23 Solomon with Dares and Dictys,
Benoît de Saint-Maure, *Roman de Troie*.
Paris, BN, MS fr. 1610, fol. 1r.

mances. A manuscript of Benoît de St-Maure's *Roman de Troie*, where the introductory text draws on the authority of Solomon, 'qui nous enseigne', to authorize the versions by Dares and Dictys over that of 'Homer' on the Trojan War, opens with Solomon seated before two ancients (Dares and Dictys) bearing scrolls, which are to be understood here as referring to the appearance of ancient books before the emergence of the codex (FIG. 23).[29] In somewhat different terms than those used for Marie, the absent author, Benoît, nevertheless here takes his place in a *translatio studii* extending from Solomon through Dares and Dictys to the modern day. His authority derives not only from that of the ancients but from the Divine Word. The same thing happens in prose romances. Author-portraits in Arthurian romance seem to occur only in works like Robert of Boron's prosification of the Grail legend, where he recasts the Perceval story in prose, the language of truth, to reveal the mysteries of revelation.[30] Of course, we should remember that the pictorial formula of the author-portrait itself appropriately merges two models, the inspired evangelist and the classical author.

The novelty of imagery in Marie's manuscripts forces us to reconsider the reception of her work in the thirteenth century. Imagery in manuscripts of the *Fables* asserts not just a female version of the *translatio studii*, or a self-consciousness about writing as a woman, or an awareness of the mixed gender of the readers, but a connection with grammar, the branch of philosophy and one of the Seven Liberal Arts which teaches how to write and read in the right manner. According to the School of Chartres in the twelfth century, philosophy, including grammar, offered an opportunity to combine human and Divine

Wisdom. The double Prologue to the *Lais*, where Marie cites the model of the grammarian Priscian among the philosophers, has previously been understood to express in Marie's poetics the close relationship between poetry, theology, and philosophy.[31] Likewise, in the textual and pictorial poetics in manuscripts of the *Fables*, we are confronted with a *translatio studii* that is not just feminine but Christian also, one that conveys the concept that the ultimate truth resides in the Book.

Notes to Chapter Two

1 A version of this paper was delivered as a talk at The Medieval Institute, Kalamazoo, Mich., May 1993. For a bibliography on Marie de France and her works, *see* G.S.Burgess, *Marie de France: An Analytical Bibliography* (London, 1977) and *Supplement No. 1* (1986). The first modern edition of the Fables is J.-B.B.de Roquefort, *Poésies de Marie de France, poète anglo-normand du XIIIe siècle* (Paris, 1819–20) (vol.ii, on the Fables and the Espurgatoire). Modern editions of the Fables are edited by C.Bruckner, *Les Fables* (Louvain, 1991) and K.Warnke, *Die Fabeln der Marie de France* (Halle, 1898). For a translation of the Fables, *see* H.Spiegel, *Marie de France, Fables* (Toronto, Buffalo, and London, 1987). Quotations here are taken from Warnke; English translations from Spiegel.

2 A.Foulet and K.D.Uitti, 'The Prologue to the *Lais* of Marie de France: A Reconsideration', *Romance Philology*, 35 (1981), pp.242–49.

3 L.Spitzer, 'The Prologue to the *Lais* of Marie de France and Medieval Poetics', *Modern Philology*, 41 (1943), pp.96–102; D.W.Robertson, 'Marie de France, *Lais*, Prologue, 13–16', *Modern Language Notes*, 64 (1949), pp.336–38; R.Pickens, 'La Poétique de Marie de France d'après les Prologues des Lais', *Les Lettres Romanes*, 32 (1978), pp.367–84; A.Foulet and K.D.Uitti, *ibid.*; M.Freeman, 'Marie de France's Poetics of Silence: The Implications of a Feminine *Translatio*', *PMLA*, 99 (1984), pp.860–83; T.Sankovitch, *French Women Writers and the Book: Myths of Access and Desire*, (Syracuse, NY, 1988), *esp.* ch.1, 'Marie de France: The Myth of the Wild', pp.15ff.; A.Leupin, 'The Impossible Task of Manifesting "Literature": On Marie de France's Obscurity', *Exemplaria*, 3/1 (1991), pp.221–42.

4 *See esp.* Freeman, 'Marie de France's Poetics'.

5 On this subject, *see* M.M.Malvern, 'Marie de France's Ingenious Use of Authorial Voice and Her Singular Contribution to Western Literature', *Tulsa Studies in Women's Literature*, 2/1 (1983), pp.21–41.

6 The only study on illuminations in manuscripts of Marie's texts remains K.Ringger, 'Prolégomènes à l'iconographie des oeuvres de Marie de France', in *Orbis Mediaevalis. Mélanges de langue et de littérature médiévales offerts à Reto Radulf Bezzola à l'occasion de son quatre-vingtième anniversaire*, ed. G.Güntert, M.-R.Jung, and K.Ringger (Berne, 1978), pp.329–42.

7 For a list of the manuscripts, *see* Burgess, *Marie de France*, pp.11–12; and A.Ewert and R.C.Johnston (eds.), *Marie de France: Fables* (Oxford, 1942) pp.xii–xiii. For the *Lais*, *see esp.* E.Hoepffner, *Les Lais de Marie de France* (Strasbourg, 1921; Paris, 1966), and id., 'La Tradition manuscrite des lais de Marie de France', *Neophilologus*, 12 (1927), pp.1–10, 85–96. For the *Fables*, *see esp.* Warnke, *Fabeln*, pp.iii–xiii; and G.Keidel, 'The History of French Fable Manuscripts', *PMLA*, 24 (1909), pp.208–12.

8 Warnke, *Fabeln*, p.vi, no.11; *Catalogue des manuscrits français: Anciens fonds*; and F.Avril and M.-Th.Gousset, with C.Rabel, *Manuscrits enluminés d'origine italienne*, ii, *XIIIe siècle* (Paris, 1984), pp.9–10, no.9, plate iv.

9 Warnke, *Fabeln*, p.xi, no.21; H.Martin, *Catalogue des manuscrits de la Bibliothèque de l'Arsenal*, iii (Paris, 1887), pp.256–64. *See also* P.Paris, 'Adam ou Adènes, surnommé Le Roi: Sa vie', *Histoire littéraire de la France*, 20 (1842), pp.710–18; H.Martin, 'Cinq portraits du XIIIe siècle: Marie de Brabant; – Blanche de France; – Jean II de Brabant; – Robert II d'Artois; – Adenet le Roi, ménestrel', *Société nationale des Antiquaires de France. Centenaire (1804–1904). Recueil de mémoires* (1904), pp.269–79, plate xv; H.Martin and P.Lauer, *Les Principaux manuscrits à peintures de la Bibliothèque de l'Arsenal à Paris* (Paris, 1929), p.21, plate xix; A.Henry, *Les Oeuvres d'Adenet le Roi*, i. *Biographie d'Adenet: La tradition manuscrite* (Bruges, 1951), *esp.* pp.95–100; id., *Adenès: Dernier grand trouvère* (Paris, 1971), *esp.* pp.24–25.

10 'Cil, ki sevent de letreüre,/devreient bien metre lur cure/es bons livres e es escriz/e es essamples e es diz,/que li philosophe troverent/e escristrent e remembrerent./Par moralité escrivient/les bons proverbes qu'il oeient,/que cil amender s'en poïssent/ki lur entente en bien meïssent./Ceo firent li anciën pere'.

11 On the origins of the author-portrait *see* A.M.Friend, 'The Portraits of the Evangelists in Greek and Latin Manuscripts', *Art Studies*, 5 (1927), pp.115–47 and *Art Studies*, 7 (1929), pp.3–29.

12 'Al finement de cest escrit,/qu'en Romanz ai traitié e dit,/me numerai pur remembrance:/Marie ai num, si sui de France'.

13 'Puet cel estre, cil clerc plusur/prendreient sur els mun labur:/ne vueil que nuls sur lui le die;/cil uevre mal ki sei ublie'.

14 For a related analysis of the content of these two fables, *see* H.Spiegel, 'Male Animal Fables of Marie de France', in *Medieval Masculinities: Regarding Men in the Middle Ages*, ed. C.A.Lees, with the assistance of T.Fenster and J.A.McNamara (Medieval Cultures 7, Minneapolis and London, 1994), pp.111–26, *esp.* pp.122–23.

15 L.Hervieux, *Les Fabulistes latins, depuis le siècle d'Auguste jusqu'à la fin du moyen âge* (Paris, 1893–99); H.R.Jauss, *Untersuchungen zur Mittelalterlichen Tierdichtung* (Tübingen, 1959) pp.30–31.

16 For the *Romulus Nilantii*, *see* Hervieux, *Fabulistes*, ii, pp.513–48; fable: 413–14. *See* remarks on transformations to this fable by A.C.Henderson, 'Medieval Beasts and Modern Cages: The Making of Meaning in Fables and Bestiaries', *PMLA*, 97 (1982), pp.40–49.

17 *See* also B.E.Perry (ed.), *Babrius and Phaedrus* (Cambridge, Mass., 1965).

18 *See* Hervieux, *Fabulistes*, ii (1893–99), pp.647, 650.

19 Jauss, *Untersuchungen*, pp.33–34.

20 'que nuls ne deit nïent entendre/a fable, ki est de mençunge,/n'a peinture, ki semble sunge;/c'est la creire dunt hum veit l'uevre,/ki la verité en descuevre'.

21 'la buche mustre le penser,/tut deïe ele d'el parler'.

22 S.Hindman, *'Sealed in Parchment': Rereadings of Knighthood in the Illuminated Manuscripts of Chrétien de Troyes* (Chicago, 1994), *esp.* pp.4, 8, 39.

23 On Alard, *see* R.Bargeton, *Le Livre de philosophie et de moralité, par Alart de Cambrai, étude et édition*, in *Positions des thèses de l'Ecole des Chartes* (1942), pp.9–13; Alard de Cambrai, *Le Livre de philosophie et de moralité d'Alard de Cambrai*, ed. J.-Ch.Payen (Paris, 1970).

24 'deus dames en cui maint la flour/de sens, de biauté, de valour,' Henry, *Adènes*, vv.23–24.

25 Though probably not an audience largely composed of children, as suggested by H.Spiegel, 'Instructing the Children: Advice from the Twelfth-Century *Fables* of Marie de France', *Children's Literature*, 17 (1989), pp.25–46.

26 On this subject, *see* Hindman, *Rereadings*, pp.83–84, 197–98.

27 *Ibid.*, p.83, Fig.35.

28 *Ibid.*, pp.53–54, Figs.23, 40.

29 Paris, BN, MS fr. 1610. Excepting H.Buchthal, *Historia Troiana: Studies in the History of Mediaeval Secular Illustration* (London, 1971), there is no systematic study of these illustrations. For the text, cf. Benoît de Saint-Maure, *Le Roman de Troie*, ed. L.Constans, (6 vols., Paris, 1904–12).

30 Hindman, *Rereadings*, pp.197–98, Fig.104.

31 'Les Anciens avaient coutume,/comme en témoigne Priscien,/de s'exprimer dans leurs livres/avec beaucoup d'obscurité/à l'intention de ceux qui devaient venir après eux/et apprendre leurs œuvres:/ils voulaient leur laisser la possibilité de commenter le texte/et d'y ajouter le surplus de science qu'ils auraient./Les poètes anciens savaient/et comprenaient eux-mêmes/que plus le temps passerait,/plus les hommes auraient l'esprit subtil/et plus ils seraient capables/d'interpréter les ouvrages antérieurs.' Marie de France, *Lais*, transl. L.Harf-Lancner, ed. K.Warnke, (Paris, 1990), vv.9–22.

CHAPTER THREE

Interpreting Images of Women with Books in Misericords

WENDY ARMSTEAD

MISERICORDS EVOLVED IN the medieval Western European Church as a response to specific historical and cultural forces. Plain or decorated, the ledges acknowledged, literally and allegorically, the weakness of struggling humanity,[1] and became an integral part of the structure of choir-stalls for a period stretching, roughly speaking, from the mid-eleventh century to the Reformation and the outlawing of the Feast of Fools.[2] So many misericords have been lost – destroyed or censored – that it is impossible to know how many were created, but some 3,400 survive in Britain.[3] Often they are depreciated, historically and artistically, and thought lightweight.[4] Thematically, it has been felt necessary to look for reasons to explain (and in some sense excuse) this 'levity'; artistically, the artisans who created them are not admired for their skill with the chisel, but rather are blamed for their crudity, imagination, or ignorance. The highly placed clergy who commissioned the work, it is assumed, were not responsible (whether through absence or oversight) for content which we consider to be reprehensible or unintelligible, the blame for which falls squarely on the shoulders of the carvers. But this begs a question: who were the carvers? Misericord researchers such as Francis Bond at the turn of the century, and more recently Mary Anderson and others, have tended to portray misericord carvers, the patrons-by-default, as jolly, good-humoured 'ignorant men', prey to superstition and fancy: humble craftsmen whose wild imaginations sometimes got the better of them. According to this popular myth, the wise, prayerful bishop was a man so intent upon his religious duties that he was inclined to overlook the occasional sexually explicit or impious image that a mischievous carver slipped past him. After all, it was said, what could one expect of the creations of illiterate artisans who simply offered a mirror of daily life in the village?

This seductive 'carver as culprit' theory still exerts its influence today. In 1910, Francis Bond contended that misericords are 'a record of just what stately historians omit … not the ways of courts and politicians … but the simple everyday life of ordinary folk … a picture – realistic and true – of that history which does not find its way into books';[5] in 1954, Mary Anderson maintained that 'the carvers were … free to draw their inspiration from the world around them'[6] (a view, incidentally, which conflicts with her statement in 1935 that 'we can learn little of how they [the carvers] lived from what they carved, and yet the choice of their subjects sheds some light upon their mental attitude'[7]). Even if, by 1969, she rather reluctantly concludes that the clerical patrons must logically have been involved to some degree in artistic choices, she still argues that the lack of 'scholarly planning' in the iconography of misericords argues for a 'considerable measure of freedom in [the carver's] choice and treatment of designs'.[8] For Anderson, the carver's influence can be seen in the fact that misericords provide a hotchpotch 'picture of the lighter side of medieval life', including 'sardonic commentaries on social abuses at home'.[9] More recently, Kraus and Kraus in 1975 emphasize the way in which the 'freedom of the medieval misericord-maker's work' apparently 'resulted in a kind of anarchy', and suggest that the subjects of any set have a 'haphazard' quality with only a stylistic relationship with other carvings; the reason for this state of affairs, they maintain, is that clerics 'rarely had a role in initiating subject matter'.[10] The argument presumes that if clerics had been handling the matter, they would necessarily have used the underseats of the choirstalls for sequences of religious subjects; since no such ideational pattern is obvious to us, clerics must have taken no interest and the carvers were free to do as they liked. A recent misericord picturebook still claims that 'the craftsmen felt free to carve everyday scenes and animals from their own imagination, rather than the religious subjects one might expect';[11] most recently, Michael Camille concludes that 'ribald' misericord imagery is proof that 'ecclesiastical patrons left the non-essential parts of programmes to the imaginations of their makers'.[12] All misericord theorists agree that the clergy was in some way involved in the choice of misericord ornamentation; none of them allows this to impinge on the stereotypical uneducated carver with his skilful jumble.

The myth of the fanciful, mischief-making carver unwittingly creating genre art, however, deflects attention from some interesting questions. Misericords were widely accepted by collegiate institutions across Europe. Not all clergymen reacted well to profane art in church,[13] but by and large, it seems, no prohibition prevented their sustained creation over some six centuries. Indeed, the evidence of the imagery would suggest that it was precisely the learned élite of medieval society, the powerful, literate clergymen – and in at least one case, nuns[14] – who would have enjoyed the visual puns and surreptitious references to legends and tales that characterize misericord imagery. Were the misericords not a source of private enjoyment for the élite who knew about them?[15] Is it perhaps the case that when what has been called 'pagan' and 'folk' imagery is invited into the confines of the church, the very contrast makes a confident, self-conscious statement concerning the higher status of the monks, and the rightness and dominance of their higher-order Christian perspective?

As the study of the iconography of misericords has recently developed, it has become clear that a careful, comparative reading of individual misericords frequently turns up information that defies the broad 'social history of folk' and 'carver's folly' hypotheses. In some instances, it seems, generations of clergy and selected lay brethren inherited, without disquiet, misericords which satirized women (from wives to witches, prostitutes to young innocent maidens), mendicant priests, peasants, foreigners, and Jews, or which alluded disturbingly to ancient gods and goddesses, or included Roman and Celtic motifs. A misericord is, of course, a marginal decoration only a shadow away from the posterior of clergymen; this truism is frequently invoked by misericord researchers to explain what are often, disparagingly, considered to be their unsystematic and secular misericord programmes.[16] But this is insufficient: one has only to consider the similarities of misericord design with that of other medieval media (early stone-work, roof bosses, wall-paintings, bench ends, stained glass windows, manuscript marginalia, and the decorated household objects of the aristocracy such as musical instruments, chalices, or the backs of ivory mirrors) to realize that it is possible to exaggerate the 'shadow side' of misericords while ignoring intriguing contradictions and neglecting the more profound implications that the profane image takes on in its sacred setting.[17] What I shall suggest here is that a Bakhtinian approach to misericord analysis makes possible a reading of certain misericords which might otherwise remain mysterious, and that in particular, when we read images of women with books in misericords we must acknowledge not just the possibility, but the high probability, of irony, so that the type of humour exemplified by misericord imagery can be seen as a manifestation of the social bond that distinguished the monks and canons as a group. What could be threatening – the female, for example – was now laughable; images belonging to the old order were domesticated and made safe.

What, then, is the best theoretical framework within which to examine images of women with books in misericords? However tempting it is to conclude that a female figure with a book in hand is a rare respectful representation of a serious woman engaged in a scholarly or devotional act, this literal reading of the image is just as much of a mistake as the common error of assuming that if a woman in a misericord is beating a man over the head then this is proof positive that medieval women were in actuality violent husband-beaters.[18] It may be that there is no ironic or comic intent in the image of the woman with her open book; it may be that medieval women did hit their husbands; but upon what basis are we passing this judgement in relation to the carved image in front of us?

Mikhail Bakhtin's study of Rabelais has enabled a generation of medievalists to begin to comprehend a vast archaeological reservoir of images previously denounced as silly and meaningless;[19] in the present case, a Bakhtinian reading helps to make sense of the misericord narratives which emphasize the comedy of the human body and the tragedy of unredeemed human life. Rather than being chaotic godless gropings in the dark, misericord images eloquently remind the viewer of what it is to be weak and human, trapped in the realm of the flesh, the devil's realm. The key, perhaps, properly understood, is Bakhtin's phrase, 'the material lower bodily stratum'. This has become popularly associated with misericords in a sense limited to 'bottoms' or 'naughtiness'; but for Bakhtin, it describes the dynamic at the heart of Gothic grotesquery, and we shall need to look at his holistic envisioning of the 'medieval logic' of the grotesque image.[20]

One of the more useful intersections between Bakhtin's study of Rabelais and an iconographic study of misericords is the relationship between speech and image, and in particular between official and unofficial realms of speech, behaviour, and art in the world of the medieval élite. Of necessity, the élite, of all medieval social groups, possesses the greatest flexibility and self-consciousness, and it is their formal, schooled speech that can best accommodate and explicate the free and unschooled speech of the fair and the marketplace; the two meet, typically, in the church, literate speech encountering what Bakhtin refers to as 'the folk culture of humour'. Folk culture, for Bakhtin, is a 'boundless world' of 'humorous forms and manifestations' created in opposition to the official and serious tone of the ecclesiastical and feudal culture: 'in spite of their variety, folk festivities of the carnival type, the comic rites and cults, the clowns and fools, giants, dwarfs, and jugglers, the vast and manifold literature of parody – all these forms have one style in common: they belong to one culture of folk carnival humour'.[21] Bakhtin, of course, emphasizes the egalitarian nature of this folk 'culture of humour', but it is easy to oversimplify or romanticize: 'carnival', the meeting place of citizen and non-citizen, Christian and Jew, man and woman, in so-called rejuvenative laughter does not reflect in any sense a democratic meeting of equals, but rather its opposite: 'high' intersects with 'low' in a particular, predictable way that ultimately empowers the privileged classes. The community in general can be empowered only ritualistically, as symbolized by the metaphorical carnival crowning: the debasement and reinstatement of an individual signifying the renewal of the dominant social group. The appropriation of folk-cultural motifs for use in 'high' art and literature is a demonstration of power as much as it is a symbol of interdependence and universality. For the image changes as it changes hands: a depiction in the margin of a manuscript – or on a misericord – of a mummer's mask, a woman dancing, or a peasant at work is not necessarily mimetic, but may be richly comic or diminishing.

That unexceptionable motifs are transformed into comedy shows, perhaps, how far higher classes 'owned' speech idioms, images, and practices, and how far the educated, more privileged élite – the masters of language and image – were able to use and refine them for their own social needs. When Bakhtin, for example, refers to 'speech' or 'language', he invests the terms with an appealing poetic universality, but clearly it must be the speech of the higher orders of society that is invigorated and renewed by its familiarity with the unlettered, and therefore unencumbered, speech – or world-view – of the lower-order labouring and servant classes. Rabelais himself, after all, was a sophisticated man of the world who skillfully and creatively manipulated folk culture to create literary sensations designed to shock, excite, delight and dazzle the literate. Metaphorically speaking, he is not the clown but the ringmaster, his formalized model of low culture producing something other than genuine 'folk art'. This does not prevent Bakhtin from claiming that the folk culture of humour found in Rabelais's *Gargantua* and *Pantagruel* embodies 'its greatest literary expression'. I would suggest, on the same point, that its greatest *visual* expression is found in the art of misericords, an art which leads us not to the folk so much as to those highly cultured individuals who could move in and out of folk culture at will; in this case, the educated ecclesiastical community.

Misericords, after all, express the forms of folk culture as delineated by Bakhtin, but in a virtually non-literate, non-linguistic style. In misericords one can find traces of oriental influence on the medieval European imagistic corpus: dragons and griffons, pagan gods and goddesses, and traces of a reproductive, female-tainted lost world. We also find traces of the Bakhtinian paradox which contends that in the context of the élite culture, as here in the cathedral and in the church, status is also a reminder of its reverse, lack of status, life a reminder of death. If we bear these Bakhtinian models in mind, we may well see a certain misericord from Norwich Cathedral, for example, in a slightly altered light. Here one finds a husband and wife in perfect positional equality (both, unfortunately, equally damaged) with no misogynist motive apparent: 'A man and woman stand side by side. The woman on the left holds a book in both hands ... The man ... holds by both hands a scroll'. Under the ledge 'a crown has been carved with W, standing for William, the christian name of the man who stands beneath'. A greyhound, 'the aristocrat of dogs', lies at the feet of the pair. The supporters on either side bear coats of arms which positively identify the two figures as 'Sir William Clere of Ormesby, who died in 1384, and his wife Denise Wichingham'.[22] The effect of the whole is reminiscent of the sister art of effigy – a word especially appropriate here in that it has come to signify either the grandness or the degradation of monumentalized persons. The Wichinghams have been made prominent at the same time that they have been lowered; their lives have been celebrated, but in a space where earthly life is held in low repute. Festoons of scrolling vines and flowers can drape a tomb or a banquet table – or concessionary seats in choir-stalls. What is alive must die, what is high is made low, what is serious is laughed at – but all in the cause of renewal. To take a Bakhtinian view of misericords is to accept that their iconography is informed by its appearance in this particular medium, that the misericord is not just the equivalent of an illustration or a wooden copy of a design from another medium, but that in all probability the carver, in conformity with the instructions of his employer and the demands of the tradition, exploited his materials to the full. For instance, the sudden, surprising equality between men and women in carnival-laughter which informed the Wichingham carving is evident too in the evenly-matched couples one finds at Ely,[23] to name one typical example from the fourteenth century. Their stance and posture suggests a levelling that ordinary society did not tolerate. Such evenly-matched 'kings and queens' and seated 'men and women', usually dismissed as of merely architectural origin, may be seen to embody the carnival spirit. We accept that in reading misericord imagery we are led back into the realm of extraordinary circumstance, a 'temporary suspension, both ideal and real, of hierarchical rank', a liberation 'from norms of etiquette and decency imposed at other times'.[24]

In viewing misericords, then, as a manifestation of carnival spirit, we are justified in assuming that a different set of rules and logic informs their creation, and the primary task becomes that of understanding 'market-place gesture and speech',[25] where ambivalence colours every move. If we accept the Bakhtinian view, we will find in misericords neither 'purely negative satire' nor 'gay, fanciful, recreational drollery deprived of philosophical content,'[26] and this raises interesting questions about whether it is enough merely to say that certain debasing, satirized, female-centred misericords are misogynistic in intent. This is not, of course, to deny that they are so: merely to ask if this is the only conclusion we

FIG. 24 Supporter (detail). Ely Cathedral.

may draw. The situation for the interpreter is complex. Tempting as it may be to use the image of a seductive misericord woman or her counterpart, the hag, to illustrate the point that medieval preachers were threatened by women,[27] obvious as the contention may be that the medieval cleric and other members of his society could be demeaning and controlling of the female population, we must accept that issues of gender are often difficult to interpret in misericords. We need to take into account the possibility of ambivalence: is the hag in a horned headdress, for example, intended only to debase the female, or has she rather a secondary function, that of encapsulating the human fear of ageing and dying? If she is relegated to the choir-stall, does this suggest more than lost fertility – perhaps even death? Misericord subjects, as one colourful outgrowth of the moral concerns of a church burdened with the lives of its parishioners, reflect these issues, and sometimes use female images to do so.[28]

In making sense of the female image in misericords, then, as in any visual image, context is everything. In the case of the misericord, the context is the choir-stall – and the creator of context is the 'clerical imagination'. In other words, interpretation of the carved image should be related to the culture – both visual and textual – of the collegiate institutions. It would be possible, for example, to take a picture of a woman kneeling in prayer, with prayer-book in hand, at face value – and even employ it to illustrate an essay on medieval female piety (FIG. 24). But this will not give the whole picture. There is a well-documented tendency for British misericords to consist of related parts, with the central carvings relating to the side carvings in an intelligible fashion;[29] and if we do indeed look at the com-

FIG. 25 Centrepiece (detail). Ely Cathedral.

plete programme, it becomes clear that to take this image of a woman with a book at face value would be to lose much of the meaning. (FIG. 25). Emma Phipson, in her 1896 guide to British misericords, describes it as follows: 'A man and horse falling to the ground; the man wears a tight-fitting cap and a hose jerkin. His hunting horn lies broken beside him. Lefthand supporter: two dogs hunting hinds through a wood'; and, on the right hand, 'a woman or saint, possibly St Giles, in a chapel praying before a small altar'.[30] Seventy-three years later, G.L.Remnant replicates her description almost word for word: 'Man wearing tight-fitting cap and loose jerkin with his horse falling to the ground. His hunting horn lies broken beside him'. Supporters: two dogs hunting hinds through a wood; and 'woman in a chapel praying before a small altar'.[31] So far so good: but is it possible to go further than this in understanding the imagery?

There seem to be three possible avenues for investigation. Firstly, Phipson suggested that the image of the woman with her psalter in her chapel praying before an altar is not a woman at all but St Giles (d. c.720). The only support given for this is the fact that another Ely misericord is most probably a depiction of the half-naked figure of the saint.[32] The legend of St Giles describes how a Frankish king or prince, while hunting in the woods, disturbed a doe who inadvertently led him to the hermit '*in pe woodis wylde*'[33] who, wounded by a stray arrow from the hunter, had survived only on the doe's milk. The king was so moved by this holy man that he built a monastery upon the site of his grotto.[34] In Phipson's reading, then, the fallen hunter represents one of the hunters in the royal entourage, the hinds those he pursued, and the woman with her psalter signifies the birth of the monastery

– for the figure is most certainly a woman and not St Giles. But there are problems with this reading. In the legend, the hunter is depicted in the midst of the chase, and there is no reason for him to fall; there is, moreover, no reference to a woman. Also, there is no apparent visual sign referring to the saint himself in this carving. Secondly, of course, it is possible that there is nothing especially meaningful in this trio of carvings. Each image in and of itself completely lacks an independent meaning – an imagined hunter is falling from a horse, as men do fall from horses in real life; deer are being chased, as deer do get chased in life; a lady is praying, as some ladies do. In this interpretation, in other words, this is not narrative but mere decoration, a construction blissfully devoid of connection and coherence.

If neither of the preceding seems convincing, let us return, thirdly, to a Bahktinian approach to the image as carnival. At its simplest level – and misericord meanings are frequently simple, even slapstick, when they contain anecdotal material – the stag-hunter may be seen as a common calendar motif for Spring, as he would appear depicting young manhood in the *Ages of Man* sequence. But why is he shown falling? Although knights have been known to fall from heights as punishment for their excess of pride, in this composition the emphasis is on a hunt and a hunter, and not on a knight. If the deer is cast as a concrete sign of the hunt, and the hunter as a metaphorical figure of a young man who has fallen in life's hunt (an error emphasized by the broken hunting horn) then it may be possible to decode the image in the following way: a young man in the springtime of his life has fallen from piety into sin, has fallen from grace in his foolhardy participation in the worldly chase for love, the latter meaning being reinforced by the apparent piety of this woman in her chapel with her devotional book. He has fallen for her charms and she is desperately beseeching God to help her maintain her purity in the light of this apparently fatal attraction. Of course, there could be an explicit reference here to a tale or proverb that we are as yet unaware of, but even this is not necessarily straightforward. James Rushing maintains, for example, that the Lincoln misericord which apparently depicts a scene from *Yvain* is less an illustration of *Yvain* itself than a comic allusion to the tale, the emphasis being on the comedy of a horse's crupper being trapped in the portcullis.[35] To that extent, bearing in mind the probability of a multivalent image, it is still possible that a loose reference to the saint could have been perceived here by men well-versed in the St Giles legend, a humorous reference to the difficulty of renunciation, and for hermits and monks in particular, of celibacy.

Context, then, is paramount – but still we cannot pronounce with any great certainty: our analytical options are not unlimited, and we are tied to the plausible. We can suggest probabilities based upon reasoned arguments, arguments firmly founded on our knowledge of the workings of medieval culture. With these qualifications in mind, we can attempt to read the elements of this visual image by comparing it with similarly constructed narratives found in other medieval media. We can then argue that the image of the fallen hunter with the devout woman is an embodiment of the folklore motif of Love as a Hunt. Woman is an object of prey; hidden away, she makes tantalizing quarry. Man is the hunter, and Ovid has told us that 'For the hunter, pursuit is all'. Indeed, the fallen hunter in the carving brings to

FIG. 26 Left: The demon Tutivillus. Ely Cathedral.

FIG. 27 Above: Woman with package of books. Winchester Cathedral.

mind Ovid's complaint, 'Why should I/Be the one who gets shot from behind?'.[36] In this misericord, the hunt does appear to have had disastrous consequences for the man. As Ovid, again, says in the *Art of Love*, Book i: 'Then there's Diana's woodland shrine ... /Diana's a virgin, detests the shafts of Cupid: That's why/People who go in the woods/Always get hurt, always will'.[37]

Some other examples of women with books are less problematic, apparently illustrating neither piety nor devotion, but rather inappropriate speech. Such images can be found in misericords from Ely, Winchester, Whalley and Nantwich St Mary. The misericord from Ely (FIG. 26) 'shows the demon Tutivillus at his work. His special function was to gather up the idle chatter of people in church, and to record them on scrolls, to be read out at the Day of Judgement'.[38] He is shown happily eavesdropping on two women, with left- and right-hand supporters depicting devils with scrolls. One woman has a book, perhaps a psalter, in her hand, and the other a rosary. There may be an indication of the contested social status of the women in their headgear, similar to that indicated in Dürer's woodcut 'The Four Witches', and with similar intent – to indicate the weakness of women of all social classes. The carving from Winchester Cathedral (FIG. 27) may have a similar derogatory purpose. It shows a woman seated sideways with a parcel of books or papers bound with a strap in her right hand. The supporters on both sides show a boy with foliage. In considering this image it is worth remembering that there are many misericords at Winchester of the mocking type.[39] In this context, and bearing in mind the distaste with which the clergy viewed this type of dramatic feminine fashion, it seems likely to me that the books in her hand signify religious devotion in contrast with worldly vanity, and that the figure mocks pretension, especially female pretension.[40]

Less obviously, the misericord from Whalley (FIG. 28; c.1435) shows what is usually described as a satyr, but what is probably a Wildman, and a woman holding a scroll upon which is inscribed in French: *Penses molt et p[ar]les pou*, 'think much and speak little'.[41] It is one of a few misericords containing images of women with scrolls: there is another female

FIG. 28 St Mary. Whalley.

figure in a misericord from Stratford-upon-Avon, thought to be a possible representation of Luxuria, bearing a blank scroll,[42] and at Lincoln Cathedral an Assumption of the Virgin with an angel and the Virgin Mary bearing a scroll.[43] But in the Whalley example the scroll has a text, which makes it extremely unusual among misericords.[44] It should be one of the most simple of images to read, tied as it is to a textual anchor; but despite this help, misericord researchers have still found the carving mystifying. Mary Anderson, for example, wrote that 'the connection between that adage and the subject of a woman confronting a wodehouse is mysterious'.[45] Why a wildman, why a woman? How does the visual content connect with the verbal? Women were widely associated in this period with 'creaturely-ness' as opposed to humanity, and silence was thought of as a form of obligatory feminine obedience; this arguably influenced the choice of a female figure in alliance with an uncivilized, dangerously sexual pagan figure. It seems possible that the ridiculously phallic club in the hand of the male figure, held high over the head of the smiling female, indicates a kind of threat: 'Think what you like but keep your mouth shut'. But that has an ominous tone out of keeping with the laughing figures. The answer may be that, in topsy-turvy fashion, the humour of this image derives from stating the antithesis of what was perceived as true – in other words, the wild man with his brutish club does not think much and the woman does not speak little.

A misericord from St Mary's Church, Nantwich, shows a woman in a widow's neck-cloth reading a book (FIG. 29). On her left is a falcon, and on the right a begging dog missing, through damage, what should be another outstretched paw.[46] Here again we can read a connection between the central carving and the supporters, using the theme of the carnival of life. The prayerful, pious young widow is juxtaposed to the hawk, a sign of woman's less-than-nunlike weakness for, or attraction to, the things of this world, including love;

FIG. 29 Woman reading a book. Parish Church of St Mary, Nantwich.

and the begging dog is a sign of the proverbial fate of the unlucky widow who may well end her days begging for scraps like a dog if her prayers are not answered with the likes of a husband.

A more complex interpretational problem is posed by a misericord from Worcester Cathedral. FIG. 30 shows a woman (once thought to have been a monk) sitting on a bench, the end of which is delicately ornamented with an ogee trefoiled arch, interior roses, and foliage. The figure wears a hood and cape, or gown, tight fitting at the neck, with large loose sleeves. She is writing in a book on a lectern, while her left hand is touching something, perhaps an ink bottle, held in the beak of the large bird standing at her feet. A smaller bird is being attacked and gobbled up by a small dog snaking out from the woman's hood.[47] Anderson suggests that the woman may be Dialectica,[48] and that the design is a copy from an unknown early manuscript. She points to a close parallel in the *Hortus Deliciarum* of Herrad von Hohenberg, where a central figure of Philosophia is surrounded by seven radiating arches in each of which stands one of the Liberal Arts. Dialectica makes a gesture of speech with one hand, while in the other she holds the head of a snarling dog. Anderson notes that the dog-headed snake is associated with Dialectica elsewhere. Whatever the precise design source used for this carving, however (and similar designs can be seen on a misericord from Bristol cathedral[49] and a roof boss from Westminster Abbey, the latter said to depict the Annunciation[50]), the final image probably has less to do with a depiction of Dialectica for its own sake than with a determination to exploit whatever comedy could be made of depicting a bold female in this clerical, all-male space. Thus, the humour of this piece may amount to nothing more than the wit of the composition itself. The central carving contains what I believe to be a playful reference to the supporters (described below), but more specifically, there is shock value in a strong female figure that has the audacity to hold a pen in the act of writing in a book; she commands immediate attention in a society that repressed the intellectual capabilities of its women. In addition, as Dialectica was known allegorically to allude to the human intellectual capacity to rationalize as much what is false as what is true, she is an ambiguous figure who necessarily lacks integrity.

But the wit of the image may go beyond the simple depiction of Dialectica in the misericord context. It is interesting that in some of her well-known incarnations, she is armed not only with a pen, but also with a helmet bearing two feathers, one white and one black; she carries a double-edged sword and is shown clenching her fist in the manner of more warlike goddesses. Indeed, the dog in such close association with the woman, and the hunting dog with the supporters, remind one of the importance of dogs to Diana, who has been depicted with a dog in her lap, while the bird as an attribute is reminiscent of other warlike Romano-Celtic gods and goddesses; bird-feathered helmets were common elements of their iconography, along with the companionship, assistance, and promise of transformation offered by a variety of animals, but especially of hares, hounds and birds.[51] Although the bird may be serving a negative function here, signifying power gone wrong or 'evil thoughts', we know that the mythological association of birds with prophecy and, even more pertinently here, with prophetic women, is of ancient standing, signifying a certain ennobling, respectable power to enlighten, heal, and uplift.

That power is probably turned on its head in the case of the birds of Worcester, which pose an iconographical problem. Anderson's theory would link the image to a twelfth-century Westphalian engraved bronze bowl. In this composition Philosophia stands between Socrates and Plato, the whole being encircled by six wise men. Beside each of these sages 'is a smaller figure of one of the Liberal Arts'; each Art is associated with a named bird. Since Geometry takes the eagle, and Dialectica is given what appears to be 'Monerus', the possibility of the large bird in question being an eagle is discarded in Anderson's argument. However, a nineteenth-century suggestion that the carving represented St John with his emblematic book and eagle has been disregarded not so much because of this theory as because of the figure's feminine characteristics; so the validity of Anderson's iconographical link remains an open question. Anderson admits that the association between the Worcester carving and the Continental bowl would be of small importance if it were not for its close relation to two twelfth-century engraved bronze bowls in the British Museum, known as the Cadmus and Scylla bowls, both found in the river Severn below Worcester. Whatever one makes of the particulars of Anderson's theory, the figure does seem likely to be an allusion to the dangerous and beautiful Dialectica, with the 'crafty device of the snake hidden under her cloak', a sorceress 'well-versed in every deceptive argument', whose words charm snakes and men.

It is likely that, as with previous examples, a complete reading of this misericord should take into account the supporting carvings. Indeed, it seems probable that there is some related irony within them. The left-hand supporter (FIG. 31) has previously been described as 'a hunter bearing a rabbit on a pole upon his shoulder; other rabbits retreating into burrows in a bank of earth, with a greyhound seizing one of them'.[52] It is visually interest-

FIG. 30 Above: Seated woman. Worcester Cathedral.

FIG. 31 Right: Supporter (detail). Worcester Cathedral, late 14th century.

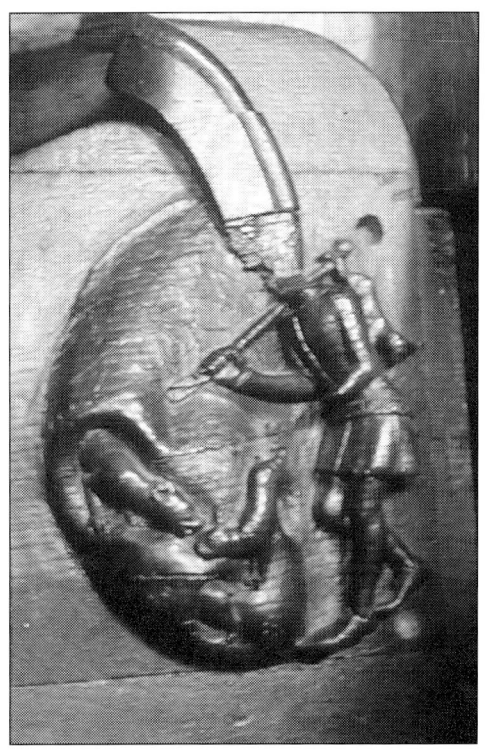

ing, and typical of the 'carnival' misericord spirit, that the dog is emerging from its earthen hole in a way that artistically echoes the feisty dog emerging from the hole of the woman's hood. The right-hand supporter has been described as 'a boy picking fruit'; however, it seems not to be a separate image, but rather the hunter depicted in the first stage of the hunt, lying in wait for the right moment to spring upon his prey. The male figures in both supporters are identically costumed, with pleated tunic, well-carved belt, and pointed shoes. The right-hand carving shows marks of flowery foliage, outlined by the carver on the blank surfaces of the wood; had the carver completed the foliage, duplicating that on the other side, the unity between the two supporters might have been clearer.

In considering the female in the central carving, it may help to remember bawdy songs like the following:

> I hunted up a hill,
> a Coney did espye;
> my fferrett seeing that,
> into her hole did hye;
>
> my fferrett seeing that,
> into her hole did run;
> but when he came into her hole,
> noo Coney cold he ffound.

> I put itt in againe,
> itt found her out att Last;
> the Coney then betwixt her leggs
> did hold my fferrett ffast,
>
> Till that itt was soe weake,
> alacke, itt cold not stand!
> my fferrett then out of her hole
> did come unto my hand . .... (etc.)[53]

In the context of misericords I think it likely that the Worcester example is a pastiche of mythological elements brought together to encapsulate a humorous reflection on female sexual allure. But this humour cannot be separated from the seriousness of the clerical imagination that fostered it. The threat and comedy of female wisdom – inseparable from female sexuality – is emphasized by the juxtaposition of a woman with a book with scenes of women in alliance with nature, and the control of man over nature.

In a brief space, I have tried to show that the images of women with books in misericords have to be considered not as individual oddities, but in their correct context; that is as a successful and meaningful part of church architecture, inspired artistically by the desires of the clergy to see reflected therein comment on their own social interests and religious status. In this way we move away from an unquestioned dismissal of misericord programmes for their failure to offer well-planned iconography with appropriate Christian subjects, away from planting the blame for this failure on the ignorant carvers, and on to the task of comprehending the complexities of the interrelationship of ecclesiastical culture with a visual tradition which evolved over several centuries.[54]

Notes to Chapter Three

1. It was the devil, the world and the 'woman' (fleshly weakness) in man which were addressed by this concession to human frailty. In the Western church, human salvation depended on the practice of constant virtue (virility), and weakness could lead to damnation. Misericords were an architectural admission of weakness and consequent Christian mercy. On mercy, *see Vices and Virtues,* ed. F. Holthausen, EETS, o.s. 89 and 159 (London, 1921), pp.110–20.

2. Christianity developed in such a way that eventually it could not tolerate parody of itself; the Feast of Fools, for example, was outlawed in 1542. On the relationship of the Feast of Fools to art, *see* a series of studies by K.P.F.Moxey, 'Pieter Bruegel and the Feast of Fools', *Art Bulletin,* 64 (1982), pp.640–46; 'Master ES and the Folly of Love', *Simiolus,* 11 (1980), pp.125–48.

3. According to G.L.Remnant, *A Catalogue of Misericords in Great Britain* (Oxford, 1969). *See also* D. and H.Kraus, *The Hidden World of Misericords* (London, 1975).

4. The following 3 examples are typical: M.D.Anderson's introductory essay to Remnant, *A Catalogue*, p.xxiii, 'Misericords are a very humble form of medieval art'; Kraus and Kraus, ibid., p.x, 'the humble background of the misericord-carvers reduced the availability to them of many ... cultural sources, resulting in their depending to a great extent on their own resources. The art of the misericord-carvers was based essentially on life: ... the life they themselves lived'; M.Jones, 'The Misericords of Beverley Minster: A Corpus of Folkloric Imagery and its Cultural Milieu, with Special Reference to the Influence of Northern European Iconography on Late Medieval and Early Modern English Woodwork' (unpubl. Ph.D.dissertation, Polytechnic of the South West in collaboration with the University of Cambridge, 1991), 'my project ... so far from Cantabrigian in its preoccupation with so humble an art-form'.

5. F.Bond, *Misericords* (Oxford, 1910), p.87.

6. M.Anderson, *Misericords: Medieval Life in English Wood-Carving* (Harmondsworth, 1954), p.5.

7. Id., *The Medieval Carver* (Cambridge, 1935), p.35. Significantly, when she discusses 'high' sculpture, there is a sudden insistence on clerical genius: 'no unlettered mason could have marshalled the complex hierarchies of statues that adorn the west fronts of Exeter and Wells' (p.16).

8. Anderson, in Remnant, *Catalogue,* p.xxiv.

9. *Ibid.,* p.xl.

10. Kraus and Kraus, *Hidden World,* pp.x, xiv. In *The Gothic Choirstalls of Spain* (London and New York, 1986), the Krauses elaborate on their view that the sculptors were virtually independent creative agents – that secular art was the invention of secular man, and that one is wrong to 'seek out moralistic interpretations' (p.50).

11. M.Laird, *English Misericords* (London, 1986), publisher's preface; see *also* pp.12,13.

12. M.Camille, *Images on the Edge: The Margin of Medieval Art* (London, 1992), p.95.

13. St Bernard of Clairvaux's famous but sometimes misunderstood 'Apology' addressed to William, Abbot of St Thierry, in the 12th century is popularly associated with misericords: rather than being *mystified* by mythological imagery, Bernard was clearly upset by it. Veronica Ortenberg's recent work helps clarify the intricacy of the art-historical network that paved the way for early misericord phenomena: *The English Church and the Continent in the Tenth and Eleventh Centuries: Cultural, Spiritual, and Artistic Exchanges* (Oxford, 1992).

14. The priory of Swine was a Cistercian nunnery of fifteen sisters and a prioress, with a small community of lay brethren; there were, it seems, originally misericords for the women. *See* T.Tindall Wildridge, *The Grotesque in Church Art* (London, 1899), pp.109–10 (with an illustration of 'The Winking Nun, Swine, Yorkshire'); and cf. Remnant, *Catalogue,* pp.184–85: 'The church of St Mary'. Wildridge implies (questionably) that this image of a coy nun should be read in relation to the history of this particular nunnery. Likewise, he would trace the origin of the rather conventional hybridized creature, identified perhaps prematurely as a 'papal minister', to historical circumstance which 'on the occasion of the contumacy of the [13th-century] nuns in refusing to pay certain tithes, caused the church, with that, adjoining, of the

WOMEN AND THE BOOK

15 lay brethren, to be closed. The nuns defied all authority, broke open the chapels, and in general during the long contest acted in a curiously ungovernable, irresponsible manner'.

15 The dividing line between the educated and wealthy bishops, deans, and abbots who commissioned misericords to beautify the 'House of God', educated and wealthy laypeople, and ordinary Christian folk, may not have been as impenetrable as is often supposed. See M.Barasch, *Theories of Art from Plato to Winckelmann* (New York and London, 1985), p.87: 'It would be very hard to draw a precise dividing line between ... the learned and the ignorant'.

16 The presupposition is that misericord iconography *should* be systematic; the argument for its 'hiddenness' is thus one explanation for assumed 'error'. For a hypothesis that moves beyond this narrow view, *see* H.-J.Raupp, *Bauernsatiren: Entstehung und Entwicklung des bäuerlichen Genres in der deutschen und niederländischen Kunst, ca.1470–1570* (Niederzien, 1986).

17 *See* M.Bakhtin, *Rabelais and His World*, transl. H.Iswolsky (Bloomington, Ind., 1984), p.5, on suspension of hierarchies which, paradoxically, reinforce them. This has implications for women's history: guild activity and women's association with it, for instance, should be considered in relation to carnival and the Church; *see* M.Howell, *Women, Production and Patriarchy in Late Medieval Cities* (Chicago, 1986), and cf. Bakhtin's portrayal of the female principle and person in carnival.

18 Anderson, to name just one example, misses the irony when she writes of the 'sufferings inflicted by an ill-tempered wife', thus taking the misericord as a sociological document for wifely behaviour; *see* her *History by the Highway* (London, 1967), p.146. But this class of misericords – one of those most frequently reproduced – is nevertheless visual evidence of the gender confusion and struggle that can be traced throughout the Middle Ages – a cultural obsession of historical importance.

19 Bakhtin, *Rabelais*, demonstrates that the use of church art goes beyond the 'merely ornamental'; *see* Wildridge, *Grotesque*, p.1.

20 *See* Bakhtin, *Rabelais*, ch.6: 'The Material Bodily Lower Stratum', i.e. 'the downward movement', or debasement, immanent in 'all popular-festive merriment and grotesque realism. Down, inside out, vice versa, upside down ... both in the literal sense of space, and in the metaphorical meaning of the image' (p.370). In relation to misericords, *see* M. Jones, 'Folklore Motifs in Late Medieval Art I: Proverbial Follies and Impossibilities', *Folklore*, 100 (1989), pp.201–17, and C.Grossinger, 'Humour and Folly in English Misericords of the First Quarter of the Sixteenth Century', in *Early Tudor England*, ed. D.Williams (Woodbridge, 1989), pp.73–85.

21 Bakhtin, *Rabelais*, p.4.

22 I am grateful for this citation to Martial Rose, who researches the Norwich Cathedral misericords and who has recently (1993) compiled a fully-illustrated volume on the subject to be housed in the Cathedral Library and the Sacrist's Office. See also A.Whittingham, *The Stalls of Norwich Cathedral* (Norwich, 1949).

23 Those Ely misericords which contain female images stand out for their sympathetic treatment; in addition, there are several evenly matched couples. Remnant, *Catalogue*, p.16: 'No. 18, N side from W, upper row'; p.17: 'No. 10, S side from W, upper row'; p.17: 'No. 13, S side from W, upper row'; p.18: 'No. 21, S side from W, upper row'.

24 Bakhtin, *Rabelais*, p.10; *see also* p.5: 'comic protocol, as for instance the election of a king and queen to preside at a banquet "for laughter's sake" (*roi pour rire*)', and p.235: 'kings and queens of the "feast of fools"'. I deal more fully with this topic in a paper given at the University of Wales Conference of Medievalists, Apr.1988: 'The Misericord as Document: The Female Image in the Misericords of Ely Cathedral'.

25 Misericords can sometimes be seen as a kind of picture-writing of proverbs, comic tales (*fabliaux*), invective, curses, oaths, and parody, the medium itself being seen as a hybrid of market-place speech and image. This development suggests clerical interest – just as, for instance, 'The Land of Cokaygne' seems to be a comic fantasy by an author 'likely to have been a goliardic cleric'. In the MS containing the sole copy of this piece there are similar works of a goliardic character, such as a 'Tippler's Mass' (*Missa de Potatoribus*); *see Early Middle English Verse and Prose*, ed. J.A.W.Bennett and G.Smithers (Oxford, 1966), pp.137–38.

26 Bakhtin, *Rabelais*, p.12.

72

27 As discussed in relation to misericords in Wendy Armstead, 'A Catalogue of the Misericords of St David's Cathedral' (unpubl. M.A.thesis, Univ. of Wales, 1986), pp.21–35. *See also* Jones ('Misericords', n.4), and E.C.Block, 'Half-Angel Half-Beast: Images of Women on Misericords', *Reinardus*, 5 (1992), pp.17–34, with a comprehensive list of women on misericords in Europe (including the U.K.).

28 In exploring the content of human images in misericords we have to consider their relationship with personifications and allegorical figures – and the possible gendered meanings injected into such figures. *See* M.Evans's discussion, 'Allegorical Women and Practical Men: The Iconography of the *Artes* Reconsidered', in *Medieval Women,* ed. D.Baker (Oxford, 1978),

29 Laird (*English Misericords*, p.9) claims that 'only 2 percent of the supporters have the same design as, or a similar one to, that of the centre piece, or are known to interact with the latter'; but he himself gives two new examples of interaction, and Jones, Camille, Kraus and Kraus, Grossinger, et al. have all independently argued for the coherence of individual examples previously thought separate. Laird's '2 percent' is thus not very useful, and the whole concept requires further analysis. I would argue in most cases for a poetic relationship.

30 E.Phipson, *Choir Stalls and Their Carvings: Examples of Misericords from English Cathedrals and Churches* (London, 1896), p.31.

31 Remnant, *Catalogue*, p.16: 'No. 16, N side from W, upper row'.

32 On St Giles, *see* the Rev.S.Baring-Gould, *The Lives of the Saints* (London, 1898), x, pp.8–10. The Rev.A.Butler, *The Lives of Fathers* ... (London, 1814), ix, makes the point that the hermit brings to mind 'the ancient Christian proverb ... that he who lives alone is either an angel or a devil. The state is not without snares and dangers' (p.3). Pictured in Laird, *English Misericords*, no.134: bearded, and with rosary in hand, St Giles tends the miraculously milky doe that is here shown with an arrow in the neck: 'The supporters show the offending bowmen'.

33 Note John Lydgates's description, ll.32–40 in his 'Prayers to Ten Saints', in *The Minor Poems of Lydgate,* ed. H.MacCracken, EETS o.s. 107 (London, 1911), p.122.

34 Hugolina, a devout woman of Cambridge, founded a church for him in the late 11th century, and 12th century monks wrote about him; but St Giles appealed most to society's most vulnerable members, 'village labourers'. He was the patron of cripples, lepers, and nursing mothers, and the only saint whose name was as powerful as 'sacramental confession' in absolving sins, according to F.Brittain, *Saint Giles* (Cambridge, 1928), p.38. St Giles's appearance at Ely might then have a humorous slant, a reference to superstitious peasants and magical claims to virtue.

35 See J.A.Rushing, Jr., *Adventures Beyond the Text: Ywain in the Visual Arts* (unpubl. Ph.D.dissertation, Princeton Univ., 1988), ch. 6. On the multivalency of the medieval symbol, *see* M.Schapiro, *Words and Pictures* (Paris, 1973).

36 *See* 'The Amores', 2/9, in Ovid, *The Erotic Poems*, transl. P.Green (Harmondsworth, 1982), p.122.

37 The Art of Love', i, p.174 . *Cf. also* the popular verse: 'Ef thou wolt fleysh lust overcome,/Thou most fist and fle y-lome,/With eye and with huerte;/Of fleysh lust cometh shame;/Thath hit thunche the body game,/Hit doth the soule smerte:/Wel fytht that wel flyth'. Attributed to Hending, medieval collector of proverbs, in BL, MS Harl.2253, fol. 125; discussed in Thomas Wright's *Essays on the ... Literature, Popular Superstitions and History of England in the Middle Ages* (London, 1846), i, p.142.

38 Anderson discusses this in relation to one of Jacques de Vitry's exempla in *The Imagery of British Churches* (London, 1995), p.155. In Islam, a devil and an angel are said to look over a person's right and left shoulders; from the right, the angel recording good works, and the devil recording bad from the left; at death, God will scrutinize the book of one's life and mete out reward or punishment.

39 Remnant, *Catalogue*, p.56–59; there is, for instance, a mock-bishop, fools, ape with arm round ape in female dress, and posturers, including female tumblers and musicians. Winchester has a high proportion of female figures.

40 Compare e.g. the depiction of the female in the poem 'La contenance des fames', ll.75–78: 'And then, more wondrous thing to say/She goes to church both night and day/To sermons and on pilgrimage./Now she's humble, then she's sage' ('Et pour dire plus de merveilles/Yra aux vespres et aus veilles,/Au sermon,en pelerinage./Or fait le humble, puis le sage'), in *Three Medieval Views of Women: La Contenance*

des Fames, Le Bien des Fames, Le Blasme des Fames, ed. and transl. G.K.Fiero, W.Pfeffer, and M.Allain (New Haven, 1989), pp.90–91.

41 Remnant, *Catalogue*, p.83: 'No. 7, N side from E'.

42 *Ibid.*, p.164: 'No. 4, N side'.

43 *Ibid.*, p.87: 'No. 2, N side, upper tier'.

44 Another example at Whalley of a scroll with writing depicts 'shoeing the goose', inscribed with the proverbial theme: 'Whoever meddles in other people's affairs is sure to make a failure of it' ('Who so melles hy[m]of y al me[n] dos let hy[m]cu[m] heir & shoe ye ghos'); Anderson, in Remnant, *Catalogue*, p.xl. Also at Whalley is a carving of vine and grapes with initials and inscription'Let them be joyful who sit on this seat' ('Semp[er] gaudentes sint ista sede sedentes'), Abbot's stall, p.84. At Norwich Cathedral, Remnant, *Catalogue*, p.106, describes a 'wodehouse with club; two chained lions paw his knees; a scroll 'War foli: war' ('Beware of folly, man')'. The supporters consist of a wodehouse clutching the ear of a dog that bites his hand, and two lambs.

45 Anderson, in Remnant, *Catalogue*, p.xl.

46 Remnant, *Catalogue*, p.27: 'No. 8, N side from W'.

47 The Revd Canon Iain Mackenzie of Worcester kindly sends information from E.Aldis's *Carvings and Sculptures of Worcester Cathedral* (London, 1873), which questions whether 'she' might be a monk bearing a resemblance to St John.

48 Mrs Trenchard Cox (M.D.Anderson), 'The Twelfth-Century Design Sources of the Worcester Cathedral Misericords', *Archaeologia*, 97 (1959), pp.165–78.

49 Remnant, *Catalogue*, p.47: 'No. 4, S side from W'. Dr Maldwyn Mills, of the English Dept., Univ. of Wales, Aberystwyth, has drawn my attention to another example of what may be a woman with a book on a lectern at Leintwardine, Hereford; it is unfortunately very damaged.

50 This 13th-cent. roof boss shows a tree with a bird shadowing the female figure beside her lectern with a book. But the tone is completely different; the Bristol female is hagified while the young mother Mary is graceful and flanked by angels. Reproduced in *Westminster Abbey,* with contributions by Dean E.Abbott *et al.* (London, 1972), p.156, top left.

51 Examples of the iconography of Diana in the Romano-Celtic tradition can be found in M.Green's *Dictionary of Celtic Myth and Legend* (London, 1992), p.80; R.J. Stewart's *Celtic Gods and Goddesses* (London, 1990), p.51; and A.Ross's *Pagan Celtic Britain* (London, 1992), pp.276–78. Compare the description of Dialectica in *Martianus Capella and the Seven Liberal Arts*, iv, transl.W.Stahl and R.Johnson, with E.L.Burge (New York, 1977).

52 Remnant, *Catalogue*, p.171: 'No. 11. S side from E'.

53 From 'Off all the seaes', collected in *Bishop Percy's Folio MS: Loose and Humourous Songs*, ed. F.J.Furnivall *et al.* (London, 1868), pp.55–56.

54 The few surviving remnants of instructions given to carvers by their ecclesiastical patrons are all very late in the history of the misericord, and prove little regarding clerical input (although Jones, 'Misericords of Beverley Minster', p.344, argues otherwise). The tradition was so well-established by the 15th and 16th centuries that there was little need for detailed and tedious instruction.

CHAPTER FOUR

Mirrors of a Collective Past: Re-considering Images of Medieval Women

MARTHA W. DRIVER

BY THE END of the fourteenth century, women were increasingly literate, educated to assist in the family business, keep the books, manage the household, help with correspondence, and teach their children. Beginning in this period, we find a proliferation of books directed to a female audience, books which are sometimes, though not always, written in the vernacular, and which are often heavily illustrated with well-developed visual apparatus to guide the reader through the text. And it is perhaps no coincidence that images of women reading become increasingly popular in the visual arts: in the Merode altarpiece (FIG. 32), c.1425, for example, the Virgin Mary looks up from an open book, the text almost legible, interrupted in her reading by the Angel Gabriel. A famous fifteenth-century painting by Rogier van der Weyden of c.1440 (FIG. 98), now in London's National Gallery, shows the Magdalene reading a two-column bible text, while illuminations in a primer made for Princess Claude of France in 1508 (FIG. 33) depict the young princess herself engaged, like the child Virgin before her, in the process of learning to read.[1]

Women, whether holy, religious, or lay, are shown reading in late medieval art, forming one type of visual evidence for female literacy in the later Middle Ages.[2] And if we look within the pages of books read by them, we further find a wealth of pictorial information about their daily lives. Illuminations and miniatures can provide information about women's occupations, for example, about the home, living conditions, workshops, and dress. For women's history in particular, for which so much documentation has been lost, picture evidence is a valuable tool. On the other hand, the relationship of representation to historical reality is more complex than is generally thought. Non-art historians especially tend to view manuscript illumination and late medieval painting, no matter what the original context, as an unequivocal rendering of reality:

> The difference between a naive beholder and an art historian is the fact that the latter is aware of his cultural predispositions; that is, he is aware of the contemporary perspective he brings to the work of interpretation as a consequence of belonging to a culture different from the one under investigation, while the naive beholder is not.[3]

The naïve viewer takes the picture evidence at (twentieth-century) face value, though all readings, to some extent, are distorted by our contemporary perceptions of the past, by our

FIG. 32 The Merode altarpiece. Robert Campin (Master of Flemalle).
New York, Metropolitan Museum of Art, Cloisters Coll.

own subjectivity. In 'Self-Portrait in a Convex Mirror', the poet John Ashbery writes of this contemporary reception of older images:

> The gray glaze of the past attacks all know-how:
> Secrets of wash and finish that took a lifetime
> To learn and are reduced to the status of
> Black-and-white illustrations in a book where colorplates
> Are rare. That is, all time
> Reduces to no special time.[4]

It is this distance between historical time and the present in the recovery of women's work that I wish to travel here, looking at ways to retain the integrity of the image in its original context while also beginning to build a visual history of medieval women which

FIG. 33 Left: Princess Claude learning to read. Primer of Claude de France. Cambridge, Fitzwilliam Mus., MS 159, fol. 14r.

FIG. 34 Above: Untitled. Cindy Sherman.

speaks to us today. So, how might we begin to read images of women? How might the modern historian more effectively use pictures to retrieve the past? In what ways were pictures originally received? What was their original context or purpose? How are images related to actual lived experience? Can we separate fact from fiction in the historical record (if, indeed, we want to), and when is that a particularly appropriate exercise? Finally, how may images of women be used to rewrite the historical record, to emphasize women's contributions, to recreate the realities of women's lives and relate them to our own?

A medieval manuscript illumination is not a photograph or scientific diagram, both of which may themselves be technically altered, staged, or arranged to suit subjective whim or fit a particular theory. In two richly resonant examples of quasi-medieval imagery created by the contemporary American photographer Cindy Sherman (FIG. 34), for example, we find the photographer herself serving as the model for both the Virgin Mary, her bare breast grotesquely exposed in Gothic fashion to feed what seems a comparatively tiny and perhaps hypothetical infant Christ, and for the Dissolute Monk, a photograph recently acquired by the Metropolitan Museum. In these and her other History Portraits, Sherman costumes and manipulates her body to create a plurality of identities, a multiplicity of

FIG. 35 Reader. Giovanni Boccaccio, *Le Livre des Cleres et Nobles Femmes*. Paris, BN, MS fr. 599, fol. 22r.

effects. Her photographs convince 'the viewer that her various images are indeed different presences', while simultaneously exposing 'the material underpinnings of identity-production'. Her fabrications of Old Masters are rewritings of the visual text, creating lively tension between our perceptions of the past and the present moment.[5]

Just as a modern photograph may be created, is created, by the photographer, illustration in medieval manuscripts is not simply a straightforward record of reality, and it would be naïve to think so. Instead, an illumination or miniature refracts reality, becoming a mirror, whether a fun-house distortion or a real-seeming reflection, of the culture producing it. Medieval images of women, like modern photographs, reveal aspects of female identity, creating a sense of presence and immediacy, whether the image is of a powerful queen, a woman writer offering her book to her patron, or a peasant woman at work in the fields. Opening with an overview of what we might call typical or predictable images of women which illustrate late-medieval books read by women, I shall focus briefly on some specific examples in which the relationship between representation and reality remains problematic, closing with a few comments on pictures of women reading and what these suggest about actual reading practice in the later Middle Ages.

In addition to books of hours commissioned or owned by women, illustrated books read by them might include those by Giovanni Boccaccio, or by Christine de Pizan, or other works with dedications to a female readership.[6] The picture of the woman reader (FIG. 35) comes from a French translation of Boccaccio's *Of Famous Women* (*De mulieribus claris*) a text widely illustrated in the fifteenth century. Though Boccaccio focuses on classical women, the pictures illustrating the manuscripts uniformly show women in fifteenth-century settings and costume, reflecting late medieval, rather than classical, sensibility.[7] The naïve viewer might say that this is an image of an actual woman reading, and in this case she wouldn't be far wrong. The picture of the woman reader is technically an illustration of a mythical character, one fiction among many in Boccaccio's collection, but when considered in the context of the wide circulation of *De mulieribus claris* among women, she becomes representative of that book's popular female readership, particularly in its vernacular (i.e. French) translations.

Christine was a prolific and best-selling author in her own lifetime, widely read by both women and men. Portraits of her, whether writing or instructing or presenting her volumes to noble patrons, frequently appear in contemporary manuscripts of her works, creating a new identity of the woman as teacher and writer. In her poetry and prose Christine creates herself as a powerful role-model, which she remains for women to this day.[8] In the epilogue to the English translation of her *Moral Proverbs*, printed by William Caxton, she is described this way: 'Of these sayynges Cristyne was aucteuresse, Whiche in makyng hadde suche Intelligence/ That therof she was mireur (mirror) and maistresse/ Hire werkes testifie thexperience.' It is, however, interesting to note that within a hundred years of their composition (or sooner), Christine's authorship of several works, or rather the probability of female authorship in general, was already being called into question.[9]

Writings on practical subjects, conduct books, herbals, and health manuals, as well as biographies of famous women and the lives and works of woman saints, were also among the illustrated books that women read. An illustration of St Joan, from Antoine Dufour's *La Vie des Femmes Célèbres* (1504), a work composed for Anne of Brittany, shows Joan as a triumphant warrior clad in armour, 'the Renaissance suit kept in the castle of Amboise by Anne of Brittany and believed to have belonged to her'. Though there are extant sketches of Joan made during her lifetime, this miniature was painted some 70 years after her death. It is not, therefore, an actual portrait, or realistic portrayal, but an image of an heroic woman, an emblematic representation, identified in the text as Joan.[10]

Conventional representations of St Bridget of Sweden and of St Catherine of Siena, two of the most influential and prolific woman visionaries, also appear frequently in fifteenth-century manuscripts and early printed editions of their and related writings dating from the late fifteenth and early sixteenth centuries. They are variously shown receiving revelation from God, writing at desks, and giving their writings, in the form of scrolls and books, to religious and other readers. A woodcut portrait of Bridget becomes an imprimatur, or emblem of approval, of the Bridgettine nuns at the English house of Syon, occurring in a number of early printed English editions of Bridgettine texts.[11]

In other manuscript pages we find a variety of tasks undertaken by women. The calendar pages of prayer-books, for example, supply scenes of women at work in the fields and in the dairy, as we see in the Grimani Breviary and the Da Costa Hours, manuscripts which were produced for wealthy patrons (FIG. 36). Such scenes contain realistic detail, but are also idealized, painted for the pleasure of the books' noble owners. The costumes of the peasants

FIG. 36 Dairy scene. *The Da Costa Hours.* New York, The Pierpont Morgan Library, MS 399, fol. 5v.

FIG. 37 Sweeping. Barthélémy l'Anglais, *Livre des Propriétés des Choses.* Paris, BN, MS fr. 9140, fol. 107r.

are brightly coloured, the women's aprons crisply white and clean. Their hands and faces, no matter what the task at hand, whether slaughtering or grape-picking, appear freshly washed. The images are charming and sanitized, similar to the scrubbed versions of historical films produced in Hollywood in the 1940s and 1950s. Conventions of representation, readily recognizable iconography, and reaffirmation of social stereotypes were apparently as popular in the calendar pages of books of hours as they were to be later on film, types of visual shorthand promoting idealized scenes of daily life.

Encyclopaedias, like *The Properties of Things* (*De proprietatibus rerum*), a popular and widely circulating work composed by Bartholomeus Anglicus, show women engaged in distillation, scything in the fields, healing the sick, and doing familiar household tasks (FIG. 37), as we see on this page from a fifteenth-century French translation of Bartholomeus now in the Bibliothèque Nationale.[12] Health handbooks and gynaecological texts also illustrated the tools and practices relating to midwifery, practised exclusively by women for women in the Middle Ages. A manuscript illumination, from a history of the world by Guiars des Moulins (FIG. 38), shows the expectant mother seated before the midwife who firmly clasps her by the hips during labour, providing essential physical support, 'mothering the mother' during the painful process.[13] Pictures of women weaving and spinning, tasks traditionally female, are readily found in the pages of books written by Christine and Boccaccio, as well as in compilations, histories, and encyclopaedias.

The domestic side of life – that is, housework, food preparation, childbirth, and cloth-

FIG. 38 Woman in labour (detail). *Bible Historiale de Guiars des Moulins.* Geneva, Bibliothèque publique et universitaire, MS FR/T.1, fol. 22r.

making – is readily associated with medieval women. Shaped by twentieth-century culture, our assumption that the domestic role was central for most medieval women is confirmed by pictures like these. They seem to mirror accurately our perceptions of the medieval experience, and we find no quarrel with the picture evidence. But what of occupations we do not customarily associate with women? How can the picture evidence enlarge the scope of possibilities, challenging us to think more expansively, and perhaps more accurately, about women's history?

Metalwork, for example, is one field with which we do not normally associate women. And the majority of illustrative examples to be found in medieval manuscripts are allegorical. Like the woman reader in Boccaccio's *De claris mulieribus*, they illustrate fictions, not reality. Or do they? In one fourteenth-century example, from a French manuscript of the *Roman de la Rose*, Dame Nature, clad in a smock, prepares to forge humankind (FIG. 39). In the other, an illustration from *Les Douze Dames de Rhetorique*, a woman mines the gems of rhetoric to adorn the books at her feet (FIG. 40). We might, at this point, say, 'But those are allegorical women! Real women didn't do that.' However, when reading an image, our interpretation of its meaning may be too limited by our preconceived notions and modern biases. In this case, we might justifiably ask: what is the relation of these pictures to actual lived experience?

Though the woman miner is an allegorical figure, the tools she uses as well as the headcloth and garments she wears closely resemble those shown in actual mining scenes. In *On*

81

WOMEN AND THE BOOK

FIG. 39 Above: Dame Nature at the forge. Guillaume de Lorris, Jean de Meun, *Roman de la Rose*. Paris, Bibliothèque Sainte-Geneviève, MS 1126, fol. 115r.

FIG. 40 Right: Miner. Montferrant, *Les Douze Dames de Rhétorique*. Paris, BN, MS fr. 1174, fol. 29r.

Mining (*De re metallica*, 1556), by Georgius Agricola, which remained the standard work on mining and metallurgy until the end of the eighteenth century, there are numerous wood-cuts based, as the author says, on his direct observation. These illustrate women employed in the oreworks, panning for gold, and sorting in the silver mine. They are shown wearing smocks (which, however, lack the fancy gold-leaf highlights) and kerchiefs just as our allegorical woman miner does here, which suggests she may be based on actual observation.[14]

These suppositions are further supported by historical records which describe women engaging in many aspects of metalwork. Typically, these were the wives and daughters of men employed in the metal trades. Needle-makers in Nuremberg and Lübeck were allowed to train their children, both girls and boys, in the trade; and in fourteenth- and fifteenth-century accounts we find women working as metal casters, cutlers, scythe-smiths, tinsmiths, bolt grinders, and locksmiths. Women were also employed as gold-spinners, a branch of the goldsmith's trade, making gold thread to be woven into fine cloth. In this case, then, the historical sources confirm the implications of the images, however allegorical – there were indeed women working in the metal trades, wearing clothing and using tools like those seen here, in the later Middle Ages.[15]

We imagine the aristocratic lady surrounded by her maidens idly passing time in an exquisite summer garden, or in winter in a gracious castle chamber, perhaps turning her hand to a bit of embroidery. But real life was not like that, or not very often. In an example from a fifteenth-century Dutch version of the *Cité des Dames* we see a manor lady supervising a woman gardener. Again these are allegorical figures who rather improbably wear similar garments, but they may also be seen as realistic representations: the lady did super-

FIG. 41 Women Builders. *Roman des Girart von Roussillon*. Vienna, ON, MS 2549, fol. 167v.

vise and care for her servants, and she was herself required to know the proper way to carry out numerous tasks.

In the *Book of the Three Virtues* (c.1406), Christine instructs the noble lady to understand the work of labourers, the seasons for planting and harvesting, the care of animals, and which crops are best suited to different soils. Christine insists that the lady know 'which way is best for the furrow to go according to the lay of the land .... She should see that the furrows are straight and well made and of the right depth and sown at exactly the right time with such grains as are best for the land.' According to Christine, the lady must rise early and she 'should often take time to visit the fields to see how the men are getting on with the work, for there are a good many workers who will gladly abstain from working the land and give it up for the day if they think no one is keeping an eye on them'. The lady must also set her maidservants to work at tasks outdoors: 'she will employ her women and her chambermaids to attend to the livestock, to feed the workmen, to weed the courtyards and work in the herb garden, even getting covered in mud'.[16]

The illustration of two women building the church of chaste love (as the jealous husband spies from the bushes) comes from the *Roman des Girart von Roussillon* (FIG. 41), a romance manuscript copied in Flanders in 1447. The women are again not precisely attired for the job at hand. They are fictional, though the scaffolds and building tools are realistically rendered. Again, we may leave them in their fictional frame or consider the possibility that women's work included building construction in the Middle Ages, which does not seem very likely. However, when we look at other evidence from written and pictorial sources, we find that medieval women do in fact work alongside men in the building trades.

FIG. 42 Bath-house. Valerius Maximus, *Des Faits des Romains*.
Paris, BN, MS Arsenal 5196, fol. 372r.

There are woman claywall makers and women working in the lime works, along with female glaziers and masons cited in late medieval records.[17]

When confronted by scenes of men and women bathing together in medieval hot-tubs (FIG. 42), a common enough subject in manuscript illumination, the mind of the modern observer reacts immediately, thinking first of sex and then of prostitution. Prostitution is, in fact, the most documented of all medieval female occupations in twentieth-century scholarship.[18] We are products of our culture. And, to be sure, some medieval bathhouse scenes do, in fact, depict the whorehouse. But are there other aspects of bathing, and women's roles in that (necessary) process, which pictures can help us to recover?

Washing the body, whether one's own or those of others, seems to have been mainly women's work in the Middle Ages. Baths and massage, both thought to prevent plague, were frequently recommended in medieval health handbooks. A thorough cleaning might include removing lice and other vermin (a task assigned to mistresses and wives in Montaillou), scraping the skin and flagellating it to stimulate circulation, then rubbing the body with ashes and soap before rinsing with water. Female bath-house attendants also gave massage and sweat-baths as well as cupping and bleeding patrons, and clipping their hair.[19]

The humanist Poggio Bracciolini, writing in 1415, describes these and other practices in his eyewitness account of the public baths at Baden outside Zurich: 'People often take meals in the water ... tables are set on the water, and onlookers often share meals with the bathers.' Public bath-houses were a necessity for people without private baths at home, and

FIG. 43 Bath maidens washing hair. Wenceslaus Bible. Vienna, ON, MS 2759, fol. 174v.

FIG. 44 St Barbara. Breviary, Roman office for Franciscan use. New York, The Pierpont Morgan Library, MS 52, fol. 558v.

were usually strictly regulated. Guild regulations for thirteenth-century Paris, for example, set specific guidelines for bath-house-keepers, warning, 'No man or woman of the aforesaid trade may maintain in their houses or baths either prostitutes of the day or night, or lepers, or vagabonds, or other infamous people of the night.'[20]

There were, however, a few exceptions, which have been much documented: in the mid-fourteenth century the bath-houses at Southwark, outside London, were notorious as brothels.[21] The Belle, mentioned by Chaucer in his prologue to *Canterbury Tales*, was then a well-known house of prostitution. Even Poggio, our open-minded fifteenth-century humanist, seems somewhat surprised to find men and women of all ages and classes bathing together in the bath-houses at Baden, 'and in my heart of hearts I admired the innocence of these people ... who think and speak no evil'. The Baden bathers were, however, at least partially clothed, the men in bathing trunks and the women wearing the loose 'tunics which are open on top or along the side and do not cover the neck, the breasts, the arms, or the shoulders,' similar to the outfits worn by the bath-maidens in the illumination from the Wenceslaus Bible (FIG. 43).[22] Female bath-attendants performed many of the same tasks as the male barber-surgeons of the same period, the respected predecessors of the modern surgeon and doctor, and bathing, despite its sexual overtones, seems to have been generally viewed as a preventative to plague, a healthy practice occasionally performed, as necessary to one's well-being as cupping, bleeding, or cutting the hair.

Finally, the act of reading itself, as a female occupation or pastime, would seem rather surprising, because we know women were not taught Latin, nor were they prepared for the university or professions in any formal way. Literacy and books, we presume, were predominantly a male prerogative. What can pictures suggest, then, about the actual reading practice of women? Like the other pictures we have seen, medieval representations of women reading can have a number of interpretations.

The woman readers may be members of the Holy Family, presenting a model of learned piety to both men and women. Scenes of Mary's prayerful reading or contemplation of the open text of Isaiah at the Annunciation, which is interrupted by the Angel Gabriel (FIG. 32), are exemplars for, or one might say the mother of, all other images of women reading. Whether the women represented are religious or secular, reading retains a spiritual or contemplative connotation: it is Mary's occupation, not Martha's, requiring leisure time set apart from domestic or economic concerns, leisure not usually associated with women, either then or now.

Recent scholarship has focused on sacred images as models of female piety, on St Anne teaching the Virgin to read and the Virgin reading at the Annunciation.[23] Such pictures emphasize the value and spiritual rewards of female literacy, as well as providing models of learned piety to both men and women. Illuminations of St Anne instructing the Virgin begin to appear with some regularity in books of hours and in other books of devotion after papal approval of the Feast of St Anne in 1378. Pictures like these, which often include the book's female patron in the sacred scene, inspired the earthly counterparts of Mary and St Anne, women who would be like these holy ones, to take up the book and read. In the well-known illustration from the Bedford Hours, for example, Anne of Burgundy, Duchess of Bedford, kneels before Anne, her name saint, and as Pamela Sheingorn has pointed out, 'It is surely significant that the duchess mirrors not only St Anne's name, but also her activity – both have open books before them'.[24]

In fifteenth-century depictions Mary is shown reading not only at Anne's knee, or at the Annunciation, but at Pentecost, in enclosed gardens, on thrones surrounded by angels, or while visited by Old Testament Patriarchs, St Elizabeth, or the Resurrected Christ. Another frequently depicted scene is the inception of the Virgin Mary, in which the pregnant Anne appears to read to the foetus of Mary within. One such miniature of the inception of the Virgin occurs in the Da Costa Hours, illuminated by Simon Bening of Bruges; related miniatures appear in the Grimani Breviary and in another book of hours in the Pierpont Morgan Library, written and illuminated in Bruges in 1531 by Antonius van Damme.[25]

And increasingly, from the fourteenth century onward, reading becomes an attribute of woman saints who themselves emulate the Virgin. For example, St Catherine of Alexandria and St Barbara are regularly shown reading or meditating upon open books in paintings and miniatures of the later Middle Ages. In *The Golden Legend*, Barbara is said to have been converted to Christianity by her reading of True Doctrine, while St Catherine's erudition has been traced to her home, Alexandria, a city famous for its scholarly tradition. For a

FIG. 45 Madonna and child with saints. Robert Campin (Master of Flemalle) and assistant. Washington, DC, Nat. Gallery of Art, S. Kress Coll.

variety of reasons, both Barbara and Catherine are usually shown, books in hand, as the protectors of schools and students.[26]

An expensively dressed St Barbara (FIG. 44) is represented in an illumination from a breviary produced for Eleanor, Queen of Portugal, in Bruges c.1500. Seated on a manicured lawn in an urban setting (in which the buildings seem almost identifiable), Barbara muses upon her open book. In a painting of the Virgin and Child in an enclosed garden (FIG. 45), St Catherine, in the left corner, peruses a two-column manuscript, probably a Bible. Painted by the Master of Flemalle, Robert Campin, also the artist of the Merode altarpiece (FIG. 32), this painting incorporates both idealized and realistic details: ornate tapestries are draped from the cracked garden wall; the plants in the foreground are realistically rendered, and careful attention has been given to the detailing over the arched doorway.

Both examples show woman saints (who were both probably fictional) in realistic settings. The books in both cases may be simply seen as another realistic detail, giving veracity and immediacy to the scene. The conventional placing of the Virgin in a homely domestic space, as in the Merode altarpiece, or the Virgin and Child with St Catherine in a naturalistic garden setting, or Barbara in an urban one in which even the buildings seem recognizable, shows the conscious pseudo-realism of Dutch and Flemish painters. It is the hallmark

FIG. 46 Deathbed scene. *The Hours of Catherine of Cleves*, Use of the Augustinian Canons. New York, Pierpont Morgan, MS 917, fol. 180r.

FIG. 47 Left: Anne of Brittany with her book. Jean Bourdichon, the *Grandes Heures*, Use of Rome, France, Tours or Paris, Paris, BN, MS lat.9474, fol. 3r.

FIG. 48 Above: The money-lender and his wife. Quentin Massys. Paris, Louvre Mus.

of their style, wherein the book becomes a realistic detail drawn from life just like the plants sprouting from the top of the garden wall.[27]

Readers represented in late medieval art may also be nuns or laywomen who are, in turn, consciously modelling themselves on female saints and the Virgin. Female readers, noble or middle-class, may be shown with their open books in church, present with a book at a holy scene such as the Deposition or Crucifixion, or simply reading in a garden, shop or at a lectern. What is, however, often striking about scenes like these is the prominence given to worldly concerns despite the religious context. In the Hours of Catherine of Cleves (FIG. 46), for example, a nun, or perhaps the dying man's soon-to-be widow, prays from an open book at his bedside while the physician examining his urine, the two women consoling him, the priest in the foreground, and the two heirs, one of whom reappears in the lower border taking money bags out of a coffer, all contribute to the hectic busyness of the miniature. Though a deathbed scene, the emphasis here is on earthly activity.[28]

We see a similar worldly concern in half of a diptych illustration from the 'Grandes Heures', or Great Hours, of Anne of Brittany, Queen of France, illuminated by Jean Bourdichon around 1500 (FIG. 47). Anne herself appears, opulently attired, in what John Harthan has described as 'a quasi-state portrait of the Queen in her most benign aspect'.[29] With Anne are her patron saints, Anne, Ursula, and Helena. Anne's book of hours, the 'Grandes Heures', is shown open on a draped table before her. On this leaf of her book of hours, Anne would see an image of herself as a powerful, wealthy, pious woman. The open book represented in the miniature is also the same book in which Anne sees herself, the

89

ultimate exercise in reflexivity.

The book too has its own symbolic weight, representing variously (and often simultaneously) the Word of God, the beautiful object commissioned by its female patron, female piety, and status, which is, I would suggest, the main emphasis given the illuminated book of hours in the famous panel painting 'The Money Changer and his Wife' (FIG. 48), by Quentin Massys (1514). Here the wife does not so much appear to be reading the book as idly thumbing through, glancing at the pictures, perhaps appraising its worth. Does the book here represent the wife's piety or, given its context in the moneylender's shop, is it simply a beautiful object, an indication of economic status? Or is the book, in fact, a pledge for a cash loan which the money changer has just received? Does the book, presumably a book of hours to judge from the illustration, have ironic, as well as historical, significance in the scene?[30]

However we might interpret it, then, a picture of a woman reading is more than just a picture of a woman reading. The popularity of such scenes, which begin to appear in large numbers in the late fourteenth century, reaching a peak in the early sixteenth, is paralleled by increased literacy among women in this period. The picture evidence points to a 'culture in which women read', a thesis further supported by recent studies of women's wills, historical accounts, ownership marks, and other evidence.[31]

Marianne Moore, writing about good poetry, said it should present 'imaginary gardens with real toads in them', and her figurative image may be effectively extended to the visual.[32] Images can be richly suggestive, encouraging us to rethink and revisualize the past. Manuscript miniatures may be illustrative, decorative, or informational; didactic, devotional, or polemical. They may provide idealized models of behaviour or raise questions about women's roles in earlier periods which we (post)moderns have not fully considered. When we talk about pictures we must be careful to locate them in their original contexts, and we must be as precise as we can without limiting the scope of possibility. Relationships between sources – whether picture, historical document, or literary text – are complex, an intricate dance of fiction and fact, perception and reality. Picture evidence has real and important uses, and one thing it teaches is to keep an open mind, not to make judgements or assumptions based on our expectations about the lives of medieval women. In these images are encoded cultural messages from the past – if only we can adjust our spectacles to read them.

Notes to Chapter Four

1. Reproduced in J.Harthan, *Books of Hours and Their Owners* (London, 1977; repr. 1982), pp.134, 135. Versions of this essay have been presented at Women and the Book in the Middle Ages, an interdisciplinary conference held at St Hilda's College, Oxford (August, 1993) and at the seminar 'How Art Means' at the Folger Institute, Washington, DC (1994). Another, 'The Literate Lay Woman and Her Book', was given at the 1994 meeting of the Medieval Academy of America. Portions of text and some images appeared earlier in the Medieval Woman calendar, published yearly by Peter Workman Publishing (1991–95; in UK distributed by Past Times), for which I have supplied historical text and iconography. Thanks to Pamela Sheingorn and Michael Clanchy who read and commented on drafts of this essay.

2. *See* P.Sheingorn, '"The Wise Mother" The Image of St Anne Teaching the Virgin Mary', *Gesta*, 32 (1993), pp.69–80; M.T.Clanchy, *From Memory to Written Record. England 1066–1307* (Cambridge, Mass., 1979; repr. 1993), pp.191–96.

3. K.Moxey, 'Motivating History', *The Art Bulletin*, 77 (1995), p.396.

4. J.Ashbery, *Self-Portrait in a Convex Mirror* (New York, 1976), p.76.

5. N.Bryson, 'House of Wax', in R.Krauss, *Cindy Sherman 1975–1993* (New York, 1993), p.218. The chromogenic print made in 1989, 'Untitled' is reproduced in the recent *Cindy Sherman* catalogue and in the catalogue of the 1991 *Biennial Exhibition*, Whitney Museum of American Art (New York, 1991). The print of The Monk was purchased by The Metropolitan Museum of Art in 1991 and reproduced in 'Recent Acquisitions 1990–1991', *The Metropolitan Museum of Art Bulletin*, 49 (1991), p.49. For historical background on images of the Virgin's breast, *see* M.R.Miles, 'The Virgin's One Bare Breast: Female Nudity and Religious Meaning in Tuscan Early Renaissance Culture', in *The Female Body in Western Culture: Contemporary Perspectives*, ed. S.R.Suleiman (Cambridge, Mass., 1986), pp.193–208.

6. Boccaccio's *Decameron*, or 100 Stories, is a work dedicated by the author to woman readers, or as he says in his preface, to supply 'support and consolation for those ladies in love', which might, given the naughty sexual content of many of the tales, surprise even the 20th-century reader. There are several extant copies of *Decameron* manuscripts in French translation known to have been made for woman patrons. Another book written ostensibly for female readers is *The Book of the Knight of the Tower*, by Geoffroy de la Tour-Landry, which the author dedicates to his daughters.

7. Several of the French translations of Boccaccio's *De Mulieribus Claris* include illustrations of woman artists, which are fictional portraits of fictional women, but which when taken together provide the most complete visual record of the woman artist at work in the 15th century, giving information about artists' tools, conditions in the workshop or studio, and contemporary dress.

8. Portraits of Christine appear in numerous manuscripts including: Paris, BN, MS fr 1178, fol. 64v, MS fr 603, fol. 21r; Brussels, Bibl. Roy., MS 9236, fol. 136r, MSS 9009–11, fol. 118v; London, BL, MS Harley 4431, ff.3r, 259v, 261v, 290r; Oxford, Bodleian Library, MS Laud. Misc. 570, fol. 24r. Among recent English translations of Christine's works are: *The Writings of Christine de Pizan*, ed. C.C.Willard (New York, 1994); *The Book of the City of Ladies*, transl. E.J.Richards (New York, 1982); and *The Book of the Duke of True Lovers*, transl. T.S.Fenster (New York, 1991).

9. For the authorship of the verses at the end of Caxton's edition of *Moral Proverbs*, *see* N.F.Blake, *William Caxton and English Literary Culture* (London, 1991), p.143. In later manuscripts of *Les Faits d'Armes et de Chevalerie*, Christine's name is not mentioned and the pronoun referring to the author of the work has been changed to the masculine form: 'Possibly some scribe, fearing that a prejudice against a woman writing on a manly subject might detract from the book's appeal, deliberately excised or altered every reference to feminine authorship'. A.T.P.Byles, ed. *The Book of Fayttes of Armes and of Chyualrye*, EETS o.s. 189, (London, 1932), p.xvi.

10. M.Warner, *Joan of Arc: The Image of Female Heroism* (New York, 1981), p.211. The miniature of Joan is also reproduced on the dust jacket of Warner.

11. M.W.Driver, 'Pictures in Print: Late Fifteenth- and Early Sixteenth-Century English Religious Books for Lay Readers', in *De Cella in Seculum: Religious and Secular Life and Devotion in Late Medieval England*, ed.

M.G.Sargent (Cambridge, 1989), pp.241–44. *See also* Driver, 'Nuns as Patrons, Artists, Readers: Bridgettine Woodcuts in Printed Books Produced for the English Market', in *Art into Life: Collected Papers from the Kresge Art Museum Medieval Symposia*, ed. C.G.Fisher and K.L.Scott (East Lansing, Mich., 1995), pp.237–67.

12   This medieval encyclopaedia covers a range of subjects from the nature of God, angels, and Time to the composition of the elements and the human body, and the varieties of plants, animals, gems, and eggs. The woodcut illustration in the early printed editions is discussed in M.Driver, 'Illustration in Early English Books', *Books at Brown*, 33 (1986), pp.13–27, 52–53.

13   For more on midwifery, *see*: M.Green, 'Women's Medical Practice and Health Care in Medieval Europe', in *Sisters and Workers in the Middle Ages*, ed. J.M.Bennett, E.A.Clark, *et al.* (Chicago, 1989), pp.39 *et seq.*, 58–78; E.Power, 'Some Women Practitioners of Medicine in the Middle Ages', *Proceedings of the Royal Society of Medicine*, 15 (1921–1922), p.20–23; B.Rowland (ed.), *Medieval Woman's Guide to Health* (Kent, Oh., 1981); M.E.Wiesner, 'Early Modern Midwifery: A Case Study', in *Women and Work in Preindustrial Europe* (Bloomington, Ind., 1986), pp.94–113.

14   Women's work in the mines is discussed in two articles by S.C.Karant-Nunn, 'The Women of the Saxon Silver Mines', in *Women in Reformation and Counter-Reformation Europe: Private and Public Worlds*, ed. S.Marshall (Bloomington, Ind., 1989), pp.29–46, and 'From Adventurers to Drones: The Saxon Silver Mines as an Early Proletariat', in *The Workplace Before the Factory: Artisans and Proletarians, 1500–1800*, ed T.M.Safley and L.N.Rosenband (Ithaca, NY, 1993), p.85. *See also* C.Vanja, 'Mining Women in Early Modern European Society', in Safley and Rosenband, pp.100–117.

15   J.Amman, in *The Book of Trades* (1568), includes a woodcut of the needle-maker, who cuts needles from iron wire as his wife prepares them for sale to pedlars by sticking the needles neatly into sheets. Women in the metal trades are mentioned in E.Uitz, *The Legend of Good Women: Medieval Women in Towns and Cities*, transl. S.Marnie (Mt Kisco, NY, 1990), pp.60–62; E.Ennen, *The Medieval Woman* (Oxford, 1989), pp.180–84, 278. For mention of woman blacksmiths, *see English Medieval Industries: Craftsmen, Techniques, Products*, ed. J.Blair and N.Ramsay (London, 1991), pp.186–88.

16   Christine de Pizan, *The Treasure of the City of Ladies or The Book of the Three Virtues*, transl. S.Lawson (New York, 1985), pp.131–32.

17   Uitz, *Legend*, p.61; Blair and Ramsay, *English Medieval Industries*, p.193.

18   *See* J.A.Brundage, 'Prostitution in the Medieval Canon Law', and V.L.Bullough, 'The Prostitute in the Early Middle Ages', 'Prostitution in the Later Middle Ages', in *Sexual Practices and the Medieval Church*, ed. V.L.Bullough and J.A.Brundage (Buffalo, NY, 1982), pp.34–42, 149–60, 176–86; D.Herlihy, *Opera Muliebria: Women and Work in Medieval Europe* (New York, 1990), pp.18, 20 passim. For other sources, *see* R.M.Karras, 'The Regulation of Brothels in Later Medieval England', in Bennett and Clark, *Sisters and Workers*, pp.100–34.

19   G. Duby (ed.), *A History of Private Life II: Revelations of the Medieval World*, transl. A. Goldhammer (Cambridge, Mass., 1988), pp.363–66, 504, 524–25, 600–10.

20   Duby, *History*, pp.603–7; E.Amt (ed.), *Women's Lives in Medieval Europe: A Sourcebook* (New York, 1993), p.197.

21   Karras, 'The Regulation of Brothels', in Bennett and Clark, *Sisters and Workers*, pp.100–34.

22   Duby, *History*, pp.630ff. In another translation, Poggio describes Baden bathing dress this way: 'In many places, the entrance to the baths is the same for men and women, so that it often happens that a man and a half-naked woman or a woman and a naked man come face to face. The men wear nothing but a leather apron, and the women put on linen shirts down to their knees, so cut on either side that they leave uncovered neck, bosom, arms, and shoulders'. P.W.Goodhart Gordan (ed. and transl.), *Two Renaissance Book Hunters: The Letters of Poggius Bracciolini to Nicolaus de Niccolis* (New York, 1974; repr. 1991), p.27.

23   *See* Clanchy, *Memory to Written Record*, pp.13, 188–89, 191–92, 255–56, 290; Sheingorn, *Gesta*, pp.69–80; K.Ashley and P.Sheingorn (eds.), *Interpreting Cultural Symbols: Saint Anne in Late Medieval Society* (Athens, Ga., 1990), pp.1–68.

24   Sheingorn, *Gesta*, p.74, Fig.11. The miniature is also reproduced in J.Backhouse, *The Bedford Hours* (New York, 1990), plate 47.

25   NY, Pierpont Morgan Library, MS M 451.

26 A.Arnould and J.M.Massing, *Splendours of Flanders* (Cambridge, 1993), p.46.

27 *See* J.de Coo, 'A Medieval Look at the Merode Annunciation', *Zeitschrifte für Kuntsgeschichte*, 44 (1981), pp.114–32. Thanks to Michael Clanchy for sending me this article.

28 J.Plummer, *The Hours of Catherine of Cleves* (New York, 1966; repr. 1975), p.41. *See also* S.Penketh, 'Women and Books of Hours', ch.14 in this volume.

29 Harthan, *Books of Hours*, p.128.

30 Suggested by Michael Clanchy in a recent letter. A companion painting, titled 'The Banker and his Wife', also by Massys, shows another husband-and-wife team in their shop. The wife, in this case, leafs through what is clearly an account book, laid on the empty money-bags before her. Uitz describes her activity this way:'Well-versed in money matters, the wife takes over the task of bookkeeping', pp.30–31.

31 Sheingorn, *Gesta*, p.75.

32 M.Moore, 'Poetry', in *The Norton Anthology of Poetry*, ed. A.W.Allison, H.Barrows, *et al.* (New York, 1975), p.1016.

Part Two
IMAGES AND BOOKS BY WOMEN

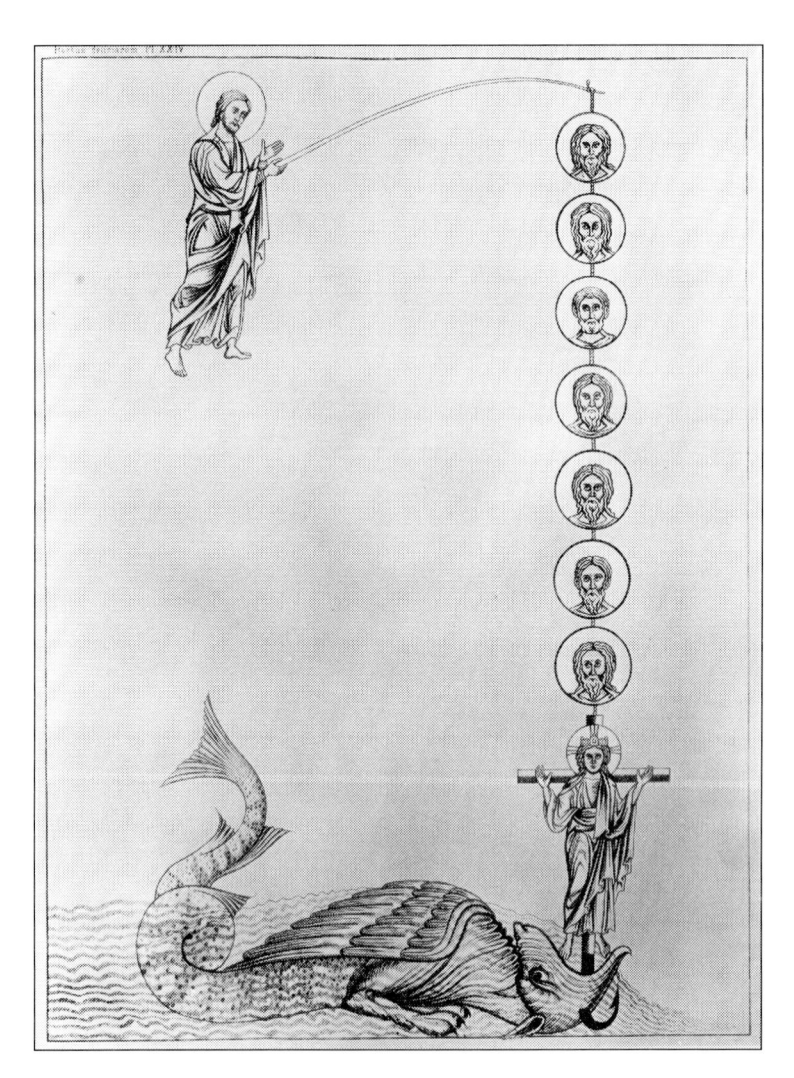

FIG. 49 God the Father capturing Leviathan.
Herrad of Landsberg, *Hortus deliciarum*, fol. 84r.

CHAPTER FIVE

Two Twelfth-Century Women and Their Books

THÉRÈSE MCGUIRE

T o SPEAK OF women and the book in the Middle Ages is inevitably to speak of learned nuns who often played vital roles in scholarship and culture in every Christianized area of Europe during the period. In the seventh century, Hilda of Whitby helped to lay the foundations of English poetic tradition by discovering and instructing her herdsman, Caedmon, the father of English poetry; while in the tenth century the playwright Hroswitha of Gandersheim (c.935–c.1000)[1] gleams as a shining light focusing a slender but steady beam on classical learning, at a time when it was supposed that the classics were suffering a severe setback and were scorned by scholars and writers alike. In the twelfth century two notable women, Herrad of Landsberg (or Hohenburg) and Hildegard of Bingen, were elected to be abbesses of their respective communities. Evaluating the importance of the role of abbess led Joanne McNamara and Suzanne Wemple to assume: 'For any [woman] to rise from obscure origin to the highest position [her] world can bestow upon [her] implies the possession of an unusual personality ... talent and ability of the rarest kind are required of any [woman] for her to overshadow [her] contemporaries.'[2]

Responsible for and concerned about the education of the nuns, some abbesses composed secular as well as religious texts for the instruction of their dependents. The knowledge gained through reading and study needed to be shared. Herrad and Hildegard accomplished this sharing through writing and through illuminations which accompanied their texts, and in later years their works served to inspire and to teach beyond the confines of their individual monasteries. Today scholars must rely on the two definitive resources produced by A. Straub and G. Keller[3] and that of Rosalie Green[4] in order to examine copies of Herrad's *Hortus deliciarum*. Many copies of Hildegard's *Scivias* exist, and the extraordinary illuminations of the Rupertsberg codex were copied in colour by Dame Josepha Knips, a nun of St Hildegard's Monastery in Rüdesheim, Eibingen,[5] before the original manuscript was lost in the Second World War.[6]

Herrad, the twelfth-century abbess of the Hohenbourg in Alsace,[7] compiled an encyclopaedia of history, philosophy, ethics, and profound learning, in addition to the teachings of biblical and secular themes. As a citizen of the twelfth century, she went beyond the scope of earlier encyclopaedic works and included new sources from Arabian writings which reached the northern countries in Europe via Spain.

Arabic scholars avidly sought to discover the philosophical and scientific findings of the ancient Greeks. Around 800 AD, an Arabian caliph purchased a copy of Euclid's *Elements* from Constantinople. This work, when translated into Arabic, became the first pebble cast into the waters of knowledge, creating ripples which spread to embrace more and more of the Greek Classics. Arabic translations were converted next into Latin and Hebrew at their European point of entry (most likely at the college of translators at Toledo, Spain).[8] Fritz Saxl believes that the Jewish and Christian scholars who translated the Arabic works were responsible for a clear revolution in the development of Western European thought;[9] and the advent of Byzantine and Arabic ideas in Western Europe allowed the fresh cool draughts of the breath of Greek and Arabic wisdom to blow through the dusty shelves of monastic libraries.

This exciting discovery and rediscovery in scholastic circles of reformation and education which were occurring in her convent milieu engaged Herrad and gave her the inspiration and impetus necessary to create and assemble her encyclopaedic work, *Hortus deliciarum*, which consisted of about 45,000 lines of text and approximately 400 illustrations. She based her precise meaning of the title *Hortus deliciarum* on definitions given by Isidore of Seville: 'Paradise is a place located in the East, the name ... translated from the Greek into Latin is *hortus*, a garden. In Hebrew it is called Eden, which means in Latin *delicie* – delights. Together this creates the phrase, *hortus deliciarum*, the garden of delights.'[10]

In the preface to her encyclopaedia, Herrad explained to the nuns why she wrote the *Hortus*:

> I was thinking of your happiness when, like a bee guided by the inspiring God, I drew from many flowers of sacred and philosophical writing, this book, called the 'Garden of Delights'; and I have put it together to the praise of Christ and of the Church, and to your enjoyment, as though into a sweet honeycomb. Therefore, you must diligently seek your salvation in it and strengthen your weary spirit with its sweet honey drops.[11]

Monastic scholars, whose work of extraction and arrangement constituted their major occupation in writing, likened themselves to bees who gathered the nectar of knowledge from far and wide and stored this learning in the secret cells of their minds. Not for them was it necessary to propose new ideas or envision new and dangerous horizons: adapting the wisdom of the centuries to enhance their teaching was their goal, and this method of gathering together and recording the wisdom of the ages was considered most necessary and trustworthy in an age that feared the ugly demon of heresy and the dragon of schism.

Herrad worked on the *Hortus* between the years 1159 and 1175. The Abbess Relindis was still alive when she began work on her masterpiece; many historians surmise that Relindis contributed advice and encouragement to her pupil. Annemarie Carr stated: 'Relindis ... was an inspired educational reformer, and a tangible example of the tradition of learning which passed from woman to woman in the German convents.'[12] Examining the tracings and notes preserved from the work of the Count de Bastard d'Estang it would seem that Herrad planned whole sections before she worked on any given part, co-ordinating a pictorial dogmatic and didactic history with a text derived from many authorities. Although she composed her manuscript in Latin, she added German glosses to explain less common or

FIG. 50 The woman clothed with the sun.
Herrad of Landsberg, *Hortus deliciarum*, fol. 261v.

generally misunderstood expressions. Intending the manuscript to be used at the monastery of St Odile by her nuns alone, she did not have the work bound, preferring to have the freedom of being able to insert additional stories and paintings as the need arose and as the lessons evolved.[13]

In the *Hortus*, Herrad dealt with the history of the world from the moment of creation; her text spanned the Hebrew and the Christian Testaments, the writings of the Fathers of the Church, and the history of the Church from Calvary to the Last Judgement. One painting that exemplifies her combination of the Hebrew and the Christian Testaments is the illustration 'God the Father catching Leviathan,' (FIG. 49) in which she uses the Cross as 'hook' and Christ as 'bait' to capture the beast from the depths of the sea. Pictures of prophets of the Hebrew Testament who, according to Christian tradition, foretold the coming of Christ, adorn the fishing line. There is no precedent for this interpretation in all of the known medieval illuminations.

The *Apocalypse* supplied Herrad with themes for several of her monumental paintings. Standing over a foot high on the folio, the figure of 'The woman clothed with the sun' (FIG. 50) is taller than many panel paintings. This figure is no ordinary woman; according to Herrad's inscription, 'The woman seen in heaven is the Church whom Christ introduces into the celestial kingdom.' Her frontal position sets the woman apart as a cult image of great importance; her dress is the rich crimson of royalty, while her crown is adorned with twelve stars. Her wide-open eyes signify knowledge; the elegant movement of her hands symbolizes power; her straight, firm legs beneath the dampfold of the drapery portray stability; her aristocratic bearing emphasizes royalty; and her ears, bent forward slightly, reveal her willingness to listen to God's Word. She is clothed in a trinity of light, which both enlightens and protects her. In direct contrast to her is the dragon, king and high priest of evil, depicted with his seven crowned heads, who waits to snatch the child away from the woman. An angel swoops down to rescue the child. In anger, the dragon spews forth a torrent of water to drown the woman, but the earth opens its mouth to swallow the torrent. Leviathan, wielding a great sword, rises from the depths of the sea. In the inscription on the illumination Herrad explains, 'The beast which then appeared and to whom the dragon had given his power, is the Antichrist ... [who] armed with a sword, strikes the saints who resist him.' But Yahweh gives the woman great wings that she might fly into the desert away from danger. 'In both text and pictures, multiple sources are apparent; but the wonder of the *Hortus deliciarum* is not that it combines so many threads but that it is woven of so few. It is not by any means a seamless garment, but it is far from the patchwork quilt that some have seen.'[14]

Particularly interesting are the excerpts taken from the writings of her contemporaries: Peter Comestor, Peter Lombard, Rupert of Deutz, and Honorius Augustodunensis. Auxiliary themes dovetail into the main themes: the confusion of tongues at the Tower of Babel provides the opportunity to discuss pagan theology and philosophy; the story of the Exodus becomes the springboard for a lesson on geography; and the story of the Magi following the star to Bethlehem allows Herrad to propound the fundamental theories of astronomy and medical astrology.

Both poetess and musician, Herrad composed forty-five Latin poems which are in part accompanied by musical notations. She transformed secular topics, changing the unacceptable pagan muses into the more acceptable liberal arts, and produced the only known twelfth-century drawings of 'Ulysses and the Sirens'.[15] Herrad did not create a new style in the *Hortus*; rather she embodied the styles found in the sculptures of Romanesque cathedrals, which combine literal and mystical meanings in their messages.

Some historians have questioned whether Herrad was the sole author and illuminator of the *Hortus*. The tremendous scope of the text,[16] the numerous illustrations, and the difference in size of the folios[17] tend to cause modern historians to wonder that a single dynamic energy would be capable of producing such a work.

A. Merigan expressed his disbelief in the authorship of the manuscript, not on historical grounds, but because he couldn't believe that 'this encyclopaedia which assembles all the knowledge of the twelfth century should be credited to a woman'.[18] Studying the copies of the *Hortus* cannot conclusively resolve the question of whether or not Herrad was sole author and illuminator, since only tracings of the illuminations exist today and the copies have been executed by different hands. Christian Maurice Englehardt copied numerous lines of the text and traced many of the drawings, while Count de Bastard studied and copied much of it, for inclusion in his comprehensive work, *Paintings and Decorations of Manuscripts.*[19]

In the nineteenth century C. Schmidt had the opportunity to study the original manuscript, and commented on the impression of unity which the illuminations engendered:

> Their design, their colours are so uniform from beginning to end, that it is not possible to surmise that it had more than one and only one artist; some rare differences in certain details are not important enough to weaken this judgement.'[20]

Although the monastery of St Odile suffered destruction by fire several times, Herrad's manuscript enjoyed relative safety in the convent treasury. When fire completely destroyed the monastery in 1546 the nuns decided to abandon the site, and they gave the *Hortus* to the Bishop of Strasbourg for safe keeping.[21] In 1609 it passed into the hands of the Carthusian monks at Molsheim, who made a copy of it. When all the monasteries were suppressed and their treasures confiscated in 1790, the *Hortus*, and the copy made by the Carthusians, were taken by government officials, who stored all the literary and artistic treasures of Alsace in the choir of a confiscated Dominican church. On the nights of 24 and 25 August 1870, during a heavy bombardment of the city of Strasbourg by the German army, the church was destroyed and the treasures burned. We have only the tracings and copies of the texts, made by nineteenth-century scholars,[22] to examine in discovering for ourselves the breadth and boldness of Herrad's conception of the life and beliefs of the twelfth century.[23]

Hildegard of Bingen, a twelfth century German Benedictine nun, was one of the most learned women of her century. Known by her peers as the 'Sibyl of the Rhine',[24] Hildegard excelled as artist, playwright, philosopher, musician, poet, doctor, theologian, and administrator. Her gift for administration helped her community to survive the hardships and vicissitudes connected with rebuilding the monastery of St Rupert's and with the founding of her second monastery in Rüdesheim, Eibingen.

William of Gembloux (d.1204) spent 3 years at St Rupert's, probably as confessor as well as secretary to Hildegard. In a letter to one of his confrères, he reported:

> The convent is rich in religious zeal and also in income. It has no tall buildings, but all the rooms are large, beautiful and monastic. All the workshops have running water, and are well equipped. The convent supports fifty nuns, also many guests, who are never lacking, and a number of servants. The mother is kind to all, gives good advice to everyone who asks for it, resolves the most difficult problems presented to her, writes books, instructs her sisters, leads sinners back to the right path, and is always fully occupied.[25]

Hildegard's days were indeed fully occupied; her many literary and artistic achievements remain as a testament to her productive mind. Her greatest role, however, was that of mystic, for it was from that unusual gift that she began to write about her visions and to interpret them in words and in paintings.

The three books of Hildegard's visions are: *Scivias* (*Know the Ways of the Lord*); *Liber vitae meritorium* (*Book of a Meritorious Life*); and *Liber divinorum operum* (*The Book of Divine Works*). In the most famous of the trilogy, *Scivias*, Hildegard explained, point for point, every facet of her visions which were subsequently translated into unusual paintings. 'The great theme of the *Scivias* is the way which God has taken in creation, especially with men [and women] and continues throughout salvation history down to the last day.'[26] The vision of 'Synagogue' (FIG. 51) one of the most meaningful visions from *Scivias* in both words and illumination, illustrates this great theme. Hildegard describes Synagogue as a tall stately woman whose countenance shows untold sadness. She stands with her eyes closed so that she may not be distracted by the pagan world; her arms, folded across her breast, embrace Moses, who holds aloft the tablets of the Ten Commandments. In her womb rest Abraham and all the patriarchs and prophets, for she is their mother. Her feet are stained with the blood of Christ and of all her martyrs. She stands upon a silver cloud because, as a symbol of God's chosen people, she has remained faithful to God's law, and at the end of time Israel will attain salvation, for God never revokes gifts nor forgets covenants. A circlet of gold crowns her head: the circlet symbolizes Mary, the daughter of Synagogue and mother of God's Son.

FIG. 51 Synagogue. Hildegard of Bingen. *Scivias* (Rupertsberg), i, vision 5.

Medieval mystics sought wisdom by intuition and vision; they centred on searching for the meaning in everything in nature, in science, in the purpose of all creation, and in written books. Hildegard sought to explain the ascent of the soul to God through symbolic language; the validity of allegory for her was the supreme expression of humanity's search for God and for God's love of the world:

> To such a mind it was meaningless to inquire whether the pelican really nourished her young with her own blood, or whether there really existed a phoenix who rose from the ashes, so long as these creatures, whether of God directly or of God through [one's] imagination, made manifest the Saviour who shed His blood upon the cross and rose the third day.[27]

Hildegard's *Ordo virtutum* (*The Order of Virtues*) enjoys the status of the earliest known liturgical morality play, which she produced between 1141 and 1151.[28] *Ordo virtutum* is the personification of the thirteenth vision in the third book of *Scivias*. Hildegard's skill as a writer as well as a composer of music culminated in this play, one which personifies Vice and Virtue warring with each other for the domination of the soul. All the characters, with the exception of the devil, sing their parts. According to Hildegard, when the soul is no longer affected by music the presence of evil is portended. Since music is the language of heaven, the devil, who is all evil, cannot sing. The play, complete with an original musical score, was most probably produced and performed in celebration of the dedication by the Bishop of Mainz of the monastic church at Hildegard's monastery in Rupertsberg in 1152.[29]

Throughout her lifetime Hildegard continued to enrich and enlarge her production of what she called her 'symphony of the harmony of celestial revelations'.[30] For her the Cistercian concept of music's sensual quality distracting worshippers with its beauty posed no problem. As Barbara Newman observed, 'For Hildegard, liturgical song was a medium that perfectly united soul and body ... just as Christ had united the human nature with the divine.'[31] Hildegard likened herself to a musical instrument in the hands of God: 'The marvels of God are not brought forth from one's self. Rather it is more like a chord, a sound that is played. The tone does not come out of the chord itself, but rather, through the touch of the musician. I am, of course, the lyre and harp of God's kindness.'[32] And Adelgundis Fuhrkotter proposed that Hildegard as writer of *Liber simplicis medicine* (*Book of Natural Science*) and *Liber compositae medicine* (*Book of Medical Science*), 'is the first German woman doctor to have left us, in writing, her scientific natural and medicinal knowledge'.[33]

It may be concluded that Hildegard was born at a propitious time in history; that she absorbed the atmosphere of the twelfth century, a period filled with new thoughts gleaned from the translations of the Latin classics, from the ancient Greek philosophers and Arabic scientists, and from Byzantine art; and that she was an inspired seer. Her works give us a glimpse into her unique personality and into the comprehensive knowledge which led popes, bishops, emperors, and princes to seek her prophetic, spiritual, and medical assistance;[34] while it was within the framework of her visions that she emerged as artist, dramatist, and musician.

Women by nature are creators; a remarkable example of Creation spirituality emerged in the works of Herrad and Hildegard, reflecting the feminine prerogative of the creation of new life in the midst of pain. This creative instinct in women, which emerges in the concept of creative spirituality, led Julianna Casey to conclude: 'Feminism does not end with equality for women. It begins there, and moves beyond to the healing of all persons, male and female, so that together all might rejoice in a God who does glorious things.'[35] Hildegard and Herrad, the intellectual giants among women of the twelfth century, evince in their books the intellectual climate that must have prevailed in their monasteries and the love for knowledge they attempted to instil in their sisters; and they attest to the continuance of education and of creative expression available in some women's monasteries. Examining the literary works of these two extraordinary women can bring scholars to a deeper understanding of how women found expression for their visions in the milieu of monasticism, and of how they were influenced by currents of aesthetic considerations which flowed through the scholarly tomes of the medieval world.

Notes to Chapter Five

1. J.Campbell, 'Women Scholars of the Middle Ages', *American Catholic Quarterly Review,* 43 (1938), pp.237–40.

2. J.McNamara and S.Wemple, 'Sanctity and Power: The Dual Pursuit of Medieval Women', in *Becoming Visible: Women in European History,* eds. R.Bridenthal and C.Koons (Boston, Mass., 1977) p.100.

3. A.Straub and G.Keller, *Herrad of Landsberg: Hortus Deliciarum,* ed. and transl. by A.Cararzas (New York, 1977).

4. R.Green, M.Evans, *et al., Herrad of Hohenbourg: Hortus Deliciarum* (London, 1979).

5. The abbot of Maria Laach Monastery, Ildefons Herwegen, had the manuscript Hs. I from Wiesbaden completely photographed, full size, so that the whole text and all the miniatures have been preserved in photocopy. In 1927 the manuscript was deposited at the Benedictine monastery in Eibingen where a facsimile copy was made on parchment by the nuns in the art studios of the abbey. It took 6 years (1927–33) to complete the facsimile. Adelgundis Fuhrkotter, *The Miniatures from the Book Scivias–Know the Ways–of St Hildegard of Bingen from the Illuminated Rupertsberg Codex,* transl. F.Hockey (Turnhout, 1977).

6. The original Rupertsberg Codex was housed in the Weisbaden Bibliothek, Germany until 1945, when the librarians placed it in a bank vault along with several other precious manuscripts. During the Second World War, the bank vault was emptied by the occupying Russian forces and the treasures have not been seen since.

7. S.Hilpisch, OSB, *History of Benedictine Nuns,* transl. by J.Muggli, OSB, (Collegeville, Minn., 1958) p.42.

8. H.N.Bixler, 'A Group-Theoretic Analysis of Symmetry in Two-Dimensional Patterns from Islamic Art', (unpubl. Ph.D. thesis, New York Univ., 1980), p.28.

9. F.Saxl, *A Heritage of Images: A Selection of Lectures,* eds. H.Honour and J.Fleming (Baltimore, 1970), pp.28–29.

10. F. Saxl, 'Illustrated Medieval Encyclopedias II: The Christian Transformation', in *id., Lectures* (London, 1957), p.245.

11. L.Eckenstein, *Woman Under Monasticism* (Cambridge, 1896), pp.254–55.

12. A.Wyle Carr, 'Women Artists of the Middle Ages', *The Feminist Art Journal,* 5 (1976), p.7.

13. A.Christen, *Le Jardin des délices, de l'abbesse Herrade de Landsberg* (Colmar, 1968), p.8.

14. R.Green, 'The Miniatures', in *Herrad of Hohenbourg: Hortus Deliciarum,* p.25.

15. L.D.Ettlinger, 'Muses and Liberal Arts: Two Miniatures from Herrad of Landsberg's *Hortus Deliciarum*', in D.Fraser, H.Hibbard, and M.J.Levine (eds.), *Essays in the History of Art, Presented to Rudolf Wittkower* (London, 1967) p.30.

16. B.Murphy, 'Medieval Female Education in Germany', *The Catholic World,* 33 (1881), p.382.

17. 'There were sixty-nine leaves which were smaller than the other folios.' Green, 'Miniatures', p.30.

18. 'Que cette encyclopédie, qui a réuni toutes les connaissances de l'extrême fin du XIIe siècle soit due à une femme.' A.Mérigan, cited in Green, 'Miniatures', p.25, n.21.

19. A.N.L. Munby, *Connoisseurs and Medieval Miniatures: 1750–1850* (Oxford, 1972), p.145.

20. 'Leur dessin, leurs couleurs d'ailleurs si uniformes d'un bout à l'autre, qu'ils ne peuvent appartenir qu'à un seul et même artiste; quelques rares différences dans certains détails ne sont pas assez importantes pour infirmer ce jugement.' Schmidt, cited in Green, 'Miniatures', p.30.

21. C.Bischoff, 'L'Histoire', *Herrad of Hohenbourg: Hortus Deliciarum,* p.13.

22. *Oeuvre Notre-Dame,* the sketches of Englehardt, the tracings of Straub, and the considerable contributions of the Bastard sketches and texts discovered in Paris, B.N.

23. K.Petersen and J.J. Wilson, *Women Artists: Recognition and Reappraisal from the Early Middle Ages to the Twentieth Century* (New York, 1976), p.16.

24 A.Sutherland Harris and L.Nochlin, *Women Artists: 1550–1950* (New York, 1976) p.18.

25 Hilpisch, *History*, p.12.

26 Fuhrkotter, *The Miniatures from the Book Scivias* (F. note 5) p.8.

27 J.H.Randall, Jr., *The Making of the Modern Mind: A Survey of the Intellectual Background of the Present Age* (New York, 1976), p.35.

28 The earliest copy of the *Ordo virtutum* is the 'Riesenkodex', codex 2, which comes from the Rupertsberg; it was copied c.1180 and 1190. It is housed in the Hessiche Landsbibliothek, Wiesbaden. The *Reigen der Tugenden* (*Leader of Virtue*) (Berlin, 1927) has a commentary about the play, a transcription of the text into German, and the only modern edition of the Latin text, together with its musical score.

29 B.Thornton, 'Introduction to the Libretto of the *Ordo Virtutum*', *Hildegard von Bingen: Ordo Virtutum, Sequentia Ensemble für Musik des Mittelalters*, (*Sequentia Ensemble for Music of the Middle Ages*) (Cologne, 1982), unpaginated.

30 *Ibid.*

31 B.Newman, 'Introduction', *Saint Hildegard of Bingen: Symphonia* (Ithaca, 1988), p.27.

32 Hildegard, *Meditations with Hildegard of Bingen*, ed. G.Uhlein (Sante Fe, NM, 1982), p.93.

33 Fuhrkotter, *Miniatures*, p.7.

34 E.von Quentin, 'Geschichte der Medizine: Hildegard von Bingen: Moderne Arztin – vor 800 Jahren', *Münchener Medizinische Wochenschrift*, 24 Nov. 1968, p.2509.

35 J.Casey, IHM, 'Feminism and Religious Life', *New Catholic World*, 226 (1982), p.210.

CHAPTER SIX

Worship of the Word:
Some Gothic Nonnenbücher in their Devotional Context

JUDITH OLIVER

IN RECENT DECADES scholars have recovered the names of numerous female scribes and illuminators from the colophons and occasional self-portraits in their manuscripts, amply illustrating the fact that nuns were actively engaged in book production.[1] In the high Middle Ages, the period which is the focus of this paper, these female religious concentrated their labours on books used in private devotion or in the liturgy. The majority of surviving decorated manuscripts which can be associated with nunneries are psalters and service books, especially antiphonals containing the chant of the Divine Office and graduals containing the music of the Mass. The psalter had always been fundamental to the monastic office, but ownership of private devotional psalters is largely a thirteenth-century phenomenon, and large choirbooks were also newly popular in the Gothic period.

Ownership of psalters is mentioned in the lives of many religious women. Dominican nuns in Germany (like the nuns of Engelberg in Switzerland) made many psalters for their own use, despite repeated prohibitions against book production by women under Dominican supervision promulgated in 1249, 1254, and 1263.[2] Beguines (who remained laywomen, but lived like nuns without entering established convents) very likely also engaged in writing and illuminating psalters for their own use in the mid-thirteenth century. One group of psalters from Liège, Belgium, in this period may be identified as the work of these beguines, for the books share a naïve style surprisingly Romanesque in spirit for the mid-thirteenth century, and thus professional artists (who were not active in Liège until the late 1260s anyway) may be ruled out (FIG. 52).[3] At the same period, the testament of one well-to-do beguine of the parish of Saint Christophe left money in 1266 to *filiabus* (a term beguines often employed in identifying themselves) *ad opus psalteriorum*, which might be interpreted to mean she left funds to meet the expense of making these very psalters.[4]

In the thirteenth and fourteenth centuries, encloistered nuns also produced numerous antiphonals and graduals. The colophon of one such antiphonal made in 1244 at the Cistercian convent of Nazareth in Lier, Belgium, identifies its scribe as the nun Agnes and attributes the musical notation to the nun Christina, who was most likely the elder sister of the mystic Beatrice of Nazareth.[5] Beatrice was taught to write manuscripts at the nearby convent of La Ramée, and later put her training to use writing choirbooks for her new house, Maagdendaal.

FIG. 52 Left: Tree of Jesse and Annunciation with Old Testament prophets in roundels. Liège Psalter. London, BL Add. MS 21114, fol. 8v.

FIG. 53 Above: Easter Antiphon. Nazareth Antiphonal. Bornem, Abdij Sint Bernardus, MS 1, fol. 46v.

Another prolific manuscript scribe at La Ramée was Ida of Leau (or Gorsleeuw) who is credited with a lectionary read at matins.[6] The Nazareth antiphonal is decorated with exuberantly unrestrained filigree initials, in highly original colours and patterns (FIG. 53). It is, regrettably, the sole surviving example of liturgical books made by the nuns of these convents.[7]

As these psalters and antiphonals indicate, despite the shift of book production to largely urban professional ateliers in the thirteenth century, encloistered women continued to practise this age-old monastic craft in the late Middle Ages. This was especially true in Germany and the Netherlands.[8] Indeed, only in the Gothic period are manuscripts made by nuns given a separate classification as *nonnenbücher* or 'nuns' books', a term of distinctly pejorative connotation, for their handiwork is generally dismissed in art-historical scholarship as inferior to contemporary secular professional production. A thirteenth-century German psalter once owned by nuns in Bamberg is illuminated in a highly decorative naïve style typical of *nonnenbücher* of the Gothic era (FIG. 54).[9] Quantities of gold leaf are thickly applied; patterns and bright colours dazzle the eye; but the figures are somewhat childlike in their uncertain proportions, small round heads, and tentative drapery folds.[10] Manuscripts of this type were produced by German nuns well into the sixteenth century.[11] Their distance from contemporary stylistic developments has been attributed to the encloistered isolation of the artists, for the nuns used other books produced within their walls as models.[12]

At the same time, some manuscripts of high quality may have been made by nuns in the thirteenth and early fourteenth centuries. A number of music books were signed by Poor

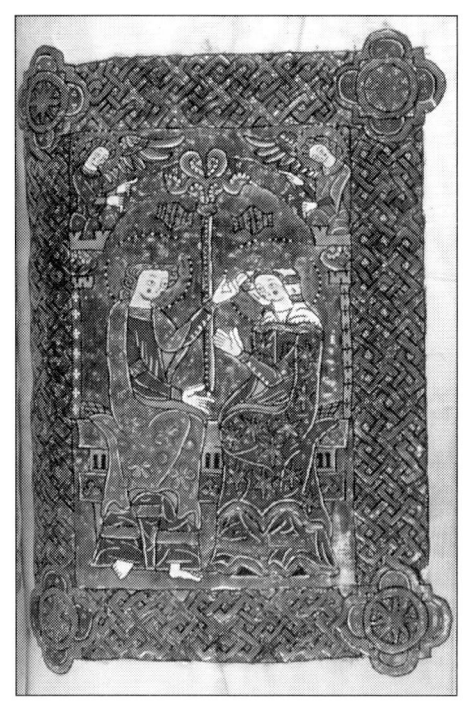

FIG. 54 Coronation of the Virgin. Rhenish Psalter. London, BL, Add. MS 60629, fol. 56v.

FIG. 55 Adoration of the Magi. Antiphonal of Loppa de Speculo. Stockholm, KB, MS A. 172, fol. 84v.

Clares of Cologne as scribe or illuminator. Sister Gertrude van dem Uorst is identified as the scribe of one gradual dating to the 1330s. One cannot rule out the possibility, however, that it was illuminated by the Franciscan scriptorium in Cologne in which Johannes von Valkenburg wrote and illuminated his two graduals in 1299.[13] It is also possible that professional illuminators from one of the active lay ateliers in Cologne decorated the Clares' books.[14] Several decades later, Sister Loppa de Speculo is identified as the scribe of one antiphonal and as the scribe and illuminator of another (FIG. 55):

> Sister Jutta Alfter paid for this book with her prebends and alms. Pray devoutly for her and for those she remembers. And Sister Loppa de Speculo completed [or perfected] it by writing, ruling, notating, [and] illuminating so that you would not exclude [her] from your hearts nor from your devout prayers. The year of our Lord 1350, great pestilence existing everywhere.[15]

Given the high quality of this manuscript and its similarity to others made for patrons outside the Clares' cloister, it has been suggested that *illuminando* may only mean Loppa did the filigree initials. It is not necessarily true, however, that the Poor Clares would not have made manuscripts for clients outside their house, as this was common practice in Italy.[16]

The *Codex Gisle*, a gradual made for the Cistercian convent of Rulle near Osnabrück in Westphalia, is equally explicit about its creator.[17] It is inscribed in a fourteenth-century charterhand on the first folio:

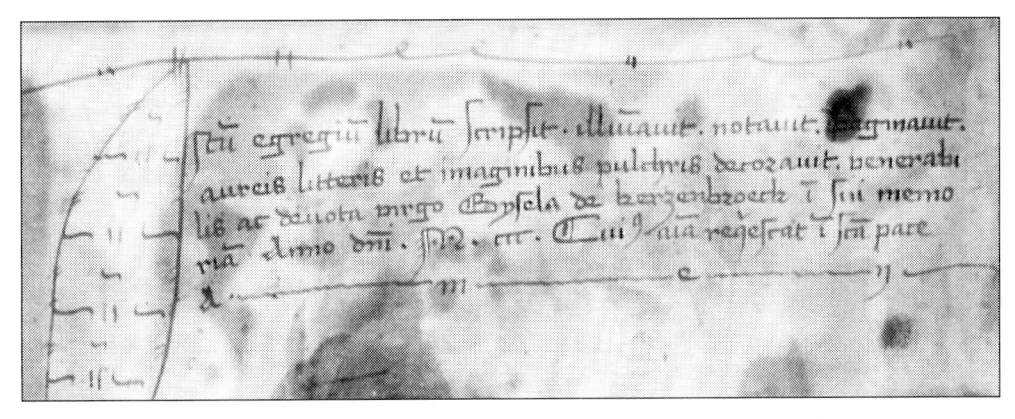

FIG. 56 Memorial inscription. Codex Gisle. Osnabrück, Gymnasium Carolinum und Bischöfliches Generalvikariat MS, p.004.

The venerable and devout virgin Gisela de Kerzenbroeck wrote, illuminated, notated, paginated, and decorated in gold letters and beautiful images this extraordinary book in her own memory, in the year of the Lord 1300. May her soul rest in holy peace. Amen (FIG. 56).[18]

In the Christmas Mass initial, Gisle is depicted with five of her sisters singing the Christmas chant *Grates nu(n)c om(ni)s reddam(us) d(omi)no deo* from an open music book, presumably this very gradual (PLATE 1). Gisle is the nun who actually holds the book open and points to its text. Appearing a second time in the manuscript, she kneels in prayer alone beside the Easter Mass introit, her pose echoing that of the Virgin Mary who kneels atop Christ's tomb at the Resurrection within the initial (FIG. 57).[19]

While the inscription and self-portraits would seem to establish beyond a doubt that Gisle was the illuminator of this manuscript, some scholars have argued (as was true for Loppa de Speculo) that because of its quality Gisle only commissioned the manuscript which would have been painted by a professional atelier.[20] Internal evidence suggests that several scribes and several artists of varying talent worked on this book. This has been taken as evidence of production in a large professional workshop, but they might just as easily be Gisela's sisters.[21] (The graduals of the Franciscan Johannes von Valkenburg also contain at least one initial by a second hand, presumably one of his brothers, yet in his colophons Johannes acknowledges no assistance.[22]) There seems no reason *a priori* to assume that all books of high style must be the work of lay professionals.[23] A fuller study of the style of the *Codex Gisle's* historiated initials and their relationship to contemporary Lower Rhenish manuscripts, however, is needed.[24]

The care with which the liturgical chant texts are embellished argues against identifying the scribes and non-figural decorators of the *Codex Gisle* with anyone except the nuns of Rulle, as will be discussed shortly. Choirbooks required scribes with a knowledge of music, local liturgical usage, and the complex repertoire of church chant. Such scribes thus almost certainly had to be clerics or encloistered religious. In addition to the Franciscan Johannes von Valkenburg and the two Poor Clares from Cologne mentioned previously, one may cite a Cistercian monk named Johannes (not to be confused with Johannes von Valkenburg) who left his self-portrait as scribe in one volume of the Beaupré Antiphonal made for Cistercian nuns in Flanders in 1289-90.[25] Two contemporaries in Liège, both of them cantors or choirmasters of their houses, also wrote music books. A miscellany containing many musical texts with notation and coloured-ink drawings was written and illuminated by Simon of Tongres, a monk at the abbey of Saint Jacques in Liège c.1296.[26] A canon of the collegiate church of Sainte Croix, Baudouin de Molin, was in charge of the production of a set of antiphonals with filigree initials in the second quarter of the fourteenth century, and most likely was their scribe, notator, and decorator.[27] Even in the late Middle Ages, monastic houses continued to be the primary centres for the production of choirbooks. Indeed, it has been argued recently that even in the sixteenth century 'the competition from lay workshops ... was minimal'.[28]

In the secular world, women were quite active in the book trade. Their names occur in Parisian records as members of ateliers; but identifying work by their hands has not proven possible, and only rarely are they explicitly identified as *illuminatrix* rather than bookseller or scribe.[29] The most famous of them, Anastasie, praised by her patroness Christine de Pizan in 1404 as the finest painter of vignettes in Paris, may have confined her activity to borders and backgrounds.[30] Thus nuns like Loppa de Speculo and Gisle de Kerzenbroeck, who have left behind signed works, provide us with our only certain evidence of the fine quality work women artists might achieve – but, as we have seen, this evidence is not uncontested.[31]

Identifying work by medieval women and assessing its merits has not been a major focus of recent research. Instead, feminist scholars have pointed out that focusing solely on questions of aesthetic quality and making comparisons with contemporary secular books is really not altogether productive for understanding manuscripts made for nuns.[32] Why these books were made, how they served to express the social context in which they were produced, and how they indeed helped to shape the devotional lives of their users have proven to be far more fruitful lines of inquiry. This focus on context threatens to lose sight, though, of the art in art history. What the artists expressed by purely aesthetic means may also shed light on the function and meaning of manuscripts in the lives of these nuns. There are distinctive ways (other than quality) in which books decorated by nuns may stand apart from other medieval manuscripts. Three such books made in the Rhineland during the late thirteenth and early fourteenth centuries are particularly striking in this regard: a homilary in the Walters Art Gallery in Baltimore, Maryland; the psalter from the house of Poor Clares in Bamberg, now in the British Library; and the gradual from Rulle, now in Osnabrück.

The Walters homilary is a collection of sermons arranged according to the liturgical year to be read at meals in the refectory. Published scholarship has dated it to the early fourteenth century and assigned it to the Rhineland.[33] It is far more richly illustrated than that painted by the German nun Guda at a Middle Rhenish nunnery in the late twelfth century, which has only two historiated initials.[34] The Walters homilary has over two dozen historiated initials and miniatures, four of them full-page. Beginning with the vigil of Easter, the book includes sermons to read from the Easter season up to and including Pentecost. It was

FIG. 57 Resurrection. Codex Gisle. Osnabrück, Gymnasium Carolinum und Bischöfliches Generalvikariat, MS p.139.

FIG. 58 Resurrection with kneeling nuns. Westphalian Homilary. Baltimore, Walters Art Gallery, MS 148, fol. 2v.

undoubtedly used by nuns, for they appear in one prefatory drawing of contemporary or slightly later date kneeling in a Gothic chapel and contemplating the adjoining image of Christ's Resurrection (FIG. 58).

Whether Walters 148 was originally illuminated by professional artists or nuns is uncertain; what is certain is that it was *redecorated* by nuns, for it has been embellished by a number of hands. Brightly coloured and patterned borders were added to some pages. Somewhat disconcertingly, the nuns even repainted sections of the text in gold leaf on coloured bars which has rendered some words less legible (FIG. 59). On aesthetic grounds, one might argue that such 'gussying up' of a high-quality book with additions of folk-art naïveté has simply spoiled the manuscript. But the additions are not mindless vandalism. The original decoration of the Walters homilary consisted of large decorative or historiated initials with the succeeding letters of the first word in gold capitals set upon blue or pink bands. The first few quires have been most thoroughly redecorated, with brightly painted decorative borders around the textblock, and many passages or short phrases of the text painted in shell-gold on bright red and blue coloured bars. Which phrases have been chosen for embellishment is significant. On fols 3 to 24, these text phrases all refer to 'this night', that is the vigil of Easter, and this section of text begins and ends with the most elaborately redecorated pages, the only ones on which entire passages have been repainted. Thus on fol. 23 a passage in Augustine's sermon is singled out as a cry of joy on the coming of the true

FIG. 59 Virgin and Child. Westphalian Homiliary. Baltimore, Walters Art Gallery, MS 148, fol. 23r.

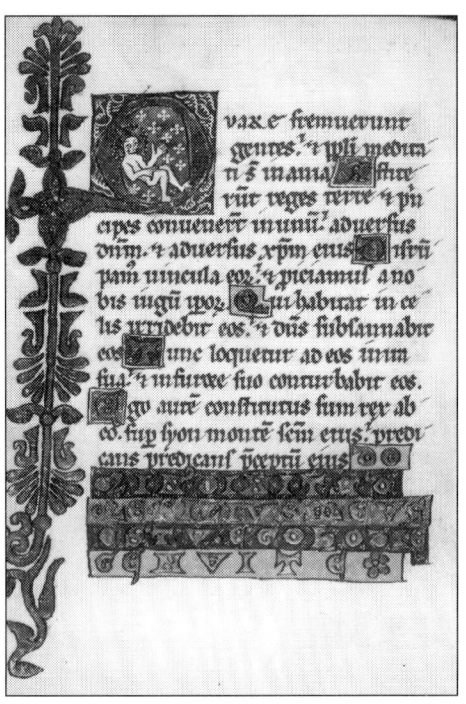

FIG. 60 Psalm 2 with Christ Child. Rhenish Psalter. London, BL, Add. MS 60629, fol. 7v.

light: 'so joyous a feast, so wonderful the brightness of the true light' (*Tam iocundam sollempnitatem tam miram veri luminis claritatem*). Ff.23 and 24, the two pages recited at dawn, ending the Easter Vigil as Easter Day itself began, flank a full-page miniature of the Resurrection on fol. 23v. In the succeeding section for Easter, the words 'day' and 'Resurrection' are repeatedly picked out in gold in a similar fashion. Use of gold leaf to mark off the incipits of texts and occasionally to write whole manuscripts is a practice found throughout the Middle Ages, which was given theological justification as a form of homage to God by Saint Boniface in the eighth century. He wrote to Eadburg, abbess of Thanet, that she should write a copy of the Epistles for him in gold letters so that her words 'may shine in gold to the glory of the Father in heaven'.[35]

A comparable liturgical consciousness lies behind the embellishment of seemingly random verses in the British Library Psalter, which are set off in gold on red, green, and blue coloured bars (FIG. 60). Psalm 2:7 is singled out: 'The Lord said to me: You are my son. Today I have begotten you' (*Dominus dixit ad me filius meus est tu. Ego hodie genui te*). The psalm is illustrated with a depiction of the naked Christ Child reclining as if in a manger. Inclusion of an historiated initial for Psalm 2 is not customary, and in the rare instances where it is illustrated, it does not have this subject.[36] Depiction of the Christ Child provides a Christian gloss for the Old Testament psalm verse, for it was interpreted as referring to the birth of Christ and was used as the introit chant for the Midnight Mass at Christmas.[37] One finds a similar image in the *Codex Gisle*, which is a gradual containing the chants sung during the

112

FIG. 61 Virgin kneels before Christ Child. Codex Gisle. Osnabrück, Gymnasium Carolinum und Bischöfliches Generalvikariat MS, p.19.

Mass. Here the child waves a scroll with the Psalm 2:7 text in illustration of the introit for the Christmas Midnight Mass (FIG. 61).

The *Codex Gisle* adopts the liturgical word-illustration seen in the Walters Homilary and British Library Psalter, and develops it to its most elaborate form. The Christmas and Easter seasons are marked off by enormous introit initials and numerous subsidiary ones for other chants (PLATE 1 and FIG. 57). Their first words are illuminated in gold on red and blue bars, and even the musical notation has been embellished, with each note in red or blue ink. Coloured musical notation alternates by line, or occasionally by word, on the incipit pages for the Advent, Christmas, and Easter Masses. It is also used in extended sections of the Easter chants (PLATE 2).[38] Ordinary text pages revert to black-ink notation and script.

Having noted the importance of textual decoration in these *nonnenbücher*, we should return to the memorial inscription prefacing the *Codex Gisle*. Johannes von Valkenburg and Loppa de Speculo both report their accomplishments in the order in which their books were produced: 'I, brother Johannes de Valkenberg, wrote and notated and illuminated this gradual'. 'Sister Loppa de Speculo completed the writing, ruling, notating and illuminating' (*Ego frater Johannes de Valkenburg scripsi et notavi et illuminavi istud graduale. Soror Loppa de Speculo perfecit scribendo, liniando, notando, illuminando*). Writing the text is followed by ruling and notating the music. Illumination comes last after scribal work is finished. Yet, perplexingly, Gisle's annotator reports: 'Gysela de Kerzebroeck wrote, illuminated, notated, paginated, and decorated in gold letters and beautiful images this extraordinary book' (*Istum egregium librum scripsit, illuminavit, notavit, impaginavit, aureis litteris et imaginibus pulchris decoravit ... Gysela de Kerzenbroeck*).[39] The term *illuminavit* is used interchangeably with *decoravit* and *pinxit* in artists' colophons and may refer to pen filigree as well as painted ornament, to purely ornamental forms or to figural decor. Sometimes illuminating is distinguished from historiating to set ornament apart from figures.[40] Here, however, *decoravit* specifies that she decorated the book with gold letters (presumably the large blue- and gold-lobed initials on penwork filigree grounds) and with beautiful images (the fifty-five historiated initials).[41] Why then mention illumination when a fuller description of her artwork is added? Why, indeed, mention it between writing and notating the book, which seems totally out of order? Perhaps because it refers precisely to the gold and coloured text which is so painstakingly picked out at important places in these chants. Writing and illuminating the script, notating and paginating thus all preceded illuminating large-scale filigree and historiated initials.[42]

This sort of liturgically based embellishment of individual words with special significance is an unusual trait which is not in fact typical of monastic service and devotional books, but which does give visual expression to fundamental elements of monastic culture. *Lectio divina*, or pious reading, filled much of a nun's day. Reading was an active process of memorization in which one recited words orally 'in order to sound the depths of their full meaning'.[43] Each word was an object of meditation.

This form of monastic reading permeates the writings of Mechtild of Hackeborn (d. 1298), a nun at the Benedictine (or possibly Cistercian) nunnery of Helfta in Saxony.[44] Her book of meditations, *The Book of Special Grace*, is arranged according to the feasts of the liturgical year, and was written in the late thirteenth century.[45] It is an extended meditation on the meanings of individual words recited in the chants of the Mass, texts which had particular resonance for her because she was the choirmistress of the convent.[46] At the feast of the Ascension, for example, Christ appeared to her and she asked Him what spiritual fruit she should extract from the words of the second responsory. Christ replied that the word *incarnatio* recalls charity, the words *gloriosa passio* recall fidelity, the words *pretiosa mors* recall the price of His sacrifice, and in like manner He continued to gloss the entire chant word by word.[47] The liturgy became a spiritual drama and inspiration for personal visionary experience in nunneries of the Gothic period. It was no longer just a service performed by the nuns, but one in which they were accompanied by hosts of angels. Christ or the Virgin or various saints made frequent appearances.[48]

Recitation of the liturgy was the foremost function of monastic life, and each word was to be spoken (or most likely chanted) with undivided attention and fervour. Gertrude of Helfta, Mechtild's contemporary, related in her book of meditations, *The Herald of Divine Love*, that she recited the canonical hours one day inattentively, hastily slurring over and suppressing words and syllables. The devil appeared and finished a psalm for her and then reproached her, 'Your words are so hasty and careless that just now in this psalm you left out this number of letters, this number of syllables, and this number of words'. Gertrude was immediately panic-stricken that each letter, syllable, and word omitted would be held against her at her death.[49]

FIG. 62 Nativity. Embroidery from Wienhausen.

Words were thus laden individually with great spiritual merit, and Mechtild visualized them as jewels. On the feast of Saint Agnes, Christ and the saint appeared to Mechtild in red robes. All the saint's words (that is, the text of her office) were embroidered in golden letters on Christ's robe and gave off light which entered the hearts of the choir singing the psalms.[50] In Mechtild's visions, angels and saints carried books, magnificently decorated to symbolize their faith. At the memorial service for Abbess Gertrude, she saw the apostles bearing large, richly ornamented books, acknowledging the abbess's apostolic calling as spiritual teacher of her nuns.[51] Abbess Gertrude herself appeared adorned in a vestment of green embellished with innumerable gold stars, its seams studded with white pearls and small rubies.[52] Such splendour immediately recalls embroidery, the art form in which German nuns excelled in the Gothic period.[53] Gold and silk thread enriched with pearls, stones, and small metal and enamel ornaments added opulence to altar-cloths, wall-hangings, and vestments. Several extant Saxon embroideries have backgrounds strewn with gold stars, and inscriptions drawn with strings of seed pearls are common.[54] While we have no pieces attributable to Helfta, we can be sure that these nuns also practised this traditional convent craft. Gertrude used embroidery as a metaphor in her *Herald of Divine Love*, describing how a mother put her child in a place above her to hold the thread of pearls while she did silk and pearl embroidery.[55]

Mechtild's visions of Saint Agnes and Abbess Gertrude in their embroidered robes call to mind the miniature showing the Coronation of the Virgin in the British Library Psalter, discussed earlier (see FIG. 54). Its opulent use of gold leaf on hems, armbands, and collars, and its richly patterned draperies with gold stars and roses derive directly from embroidery work. The basic aesthetic elements which distinguish the *nonnenbücher* – a love of bold patterns and exquisite detail, large areas of bright solid colour, and flat compositions with figures heavily outlined in black ink – are those one would note routinely in describing embroidery. An altar-cloth depicting the life of the Virgin and the infancy of Christ, contemporary with or somewhat later than Mechtild's and Gertrude's writings, from the Saxon convent of Wienhausen near Helfta, illustrates all of these characteristics. Seen here is a detail of the Nativity panel (FIG. 62).[56] It thus seems clear that much of the illumination of manuscripts in nunneries was not only largely isolated from secular developments, but pursued a very different aesthetic inspired by needlework.

The motivation for this book production was also completely different from that of secular artists, preserving the venerable monastic tradition of self-contained scriptoria. Focus on the spiritual power of individual words, which is so insistent a feature of these German Gothic *nonnenbücher*, is equally traditional, for it shares in its essence the same worshipful attitude which informs great works of Celtic monastic art.[57] In the Lindisfarne Gospels and the Book of Kells the name of God is treated as a precious object, and the incipit pages of the gospels are embellished in cascading hierarchies of script, scarcely legible, demanding close meditative attention from their readers as do the gold letters and coloured notes of Gisle's gradual. While the secular world and male monasteries became ever more involved in classical learning and the recovery of realistic three-dimensional image-making in the Gothic period, the *nonnenbücher*, one may well argue, remained far more faithful to the essential monastic tradition of *lectio divina*, the worship of the Word.

Notes to Chapter Six

1. D.Miner, *Anastasie and Her Sisters* (Baltimore, 1974), and A.Weyl Carr, 'Women as Artists in the Middle Ages', *Feminist Art Journal*, 5 (1976), pp.5–9 and 26 are still fundamental reading. *See also* the recent exhibition: Ludwigshafen, Wilhelm-Hack Museum, *Frauen und Kunst im Mittelalter*, eds.E.Schraut and C.Opitz (Braunschweig, 1983), pp.28–34; and J.J.G.Alexander, *Medieval Illuminators and Their Methods of Work* (New Haven, 1992), pp.18–20. For a recent survey of the growing literature on women artists, *see* P.Sheingorn, 'The Medieval Feminist Art History Project', pp.5–10 and L.Yawn-Bonghi, 'Medieval Women Artists and Modern Historians', pp.10–19 in *Medieval Feminist Newsletter*, 12 (1991). *See too* the forthcoming essay by A.Weyl Carr et al, 'Women as Artists in the Middle Ages: The Dark is Light Enough', *Dictionary of Women Artists*, ed. D.Gaze (London, in press).

2. E.Beer, *Beiträge zur Oberrheinischen Buchmalerei in der ersten Hälfte des 14. Jahrhunderts unter besonderer Berücksichtigung der Initialornamentik* (Basel, 1959), pp.25 and 38. A late 12th-century south German psalter (Baltimore, Walters Art Gallery, MS 26) contains an image of a nun praying at Psalm 101, the most common place to find an image of a psalter's owner. D.Miner, *Anastasie*, pp.11–12 argued that the multiplicity of hands of varying quality decorating this psalter reflected its creation by nuns. However, the manuscript is made up of disparate sections of perhaps slightly varying date. The calendar and prefatory full-page miniatures (fols 1–9) form a quire by one hand; fol. 10 is a tipped-in leaf by a second hand. The psalter itself has two historiated initials and two full-page miniatures on fol. 131r–v, all by a third artist (Miner, Figs.2–3), and two smaller miniatures (on fols 63v and 115r) by a fourth hand. At Psalm 51 the figure of a young laywoman named Claricia swings from the tail of the letter Q. Alexander, *Medieval Illuminators*, pp.18–21, rejects Miner's identification of Claricia as a convent student-illuminator as she is a laywoman and the text of the psalm is highly derogatory.

3. London, BL, Add. MS 21114 contains a unique portrait of the purported 'founder' of the beguine community of Saint Christophe, the 12th-century cleric Lambert le Bègue. For evidence dating this and related psalters to the period *c.*1235–60, *see* J.Oliver, *Gothic Manuscript Illumination in the Diocese of Liège c.1250–c.1330* (Louvain, 1988), i, pp.130–2.

4. *Ibid.*, i, p.206; *idem*, 'Devotional Psalters and the Study of Beguine Spirituality', *Vox Benedictina*, 9 (1992), pp.202–3 (reprinted in *Vox Benedictina*, 11 (1994): *On Pilgrimage. The Best of Vox Benedictina 1984–1993*, eds.E.Durie and D.Kramer (Winnipeg, 1994), pp.210–34); and *idem*, 'Reflections on Beguines and Psalters', *Ons Geestelijk Erf*, 66 (1992), pp.254–56.

5. Bornem, Abdij Sint Bernardus, MS 1, fol. 182v: 'Anno d(omi)ni m.cc.xliiii scriptus et notatus est liber iste. finit(us) au(tem) i(n) crastino ambrosii anni m.cc.xliv. Q(uaesi)m(u)s q(ui) videri(n)t eu(m) orent p(ro) scriptrice agnes et notatrice xp[christ]ina q(uae) laboraver(un)t in eo'. Lier, Stedelijk Museum, *750 Jaar Abdij van Nazareth* (Lier, 1986), no.16, pp.132–40 by P.Valvekens; F.Masai and M.Wittek, *Manuscrits datés conservés en Belgique I. 800–1400* (Brussels, 1968), no.9, p.21 and pls.34–36.

6. *The Life of Beatrice of Nazareth 1200–1268*, transl.R.de Ganck (Cistercian Fathers Series 50, Kalamazoo, 1991), pp.xvii, 60–61, and 268–69. A 1490 inventory of the manuscripts of Nazareth cites a number of books written by Beatrice. *Vita Beatricis. De Autobiografie van de Z. Beatrijs van Tienen O. Cist. 1200–1268*, ed. L.Reypens, Studien en Tekst uitgaven van Ons Geestelijk Erf 15 (Antwerp, 1964), p.50*, n.15. For Ida of Leau, *see* most recently R.de Ganck, 'Chronological Data in the Lives of Ida of Nivelles and Beatrice of Nazareth', *Ons Geestelijk Erf*, 57 (1983), pp.14–29 and A.Steenwegen, 'De gelukz. Ida de Lewis of Ida van Gorsleeuw', *Ons Geestelijk Erf*, 57 (1983), pp.227–37.

7. One other La Ramée manuscript can be identified: Brussels, Bibl.Roy., MS 8895–6 is a 14th-century copy of the lives of Ida of Nivelles and Ida of Leau in a very utilitarian charterhand on stiff parchment, decorated with a few rudimentary red capital letters.

8. For the nunnery of Adelhausen in Freiburg in the late 13th and 14th centuries *see* Freiburg, Augustiner Museum, *Kunstepochen der Stadt Freiburg. Ausstellung zur 850. Jahrfeier*, ed. I.Krummer-Schroth (Freiburg, 1970), nos.85–90 and 114–5; for upper Rhenish cloisters in the 14th and 15th centuries *see* C.von Heusinger, 'Spätmittelalterliche Buchmalerei in Oberrheinischen Frauenklöstern', *Zeitschrift für Geschichte des Oberrheins*, 107 (1959), pp.136–60; for Engelberg in Switzerland, *see* E.Beer, *Beiträge zur Oberrheinischen Buchmalerei*; for

Gnadenthal (in the diocese of Basel) in the 16th century *see* A.Bruckner, 'Zum Problem der Frauenhandschriften im Mittelalter', *Aus Mittelalter und Neuzeit: Gerhard Kallen zum 70. Geburtstag*, ed. J.Engel and H.Klinkenberg (Bonn, 1957), pp.171–83; for Nurnberg in Franconia in the 15th century *see* E.Schraut, 'Kunst im Frauenkloster. Uberlegungen zu den Möglichkeiten der Frauen im Mittelalterlichen Kunstbetrieb am Beispiel Nürnberg', in *Auf der Suche nach der Frau im Mittelalter. Fragen, Quellen, Antworten. Interdisziplinäre Beiträge*, ed. B.Lundt (Munich, 1991), pp.81–114; for Saxony *see* B.Uhde-Stahl, 'Drei Miniaturen aus den Ehemaligen Klöstern Lüne und Ebstorf', *Niederdeutsche Beiträge zur Kunstgeschichte*, 15 (1976), pp.63–70 and *idem*, 'Figurliche Buchmalereien in den Spätmittelalterlichen Handschriften der Lüneburger Frauenklösters', *Niederdeutsche Beiträge zur Kunstgeschichte*, 17 (1978), pp.25–60. For nuns as scribes see the bibliography in K.Christ, 'Mittelalterliche Bibliotheksordnungen für Frauenklöster', *Zentralblatt für Bibliothekswesen*, 59 (1942), 1–29, *esp*. p.7 n.3. For Augustinian nuns and Sisters of the Common Life (who like beguines were technically laity) writing and decorating books in the Netherlands in the 15th century, *see* J.Gumbert, *The Dutch and Their Books in the Manuscript Age* (London, 1990), pp.52–61, and Fig. 21. For the Sisters as authors as well as writers of books, *see* W. Scheepsma '"For Hereby I hope to rouse some to piety": Books of Sisters from Convents and Sister-Houses associated with the Devotio Moderna in the Low Countries', *Women, the Book and the Godly. Selected Proceedings of the St. Hilda's Conference 1993*, eds. L.Smith and J.H.M.Taylor (Woodbridge, 1995), pp.27–40.

9 London, BL, Add. MS 60629. Acquired by the BL in 1979, the manuscript is unpublished. I am preparing a fuller study of it. Inclusion in the litany of Saint Clara, canonized in 1255, dates it to the second half of the century. That it was made for nuns is certain as there is a petition on fol. 169r and a collect on fol. 170r for *nos famulas tuas*. Both of these invocations are underlined in red. The psalter gives special prominence to Psalm 32, one of the Benedictine psalm divisions, and marks Benedictine subdivisions at Pss. 36:27, 68:17, 103:25, and 105:32 with two-line initials. The calendar and litany include Benedictine, Cistercian, and Franciscan saints. An ownership note on fol. 170v says the book belonged to Dorothea, daughter of Margrave Albert Achilles of Brandenburg, who became abbess of the Poor Clares in Bamberg in 1498 and died in 1520. There seems no reason to assume that the book was originally made for Bamberg because the Clares were not established there until 1341. S.Krämer, *Handschriftenerbe des Deutschen Mittelalters*, i (Munich, 1989), p.74. Its calendar also does not adhere to that for Bamberg published by H.Grotefend, *Zeitrechnung des Deutschen Mittelalters und der Neuzeit*, ii (Hanover, 1891), pp.7–10; nor does it resemble the upper Rhenish and Middle Frankish calendars given by H.Swarzenski, *Die Lateinischen Illuminierten Handschriften des XIII. Jahrhunderts in den Ländern an Rhein, Main, und Donau* (Berlin, 1936), pp.166–73. Instead, the calendar has numerous saints for Trier and the Cologne region; the Two Ewalds of Westphalia are on October 3. The litany includes A(de)lheidis. Several German saints bear this name; the 11th-cent. Benedictine abbess of Villich (near Bonn) and Saint Maria im Kapitol in Cologne was most widely venerated. Thus liturgical evidence seems to point to a Rhenish origin.

10 For characterization of *nonnenbuch* style, *see* R.Kroos, 'Sächsische Buchmalerei', *Zeitschrift für Kunstgeschichte*, 41 (1978), p.298 n.117.

11 Uhde-Stahl, 'Figurliche Buchmalereien'. For contacts between nunneries in the 15th century *see* E.Schraut, 'Kunst im Frauenkloster', pp.108–10.

12 C.von Heusinger, 'Spätmittelalterliche Buchmalerei', p.160; G.Greer, *The Obstacle Race: The Fortunes of Women Painters and Their Work* (New York, 1979), pp.151–168; C.Opitz and E.Schraut, 'Frauen und Kunst im Mittelalter', in *Frauen. Kunst. Geschichte. Zur Korrektur der Herrschenden Blicks*, ed. C.Bischoff *et.al.* (Giessen, 1984) pp.33–52, *esp.* p.48. On the other hand, Schraut also suggests that the *nonnenbücher* style may be a reflection of popular taste, a lay 'folk' style also seen in popular crafts; *see* her 'Kunst im Frauenkloster', pp.113–14. That nunneries thus served as intermediaries between lay and learned culture is also suggested in another context by M.Zink, *La Prédication en langue romane avant 1300* (Paris, 1976), pp.161–62.

13 Cologne, Wallraf-Richartz Museum, Graphische Sammlung Inv. Nrs.67–71. Johannes' two graduals (Cologne, Diözesanbibliothek, MS 1B and Bonn, Universitätsbibliothek, MS 384) are inscribed on their first folios: 'Ego frat(er) Joh(ann)es de Valkenburg scripsi et notavi et illu(m)i(n)avi istud graduale et co(m)plevi anno d(omi)ni m.cc. nonagesimo nono'. J.Oliver, 'The Mosan Origins of Johannes von Valkenburg', *Wallraf-Richartz Jahrbuch*, 40 (1978), pp.23–37. Collaboration between a nun of Schwarzenthann, Guta, as scribe, and an Augustinian canon of Marbach, Sintram, as artist, can be seen in an 1154 martyrology (Strasbourg, Bibliothèque du Grand Séminaire, MS 37). Cologne, Schnütgen Museum, *Ornamenta Ecclesiae. Kunst und Denkmäler der Romanik*, ed. A.Legner (Cologne, 1985), no.B44, p.245, and J.Alexander, *Medieval Illuminators*, pp.18–19 and n.81.

14   R. Mattick, 'Choralbuchfragmente aus dem Kölner Kloster St. Klara', *Wallraf-Richartz Jahrbuch*, 45 (1984), pp.291–303, *esp.* p.296 and p.300.

15   Stockholm, Kungliga Biblioteket, MS 172, fol. 106r: 'Soror Jutta de Alft(er) p(er)solvit ist(um) lib(rum) cu(m) suis expe(n)sis et el(eemosyn)is orate p(ro) ea et p(ro) q(ui)b(u)s devote i(n)te(n)d(i)t et Soror Loppa de Spec(u)lo p(er)fecit sc(ri)bendo, liniando, nota(n)do, illu(m)i(n)ando q(ui)a n(on) excludatis ex cordib(us) v(est)ris n(ec) no(n) ex or(ati)o(n)ib(us) v(est)ris devotis. Anno d(omi)ni m.ccc.l. maxi(m)a pestilentia u(bique) existe(n)te.' Cologne, Wallraf-Richartz Museum, *Vor Stefan Lochner. Die Kölner Maler von 1300 bis 1430* (Cologne, 1974), nos.79–80. Individual Poor Clares are depicted kneeling in the margins with captions in the German vernacular naming them.

16   E.Galley, 'Miniaturen aus dem Kölner Klarissenkloster. Ein Kapitel Rheinischen Buchmalerei des 14. Jahrhunderts', *Aus der Welt des Bibliothekars. Festschrift für Rudolf Juchhoff*, ed. K.Ohly (Cologne, 1961), pp.15–28 argues for the existence of an atelier at the Clares' cloister associated with Loppa de Speculo, producing manuscripts for outsiders in the 1350s (pp.22–7) since a missal for Cologne use (Brussels, Bibl.Roy., MS 212) he attributes to Loppa was not for use by the Clares. The attribution to Loppa is accepted by R.Mattick, 'Choralbuchfragmente', p.302 n. 6. However, E.Beer, 'Literaturbericht: Gotische Buchmalerei. Literatur von 1945 bis 1961', *Zeitschrift für Kunstgeschichte*, 28 (1965), p.150 questions not only whether Clares would make books professionally but also whether Loppa was actually the painter of figural initials. For book production by Poor Clares serving a varied clientele, *see* K.Gill, 'Women and the Production of Religious Literature in the Vernacular, 1300–1500', in *Creative Women in Medieval and Early Modern Italy. A Religious and Artistic Renaissance*, eds. E.A.Matter and J.Coakley (Philadelphia, 1994), p.67.

17   Osnabrück, Gymnasium Carolinum und Bischöfliches Generalvikariat, MS C.Dolfen, *Codex Gisle* (Berlin, 1926); R.Kroos, 'Der Codex Gisle I. Forschungsbericht und Datierung', *Niederdeutsche Beiträge für Kunstgeschichte*, 12 (1973), pp.117–34; H.Feldwisch-Drentrup and A.Jung, *Dom und Domschatz in Osnabrück* (Stuttgart, 1980), pp.32 and 68; and most recently Braunschweig, Herzog Anton Ulrich Museum, *Stadt im Wandel: Kunst und Kultur des Bürgertums in Norddeutschland 1150–1650* (Braunschweig, 1985), no.1084, pp.1246–49 by R.Kroos.

18   The inscription, which has never been reproduced, is at the top of the page: 'Istu(m) egregiu(m) libru(m) scripsit, ill(um)inavit, notavit, i(m)paginavit, aureis litteris et imaginibus pulchris decoravit venerabilis ac devota virgo Gysela de Kerzenbroeck i(n) sui memoria(m). Anno d(omi)ni MCCC. Cui(us) a(n)i(m)a req(ui)escat i(n) s(an)c(t)a pace'. C.Dolfen, *Codex Gisle*, p.9 mistranscribes this inscription. His monograph should be used with caution as transcriptions of inscribed scrolls in the historiated initials are often inaccurate and a scroll is recorded for the Easter *Resurrexi* initial which is not there at all. The inscription's location on the first leaf rather than at the end of the text is unexceptional. Johannes von Valkenburg signed both of his graduals in 1299 on fully illuminated frontispieces (*see* n.13). A comparably grand declaration of ownership prefaces the Flemish Beaupré Antiphonal of 1290 (Baltimore, Walters Art Gallery, MS 759, fol. 1v). In contrast, the inscription in the *Codex Gisle* is strictly utilitarian, and presumably was added shortly after Gisle's death. Jaeger, 'Die Heimat der Graduale der Gisela von Kerssenbrock', *Osnabrücker Mitteilungen*, 27 (1902), p.301 calls it late 14th cent.; A.Stange, *Deutsche Malerei der Gotik*, i (Munich, 1934), p.104 also says it is certainly 14th century. In a later article, C.Dolfen claims that the inscription is in a 16th-cent. hand: 'Zur Datierung des Codex Gisle', *Osnabrücker Mitteilungen*, 67 (1956), pp.159–74, *esp.* p.160. Based on my examination of the manuscript, there seems no reason not to identify the script as an early 14th-cent. charterhand. Dolfen's main argument in this article, that the book dates to the mid-14th cent. because the nuns depicted are Brigittines, has been disproven by R.Kroos, 'Der Codex Gisle I'.

19   Gisle holds a scroll petitioning Christ for salvation, inscribed 'per tuam gloriosam victoriam aeternam confer laetitiam'. For Gisle's meditative identification with the Virgin here *see* F.Büttner, *Imitatio Pietatis. Motive der Christlichen Ikonographie als Modelle zur Verähnlichung* (Berlin, 1983), pp.116–18. The convent of Rulle, called Marienbrunn, was dedicated to the Virgin. G.Streich, *Klöster, Stifte und Kommenden in Niedersachsen vor der Reformation. Veröffentlichungen der Historischen Kommission für Niedersachsen und Bremen*, ii, 30 (Hildesheim, 1986), p.87. In a mid-14th-cent. book made at the Freiburg convent of St Maria Magdalena, the Magdalene takes the place of the Virgin, serving as a meditative role model for the nuns of this convent. K.Boskamp, 'Der Codex Adelhausen 3, Inv. Nr. 11725. Ein Dominikanisches Graduale des Freiburger Klosters St. Maria Magdalena zu den Reuerinnen', *Freiburger Diözesanarchiv*, 10 (1990), pp.79–123.

WOMEN AND THE BOOK

20 E.Beer, 'Literaturbericht', pp.152–53 summarizes the literature. A.Stange, 'Einige Bemerkungen zur Westfälischen Malerei des frühen 14. Jahrhunderts', *Westfalen*, 32 (1954), pp.201–11 argued that the style and quality of the Rulle Bible of 1278 negated any possibility that the gradual was made at Rulle some twenty years later, and Gisle was thus the patron, not the artist, of this book. The fact that the 2-volume Rulle Bible of 1278 written by sister Cristina von Haltern (Osnabrück, Gymnasium Carolinum, MS 90) has filigree initials of much more old-fashioned style than the gradual does not in itself rule out the possibility that the *Codex Gisle* was made at the convent. See R.Kroos, 'Der Codex Gisle I', p.128. Sister Cristina could well have been an aged artist working in a style learned decades earlier, first of all. Her obit is added on fol. 255v, noting that she had written many other books. Presumably then the Bible was her last creation. My thanks to Benno Suerbaum for allowing me to study his photographs of the initials and inscriptions, and his catalogue description of the Bible (which was not accessible).

21 R.Kroos, 'Der Codex Gisle I', pp.127–28 argues that the number of hands and the lesser quality of some indicates that the book must have been made in a large workshop, not in Rulle, and the 'fecit' in the inscription should be translated 'had made'. That other nuns wrote manuscripts at Rulle is indicated by 4 citations in the Rulle Memorial Book, known through a copy of 1714. These 4 nuns wrote or gave choirbooks (including antiphonals) to the nunnery: Jaeger, 'Heimat', p.301. Regrettably their dates are not given; one was a 15th-cent. abbess, as she is mentioned in a dated inscription added to the 1278 Rulle Bible.

22 J.Oliver, 'Mosan Origins', p.25. For Johannes' colophon *see* n.13.

23 J.Alexander, *Medieval Illuminators*, p.20 notes the continued involvement of monks in book production in the Gothic period, and pp.29–30 notes numerous mendicants who were illuminators in the late Middle Ages, while in an earlier article he had argued that from the 12th cent. on, few monastic scribes were also artists, Matthew Paris being an exception. *Idem*, 'Scribes as Artists: The Arabesque Initial in Twelfth-Century English Manuscripts', in *Medieval Scribes, Manuscripts, and Libraries. Essays presented to N. Ker*, eds. M.Parkes and A.Watson (London, 1978), pp.87–116. However, the long-accepted identification of the illuminator of the great Bury Bible (Cambridge, Corpus Christi College, MS 2), Master Hugo of Bury Saint Edmunds, as a lay professional may be erroneous. *See now* E.Parker and C.Little, *The Cloisters Cross. Its Art and Meaning* (New York, 1994), pp.213–22, who argue that he was a monk who was both a craftsman and a scholar.

24 Stylistic analysis of the *Codex Gisle* was promised by Renate Kroos in the 1973 article, 'Der Codex Gisle I'. A study of contemporary manuscripts from the Lower Rhine will be the subject of a future article by J.Oliver. For manuscripts in a related style *see* J.Holladay, 'The Willehalm Master and his Colleagues: Collaborative Manuscript Decoration in Early-Fourteenth-Century Cologne', in *Making the Medieval Book: Techniques of Production*, ed. L.Brownrigg (Los Altos, 1995), pp.67–91. One awaits publication of *idem.*, *Illuminating the Epic: The Patron and the Program of the 1334 Willehalm Codex*.

25 Baltimore, Walters Art Gallery, MS 760, fol. 1r. *See* most recently Paris, Caisse nationale des monuments historiques et des sites à la Conciergerie, *Saint Bernard et le monde cistercien*, eds. T.Kinder and L.Pressouyre (Paris, 1990), no.70, pp.224–25 by A.Stones. Cologne, Kunsthalle, *Rhein und Maas. Kunst und Kultur 800–1400* (Cologne, 1972), i, p.90 mistakenly calls this the Antiphonal of Johannes von Valkenburg.

26 Darmstadt, Hessisches Landes- und Hochschulbibliothek, MS 2777. J. Oliver, 'The *Crise Bénédictine* and Revival at the Abbey of Saint Jacques in Liège c.1300', *Quaerendo*, 8 (1978), pp.320–36.

27 Liège, Eglise Sainte-Croix, MSS 1–2 and Musée d'art religieux et d'art mosan, Antiphonaire pars aestivalis. J.Oliver, 'L'Héritage de Philippe Bruni, Doyen de Sainte-Croix, revenu à Liège', *Bulletin de la Société d'art et d'histoire de Liège*, 60 (1995), pp. 47–63. Another clerical artist was the priest Gerarduccius of Padua, scribe and illuminator of six choirbooks in 1306; *see* J.Alexander, *Medieval Illuminators*, p.122.

28 Cambridge, Fitzwilliam Museum, *Splendours of Flanders. Late Medieval Art in Cambridge Collections* (Cambridge, 1993), pp.138 and 140.

29 A.Farber, 'Considering a Marginal Master: The Work of an Early Fifteenth-Century Parisian Manuscript Decorator', *Gesta*, 32 (1993), p.37, n.2 surveys the documentation for women illuminators. *See also* R.Rouse and M.Rouse, 'The Commercial Production of Manuscript Books in Late Thirteenth-Century and Early Fourteenth-Century Paris', in *Medieval Book Production: Assessing the Evidence*, ed. L.Brownrigg (Los Altos Hills, 1990), p.106, for the widow Ameline de Berron active by 1298.

30 D.Miner, *Anastasie*, pp.7–8 and 21. *See now* A.Farber, 'Considering a Marginal Master', p.21.

31 For response to the assumption that good-quality work could not be done by nuns, *see* E.Schraut, 'Kunst im Frauenkloster', pp.103–4.

32 C.Opitz and E.Schraut, 'Frauen und Kunst im Mittelalter', p.50.

33 Baltimore, Walters Art Gallery, MS 148. *See* D.Miner, 'Preparatory Sketches by the Master of Bodleian Douce MS 185', *Kunsthistorisches Forschungen Otto Pächt* (Salzburg, 1972), pp.118–28. I am preparing an extended study of Walters 148, which is an outgrowth of my collaboration on the projected fourth volume of L.Randall, *Medieval and Renaissance Manuscripts in the Walters Art Gallery 4: England, the Netherlands, and Germany*.

34 Frankfurt, Stadt- und Universitätsbibliothek, MS Barth 42. Guda embellished the book with her self-portrait on fol. 110v. She carries a scroll inscribed 'Guda peccatrix mulier scripsit et pinxit hoc librum'. The other initial depicts the Virgin Mary. *Ornamenta Ecclesiae*, no.B43, pp.244–45; G.Powitz and H.Buck, *Die Handschriften des Bartholomaeusstifts und des Karmeliterklosters in Frankfurt-am-Main. Kataloge der Stadt- und Universitätsbibliothek Frankfurt-am-Main* 3, ii (Frankfurt, 1974), pp.84–88.

35 M.Heinrich, *The Canonesses and Education in the Early Middle Ages* (Washington, 1924), p.150.

36 For Ps. 2 illustrations *see* Oliver, *Gothic Manuscript Illumination* i, pp.62–65; for psalters illustrating every psalm, *see* E.Peterson, 'Accidents and Adaptations in Transmission among Fully Illustrated French Psalters in the Thirteenth Century', *Zeitschrift für Kunstgeschichte*, 50 (1987), pp.375–84.

37 F.Haberl, *Das Graduale Romanum: Liturgische und Musikalische Aspekte, Vol. i: Die Antiphonalen Gesänge. Introitus und Communio* (Bonn, 1976), pp.57–59.

38 Major feasts have text in gold at Advent (*Ad te levavi*, fol. 12r), Christmas (*Puer natus*, fol. 13v), and Easter (*Vidi aquam*, fol. 68r and *Resurrexi*, fol. 69v). Subsequent Easter chants have notes entirely in blue on fol. 70r and entirely in red on fol. 70v. Single words are also picked out in gold as in Walters 148: *hodie* and *die* in the Christmas season on fol. 14v, *dies* and *surrexit* repeatedly in the Easter season on fols 68r and 72r–74r, and *Marie hodie assumptio* in gold, red, and blue on fols 273r–74r.

39 *See above*, note 18.

40 For colophons, *see* J.Alexander, *Medieval Illuminators*, pp.6–18 passim. For uses of the term *illuminare see* P.Stirnemann and M.-T.Gousset, 'Marques, mots, pratiques: leur signification et leurs liens dans le travail des enlumineurs', in O.Weijers, *Vocabulaire du livre et de l'écriture au moyen âge* (Turnhout, 1989), pp.36 and 42.

41 C.Dolfen, *Codex Gisle*, fails to list or illustrate six historiated initials: 4 on Maundy Thursday and Good Friday (fol. 61v Last Supper and Flagellation, fol. 64r Christ carrying the cross, and fol. 66r Entombment), one for the Easter season (fol. 79r Resurrection), and one for the feast of John the Baptist (fol. 128v John holding the Agnus Dei disc).

42 The book is boldly paginated with quire numbers beginning Ai-Aviii through Si-Sviii in large red Roman numerals in the outer margins of versos. There are numerous errors in counting pages (many were skipped, and the pagination ends long before the end of the book).

43 J.Leclercq, *The Love of Learning and the Desire for God. A Study of Monastic Culture* (New York, 1961), pp.15–17 and 72–73.

44 Helfta followed Cistercian constitutions without becoming part of the order, and after 1271 spiritual direction was provided by the Dominicans.

45 *Revelationes Gertrudianae ac Mechtildianae II. Sanctae Mechtildis virginis ordinis Sancti Benedicti. Liber specialis gratiae* (Paris, 1877). *See* for translations *Le Livre de la grâce spéciale. Révélations de Sainte Mechtilde, vierge de l'ordre de Saint-Benoît* (Paris, 1907) and *The Book of Gostlye Grace of Mechthild of Hackeborn*, ed. T.Halligan (Toronto, 1979).

46 Mechtild of Hackeborn's meditations are far more pictorial and dependent on the liturgy than those of either of her contemporaries at Helfta, Mechtild of Magdeburg or Gertrude of Helfta. For the nuns of Helfta *see* M.Finnegan, *The Women of Helfta: Scholars and Mystics* (Athens, Ga, 1991), *esp.* pp.34–35.

47 Mechtild of Hackeborn, *Liber specialis gratiae*, i, cap.xx, pp.75–76.

48 S.Hilpisch, 'Chorgebet und Frömmigkeit im Spätmittelalter', *Heilige Uberlieferung: Ausschnitte aus der Geschichte des Mönchtums und des Heiligen Kultes. Festschrift für Ildefons Herwegen*, ed. O.Casel (Münster, 1938), pp.270–74.

49 Gertrude of Helfta (d.c.1301), *Legatus memorialis abundantiae divinae pietatis* in *Revelationes Gertrudianae ac Mechtildianae I. Sanctae Gertrudis Magnae, virginis ordinis Sancti Benedicti* (Paris, 1875), iii, cap.xxxii, pp.193–95. For a translation, *see The Herald of Divine Love*, transl. M.Winkworth, Classics of Western Spirituality (New York, 1993), p.205; and *see also* Gertrude the Great of Helfta, *Herald of God's Loving Kindness. (Books One and Two)*, transl. A.Barratt (Cistercian Fathers Series 35, Kalamazoo, 1991), pp.7–25.

50 Mechtild of Hackeborn, *Liber specialis gratiae*, i, cap.xi, p.34.

51 *Ibid.*, vi, cap.i, p.377.

52 *Ibid.*, vi, cap.vii, pp.385–86.

53 R.Kroos, *Niedersächsische Bildstickereien des Mittelalters* (Berlin, 1970), *passim*, and for Helfta, pp.161–62. J.Hamburger, 'Art, Enclosure and the *Cura Monialium*: Prolegomena in the Guise of a Postscript', *Gesta*, 31 (1992), pp.108–34, notes on p.122 that embroideries hung on the choirstalls themselves were decorated with scenes for different liturgical seasons and included the words of antiphons for each season: 'the decorated textiles echoed and elaborated the imagery of the chant'.

54 R.Kroos, *Niedersächsische Bildstickereien*, *passim* and especially cat.no. 6, a much faded hanging from Brandenburg Cathedral of c.1290, in which the Virgin wears a star-studded robe and John a diapered one. A typical north German example of pearl-encrusted work is a mitre from Minden of c.1400 (Berlin, Staatliche Museen Preussischer Kulturbesitz. Kunstgewerbemuseum K6156) which depicts the Annunciation in silk threads, seed pearls, and silver-gilt ornaments. *Stadt im Wandel* ii, no.1080, pp.1241–43; and K.Staniland, *Embroiderers* (Medieval Craftsmen Series, London, 1991), plate 53. *See Stadt im Wandel* ii, no.1082 for comparable 13th-cent. examples. For women as embroideresses *see also* R.Parker and G.Pollock, *Old Mistresses: Women, Art and Ideology* (New York, 1981), pp.58–60; and R.Parker, *The Subversive Stitch. Embroidery and the Making of the Feminine* (London, 1984), pp.40–59.

55 Gertrude of Helfta, *Legatus memorialis*, iii, cap.vi, p.124.

56 It has recently been dated to c.1310 by Appuhn, while Schuette dated it to the third quarter of the century. H.Appuhn, *Meisterwerke der Niedersächsischen Kunst des Mittelalters* (Bad Hannef, 1963), plate 12; M.Schuette, *Gestickte Bildteppiche und Decken des Mittelalters. Band 1. Die Klöster Wienhausen und Lüne. Das Lüneburgische Museum* (Leipzig, 1927), pp.13–4 and plate 10. For a general introduction to the Wienhausen tapestries *see* V.Moessner, 'The Medieval Embroideries of Convent Wienhausen', *Studies in Cistercian Art and Architecture* iii (Kalamazoo, 1987), pp.161–77. C.von Heusinger, 'Spätmittelalterliche Buchmalerei', p.159 notes *nonnenbücher* images are flat and tapestry-like. K.Staniland, *Embroiderers*, pp.20–22 notes the close connections between English manuscripts and the design, style, and imagery of contemporary *opus anglicanum*.

57 For Celtic 'worship of the word', *see* e.g. S.Lewis, 'Sacred Calligraphy: The Chi Rho Page in the Book of Kells', *Traditio*, 36 (1980), pp.139–59.

CHAPTER SEVEN

A Library Collected by and for the Use of Nuns: St Catherine's Convent, Nuremberg

Marie-Luise Ehrenschwendtner

In December 1428 ten sisters from Schönensteinbach, Alsace, arrived at St Catherine's, Nuremberg; they were sent there to introduce the reformed Dominican life, which consisted primarily of strict adherence to the Dominican rule and constitutions.[1] It was a date which marked a turning-point in the convent's intellectual history: during the years which followed, the sisters started establishing a library whose contents were geared towards their own interests and requirements. In Dominican convents the acceptance of reform often comes with the growth of a library, but the Nuremberg situation is extraordinary for being traceable. Many sources are still extant; in particular, we have two fifteenth-century book lists, one giving the private books of the sisters, the other registering the convent's books and their contents, and two further lists recording the table readings (readings made during dining periods in the convent) for the years 1429–31 and 1455–61.[2] Many of the volumes, moreover, remain in the Nuremberg libraries, so that it is often possible to cross-check medieval comments about the books.

St Catherine's was founded in 1295 as a Dominican convent, but until its reform it was in no way remarkable: it housed no mystics, nor did any sister compile a convent chronicle or 'Schwesternbuch'. The sisters were members of the Nuremberg upper classes, and seem to have enjoyed considerable personal liberties.[3] We only have sparse information about the St Catherine's library before the reform: the old catalogue of the library kept in the years 1455–61 enumerates forty-six books with the remark 'here before the reform'.[4] There are no other sources for the early state of the library: some of the books seem to have been private donations to promote the convent's spiritual life,[5] and none of them seems to have been written by the sisters themselves. Although the usual remarks on these early books' origins and copyists are missing from the catalogue, it is possible that they were produced in the convent.[6] The contents of many books in the early library do not differ much from what we find later. Even before the reform, the library contained collections of sermons, tracts, and prayers. One important detail, however, should not go unnoticed: as far as we can see, there were no manuscripts of the Dominican rule or constitutions, nor any interpretations of them.[7]

The turning-point is 1428: as a consequence of reform, the intellectual and spiritual life of the convent grew richer. The sisters began to be busy with spiritual matters — and with collecting books. Indeed, they became such passionate collectors that by the end of the fifteenth century the convent possessed between 500 and 600 books.[8] But the collection of books was not regarded as an end in itself: the library was assembled for a number of purposes.

First of all the nuns had to provide for their table readings. The *ordinatio* of Bartholomäus Texery given on the occasion of the reform prescribes table reading in German and Latin: "Thus I prescribe that you always have table readings during meals or collation in the refectory, in German in the morning and, in the evening, partly in Latin and partly in German."[9] The sisters did so, as the records of table reading show, but they changed Texery's instructions as to language, reading only German books at table.[10]

What did they read? Never entire books. The sisters chose extracts appropriate to the ecclesiastical year: parts of the New Testament and their explanation, texts of the Mass and their interpretation (they preferred Wilhelm Durandus' *Rationale divinorum officiorum* in the vernacular), sermons (especially those of Johannes Tauler), tracts, and saints' lives.[11] Community life was focused on the Divine Service; not surprisingly, table readings were designed to contribute to a better understanding of this fundamental duty. To illustrate this, let us look at what the sisters read at table on the first Sunday of Advent.[12] They began with a translation of the Mass of the day (*die meß in teuczsch in dem advent*)[13] and added the text of the gospel for that day (*ewangelium nach dem text von der zeit*).[14] Then followed the exposition of the Mass according to Wilhelm Durandus' *Rationale divinorum officiorum*, and the reading ended with a sermon 'on the four "states" of our Lord' (unfortunately, we have no information on the sermon's author or content). All these texts were read in German.

Not only did the sisters read as a community; according to rule and constitutions, they also had spare time for private reading. In her correspondence with St Catherine's convent in St Gall, the Nuremberg prioress informed the Swiss nuns that each sister should spend her leisure time after lunch with spiritual reading in order to improve her spiritual life.[15] For their private reading, the sisters were given the opportunity to borrow books from the convent's library. The Dominican Johannes Meyer, in his *Ämterbuch,* had given instructions on the loan of books,[16] and the Nuremberg sisters followed his advice. Some of them made use of this opportunity to write their own books for private prayer and contemplation, compiling favourite pieces which they chose from the convent's books.[17] There were also sisters who had small private libraries within the convent. Some of them had entered with a number of private books; others took to compiling their own once they had become nuns. Sister Katharina Tucherin, for example, the widow of a patrician, was equipped with twenty-four books when she entered the community,[18] and during her time in the convent she wrote down her own 'visions'.[19]

In running their library, the sisters also helped other newly reformed convents to build up libraries of their own. They lent books to be copied, for example to St Catherine's convent in St Gall which was well provided with books by the Nuremberg prioresses: the prioress of St Gall thanks the Nuremberg sisters in her so-called *Schwesternbuch* – a collection of the Nuremberg letters – for lending books and teaching the reformed Dominican way of life.[20] Some convents, especially those reformed by Nuremberg sisters such as

Altenhohenau and Frauenaurach, received some books as presents. The old Nuremberg catalogue mentions such donations to other convents.[21] This was very important for the promotion of the Dominican reform movement: the newly reformed communities needed the correct statutes of the Dominican order and correct office prayer books to fulfil the requirements of their reformed monastic life.

How, then, did the sisters of St Catherine's in Nuremberg manage to assemble their extensive library? The nuns themselves copied many of their books; from 1428 to the end of the century the names of thirty-two copyists have survived. The most important *scriptrix* was Kunigunde Niklasin (d.1457),[22] who copied thirty-one manuscripts,[23] among them the entire Bible, some books of sermons, the lives of Dominicus and Heinrich Seuse, and the legends of St Catherine and St Ursula.[24] It was also she who, as librarian, began to catalogue the convent's books; in addition, she compiled a list of texts for table readings.[25] It may be supposed that she also chose the texts, since she must have had a profound knowledge of spiritual literature.

Another important copyist was Sister Margareta Karthäuserin who was among the ten sisters from Schönensteinbach sent to incorporate the Nuremberg convent into the Dominican reform movement. Unlike Kunigunde Niklasin, she specialized in copying books for the Divine Office. Fries[26] enumerates fourteen office books, but concedes that his list might be incomplete. Her fellow sisters praised her merits as a copyist: 'She wrote such beautiful books that those who see them cannot believe a woman can do such fine work.'[27]

It is not surprising that St Catherine's provided a great number of copyists. Since the building-up of a library was regarded as an important matter pertaining to the spiritual life of the community, copyists were in demand, and the prioress Kunigund Hallerin paid particular attention to the training of the novices and young sisters. She admonished them to practise writing, and in a letter to the St Gall sister convent she recommends the copying out of St John's Gospel as a useful exercise.[28] The high regard in which the copyists' work was held can be inferred from their working conditions: *scriptrices* were exempt from normal manual labour, and had rooms of their own, suitable for their task, in which they could work undisturbed.[29]

But the sisters did not copy all their books themselves. Firstly, as mentioned above, many of them possessed their own small libraries, and some of these books were left or donated to the community and integrated into the convent's library. It is possible to trace individual volumes by means of the two separate catalogues mentioned above, listing books in the possession both of private individuals and of the convent. According to the catalogue of private possessions, for instance, Sister Clara Keyperin owned a book which contained, among other texts, Heinrich von Langenstein's (d. 1397) tract on penitence and sin (*Erkenntnis der Sünde*)[30]. She had been given this book by a secular friend.[31] Later on we find the same book listed as part of the convent's library in the other catalogue, with the names of Clara Keyperin and her friend as donors.[32]

The convent also received books from other sources. Since most of the nuns came from the Nuremberg upper classes, they had many relatives and friends outside the monastery who presented them with books, and they also received books from clergy who were on friendly terms with them.[33]

What, then, were these books? It would not be practical to describe the contents of the library in detail, and I shall confine this discussion to a brief outline of its scope, selection, and content. At the centre of the sisters' religious life were the canonical hours, sung in Latin, and the Masses, but in spite of spending a significant amount of time each day on these duties most of the nuns did not understand Latin. They were able to read and sing Latin in the choir, but were unable to understand the language as such. This is not astonishing if one considers the education received in the convent. The novices were taught how to sing, read, and pray, and to live the godly life as defined by the rule and constitutions of the Dominican order. They were also instructed in manual work or writing; the letters of the Nuremberg prioresses describe the education of the novices in detail. Never, however, do they mention the teaching of Latin.[34] The contents of the convent's library corroborate this observation: most of the manuscripts recorded contain German texts, but very few of the surviving books are written in Latin.[35] The few sisters who did have command of the Latin tongue were a small minority.[36]

This explains why much attention was paid to the translations of biblical books, office prayers, hymns, and the Latin liturgy.[37] Often the manuscripts include expositions of all these texts, so that nuns ignorant of Latin might become familiar with their contents. For the same reason translations of the rule, the constitutions, and their various interpretations were incorporated into the library.[38]

Let us consider the example of biblical manuscripts.[39] The librarian Kunigunde Niklasin used capital letters to refer to the books' subjects and Roman numerals to designate individual volumes. 'A' marks the translations of both the Old and New Testaments (except A XIV: Hugo Ripelin, *Compendium theologicae veritatis*[40]). Under 'B' we chiefly find expositions of the Bible, in particular of the Ten Commandments; 'C' designates manuscripts of the Psalter, partly with commentary, and 'D' refers to extracts from the New Testament, with special respect to the gospels. This, of course, points to the main principle underlying the selection of the texts: the books accepted into the library corresponded to the aims of the sisters' religious life. The life of reformed Dominican nuns focused on prayer, contemplation, and strict adherence to the statutes of the order; the books contained in the library were intended to promote these aims by translating and explaining the principal sources of this life so as to deepen the sisters' knowledge, insight, and devotion, and since the nuns had to understand what they read or heard at table it was important that these be written in the vernacular.

Collections of prayers, sermons, meditations, and tracts vary the themes of devotion towards God the Father, the Son, and the Holy Ghost, to the Blessed Virgin Mary, and to the saints. Many texts concern the life and humanity of Jesus Christ (His birth, passion, death, and resurrection), which is typical of the period and consonant with the piety of the nuns. Other texts deal with the means to obtain a perfect life and blissful dying, or with the sacraments and appropriate preparation for receiving them.[41] Fewer texts treat mystical matters, since the Dominican reform movement in general distrusted mystical experience which was regarded as detrimental to the aims of the reformed way of life.[42]

Whereas the works of medieval academic theology are missing (the name of Thomas Aquinas is mentioned only in connection with certain prayers and sayings ascribed to him), we find texts by, or handed down in the name of, such spiritual authorities as Jerome, Bernard of Clairvaux and others.[43] But the lack of works, strictly speaking, of academic theology should not mislead us: sermons, meditations, treatises, and tracts were themselves influenced by academic theology; their authors were theologians, and they meditated on theology in a form which was accessible to the sisters and matched their way of life. As Humbert of Romans, fifth *magister generalis* of the order, put it in his *Expositio super constitutiones fratrum Praedicatorum*: 'In studying we have to consider to be fruitful to the souls of our fellow-men; ... we need not be very learned to be saved ourselves; but we must be very learned to teach others.'[44] But while the study of academic theology was indispensable for those who wanted to become preachers or confessors, it was not considered necessary for salvation. Since nuns could not aspire to the priestly office, they simply read what was considered suitable for their duties and way of life, and although the sisters were not prevented from reading works of academic theology, there is no evidence that any of them was interested in this field of study.

Secular works, with very few exceptions, are also missing from the library; they would have been irrelevant, if not detrimental, to the nuns' way of life. A prioress of the Nuremberg convent, for instance, expressed her disapproval of the singing of worldly songs and strictly forbade her sisters to practise it.[45]

The choice of texts accepted into the library was mainly determined by the sisters, since they produced and compiled the manuscripts themselves. In so doing they followed the advice of sisters of their own or related convents. The close relations between Nuremberg and St Gall are not the only example of such a network of communities. There were several other monasteries with which St Catherine's, Nuremberg, was in touch and with which it exchanged letters and books. Sometimes the sisters were supported by confessors or other clergy; we still have a list of devotional books which the sub-prior of the Nuremberg Dominicans, Johannes Forster of Ansbach, lent to the nuns in 1474.[46]

Not only did the sisters copy books for their convent library; in some cases they also had the manuscripts illuminated. Most illuminations consisted simply of historiated initials; only a few of the extant manuscripts display miniatures. Rather than reflecting a particular programme or policy in the interpretation of the texts, these pictures simply illustrate them. In two manuscripts which contain parts of the Old Testament in the vernacular we find scraps of paper attached to the margins of some pages, telling the illuminator what to paint;[47] the manuscripts were presumably written in the convent of St Catherine's, but the illuminations were not produced by the sisters themselves.[48] The illuminations in these two manuscripts relate either to the contents of the first chapters of the biblical books (e.g. Anna and Elkana in I Samuel: 1; Abishag and David in I Kings: 1) or depict their main features (e.g. Judith killing Holofernes; Esther meeting Ahasuerus; Vanity at the beginning of Ecclesiastes).[49] Another illumination introduces the Song of Songs: the sister responsible for the instructions orders a picture 'of a king embracing a woman'.[50] The wording is revealing: the Song of Songs and its bridal mysticism were very important to the Dominican sisters' spirituality, and they collected books on this matter for both private and public reading. The instruction for the painter, however, literally reflects the contents of this biblical book: Solomon embracing a woman.[51] The numerous illustrations within the Psalter[52] are also highly literal.[53] It is not clear in what context the sisters used these translations of Old Testament books, whether they were only provided for private reading or also had a public function; none of the volumes is referred to in the list of table readings. Whatever their function, however, it seems surprising that the nuns did not trouble to remove the instructions for the painter.

Whereas in these volumes the illustration of the text may be regarded as the main objective of the pictures, in other cases the illuminations seem also to aim at deepening contemplative experience. The miniatures of a manuscript containing sermons and tracts on the suffering of Christ [54] show the crucified Christ with Mary Magdalene kneeling, and the birth of Jesus, with God the Father, the Holy Ghost (as a dove), and Mary.[55] Other manuscripts are illustrated with miniatures or woodcuts of saints[56] or the crucified Christ.[57] Compared to the great number of preserved manuscripts, however, the number of illuminated manuscripts is small; it seems as if the sisters' interest in collecting texts did not extend to their illumination.[58]

The same is true for the liturgical manuscripts. Only a few of the preserved choirbooks are illuminated at all, and most of these are decorated with the kind of ornament which might be called typical for St Catherine's.[59] The few illuminations show Catherine of Alexandria, the convent's patron saint[60] (sometimes with a Dominican sister),[61] the crucified Christ, or His transfixed heart.[62] There is no reason to assume that the sisters of St Catherine's were more keen to illuminate their liturgical manuscripts than those collected in the convent library.

Whereas the names of many copyists have survived, the name of only one illuminator among the Nuremberg sisters is known, that of Barbara Gewichtmacherin. She is mentioned together with the copyist on the back of a liturgical book (1452): 'This lectionary was written by sister Margaretha Karthäuserin ... it was illuminated by Barbara Gewichtmacherin'.[63] Nothing is known of her life except the year of her death (1491).[64] As well as illuminating this breviary, she also participated in the artistic design of several liturgical books;[65] she illuminated a missal, copied and noted by her fellow sisters Margareta Imhoff and Margareta Karthäuserin,[66] and added two pictures to an antiphonary and gradual in eight volumes (1458–70).[67] These could be considered her masterpieces; however, she probably did no more than ornament her copies, and seems not to have been responsible for the paintings themselves.[68] The eight volumes include seven miniatures illustrating the texts of the liturgy; they show, for instance, the birth of Jesus (twice),[69] the crucifixion of St Andrew,[70] the resurrection of Christ,[71] and the adoration of the Magi.[72] Barbara Gewichtmacherin is the only named painter, but it is generally agreed that the other illuminations were made by five different artists.[73] Traces of Barbara Gewichtmacherin are to be found in other manuscripts as well, though it is not clear whether she herself or a disciple undertook the illuminations.[74] Even if, as scholars agree, she was not a particularly gifted painter,[75] she seems to have been very influential, finding followers not only among her fellow sisters, but also, for instance, a Dominican friar from the Nuremberg priory whose illuminations resemble her style.[76]

One of the manuscripts she or one of her disciples illuminated is the convent chronicle of Töss.[77] The Nuremberg sisters had a collection of convent chronicles in their library,[78] describing the lives of past Dominican sisters with an emphasis on their religious and mystical experiences, and mostly written by fellow-sisters in the first half of the fourteenth century. The members of the Dominican reform movement idealized the religious fervour of the early friars and sisters and were highly interested in these writings, and the Nuremberg sisters were no exception. The only extant manuscript with illuminations from this collection is the convent chronicle of Töss: it contains twenty-three initials each showing episodes in the *vitae* of the Dominican nuns whose lives are described. The author herself, Elsbeth Stagl, is portrayed sitting at her desk.[79]

To summarize this brief survey of the illuminations in manuscripts from St Catherine's, we can say that the sisters were not as interested in illuminating their manuscripts as they were in copying texts, as also indicated by the absence of information on this matter in their letters to St Catherine's in St Gall. The topics of the comparatively small number of miniatures, however, seem to have been chosen by the sisters themselves and to have been designed to illustrate the texts literally. It is notable that certain illuminations include depictions of Dominican sisters wearing their habits; perhaps they were introduced to encourage identification with the exemplary characters portrayed in the texts. All these observations, however, confirm that the main interest was the texts and their contents. This may have been due to the objectives of the reform movement, demanding strict adherence and total obedience to the letter of the Dominican law which, in their view, represented the precepts of divine law for religious people. The sisters were, of course, not hostile to pictures, but they seem not to have been particularly interested in including them in their everyday manuscripts. And of course there may have been another reason. As our investigation has shown, the Nuremberg sisters had many copyists but only a few illuminators; a manuscript could be copied easily and inexpensively, but to have a manuscript illuminated was expensive, unless it could be done inside the convent.[80] This might explain the comparatively large number of manuscripts which were simply decorated with ornaments.

The Nuremberg sisters, passionate collectors of books, gathered together a great variety of the most diverse works of spiritual literature with one thing in common: that they should cater to the specific aims and needs of the reformed Dominican life. However, their library is not one for diverging interests; as their life focused on their central objective, the Divine Service, so too did their library and the choice of their books. In all respects, their interests were focused on the texts. Only a few manuscripts were illuminated, and in these cases the pictures literally illustrate the written words. This could not have happened by chance; the sisters must have seen the function of illuminations simply as illustrating the text.

Notes to Chapter Seven

1 T.von Kern, 'Die Reformation des Katharinenklosters zu Nürnberg im Jahre 1428', *Jahresbericht des historischen Vereins in Mittelfranken,* 31 (1863), pp.1–20.

2 P.Ruf, *Bistum Augsburg, Eichstätt, Bamberg, Mittelalterliche Bibliothekskataloge Deutschlands und der Schweiz,* iii (München, 1932), pp.578–670.

3 On the history of St Catherine's, *see* W.Fries, 'Kirche und Kloster zu St Katharina in Nürnberg', *Mitteilungen des Vereins für Geschichte der Stadt Nürnberg,* 25 (1924), pp.1–143.

4 'Vor der reformyrung hinnen gewest'; *see* I.Metschkoll, 'Der Bibliotheksbestand des St Katharinenklosters vor der Klosterreform von 1428' (unpubl. MA thesis, Univ. of Munich, 1987), p.28; Ruf, *Bistum Augsburg,* pp.599–637.

5 Metschkoll, *Bibliotheksbestand,* p.107; *see* the dedication in Munich, Bay.Staatsbibl., cgm 6396 (H IV; Ruf, *Bistum Augsburg,* p.613), which mentions the donors and the purpose of their donations.

6 K.Schneider, *Die deutschen mittelalterlichen Handschriften, Die Handschriften der Stadtbibliothek Nürnberg,* i (Wiesbaden, 1965), p.xv.

7 Metschkoll, *Bibliotheksbestand,* p.106.

8 Ruf, *Bistum Augsburg,* pp.570–71.

9 'So wil ich, daz ir all zeit in dem refenter, wenn man da ysset oder collacion trinckt, ze tisch lest des morgens teütsch und ze abend ein teil latein und den andren ze teütsch.' Kern, 'Reformation', p.19.

10 This emerges from the list of table readings, Ruf, *Bistum Augsburg,* pp.638–50 (1429–31); 650–70 (1455–61).

11 Both of these books are often mentioned in the later list of table readings; the sermons of Johannes Tauler were originally in the private possession of a sister who gave them to the convent's library (Ruf, *Bistum Augsburg,* p.604, 27–9). Durandus' *Rationale officiorum divinorum* is also found in the old catalogue (Ruf, *Bistum Augsburg,* p.613, 5–6).

12 *Ibid.,* p.651.

13 *Ibid.,* p.606, 5.

14 *Ibid.,* p.604, 17.

15 Wil, MS *Schwesternbuch,* fol. 174r. Today the manuscript of the *Schwesternbuch* is in the possession of the Dominican nuns of Wil, who very generously permitted me to read and copy parts of it.

16 J.Meyer, *Ämterbuch,* Freiburg im Breisgau, Municipal Archive, MS B1 (H), Nr.108, fol. 115r.

17 *See* the list of the sisters' private books, Ruf, *Bistum Augsburg,* pp.579–96.

18 K.Schneider, 'Die Bibliothek des Katharinenklosters in Nürnberg und die städtische Gesellschaft', in *Studien zum städtischen Bildungswesen des späten Mittelalters und der frühen Neuzeit. Bericht über Kolloquien der Kommission zur Erforschung der Kultur des Spätmittelalters 1978–1981,* ed. B.Moeller, H.Patze, K.Stackmann, Abhandlungen der Akademie der Wissenschaften in Göttingen, Phil.-Hist. Klasse, 3. Folge; 137 (Göttingen, 1983), pp.70–82; p.73.

19 *Ibid.,* p.193.

20 Wil, MS *Schwesternbuch,* fol. 26r–v.

21 Ruf, *Bistum Augsburg,* p.637.

22 Fries, 'Kirche und Kloster', p.51ff.

23 Schneider, *Handschriften,* XVI.

24 Fries, 'Kirche und Kloster', pp.52–53.

25 Schneider, 'Bibliothek', pp.394–95.

26 Fries, 'Kirche und Kloster', pp. 55–56.

27 '[Sie schreib] sölichi schöni bucher, wer die siecht, dem ist es nit wol zuo gelobind, daz ain frowen bild so wol kan arbaiten'. Wil, MS *Schwesternbuch,* fol. 177r.

28 *Ibid.*, fol. 176r.

29 *Ibid.*, fol. 233r.

30 T.Hohmann and G.Kreuzer, *'Heinrich von Langenstein', Verfasser-Lexikon,* iii, 2nd edn. (Berlin, 1981), cols. 768–70.

31 Ruf, *Bistum Augsburg,* p.594, 19–21.

32 *Ibid.*, p.634, 28–9.

33 *See* the numerous entries in the old catalogue, *ibid.*, pp.599–637.

34 Wil, MS *Schwesternbuch,* fols 240r–51r.

35 In the Stadtbibliothek of Nuremberg, for instance, one finds only 9 Latin MSS which used to belong to St Catherine's (*see* K.Schneider, *Theologische Handschriften, Handschriften der Stadtbibliothek Nürnberg,* 2/1 (Wiesbaden, 1967), the MSS Cod. Cent. IV, 17; IV, 20; VI, 46g; VII, 14; VII, 15; VII, 30; VII, 33; VII, 37, and VII, 63. They are not mentioned in the medieval catalogue, which lists only the vernacular MSS. The Latin books mainly contain sermons which were probably written by Nuremberg Dominican friars.

36 Unfortunately we have no details about the Latin-speaking sisters of St Catherine's and so have to rely on circumstantial evidence. But the number of reformed Dominican nuns with command of the Latin tongue must have been comparatively small.

37 *See* Ruf, *Bistum Augsburg,* pp.612–13.

38 *Ibid.*, pp.613–15.

39 *Ibid.*, pp.599–604.

40 *Ibid.*, pp.600–1.

41 *Ibid.*, pp.579–96 and 599–637 *passim.*

42 *See* J.Nider, *Formicarius* (*s.l., s.a.*; University Library of Tübingen), fols J 4v–J 5r.

43 *See* Ruf, *Bistum Augsburg,* pp.618–24.

44 'Studium nostrum ad hoc debeat principaliter intendere, ut proximorum animabus possimus utiles esse... Modica scientia sufficit ad salutem propriam; sed non sufficit modica ad alios docendum'. *B. Humberti de Romanis Quinti Praedicatorum Magistri Generalis Opera de vita regulari,* ed. by Fr. J.J.Berthier, ii: *Expositio in Constitutiones* (Turin, 1956), pp.41–42.

45 Wil, MS *Schwesternbuch,* fol. 138r.

46 Ruf, *Bistum Augsburg,* pp.637–38; Schneider, *Handschriften,* p.295.

47 Nuremberg, Stadtbibliothek, MSS Cod. Cent. III, 40; III, 41 (*see* Schneider, *Handschriften,* p.3).

48 Fries, 'Kirche und Kloster', p.53.

49 The contents of the instructions for the illuminator and a description of the illuminations is to be found in Schneider, *Handschriften,* pp.2 and 4.

50 *Ibid.*, p.4: 'Vber Cantica molt ein kunck der umbhalset ein frawen'.

51 The illuminator is explicitly instructed to paint a woman (*frawen*), not a virgin (*iunckfrawen*).

52 *See* W.Walter, *Die deutsche Bibelübersetzung des Mittelalters* (Braunschweig, 1889–92), p.312. There are illuminations to Psalms 1, 26, 38, 52, 68, 80, 97, and 109; this division of the Psalter into 8 groups or 'liturgical divisions' was quite common; *see* G.Suckale-Redlefsen, 'Psalmen, Psalterillustrationen', *Lexikon der christlichen Ikonographie,* iii (Rome, Herder, 1971), cols.466–81, col.468.

53 *Ibid.*, 1971, col.468.

54 Nuremberg, Stadtbibl., MS Cod. Cent.IV, 37.

55 *See* Schneider, *Handschriften,* pp.36–37.

WOMEN AND THE BOOK

56 Nuremberg, Stadtbibl., MS Cod. Cent.VI, 43f (*see* ibid., pp.96–97).

57 E.g.Nuremberg, Stadtbibl., MS Cod. Cent.VII, 88 (cf. ibid., p.401).

58 In considering this, we must of course take into account only the MSS which were actually written by the nuns themselves.

59 Neske, *Bibelhandschriften und Liturgica einschließlich der griechischen Texte, Die Handschriften der Stadtbibliothek Nürnberg*, ii, 2 (Wiesbaden, 1987), p.59 (plate no. 17).

60 Nuremberg, Stadtbibl., MS Cod. Cent.III, 86, fol. 20r (*see* ibid., p.24).

61 Nuremberg, Stadtbibl, MSS Cod. Cent.VII, 11b, fol. 29r; VII, 100, fol. 2r (*see* ibid., pp.106–7; p.123).

62 Nuremberg, Stadtbibl, MS Cod. Cent.VIII, 18, fols 51v, 78v, 84v (*see* ibid., pp.126–28).

63 'Lectionarius iste scriptus per sororem Margaretham Cartheuserin ... illuminatus per barbaram gewichtmacherin'. F.Falk, 'Der Stempeldruck vor Gutenberg und die Stempeldrucke in Deutschland', in *Festschrift zum fünfhundertsten Geburtstag von Johann Gutenberg, 23. Beiheft zum Centralblatt für Bibliothekswesen*, ed. O.Hartwig,(Leipzig, 1900) pp.73–79, p.75. Barbara Gewichtmacherin has often been confused with the copyist Margareta Karthäuserin. K.Fischer, *Die Buchmalerei in den beiden Dominikanerklöstern Nürnbergs* (Nuremberg, 1928) has finally proved that the illuminations wrongly ascribed to her were done by Barbara Gewichtmacherin. This mistake, however, is often repeated; *see* e.g. E.Schraut and C.Opitz, *Frauen und Kunst im Mittelalter* (Braunschweig, 1983), pp.30–31; the authors also confuse the name of the Nuremberg convent with that of another one, situated in Switzerland (St Katharinenthal).

64 Fischer, *Buchmalerei*, pp.69–70.

65 *Ibid.*, p.73.

66 Nuremberg, Stadtbibl., MSS Cod. Cent.III, 86; III, 87 (cf. Neske, *Bibelhandschriften*, p.23–7; *see also* n.60).

67 Nuremberg, Stadtbibl., MSS Cod. Cent.V, App. 34p-w: Cod. Cent.V, App. 34p, fol. 20v, birth of Jesus; Cod. Cent.V, 34q, fol. 4r, crucifixion of St Andrew (cf. Neske, *Bibelhandschriften*, p.65).

68 *Ibid.*, p.65.

69 Nuremberg, Stadtbibl., MSS Cod. Cent.V, App. 34p, fol. 20v; V.App. 34t, fol. 22r (*see* Neske, *Bibelhandschriften*, p.65, plates 2 and 3).

70 Nuremberg, Stadtbibl., MS Cod. Cent.V, App. 34q, fol. 4r (*see* ibid., p.65).

71 Nuremberg, Stadtbibl., MS Cod. Cent.V, App. 34v, fol. 3r (*see* ibid., p.65, and plate 4).

72 Nuremberg, Stadtbibl., MS Cod. Cent.V, App. 34w, fol. 2r (*see* ibid., p.65).

73 *Ibid.*, p.65.

74 Fischer, *Buchmalerei*, p.70. The MSS are Nuremberg, Stadtbibl., MS Cod. Cent.V.10a (cf. Schneider, *Handschriften*, p.67) and Cod. Cent.VI, 43g (ibid., p.98–99; since the MS contains the legend of Vincent Ferrer, the illumination depicts him).

75 Fischer, *Buchmalerei*, p.75.

76 *Ibid.*

77 Nuremberg, Stadtbibl., MS Cod. Cent.V, 10a.

78 Ruf, *Bistum Augsburg*, p.633 (medieval signatures: N XXII; N XXIII; N XXVII).

79 *See* Schneider, *Handschriften*, p.67.

80 Of illuminators from outside the convent, it was probably the Nuremberg friars who did some illuminating on behalf of the sisters; they also helped them with book-binding (Fries, 'Kirche und Kloster', pp.53–57).

CHAPTER EIGHT

Women's Work at the Benedictine Convent of Le Murate in Florence: Suora Battista Carducci's Roman Missal of 1509[1]

Kate Lowe

BEING ABLE TO attach a nun's name to a particular extant manuscript copied at the beginning of the sixteenth century in Italy is significant chiefly because it is rare. There are a number of reasons for this, the most obvious one being that it was traditional for female scribes not to reveal their identity or claim credit for their work. This article will focus on a missal written by a Florentine nun and will elaborate on the set of circumstances surrounding its production. In this instance, a number of elements combined to allow the initial writing of the missal, the subsequent survival of the manuscript, and the independent preservation of the scribe's name.

One of the Benedictines' main contributions to the Christian church was the care and transmission of the liturgy. Followers of Benedict's rule came to be seen as 'especial custodians of the ... rich heritage of official prayer',[2] and one way in which both the monks and nuns of this order played their part was by copying and disseminating texts of the Divine Office. The illuminated Roman missal now in the Bibliothèque Nationale in Paris – MS lat. 17323 – is known to have been written in the Benedictine convent of Le Murate in Florence, but the name of its scribe has hitherto been unknown. The manuscript is written in gothic rotunda script in Latin on membrane, and consists of 385 folios which measure 352 mms by 235 mms, with two columns of twenty-nine lines to the page (FIG. 63). The colophon states that the manuscript was completed in Le Murate on 12 October 1509 (FIG. 64),[3] and internal evidence backs this statement up. In the section on the blessing of the candles on Holy Saturday, the Pope is designated by the initial I which represents Julius II (1503–13) (FIG. 65), and the emperor by the initial M which stands for Maximilian (1493–1519); so the manuscript, even without the colophon, can be dated to between 1503 and 1513.[4]

The *editio princeps* of the Roman missal was printed at Milan in 1474,[5] setting a new standard for the text, but initially texts were still copied from other manuscripts rather than from the printed edition. The Paris missal is bound with a Roman calendar which can be dated to 1481. The calendar's most recently canonized saints are Bérard and Otto, both canonized in 1481, whereas St Bonaventure, who was canonized in 1482, is absent.[6] However, as calendars and liturgical texts travelled separately, the content of the calendar and its date do not reveal anything about the model for the missal. The liturgy in general was

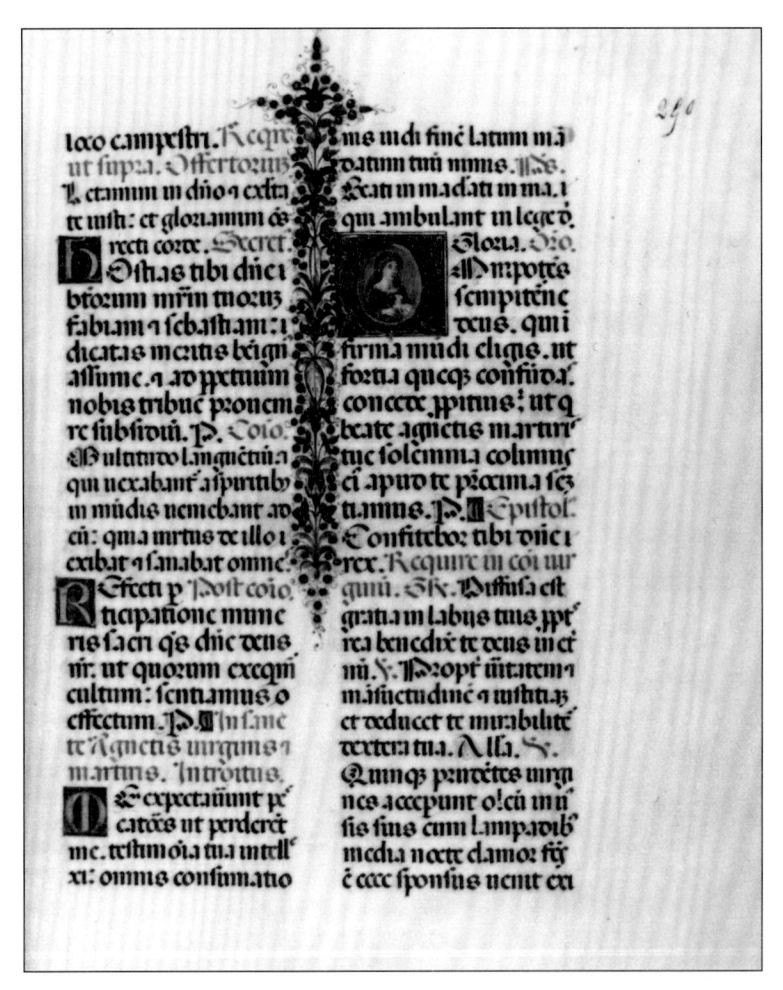

FIG. 63 The end of the Office of the Feast of SS. Fabian and Sebastian (20 Jan.),
and the beginning of the Office of the Feast of St Agnes (21 Jan.).
Roman missal of 1509 written by Suora Battista Carducci and illuminated
by Attavante Attavanti. Paris, BN, MS lat. 17323, fol. 250r.

widely believed to be in a state of decline in the fourteenth and fifteenth centuries,[7] and 'liturgical uniformity' was not achieved until after the Council of Trent.[8]

The missal was one of the chief liturgical books[9] of the Roman rite and contained all that was needed for the celebration of the Mass, and for certain other functions related to it, such as the blessings on Ash Wednesday.[10] The three principal components of the missal are the sacramentary, a book containing the prayers used at Mass and some other rites, the lectionaries for the Gospels and Epistles, and the gradual, the choirbook containing at least the textual part of the plainsong settings for the Mass. The Paris missal also contains the musical notation, proving that the scribe was well enough acquainted with music to be able to copy it with some degree of accuracy (FIG. 65). In general, a higher rate was paid for copying both music and text than for text alone, as an ability to copy musical notation was considered an additional skill.

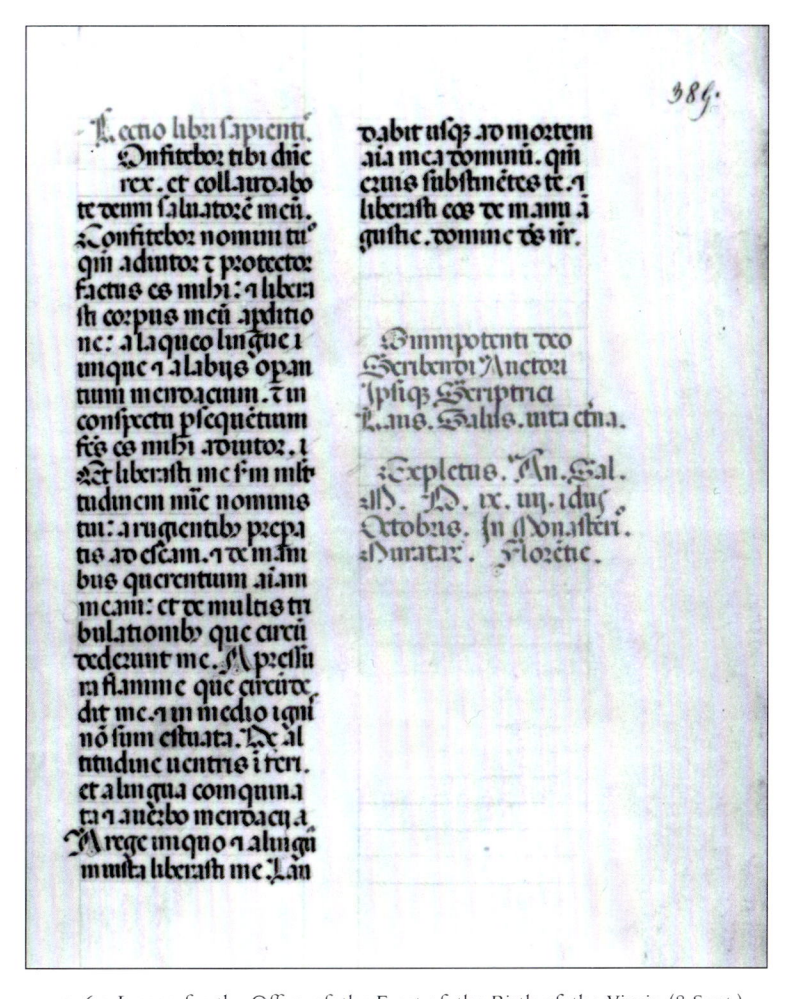

FIG. 64 Lesson for the Office of the Feast of the Birth of the Virgin (8 Sept.).
Paris, BN, MS lat. 17323, fol. 385r.

In addition to being famed for their efforts as scribes on behalf of the liturgy, Benedictines are also known for their writing of annals and their record-keeping in general. In sixteenth-century Italy Benedictine women, like their male counterparts, sometimes wrote chronicles of their convents. Le Murate not only educated and trained a number of female scribes, but also produced a female chronicler. In 1597 Suora Giustina Niccolini finished a chronicle of her convent which ran from its inception at the end of the fourteenth century to that date,[11] and which still remains unpublished. It was based on a mixture of written records, official documents from the convent archive, and oral recollection from the older nuns, and can be proved to be largely accurate. Many details of convent life in these years are therefore available which would otherwise have been lost, among which are further pieces of information about the scribe of the Roman missal, most importantly her name.

It is already known that Pope Leo X, on his way back from Bologna and his famous

FIG. 65 Part of the blessing of candles at the Easter Vigil (Holy Saturday). Paris, BN, MS lat. 17323, fol. 147r.

meeting with King Francis I of France, stopped in Florence, the city of his birth. According to the chronicle, he also visited Le Murate, which he knew his father Lorenzo de' Medici had favoured, on 12 January 1516,[12] accompanied by nine cardinals and many bishops and archbishops. The convent had attained a certain level of fame due to the excellence of its various activities such as singing and producing manuscripts, so that visiting dignitaries and ambassadors felt that it was one of the sights of Florence and tried to include a visit on their itinerary. For example, Antonio da Montecatino from Ferrara wrote to Ercole d'Este on 21 August 1480 describing a visit he made there, between ones to the Medici palace and San Marco.[13] He remarked upon the work of the scribes, who fashioned the most beautiful letters imaginable, but who, in common with the other nuns there, never raised their eyes from their work. Leo, as a Florentine rather than a tourist, must also have been aware that patronage of Le Murate was disputed by his family and their most important political rivals, the Soderini, and that to carry out a visit at this juncture when the Medici were firmly in power and the Soderini firmly out of power was a politic thing to do.[14]

The chronicle records that at a certain point during his tour Leo was presented with 'a missal written in beautiful script by Reverend Mother Suora Battista Carducci, all illuminated and decorated according to what was suitable, which His Holiness accepted with evident delight; and with great courtesy he handed the abbess 200 *scudi d'oro* in alms'.[15] Previously, it might have been surmised that this manuscript had been made for Cardinal Giovanni de' Medici before he was elected pope and took the name Leo X, as its date of 1509 was so unambiguous, and the papal arms and insignia of Leo were prominently displayed (Fig. 66).[16] Now it is clear that this manuscript, completed in 1509, probably stayed in the convent until 1515 when, on account of its great beauty, it was selected as a suitably magnificent gift for the visiting pontiff.

The illumination has been identified by Albinia de la Mare as being by the Florentine illuminator Attavante Attavanti (Figs 67 and 68).[17] Originally it might have been thought that Attavante had added the decoration after the manuscript had been acquired by Leo, but the chronicle makes this hypothesis unlikely by stating that it had already been illuminated at the time of its presentation to the Pope in 1515. Nonetheless, according to Patricia Stirnemann, Attavante's decoration seems to have taken place in two stages. Visual evidence suggests that most of it was executed in 1509 when the manuscript was completed, but that the papal coat of arms was not painted at precisely the same time, and may have been added at the moment of donation in 1515.[18]

It was accepted procedure in Tuscany in the second half of the fifteenth and the beginning of the sixteenth centuries for liturgical books to be copied by nuns and illuminated afterwards by secular male illuminators. For instance, a breviary copied by Suora Giovanna, a nun at the Augustinian convent of San Gaggio just outside Florence,[19] was decorated by Andrea (who may possibly have been the illuminator Andrea di Paolo di Giovanni da Firenze) in 1457.[20] And Suora Maddalena di Luigi di Guido, a nun at San Francesco in Florence, copied a breviary for Santa Maria Nuova in the late 1480s which was then illuminated by Gherardo and Monte di Giovanni.[21] A different example is provided by the nuns of Santa Maria Maddalena in Siena, who from the 1440s to the 1470s themselves copied and illuminated religious manuscripts for the Ospedale della Scala and the Opera del Duomo in Siena at competitive rates,[22] thereby dispensing with the need to have male illuminators. However, convents whose nuns possessed a combination of scribal and artistic skills were extremely rare.

The fact that the moment of completion and the moment of presentation of the 1509 missal are separated by five and a half years is unusual, and it is probably to be explained by the value of the book. For whatever reason, it seems that the missal remained in the convent, possibly in use, and was chosen for presentation as a worthy token of the nuns' gratitude for Medicean and papal patronage of the convent over the years.[23] The only two known owners of the book before the Bibliothèque Nationale are Leo X and Louis Fouquet, the bishop of Agde in L'Hérault from 1657 to 1702,[24] whose ex-libris is still in the missal; the reasons for the book's passage from papal to episcopal to French national library are not clear.

FIG. 66 Part of the Order of Mass for the first Sunday of Advent, with the arms of Pope Leo X.
Paris, BN, MS lat. 17323, fol. 13r.

FIG. 67 Full-page illumination of the Crucifixion.
Paris, BN, MS lat. 17323, fol. 177v.

Suora Battista Carducci came from a large and important clan in fifteenth-century Florence. Five male members of the Carducci family from this period have been included in the *Dizionario biografico degli italiani*, and many Carducci were involved in politics, both as Mediceans and as republicans. Information from the records of the dowry fund in Florence kindly supplied by Anthony Molho makes it possible to surmise that Suora Battista may have been related to Maria or Francesca Carducci. These women were allegedly the daughters of Lorenzo di Agnolo Carducci (1427- after 1493),[25] and themselves had daughters who were born in 1484 and 1487 respectively, and who later became nuns. A nun called Suora Battista (but without a surname) is listed in a notarial document of 10 November 1505 naming all the nuns present at Le Murate at this date, and this Battista is surely the scribe of the missal.[26]

The history of the nuns' scriptorium at Le Murate has yet to be written, but Suora Giustina Niccolini's chronicle provides some helpful pointers. The most famous abbess of

FIG. 68 Part of the canon of the Mass, with an illuminated initial of
Christ and the instruments of the Passion.
Paris, BN, MS lat. 17323, fol. 178r.

the convent, Suora Scolastica Rondinelli (abbess from 1439 to 1475), early in her rule ordered two psalters and two breviaries written 'in the hand of a good master' (*di mano di buon maestro*) for use in the convent church. These cost in total 100 ducats and were paid for with money generated by the nuns' production of gold thread[27] during Lent.[28] It must have occurred to Scolastica, who had come to the convent as a widow and who was blessed with an enterprising entrepreneurial spirit, that in addition to other skills the nuns could learn how to become scribes. In this way the convent would move one step further towards self-sufficiency, and at the same time would be able to earn some much-needed cash. A breviary written by 'don Nicholo tedescho' and illuminated by Filippo di Matteo Torelli for use in Le Murate is recorded in the account books of the Badia in Florence in 1436 and 1437.[29]

In the 1470s Scolastica seems to have turned an apparent disaster – a fire on 13 August 1471 – to her own and the convent's advantage by rebuilding in such a way as to include space for a scriptorium. In this she was helped by the patronage and largesse of Lorenzo de' Medici.[30] On top of the repaired loggia of the main courtyard, a *verone* or upper loggia was built, where a few years later ten small writing cubicles or study compartments, separated by wooden partitions, were constructed.[31] The three studies or scriptoria of the Benedictine convent of S. Croce della Giudecca in Venice were planned to be in the same position, on the upper floor above the central courtyard, with small windows facing west and a western door to make the most of the light.[32] On 14 April 1498 another fire broke out at Le Murate, this time in the ten scriptoria themselves, which quickly spread, again causing much damage. At this time, the Medici had been expelled from Florence and it was the turn of the republican government to fund the rebuilding programme.[33]

According to Le Murate's chronicler, the number of scribes or copyists in the convent hovered around eight at this period;[34] presumably the maximum number was ten, for there were ten writing cubicles before the 1498 fire (the number had risen to twenty-six by the end of the sixteenth century). This was a relatively restricted percentage of the convent, which expanded greatly under Scolastica's guidance, and which may have had between 150 and 170 nuns from the 1460s to the end of the century, when it was the largest in Florence.[35] However, one of the secrets of Le Murate's success was diversity of occupation. By comparison, the nuns of the convent of the Poor Clares at Monteluce near Perugia were much smaller in number in the fifteenth century, but seem proportionately to have produced more scribes.[36]

Given the number of scribes at Le Murate, and the number of years the scriptoria were in use, well into the sixteenth century, few known or identifiable manuscripts penned by the nuns have been traced. As one would expect, all of them are copies of works used in the celebration of the Divine Office. These specialized liturgical manuscripts appear to have been copied in the main by monks, friars, priests, and nuns.[37] It is not known what percentage of manuscripts was commissioned rather than being written on speculation, but they served a variety of functions, from commemoration of marriage, to use in the Duomo and in other convents, to presentation as valuable gifts to past or potential patrons.

A number of missals written at Le Murate are mentioned in the account books and deliberations of the Opera and sacristy of the cathedral in Florence between 1476 and 1478,[38] but no known ones are extant. Some of these missals were very expensive, costing hundreds of *lire*, which suggests that they were large and opulent. A manuscript of the Office of the Passion and fifteen collects of St Bridget of Sweden, comprising 182 leaves on parchment in Latin, copied at Le Murate in 1510, was sold at Sotheby's on 19 June 1989, lot 3034, as part of the J. R. Abbey collection.[39] The illumination has been attributed to Tommaso di Stefano Lunetti.[40] On folio 1 are the partially-erased arms of Pope Julius II, and those on the binding are of King Ferdinand VI of Spain, who ruled from 1746 to 1759;[41] once again, this manuscript, penned by an unknown nun, was considered worthy of papal (and in this case also of royal) ownership.

A year later, in 1511, the nuns of the nearby convent of Sant'Ambrogio in Florence ordered a small diurnal which cost twenty-eight *lire* from the scribes at Le Murate.[42] The illumination of this manuscript cost eight *lire* and was again carried out by Attavante.[43] Perhaps Attavante had some sort of contract or merely an agreement with Le Murate whereby he illuminated certain of their manuscripts, or possibly Le Murate manuscripts were so highly praised for their excellence that Attavante, as the best-known illuminator in Florence at the time, was sometimes called upon to decorate them. The relationship between nuns and male illuminators has yet to be explored in detail. For instance, when the illuminator Mariano del Buono was declared to be 'at Le Murate' in 1471, having previously paid rent to the Badia, what exactly did this mean?[44] Was he able to carry out some of his work in the convent or was he merely renting a piece of property from the nuns?

A further prayer-book copied, according to its colophon, at Le Murate, and finished on 9 November 1517,[45] was included in an exhibition of sacred art in Turin in 1898, when it was in the possession of Leone Fontana. The present whereabouts of the manuscript are unknown, so it is impossible to see it, but due to the presence of Ricasoli and Mannelli coats of arms on the one folio that was reproduced in the exhibition catalogue it has been suggested that it was intended to record the marriage of Jacopo di Gaspare Ricasoli and Lucrezia di Niccolò Mannelli in 1497.[46] This date seems too early, but if the manuscript had been commissioned as a piece of wedding memorabilia it would be evidence of another lucrative sideline widening the earning potential of the female scribes. Yet again, the illumination was provided by a secular illustrator; Albinia de la Mare believes it to be in the style of Boccardino Vecchio.[47] It is noteworthy that four manuscripts emanating from Le Murate during the 8-year period from 1509 to 1517 are known, which might suggest that one or more particularly able scribes were at work at this date.

A final manuscript partly copied at Le Murate, and completed on 2 October 1567, was sold at Sotheby's on 11 December 1979, as lot 61. This prayer-book is a curious amalgam, with decoration taken from several earlier fifteenth-century manuscripts pasted into it. There are a few small initials in the hand of the Le Murate scribe, which is the only example so far of a nun from the convent also engaging in illumination. According to Albinia de la Mare, who saw the manuscript at this time, most of the pasted-in decoration is taken from a manuscript illuminated by Bartolomeo Varnucci, while the first main border appears to be by Gherardo di Giovanni.[48]

A few questions remain to be asked. What kind of activity was copying for nuns? How did the nuns view it and how was it perceived by the male hierarchy of the church? In fifteenth-century Italy nuns appeared to have the freedom to be as self-sufficient as possible, and clever abbesses were quick to make the most of the window of opportunity. Their choice of work was of course limited, as it had to take place within the confines of the convent walls, but nevertheless it could and did encompass many different activities. Suora Giustina Niccolini writes in her chronicle of the money-spinning skills which were in fashion at Le Murate in the mid-fifteenth century: in addition to copying manuscripts, the nuns produced gold thread,[49] wove shirts, woollens, tablecloths, and other linen, netted seeds of perfume, and cast gesso reliefs.[50] These cottage industries earned them the sum of 500 *scudi* a year. The only one of the above skills which could be classified as an art was that of a scribe; it was also the sole one that could earn considerable sums of money, and it alone left enduring traces.

Copying manuscripts had the advantage of being a traditional Benedictine activity which had been taking place (admittedly only in selected monasteries) for centuries. Although no rule, not even that of St Benedict, stipulated that books should be copied, liturgical books for daily prayer and other texts for reading and teaching were required in both male and female religious communities. According to Rosamond McKitterick, 'there is ample religious justification for scribal activity, both in classifying it as labour, and in defining its holy purpose.'[51] The problem was rather that surplus books should not be produced for profit, which is certainly what was happening at Le Murate in the late fifteenth and early sixteenth century. This type of independence was not to be tolerated by the church hierarchy, who in wave after wave, starting with Girolamo Savonarola[52] and ending with the bishops at the Council of Trent, raged against the very idea of productive and profitable work for religious women. At Trent it was decreed that the vow of poverty had to be observed and enterprise could no longer be rewarded.[53] Women's work, by definition, should be trifling or homely or both, and should not be of financial benefit to the woman concerned. The preferred relationship between religious women and the book envisaged by male Church reformers can best be understood by examining a woodcut of Savonarola presenting his book on the Ten Commandments to the abbess and nuns of Le Murate.[54] The Dominican friar stands on the right while the nuns are on their knees on the left, receiving his gift. The book has been written by him; they have created and achieved nothing, and their lot is to be pleased to be in receipt of his favour and wisdom.

The gap between permissible self-sufficiency and a not-to-be-countenanced successful and skilful cash economy, not based on barter, was crossed by the nuns of Le Murate in Florence in the late fifteenth and early sixteenth centuries, with serious consequences. Scribal activity for profit by nuns was later outlawed in the gloomy patriarchal years of the Counter-Reformation. Instead, nuns were to revert to their long-standing passive role as recipients of charity rather than generators of income. In any case, copying by the mid-sixteenth century had largely given way before the advent of printing, as a breviary printed in Venice for Le Murate in 1545 shows.[55] But although the nuns fought hard for their right to be scribes, they seem not to have questioned the tradition that most scribes (and virtually all female scribes) should remain anonymous. Before the unlocking of Suora Battista Carducci's identity, no copyist at Le Murate could be ascribed a name, and no manuscript could be ascribed a copyist.

Notes to Chapter Eight

1. I am indebted to the Nuffield Foundation for its financial support. I would also like to thank Albinia de la Mare, without whose generosity and knowledge this article would not have been possible; and I am grateful to Sarah Falla, Megan Holmes, Amanda Lillie, Tony Molho, Patricia Stirnemann, and Robert Swanson for their help in various ways.

2. D. H. Turner, 'The Work of God', in *The Benedictines in Britain*, British Library Exhibition Catalogue (London, 1980), p.52.

3. Paris, BN., MS lat. 17323, fol. 385r. The whole colophon runs: 'Omnipotenti Deo, scribendi auctori ipsique scriptrici, laus, salus, vita eterna. Expletus anno Salvatoris MDIX, IIII idus Octobris in monasterio Muratarum Florentie'.

4. *Ibid.*, fol. 147r–v. See also C.Samaran and R.Marichal, *Catalogue des manuscrits en écriture latine*, iii, texte (Paris, 1974), p.575.

5. *Missale Romanum Mediolani, 1474*, ed. R.Lippe, *Henry Bradshaw Society*, 17 (1899).

6. V.Leroquais, *Les sacramentaires et les missels manuscrits des bibliothèques publiques de France*, iii (Paris, 1924), p.260.

7. See Paris, BN, MS lat. 17323, fol. 178r, which is fig. 68, where the copyist has written 'infra actionem' instead of 'infra canonem'. It is not known whether this mistake originated in an earlier manuscript or was the fault of the scribe of the Paris missal.

8. A.King, *Liturgy of the Roman Church* (London, 1957), p.41.

9. For information on the development of the liturgical books, see King, *Liturgy*, pp.175–80, and L.Eisenhofer and J.Lechner, *The Liturgy of the Roman Rite* (Freiburg/Edinburgh/London, 1961), pp.19–41.

10. A.Fortescue, *The Ceremonies of the Roman Rite Described*, 8th edn., further revised and augmented by J. O'Connell (London, 1948), pp.18–19.

11. For more information on this chronicle, see K.Lowe, 'Female Strategies for Success in a Male-Ordered World: The Benedictine Convent of Le Murate in Florence in the Fifteenth and Early Sixteenth Centuries', *Women in the Church*, ed. W.J. Sheils and D. Wood, *Studies in Church History* xxvii (Oxford, 1990), pp. 209–21.

12. Giustina Niccolini's chronicle is in Florence, Biblioteca nazionale, MS II II 509. Although the chronicle states (on fol. 76r) that Leo X visited the convent on 12 Febr., the papal master of ceremonies, Paris de' Grassis, recorded that the pope re-entered Rome on 5 Febr. 1516: M.Armellini (ed.), *Il diario di Leone X di Paride de Grassi* (Rome, 1884), p.29. It is therefore likely that Leo's visit took place on 12 Jan. and not 12 Feb. Paris de' Grassis' diary makes no mention of it, but only important religious services in Florence are noted. It is interesting to compare the viewpoints of the diary and chronicle. For the Florentine convent chronicler Leo's visit was an important event, whereas for the Bolognese papal master of ceremonies it was insignificant.

13. Modena, Archivio di stato, Archivio segreto estense, Cancelleria, Ambasciatori, Firenze, busta 2a, 21 Aug. 1480.

14. K.Lowe, 'Patronage and Territoriality in Early Sixteenth-Century Florence', *Renaissance Studies*, 7 (1993), pp. 258–71.

15. Florence, BN, MS II II 509, fol. 76r: 'un messale scritto di bellissima lettera per mano della Reverenda Madre Suora Batista Carducci, tutto miniato et adorno conforme alla loro possibilità, il che da Sua Beatitudine fu accettato con allegra faccia, et con molta cortesia pose in mano alla badessa scudi 200 d'oro in limosina'. The phrase 'conforme alla loro possibilità' is ambiguous and could mean one of three things: 'according to what was suitable', 'with suitable designs', or 'according to their utmost ability'. I think the first option is the most likely one.

16. Paris, BN, MS lat. 17323, fol. 13r.

17 Private communication of 17 July 1989. For information on Attavante, *see* the entry by R.Cipriani in the *Dizionario biografico degli italiani*, iv (Rome, 1962), pp.526–30, and M.Levi d'Ancona, *Miniatura e miniatori a Firenze dal XIV al XVI secolo* (Florence, 1962), pp.254–9.

18 This information originates in a private communication from Patricia Stirnemann of 16 March 1994. In it, she contrasts the colours and floral motifs of the arms with the rest of the illumination on fol. 13r of Paris, BN, MS lat. 17323. She also compares the arms in the Paris missal to coats of arms in other manuscripts decorated for Leo by Attavante in both Florence and Rome.

19 For more information on Florentine convents, *see* G.Brucker, 'Monasteries, Friaries and Nunneries in Quattrocento Florence', in *Christianity and the Renaissance: Image and Religious Imagination in the Quattrocento*, eds. T.Verdon and J.Henderson (Syracuse, NY, 1990).

20 Levi d'Ancona, *Miniatura*, pp.8–9, 443.

21 *Ibid.*, pp.127, 136, 137, 274, 401.

22 S.Borghesi and L.Banchi, *Nuovi documenti per la storia dell'arte senese* (Siena, 1898), p.210.

23 On Lorenzo's relationship with Le Murate, *see* F.W.Kent, 'Lorenzo de' Medici, Madonna Scolastica Rondinelli and the politics of architectural patronage at the convent of Le Murate (1471–2)', a paper given at the 'Art and Patronage' conference held at the Hertziana in Rome in 1990.

24 P.Gauchat, *Hierarchia catholica medii et recentioris aevi*, iv (Münster, 1935), p.72, and R. Ritzler and P. Sefrin, *Hierarchia catholica medii et recentioris aevi*, 5 (Padua, 1952), p.72.

25 P.Conti in the *Dizionario biografico degli italiani*, xx (Rome, 1977), p.41 states that there is some uncertainty about the paternity of Lorenzo's 4 female children: Lisabetta, Cosa, Francesca, and Maria.

26 Florence, Archivio di stato (hereafter AS), Notarile antecosimiano G 9649 (Ser Giovanni di Marco da Romena), fol. 319r–v; 121 nuns are listed.

27 On this, *see* W.Bonds, 'Genoese Noblewomen and Gold Thread Manufacturing', *Medievalia et Humanistica*, 17 (1966) pp.79–81.

28 Florence, BN, MS II II 509, fol. 25r.

29 Florence, AS, Conventi Soppressi 78, filza 1, fols. 10r, 15v, 19r, 36v, 38v, 49v, 51v, 89v, 95r. *See also* E.Nunes, *Dom Frey Gomez, Abade de Florença, 1420–40*, i (Braga, 1963), p.309, and Levi d'Ancona, *Miniatura*, pp.102 and 443.

30 This story appears in the chronicle on fols 41v–42v, and is discussed in Kent, 'Lorenzo de' Medici'.

31 Florence, BN, MS II II 509, fol. 42r; the exact words used are 'scrittoini di assito'. A *scrittoio* can either be a rather elaborate desk with many compartments or a little study. Because these *scrittoini* were built into a loggia, it is more likely that they were not pieces of furniture but small study cubicles or compartments.

32 V.Primhak, 'Women in Religious Communities: The Benedictine Convents in Venice, 1400–1550', (unpubl. Ph.D. thesis, Univ. of London, 1991), p.92.

33 Florence, BN, MS II II 509, fol. 62r–v.

34 Florence, BN, MS II II 509, fol. 45r: 'stavono sempre circa otto scrivane di lettera formata, in qual virtù heron eccellentissime'.

35 For the various figures, *see* Lowe, 'Female Strategies', pp.211–12.

36 U.Niccolini, 'I minori osservanti di Monteripido e lo "scriptorium" delle Clarisse di Monteluce in Perugia nei secoli XV e XVI', *Picenum Seraphicum*, 8 (1971), pp.108–11.

37 A. de la Mare, 'New Research on Humanistic Scribes in Florence', in *Miniatura fiorentina del rinascimento, 1440–1525: un primo censimento*, ed. A.Garzelli, i (Florence, 1985), p.476.

38 *Il Duomo di Firenze*, ed. G.Poggi, ii (published posthumously with notes etc. and edited by M.Haines, Florence, 1988), pp.56–7.

39 J.Alexander and A. de la Mare, *The Italian Manuscripts in the Library of Major J.R.Abbey* (London, 1969), pp.159–60.

40 Private communication of 17 July 1989. *See Miniatura fiorentina del rinascimento, 1440–1525: un primo censimento*, ed. A.Garzelli, ii (Florence, 1985), tavole 1075–6.

41 Alexander and de la Mare, *The Italian manuscripts*, p.160.

42 Florence, AS, Conventi soppressi 79, filza 60, fol. 253r. *See* E.Borsook, 'Cults and Imagery at Sant'Ambrogio in Florence', *Mitteilungen des Kunsthistorischen Instituts in Florenz*, 25 (1981), pp.184 and 202.

43 *Ibid.*, p.202.

44 Florence, AS, Conventi soppressi 78, filza 80, Debitori e creditori, fol. 114v ('Mariano del Buono miniatore sta alle Murate') and Levi d'Ancona, *Miniatura*, p.180.

45 F.Carta, C.Cipolla, and C.Frati, *Monumenta palaeographica sacra. Atlante paleografico-artistico* (Turin, 1899), p.58.

46 *Ibid.*, p.58, quoting the opinion of Alessandro Gherardi.

47 Private communication of 17 July 1989.

48 *Ibid.*

49 The production of luxurious fabrics, both for church vestments and for wedding trousseaux, was a speciality of two Venetian convents, that of the Virgin, near S. Pietro di Castello, and that of S. Salvador. *See* R.Goy, *The House of Gold: Building a Palace in Medieval Venice* (Cambridge, 1992), pp.41–2.

50 Florence, BN, MS II II 509, fol. 45r: 'tessevono le camice, lane, tovaglie et altre biancherie…, arretavono e' grani di profumo et gittavono in forma le pitture di gesso'.

51 R.McKitterick, 'Nuns' Scriptoria in England and Francia in the Eighth Century', *Francia*, 19 (1992), p.32.

52 G.Savonarola, *Prediche sopra i salmi*, ed. V.Romano, i (Rome, 1969), pp.181–2, in a sermon of 10 May 1495 railed against most of the activities taking place at Le Murate, including book production. *See also* Lowe, 'Female Strategies', pp.216–18.

53 H.Schroeder, *Canons and Decrees of the Council of Trent* (Rockford, Ill., 1978), p.218, the 25th session of the Council, 3–4 Dec. 1563, ch. 1, concerning regulars and nuns.

54 *Immagini e azione riformatrice: le xilografie degli incunaboli savonaroliani nella Biblioteca nazionale di Firenze*, ed. E.Turelli (Florence, 1985), pp.117–18.

55 H.Bohatta, *Bibliographie der Breviere, 1501–1850* (Leipzig, 1937), p.91.

Part Three
IMAGES AND BOOKS FOR WOMEN

WOMEN AND THE BOOK

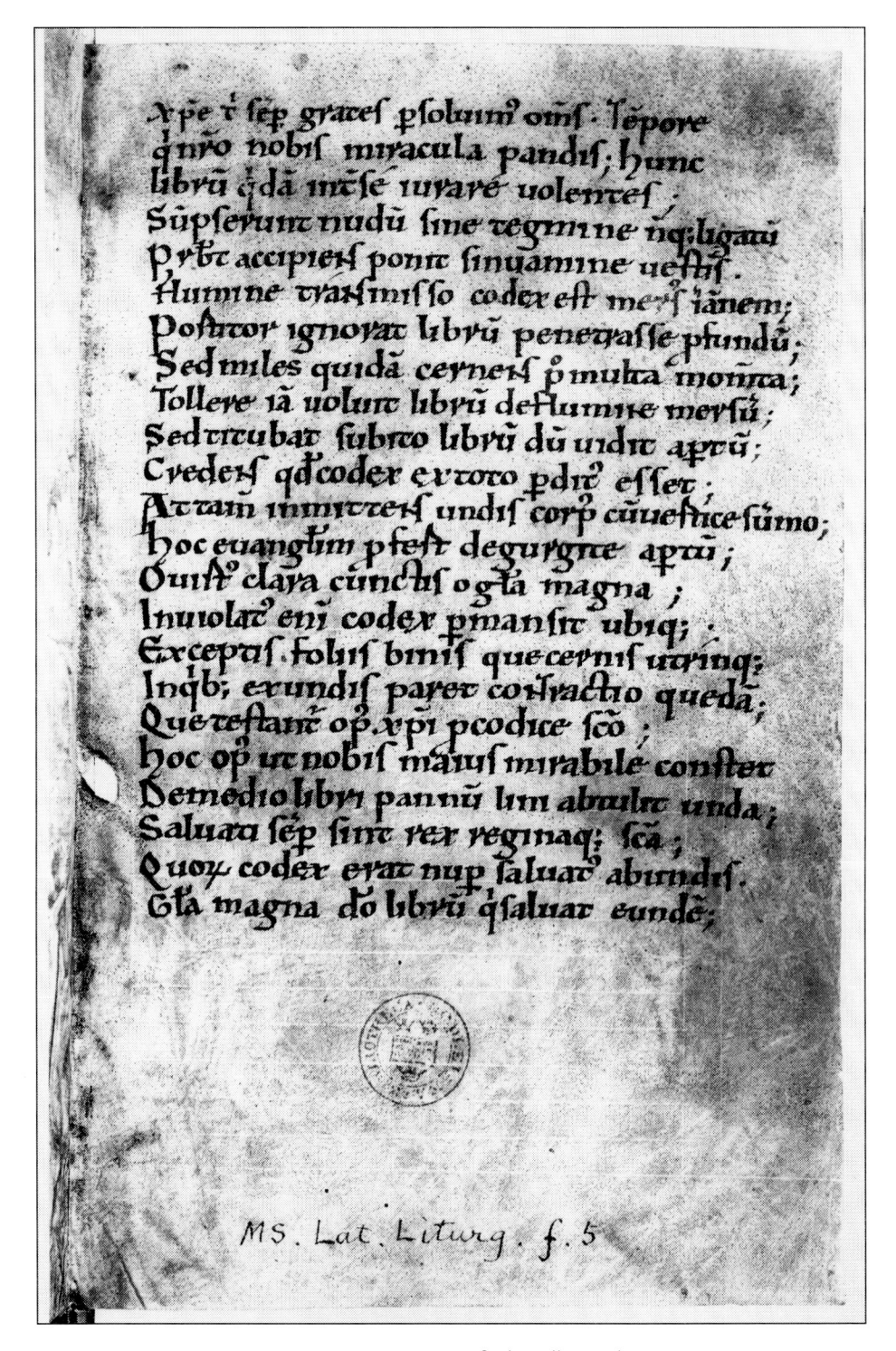

xpe ī sēp grates psolum' oīns · Tēpore
q̄ nr̄o nobis miracula pandis; hunc
librū q̄dā int̄ se iuuare uolentes;
Supserunt nudū sine regimine nq̄ligaui
p̄bt accipiens ponit sinuamine uestis.
Flumine transmisso codex est mers' ianem;
Positor ignorat librū penetrasse pfundū;
Sed miles quidā cernens p̄ multa monita;
Tollere iā uolunt librū de flumine mersū;
Sed titubat subito librū dū uidit aprū;
Credens qd' codex ex toto pdit' esset;
Attam inmitteris undis corp' cū uestice sūmo;
Hoc euanglim p̄ fest degurgite aprū;
Ouius° clara cunctis o glā magna ;
Inuiolat' enī codex pmansit ubiq;
Exceptis foliis binis que cernis utrinq;
In q̄b; ex undis paret contractio quedā;
Que restant op' xp̄i p codice sc̄o ;
Hoc op' ut nobis maius mirabile constet
De medio libri pannū lin abtulit unda;
Saluati sēp sint rex reginaq; sc̄a ;
Quoy codex erat nup saluat' abundis.
Glā magna d̄o librū q̄ saluat' eundē;

MS. Lat. Liturg. f. 5

FIG. 69 Verse inscription. Oxford, Bodleian Library,
Lat. liturg. fol. 5, fol. 2r.

148

CHAPTER NINE

The Gospels of Margaret of Scotland and the Literacy of an Eleventh-Century Queen

RICHARD GAMESON

Queen Margaret of Scotland (c.1046–93), the daughter of Edward the Ætheling and Agatha of Hungary and subsequently the wife of Malcolm III 'Canmore' of Scotland, was immortalized in a near-contemporary biography, probably written by her chaplain, Turgot.[1] One of the best-known tales in this work recounts how the Queen's favourite copy of the Gospels was dropped into a river and subsequently recovered unharmed. A gospel lectionary in the Bodleian Library bears an early-twelfth-century verse inscription which identifies it as the volume in question (FIG. 69),[2] and there is no reason to doubt the truth of this. We thus have two sources of information for the literary possessions of this eleventh-century queen; and considered in tandem, the anecdotes in the *Vita* and the surviving gospel lectionary offer complementary perspectives on the roles that her books and her reading performed.

What type of volume, then, was the favourite book of an eleventh-century queen? How is she likely to have used it? What form, according to her biographer, did her reading generally take? And what was its function? We shall begin our investigation of this material with the surviving manuscript; we will then turn to the evidence of the *Vita*; and we will conclude with some observations on Queen Margaret's literacy and on the general significance of her use of books.

The gospel lectionary of Queen Margaret (Oxford, Bodleian Library, MS Lat. liturg. fol. 5)[3] is a small codex which can be carried comfortably in one hand (PLATES 3–4; FIGS 70–72). It comprises thirty-eight medieval folios (of which the first and last were originally pastedowns)[4] and measures *c.*173 x 110 mm, with a written area of 148 x 78 mm.[5] Its dimensions are comparable to those of two other late Anglo-Saxon gospel lectionaries which are now in Cambridge and Warsaw;[6] and like them, it was presumably designed for private use by an individual reader.

The contents of the medieval volume are, in outline, as follows:

2r	Inscription recording the loss and recovery of the book
[2v–3r	Blank]
3v	Portrait of St Matthew
4r–13r	Readings from Matthew's gospel

149

13v	Portrait of St Mark
14r–20v	Readings from Mark's gospel
[21r	Blank]
21v	Portrait of St Luke
22r–29v	Readings from Luke's gospel
[30r	Blank]
30v	Portrait of St John
31r–37r	Readings from John's gospel
[37v–38	Blank].

Inscriptions relating to the post-medieval ownership of the volume were added to fols 1v, 2r, 3r, 30r, and 38v.[7]

The actual gospel texts included and their subject matter are given below. In a couple of cases, the extracts are contiguous; the divisions that are shown here are those marked in the book itself. I supply in parentheses the occasion for which the reading was liturgically appropriate.[8]

Matthew

1:1–21	Genealogy [24 December]
2:1–12	The Magi [Epiphany]
3:13–17	The Baptism [Epiphany]
4:1–11	Temptation [Quadragesima]
4:18–22	Calling of Apostles [30 November: St Andrew]
20:17–19	Jesus predicts his death [22 November: St Cecilia]
26:2–28: 7	Passion [Easter]
28:16–20	Post-resurrection commission to Apostles [Feria vi after Easter]

Mark

1:1–8	John the Baptist
6:17–29	Death of John the Baptist [30 August]
14:1–15: 46	Passion
16:1–7	Maries and Salome at the tomb [10th Sunday after Pentecost]
16:14–20	Post-resurrection appearances [Ascension]

Luke

1:1–4	Preface to Theophilus
1:26–38	Annunciation [25 March]
2:1–14	Nativity
2:21	Circumcision [1 January]
2:22–32	Symeon [2 February]
10:38–42	Mary and Martha [15 August: Blessed Virgin Mary]
22:1–23: 53	Passion
24:1–12	Maries and Peter at the Tomb

John

1:1–14	*In principio* [25 December]
14:23–31	Christ's prophecy of his departure and return; his promise of peace [Pentecost]
17:1–11	Christ as witness to men [Vigil for Ascension]
18:1–19: 42	Passion
20:1–9	Mary, John, and Peter at the tomb.

FIG. 70 Mark. Oxford, Bodleian Library, Lat. liturg. fol. 5, fols 13v–14r.

There are four main observations to make about the content. First and most fundamental, the readings are arranged following their order in the Gospels and not in a liturgical sequence. Thus this lectionary is conceived according to the model of a gospel book and not a pericopes book – that is a volume of gospel readings for the liturgical year following its calendar order. Given this fact, it appears mildly anomalous that each passage is preceded by a heading, stating from which gospel it comes – something appropriate to a pericopes book[9] and seemingly out of place in a volume arranged by gospel. Be that as it may, the headings do help the reader to navigate around the book (functioning like running headings); moreover, their inclusion reflects the fact that the individual passages were designed to be read independently, and not continuously and sequentially.

Secondly, although there is inevitably common ground between the content of Margaret's volume and that of the other Anglo-Saxon gospel lectionaries,[10] overall the correspondences are not particularly close. Anglo-Saxon gospel lectionaries varied appreciably in the amount of text they included, not to mention the way in which they arranged them. In terms of the amount of text, there is a sliding scale. One extreme is represented by a couple of the gospel books associated with Judith of Flanders, which are virtually complete;[11] in the 'middle' there is the Hereford gospel lectionary, which includes substantial extracts from each gospel;[12] while at the other extreme we have Margaret's volume

151

which omits more than it includes. What such comparisons underline above all is that the Queen's book was highly selective, and it has only a small number of readings (twenty-six in total).

Thirdly, while the particular group of extracts in Margaret's manuscript could conceivably have been read as a modest synopsis of the Gospels, the absence of any parables or miracle stories, and the lack of key texts like the beatitudes, underlines the fact that this was not its rationale. The selection does, however, include readings for all the main christological and Marian feast-days of the church year, highlighting the fact that the main character of the text was indeed liturgical. Yet as such, far from being comprehensive, it focused on the most important and universal feasts – this was hardly a service book for a cleric. There are two main exceptions to the concentration on 'high days', namely the readings for 22 and 30 November. Why were lections included for the feasts of St Cecilia and St Andrew? If perchance the book was made for a woman with Scottish connections, the inclusion of readings for both occasions would be explicable. It should, however, be said that the likely age of the codex (discussed below) is not easily reconciled with the attractive theory that Margaret herself was the figure in question.

Fourthly, in addition to the widely used liturgical readings, the book also contains the start of all four gospels, and the four passion narratives in their entirety. These texts underline the hybrid character of the manuscript. The importance of the passion narratives (which were almost invariably highlighted in gospel books by means of gold initials or other graphic devices) hardly requires explanation. It is, however, worth noting that because of their length, and given the brevity of the other readings, they occupy the greater part of the volume. In this respect Margaret's gospel lectionary is reminiscent of Anglo-Saxon prayer-books such as the Books of Nunnaminster and Cerne,[13] in which the biblical passion-narratives are also the longest single texts. The presence of all four incipits in the manuscript attests to the wish to keep the collection of texts firmly within the framework of a gospel book. If the volume was to be organized following the biblical order and not a liturgical one, and was to evoke a gospel book and not a pericopes book, all four incipits were essential; and their inclusion permitted the traditional decorative format of evangelist portrait facing incipit initial at four places in the manuscript.[14]

In sum, this little volume combines elements of a gospel book, a liturgical reading book, and a private prayer-book – all within a brief compass. Furthermore, because it was conceived according to the general schema of a gospel book, it had the additional resonances peculiar to such volumes. And these were, in fact, put to use, as we shall see.

Before we leave the text, two other aspects deserve brief mention, namely its character and the accuracy with which it was copied. The text is the Vulgate, with a fair number of 'Italian' and 'Alcuinian' readings. I have not collated it against other late Anglo-Saxon gospel books;[15] however, I provide in Appendix 2 a full list of the variant readings, which should facilitate such comparison in due course. The scribe was reasonably careful in his transcription, and himself corrected – via erasure and re-writing – most of the errors he had made. The number of mistakes that remained uncorrected is small.[16]

FIG. 71 Luke. Oxford, Bodleian Library, Lat. liturg. fol. 5, fols 21v–22r.

The text was entirely the work of a single scribe, who wrote an English Caroline minuscule of modest quality (*see* FIG. 72). The hand is easy to read, but it is not especially calligraphic. The script is of a generous size in relation to the dimensions of the book,[17] and its general proportions are quite square.[18] At the same time, however, the overall impression is a little crowded, and the writing is slightly irregular, since the scribe did not always adhere closely to the ruled lines, and was not adroit either at making his letters the same height, or at aligning vertical strokes at a consistent angle. The rough texture of some of the hair sides of the parchment sometimes exacerbated his propensity to irregularity. The text is clearly punctuated, with medial points used for pauses within sense units, while high points and *punctus elevati* indicate the ends of sentences. High points were also used to introduce reported speech. Abbreviation is restrained: 'm's are contracted or suspended, the ampersand regularly replaces *et*, and the standard sigla are deployed for *orum, per, pro*, and *que*. Otherwise, only easily construable elements of words were abbreviated. The main point that emerges here is that ease of legibility was clearly a priority: although his hand was not of the highest quality, the scribe did his best to make the text as accessible as possible.

What is the date of the script? One would most naturally assign it to the mid-eleventh century.[19] If the letter-forms themselves favour earlier rather than later within this period, the circumstance that the book was probably not produced in one of the better-known centres counsels against interpreting the formal evidence too rigidly. Palaeographically a date anywhere between c.1030 and c.1070 is possible.

The visual articulation of the text presents a similar picture: a broad range of graphic devices was deployed to subdivide the text and enhance its legibility. A form of rustic capitals was used to mark the beginnings of sentences,[20] gold being employed to distinguish passages of direct speech by Christ. Each lection was introduced by an enlarged gold initial in the margin, and preceded by a heading written in red uncials,[21] the passion narratives being signalled by titles in golden rustic capitals (*see* FIG. 72).[22] The incipit of each gospel was, naturally, marked by the most impressive visual accent: a large gold initial plus one or two lines of monumental gold capitals,[23] followed by one or more lines of gold rustics and preceded by rubric in red uncials (*see* FIGS 70, 71, and PLATE 4).[24] The only decorated initial in the manuscript is the 'L' of Matthew's gospel (which is rendered in an Anglo-Saxon version of the Franco-Saxon style[25]), thus giving an additional emphasis to the start of the text as a whole (PLATE 3). The scribe was evidently familiar with the range of contemporary display scripts and, although his realization of them was slightly gauche, he deployed them effectively to make the text as accessible as possible.

The decoration comprises four evangelist portraits, one prefacing each set of gospel extracts (PLATES 3 and 4; FIGS 70, 71). The portraits are framed by simple gold and coloured bars, and the incipits on the facing rectos are presented in matching borders.[26] Although late Anglo-Saxon manuscript art is renowned for its exuberant foliate frames, a fair number of decorated books do have plain ones (particularly those produced towards the middle of the eleventh century),[27] so that this is not in itself a distinguishing feature.

The images are competently drawn, and the evangelists are slightly corpulent men, wearing swirling robes with agitated hemlines. Whereas the figures themselves and their 'props' were fully painted, the backgrounds were left as light or bare parchment, a common approach in late Anglo-Saxon art.[28] The palette was restricted to orange-red, blue, olive-green, and yellow, plus white and gold. The paint was sensitively applied in washes of varying intensity to suggest form and drapery folds, highlights being added in white and occasionally yellow.[29] The gold, which was used in ink, not leaf form, was applied last, and overlaps the other colours. Although it was used for different details in the four images, the book (or scroll) in which the evangelist writes is always golden.[30] Stylistically the images look slightly earlier than the script, and would fit comfortably in the second quarter of the eleventh century.

The portraits are iconographically simple,[31] and as they lack symbols, specific identity is provided only by a titulus in rustic capitals.[32] Nevertheless, the artist has carefully differentiated the four figures. Matthew and Mark, for example, are framed by pulled-back curtains, while Luke and John appear under an arch with architectural pinnacles. Matthew and Luke are beardless and seated in profile, Mark and John are bearded and frontal. Matthew writes in an open book on a lectern, Mark holds a closed one, Luke clutches a scroll, and John writes in a book that is perched on his knee. Matthew and Mark sit on low-backed thrones, and John on a high-backed one, while Luke is seated on a stool. Matthew and Mark have foliate-topped lecterns (whose feet and stems are of a different design), Luke has a draped

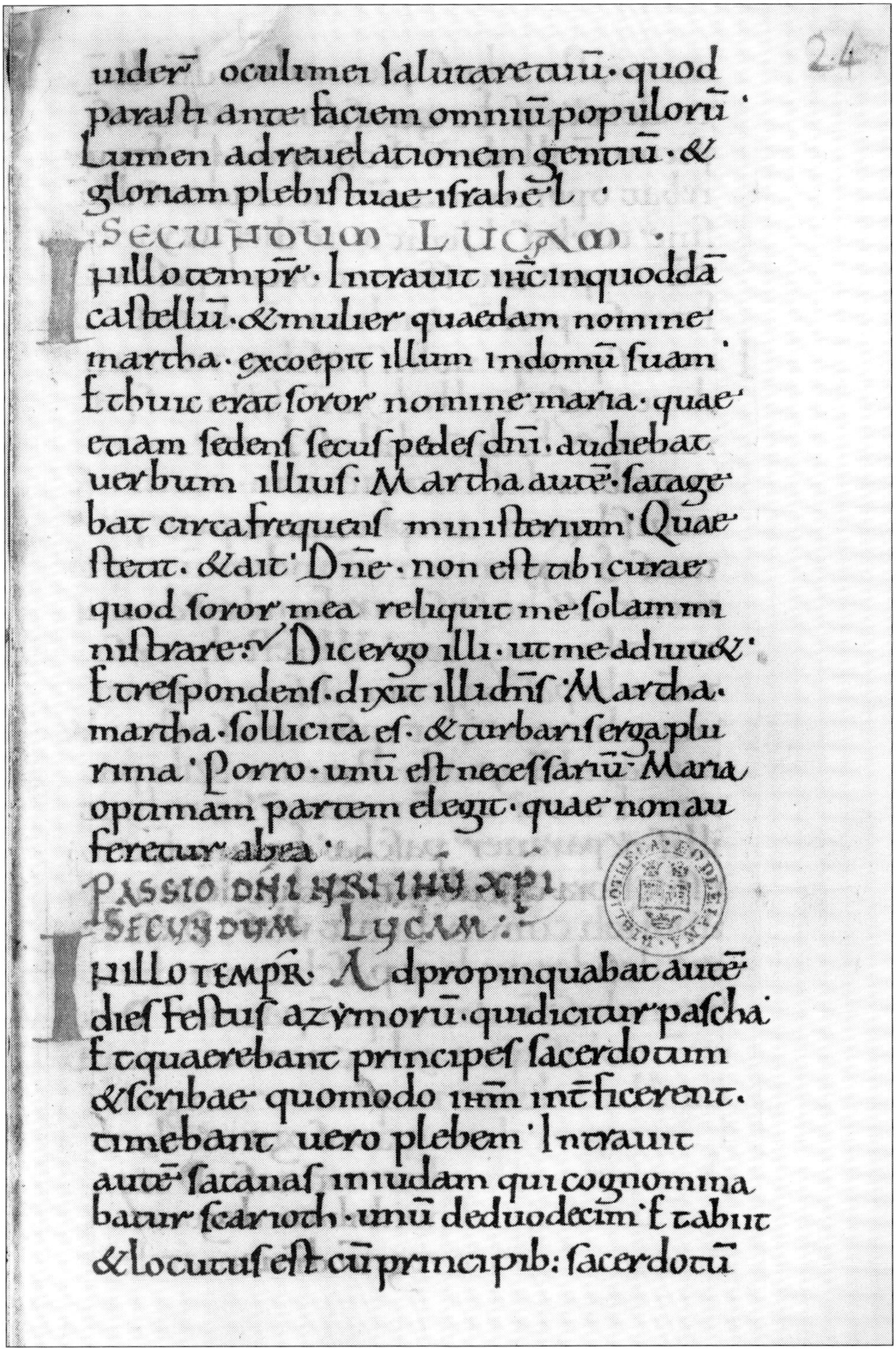

uiderūt oculi mei salutare tuū · quod
parasti ante faciem omniū populorū ·
Lumen ad reuelationem gentiū · &
gloriam plebis tuae israhel ·

SECUNDUM LUCAM ·

In illo tempr̄ · Intrauit ihc in quoddā
castellū · & mulier quaedam nomine
martha · excoepit illum in domū suam ·
Et huic erat soror nomine maria · quae
etiam sedens secus pedes dn̄i · audiebat
uerbum illius · Martha aūt · satage
bat circa frequens ministerium · Quae
stetit · & ait · Dn̄e · non est tibi curae
quod soror mea reliquit me solam mi
nistrare? · Dic ergo illi · ut me adiuuet ·
Et respondens · dixit illi dn̄s · Martha ·
martha · sollicita es · & turbaris erga plu
rima · Porro · unū est necessariū · Maria
optimam partem elegit · quae non au
feretur ab ea ·

PASSIO DN̄I NR̄I IHŪ XP̄I
SECUNDUM LUCAM :

In illo tempr̄ · Adpropinquabat autē
dies festus azymorū · qui dicitur pascha ·
Et quaerebant principes sacerdotum
& scribae · quomodo ihm interficerent ·
timebant uero plebem · Intrauit
autē satanas in iudam qui cognomina
batur scarioth · unū de duodecim · Et abiit
& locutus est cū principib; sacerdotū

FIG. 72 Pericopes from Luke. Oxford, Bodleian Library, Lat. liturg. fol. 5, fol. 24r.

lectern, John has none.[33] The artist contrived to engineer the maximum amount of variation with the smallest number of elements; and it is in this context that the depiction of Luke as left-handed – an extremely rare phenomenon – is to be understood.[34]

The artist was evidently familiar with the general repertoire of late Anglo-Saxon manuscript art, but there is nothing in his work to link him to one particular centre. The principal contributions that the evangelist portraits make to the volume are to enhance its beauty, to stress its affinity to a gospel book, and to illustrate the inspired authorship of the readings. These decorated openings are very pretty, and because of the brevity of the text one occurs approximately every nine folios, giving the illusion that the volume is quite heavily illuminated.

Of the various points that have emerged from our brief examination of this manuscript, three deserve to be stressed above all. First, in terms of size and content, the volume was eminently suitable for use by a private individual; and it was arguably more appropriate for a lay person than for a cleric. The presentation of the text which, as we have seen, is marked by clarity and simplicity, was designed to afford its user as much help as possible. This is a small, easy-to-use selection of well-known texts.

Secondly, the probable date range for the volume's production, c.1030 to 1070, casts doubt on whether Margaret was the original owner. The book is unlikely to have been written for Margaret when she was in Scotland; it could have been written for her while she was in England (i.e. between c.1058 and 1066/8); but equally it might not have been written for her at all. It is quite possible that the volume was actually made for someone else, and subsequently came into her possession, perhaps as a gift.

Thirdly, despite its charm and notwithstanding the gold, this is hardly a deluxe book. It is modestly written and attractively but not opulently decorated. It is less luxurious, for instance, than the broadly contemporary Hereford gospel lectionary; and it is considerably less handsome than the Anglo-Saxon gospel books owned by Countess Judith of Flanders,[35] or the one that Ealdorman Ælfgar of Mercia gave to Saint Remi at Rheims in the mid-eleventh century.[36] Margaret may have been a queen, but her favourite copy of the gospels was a modest one. Whether this tells us more about Scotland, Margaret, or the manuscript itself is a moot point. There is likely to have been a dearth of fine books that would appeal to Anglo-Saxon royalty in late-eleventh-century Scotland; and as a refugee Margaret may have had limited opportunity for acquiring more splendid ones.[37] On the other hand, this little codex may have had great sentimental value for her; and we are specifically told that its miraculous deliverance from the river enhanced its worth in her eyes. The gauche illuminations in the otherwise deluxe Prayer Book of Otto III (an emperor who also owned some undeniably fabulous books) make the point that even one of the wealthiest patrons could have surprisingly low-quality work in a volume designed for his private use.[38] Similarly, we know that the copy of Anselm's Prayers and Meditations owned by Princess Adelaide, the daughter of William the Conqueror, was unadorned and relatively humble; however, it is still likely to have been valued highly because it had been presented to her by the author himself.[39] The circumstances behind Margaret's love of her little gospel lectionary are now irrecoverable; but it is possible that the very simplicity of the manuscript and the fact that it was small and easy to carry around were part of its appeal.

We turn now to the evidence of Margaret's biography. The life of the Queen was probably written by Turgot between 1104 and 1107, that is just over a decade after her death, and it was dedicated to her daughter, Matilda, the wife of King Henry I of England.[40] Turgot was Prior of Durham during the period in question, subsequently becoming Bishop of St Andrew's (1109–15). The work comprises thirteen chapters which fall into four main sections. Their general subject matter may be summarized as follows: 1. (chaps. 1–5) Margaret's background, family circumstances, and character; 2. (chaps. 6–8) her role in the Scottish state and church; 3. (chaps. 9–11) her personal spirituality and its practical expressions; and 4. (chaps. 12–13) her death and the events surrounding it. The lack of fabulous elements in the Vita and, correspondingly, its superficially straightforward nature have often been remarked upon; this does not, however, mean that the work is not stylized and carefully crafted. Turgot was writing a *speculum regale*; moreover, he wanted to depict Margaret as a saint and, lacking the requisite portents and healings, he made the best of the resources that were available to him for doing so. Books are among the devices he deployed, and this is of considerable interest to us. The inclusion in this short work of no fewer than three passages mentioning books might seem to imply that Margaret was a particularly literate woman. This, however, would be to go beyond the evidence, or at least to misread it. It is worth bearing in mind that the dedicatee, Matilda, was herself a cultured patron of learning whom such material would interest; but the key point is that all three passages have more to do with sanctity than with literacy, and they reflect the firm associations of reading with spirituality.

The first such passage appears at the start of 'Section 2'. Turgot stresses that the Queen's good judgement arose from her knowledge of scripture.[41] 'Amidst the bustle of litigation,' he states, 'amidst the manifold cares of state, she continued to devote herself with admirable zeal to divine reading,' later adding that she urged him to acquire sacred volumes for her. At one level, Turgot here paints a picture of the Queen as an avid reader and book collector. From the point of view of cultural history, it is a shame that he did not provide fuller details of the volumes in question and the methods he employed to acquire them; however, even if he were not exaggerating, this was irrelevant to his purpose. The principal function of the allusion was to stress the Queen's spirituality. The language Turgot used shows that he was at pains to underline this point: it is divine writings that she studied; it is sacred volumes she pursued; and she did so with a religious earnestness. No doubt Margaret did read scripture; however, the impact of this information in the context of the Vita arises not from any implications of literacy and scholarship, but rather from the hagiographic resonances of reading. Margaret's devotion to reading shows that she had the characteristics of the good Christians adumbrated by influential writers such as John Cassian[42] and Caesarius of Arles. The latter, in a letter to his sister, described the virtues of such reading with particularly feminine imagery: the soul 'should perpetually draw the water of salvation from the fountains of divine scripture – that water assuredly about which the Lord states, "Whoever believes in me, rivers of living water shall flow from his innermost self" [John 7:

38]. The holy soul should also perpetually strive to embellish itself with the flowers of paradise, that is with the meaning of the holy scriptures. From these it should continuously hang precious pearls from its ears ...'.[43] Margaret's reading thus represented practical spirituality. At the same time, it provided an antidote to the worldliness that was an inevitable part of her royal life. The benefits of reading in this respect were underlined, *inter alios*, by Isidore of Seville (d. 636), being repeated in the ninth century by Smaragdus of Saint-Mihiel: 'The reading of the holy scriptures confers a twin gift: on the one hand it improves the understanding of the mind; on the other, it leads the man who has been drawn away from the vanities of the world to the love of God.'[44] The point is exemplified in other saints' lives, such as that of Wulfstan of Worcester (d. 1095),[45] where reading is depicted as a key device for enabling the holy man to withdraw from the world.

The allusion to Margaret's use of books carried yet further resonances. The act of such reading could in itself imply spiritual reward, as Jerome declared: 'He who applies himself assiduously to reading in the present life assuredly works hard, but afterwards he shall be rewarded, since he shall come to pluck sweet fruit from the bitter seed of letters. ... Blessed is the man who, reading divine scripture, turns words into deeds.'[46] This, of course, is precisely what Margaret did. Moreover, her eminent suitability for ruling is underpinned by her continuous perusal of scripture. Again, other saints' lives, such as that of Maiolus of Cluny (abbot 954–94), demonstrate the point. Maiolus, we are told, 'ruled himself and others by the reading of sacred scripture. As one is wont to do by looking in a mirror, so he by divine reading meditated on his inner life .... From this he was equipped to put his own life in order, and to teach and correct those committed to him.'[47] Thus, while there is no reason to doubt that Margaret did collect books and read them, this is not why Turgot tells of it; he does so because it has highly potent, spiritual overtones.

The second incident in Margaret's Vita which involves books follows shortly afterwards.[48] It appears as the culmination of a passage concerned with how Margaret civilized her warrior husband, King Malcolm. We are told that the king learned devotional practices from her, and adopted her standards: 'Whatever she rejected, he also rejected; whatever she loved, he loved through his love of her love.' This is then illustrated by his attitude to her books: 'Thus [Malcolm], although illiterate, would often leaf through and gaze upon the books that she was accustomed to use for prayer and reading; and whenever he gathered from the queen that one of them was particularly dear to her, he too considered it as particularly precious, kissing it and often touching it. Sometimes he even summoned a goldsmith and ordered him to adorn that volume with gold and gems; and when it had been ornamented, the King himself used to carry the book to the Queen as a token of his devotion.'

For the historian of manuscripts this is a fascinating record of how and why a group of books were adorned with precious bindings; and for the student of literacy it presents an interesting contrast between the literate female and the illiterate male. Once again, however, such insights are incidental to the purpose of the story. As hagiography within the context of the Vita, the episode is designed to demonstrate the intellectual and spiritual superiority of the Queen, simultaneously underlining her role in educating and elevating her husband.

Malcolm's human love for Margaret leads him to honour the objects of her spiritual love; she is the instrument through which he accepts civilization and learns to honour the Holy Word. In addition, the story depicts Margaret as the superior of the two by virtue of her Christian literacy, while the King is portrayed in the role of her servant, carrying the books to her.

The passage is a verbal counterpart of the various early medieval images of royal or noble couples presenting or receiving books, and it deserves to be considered alongside them. Viewed in this context, the most remarkable aspect of the 'depiction' in the Vita, namely the fact that the woman is the dominant party, appears even more striking. Women rarely feature in such presentation images before the Ottonian period;[49] and when they do subsequently appear as part of a couple, it is invariably the male that receives the greatest emphasis. An outstanding eleventh-century example of the phenomenon, where a standing woman offers a book to an enthroned man, is the image of Matilda of Lotharingia presenting a copy of the *Ordo Romanus* to King Mieszko II of Poland.[50] This, however, is an extreme case resulting from unusual circumstances, and the figures involved were not husband and wife. The early eleventh-century pericopes books of Saint-Mihiel, which was commissioned by a certain Irmengarde for the soul of her dead husband, provides a more subtle and typical example.[51] Although Irmengarde is prominently named in the accompanying inscription, the dedication miniature shows Werner and Irmengarde presenting the book together, and it is Werner who takes the lead and actually bears the book, while his wife follows, supporting his arm. In the 1045/6 Speyer Gospels of Henry III both the Emperor and his wife, Agnes, are shown beside the Virgin Mary; however, it is Henry who is stressed visually, who is the subject of the accompanying inscription, and who is shown as the donor of the manuscript.[52] Similarly, in the same emperor's Goslar Gospels (1050/6)[53] there is a full page image of Christ crowning Henry and Agnes (who are depicted as near-equals),[54] but it is Henry alone who is shown presenting the manuscript to Simon and Jude, the patron saints of Goslar, on the facing page. A gospel book dated 1067 provides a Byzantine example: Theodore Gabras is depicted standing beside Christ (whose hand is on the governor of Trebizond's head), while Gabras's wife, Eirene, appears on the facing recto, being presented to Christ by the Virgin Mary.[55] The prayer-book of Fernando and Sancha of Leon (1055) provides a complementary Spanish case.[56] We know from the colophon that it was the Queen who commissioned the book, yet the prefatory image shows the King receiving the volume from the scribe or artist at the Queen's behest.

In fact, the point holds good in general. Early medieval images that depict married couples, such as the Milan ivory of Otto II and Theophanu,[57] the Basle Altar[58] and the Pericopes Book[59] of Henry II (and Cunigunde), and the New Minster Liber Vitae (with Cnut and Ælfgifu),[60] almost invariably emphasize the man as opposed to the woman.[61] At its most blatant, the pre-eminence of the male is signalled by an inscription; at its most subtle, the figures appear virtually equal, but it is the man who is at Christ's right hand. The incident in the Vita of Queen Margaret is a remarkable instance where the reverse is the case. Now, this is her biography and not Malcolm's, so we would expect to find the Queen depicted in a particularly favourable light. We may indeed reasonably doubt whether Malcolm, who had been the protégé of Edward the Confessor, was the rough simpleton that Turgot implies, and other sources depict him in a rather different light.[62] Nevertheless, a key point behind the 'inversion' is surely Christianity: Margaret is elevated by her faith, and to that extent the King is naturally subservient to her. Significantly, the closest visual parallels for the described scene are in fact those images where an important male figure is shown presenting a book to the Virgin Mary, for instance Bishop Bernward of Hildesheim in his 'Precious Gospels' of c.1015.[63]

The final mention of books comes at the end of the third section of the Vita, following the accounts of the Queen's good works. Turgot admits, disingenuously, that he has no record of any miracles performed by Margaret which would prove she was a saint; however, he knows of one incident which provides an equivalent demonstration of the holiness of her life. The story runs as follows.[64]

Margaret had a favourite copy of the gospels, 'adorned with gems and gold, in which painting mixed with gold beautified the images of the four evangelists, and each capital letter glowed all over with gold'. One day, unfortunately, someone who was bearing the book carelessly tucked into his robe unwittingly let it tumble into a stream. It was eventually found lying open at the bottom of the river. 'Its leaves had been stirred unceasingly by the flow of the water, and the little pieces of silk which had covered the gold letters lest they should be dimmed by contact with the leaves, were swept away by the force of the current.' Nevertheless, when it was recovered, the codex was found to be virtually undamaged, and thereafter Margaret valued it more highly than ever. Turgot concludes, 'Whatever others may see and deduce, I do not doubt that this was a sign from the Lord because of his love for our revered Queen.'

The late eleventh-century inscription which identifies Lat. liturg. fol. 5 as the volume in question provides a couple of supplementary details.[65] It records that on the day in question the book was being transported so that an oath could be sworn upon it; and that when it was recovered from the water, it was undamaged except for the endleaves, which had cockled. In this version it is a linen sheet that is lost, and not silk covers.

This is a fascinating, not to mention charming, story with a wealth of interesting information. We learn, for instance, that such a book could be used for sacring oaths; we are told that originally it had a precious binding; and we discover that fabric was inserted between the leaves to protect the golden letters. Conversely, we note that, despite its importance, the volume was carelessly treated – albeit not by its owner herself. In addition, we can see that the Queen's biographer exaggerated slightly the opulence of the volume for hagiographical effect. Lat. liturg. fol. 5 is not the deluxe book that Turgot would have his reader believe.

Queen Margaret's gospel lectionary is by no means the only early medieval manuscript which is recorded to have survived a dunking. Symeon of Durham, for example, claimed that the same had happened to the Lindisfarne Gospels.[66] It was, he maintained, lost overboard when a tempest overwhelmed the ship that was misguidedly trying to take St Cuthbert's body to Ireland in the late ninth century. After three days, the manuscript was washed up unharmed, Cuthbert himself alerting one of the community to its reappearance. According to Muirchu's seventh-century Life of St Patrick, the 'Apostle of Ireland' was confident that his books would emerge unscathed when King Loegaire ordered him and a wizard to cast their books into water and fire as a means of deciding between the rival religions.[67] Books written by St Columba (c.521–97) could likewise survive immersion unharmed, according to his biographer Adomnan (d. 704), by virtue of the sanctity of the scribe.[68] Now, whereas there is no reason to doubt that Queen Margaret's gospel lectionary did indeed fall into a river, these other tales are highly doubtful. Nevertheless, they remain immensely important in the present context since they underline the magical and saintly qualities of a book which could emerge from water unscathed. The preservation of a manuscript in such circumstances reflected not only the holiness of the text it contained, but also the spirituality of the scribe or owner. In addition, the fact of its 'resurrection' gave it a Christ-like sacrality.

The information about the sheets that covered the golden letters in Margaret's book – an interesting practical detail to the modern reader – was doubtless included to underline the miraculous status of the holy text itself. These slips, which are not part of the sacred word, go to oblivion; the holy book itself, by contrast, is preserved. The wording of the verse inscription makes this point very clearly: 'In order that this work should be manifested to us as even more miraculous/the water washed away the sheet of linen from the middle of the book.' Turgot's story thus cleverly stressed the holiness of Queen Margaret in several ways: it was she she who owned and cherished this sacred volume, protecting its beauty with silk slips; and it was because of her great virtues that it survived its misfortune. He inserted the tale because he had no miracles that were more fantastic to relate (a preamble, incidentally, which subtly underlines its credibility); be that as it may, it serves its purpose admirably, providing clear supernatural proof of the extraordinary sanctity of the queen.

We have examined Margaret's gospel lectionary, and studied the written record of her interaction with books. In conclusion let us consider the nature of her literacy and its general implications. There are three main points I wish to make here.

First, because of the biography and the gospel lectionary, Margaret's reading is fairly well documented by eleventh-century standards. Nevertheless, it should be stressed that our knowledge of the Queen's literacy remains scanty and ambiguous. It is clear that she owned books, and there can be no doubt, surely, that she was personally literate. Yet it is worth remembering that we know next to nothing about her education; we have little way of knowing how proficient she was at reading, how much time she devoted to it, nor how important a role literacy played in her life as a whole. Our sources are not concerned to supply this information. The only one of Margaret's books we possess was possibly not written for her; it contained texts which will have been very familiar; it was written in such a way as to make the task of using it as easy as possible; and she made no additions to it. Whether the other volumes Turgot says she sought to acquire were fundamentally different is an open question. The only other manuscript associated with her that is in any sense described, a *textus argenteus* which she gave to Durham (presumably a gospel book or service book), was probably not.[69] Turgot's general allusions to the Queen's reading habits are deliberately suggestive, but (equally deliberately perhaps) very vague. Not a single text is specified; 'divine reading' could simply mean a selection of biblical books; and her entire 'collection' might have been restricted to biblical and liturgical volumes. The only other evidence we have for Margaret's literacy is a letter addressed to the Queen by Lanfranc which alludes to a (lost) letter he had received from her,[70] and it is open to doubt whether she will have drafted this personally. I am not, of course, trying to minimize Margaret's reading, but rather to put it in perspective. Given how little we really know about it, we should be very cautious in our use of it.

This leads on to the second point, which is that much the same holds good for early-medieval lay women in general. Students of early medieval history are accustomed to working with inadequate source material and are adept at circumnavigating the difficulties this poses; however, the problems involved in assessing reading and literacy are particularly fierce, and require exceptionally careful handling. Scholarship has grown increasingly sophisticated, and approaches to these issues have become more oblique and sensitive.[71] There is a widening awareness of the variety of ways in which people could interact with books and writing besides reading them personally. Careful attempts are made to define and distinguish between degrees and forms of literacy, and to judge 'pragmatic' literacy from the use of documents and from general levels of bureaucracy. This last tack has been proving fruitful: the sophistication of some early-medieval record-keeping provides a helpful index of functional literacy, attesting to a general awareness of the values and uses of writing – not to mention providing lists of names of those involved. We should not, however, lose sight of the contrasts between books and documents. The degree of literacy required to use many documents is different from that needed to read most books; moreover, both the nature of the reading process itself and the symbolism and resonances of the two media are very different. This is a theme to which we shall return. Equally important in the present context is the fact that women are under-represented in the surviving documentary sample. Books remain the cornerstone of evaluating early-medieval female literacy, and Queen Margaret and women like her are, *faute de mieux*, central to such debates.

By diligent investigation of extant manuscripts, and by scouring the surviving written sources, it is possible to 'excavate' a considerable number of early-medieval women who used and interacted with books, some of them undoubtedly in secular society. As outstanding examples of this latter class one thinks of the Bavarian princess Theudelinde (d. 628), who received a gospel book and a copy of the *Dialogi* from Gregory the Great himself;[72] of Ragyndrudis, the eighth-century woman who commissioned the codex that is named after her;[73] of the various women who received books from the wills of Duke Eberhard of Friuli[74] and Eccard of Mâcon[75] in the ninth century; and of Hedwig of Swabia, the niece of Otto I who studied Virgil and gave a manuscript of Horace and various other books to Saint Gallen,[76] and of the Anglo-Saxon Wynflæd, who willed her books to another woman called Æthelflæd, in the tenth century;[77] while in the eleventh and early twelfth centuries we find a few important laywomen, like Emma of Normandy, Judith of Flanders, and Matilda of Tuscany, who were commemorated visually in books they owned.[78] Armed with such examples and with general information about the education of noble women, scanty though it may be, it is possible to mount arguments about issues such as the diffusion of literacy in lay society and the role of women in its transmission; about the type of books that women owned and donated, and even about possible distinctions between the degrees of male and female literacy. Yet firm conclusions remain elusive. Possession of books is not a reliable guide to literacy. The case of Malcolm 'Canmore' demonstrates the point. It is sobering to reflect that if the King of Scotland's embellishing of manuscripts had been recorded in an inventory or a chronicle rather than in the specific words of Turgot, he would probably appear as a donor and user of them, and not as an illiterate. Thus while the available evidence shows beyond a shadow of doubt that certain early-medieval laywomen lived in a fairly cultured environment where books were available, and that some of them certainly used them, it is a slender basis for debating the niceties of female lay literacy. This may seem a pessimistic conclusion, but it is a necessary corrective in the face of a burgeoning industry.

The evidence does, however, show some things very clearly, and this is my third and final point. There is a dichotomy between what early-medieval sources tell us about books and how modern scholarship tends to use that information. In our concern for the type of themes outlined above – interesting though they may be to us – we can overlook the central message of the contemporary records. What does Turgot really tell us about Margaret's literacy? As we have seen, he portrays reading as part of Margaret's day-to-day regime, not because it was a useful skill in the abstract, but specifically because it was a devotional activity. We should also note that it is only books, and not documents, which feature in his account. Such a slant reflects the hagiographical and hortatory nature of the work Turgot was writing; but this does not vitiate his view, and it is certainly not an argument for ignoring it – particularly given that the one surviving manuscript associated with the Queen is wholly in accord with it.

Although early-medieval books could, of course, be a reflection of literacy, learning, and status, most of them were first and foremost a function of Christianity. This was inevitable, given that the Church had enjoyed a near-monopoly of book production, the transmission of texts, and the composition of new works since the time of Cassiodorus (d. c.580).[79] There were some 'secular' volumes in lay hands – Eberhard of Friuli had a selection – but, nevertheless, lay book collections, including Eberhard's, were dominated by ecclesiastical writings and service-books. Today reading is a transferable skill, central to modern secular life; and we acquire literary skills without the expectation that it is in order to read a particular canon of works. In the early-medieval period, by contrast, the reverse was the case. Recent work has demonstrated that writing did play a crucial role in early-medieval life as a whole, and that the ability to use documents was accordingly an important accomplishment. However, this is where the significance of books and documents should be carefully distinguished. Although the same basic skills were employed, the function and import of reading books was altogether different. One learned to read books principally in order to be able read specific works; and one learned to read using the Psalter because this was the fundamental text of Christian life. The key point here is that Christianity did not just dominate the canon of literature passively: it actively pervaded the very concept of reading a book – in secular society no less than in the Church. A document might be predominantly secular, but reading a book was, first and foremost, a Christian act.

It is arguable that in a few circles, such as the more progressive cathedral schools, this attitude began to be undermined as early as the tenth century. Be that as it may, many sources attest to its vigorous survival in society as a whole well after this date. Turgot's life of Queen Margaret, stylized and partisan though it is, underlines the point. Reading a book was piety; a gospel lectionary was an appropriate accoutrement for a supremely spiritual woman; and the fate of the manuscript reflected the sanctity of the owner. Turgot's work is hagiography; but his perception of books, and the value he ascribes to them, is a valid reflection of their role in much of society, secular as well as ecclesiastical, up to the end of the eleventh century. Correspondingly, he provides a useful counterbalance to modern concern with literacy *per se* and our interest in books as agents of culture. Margaret's gospel lectionary was not, as we have seen, a deluxe book and its text is very short; but its spiritual virtues were in no respect the less for that. It is a clearer indicator of the Queen's holiness than of her literacy, because in the late eleventh century reading a book – and even just possessing one – could still be, almost by definition, an act of spirituality. Correspondingly, whatever the allusive references to books and reading fail to reveal about the literacy of early-medieval laywomen, they cast an invaluable light on their piety.

Appendix 1

I provide below a text and translation of the inscription that was added to the flyleaf of Lat. liturg. fol. 5 (fol. 2r). The text was presumably composed in or before 1093 (*teste* l.21). It is in hexameters. The exceptions to this are lines 12 and 14 (*At tamen ... O uirtus ...*). Line 12 may have deliberately been given an extra foot to distinguish it, since it is the very centre of the poem (the twelfth line both from the beginning and from the end). The fact that line 14 does not scan is more puzzling.

The script suggests a date at the beginning of the twelfth century or just possibly c.1100. The scribe seems to have attempted to match his hand to that of the main text of the book, giving it a slightly archaic feel. He spaced the first two lines incorrectly – including the first word of the next 'verse' at the end of the line. From line 4 the proper divisions were observed, and henceforth each line begins with a capital.

In the following transcription, lines 1–3 have been restored to the intended form, the two words that were in fact misplaced being isolated by a bracket. Abbreviations have been silently expanded; and prepositions are presented separately (they are customarily joined to the word that follows).

Christe tibi semper grates persoluimus omnes.
Tempore] qui nostro nobis miracula pandis;
Hunc] librum quidam inter se iurare uolentes;
Sumpserunt nudum sine tegmine nonque ligatum
Presbyter accipiens ponit sinuamine uestis.
Flumine transmisso codex est mersus in amnem;
Portitor ignorat librum penetrasse profundum;
Sed miles quidam cernens post multa momenta;
Tollere iam uoluit librum de flumine mersum;
Sed titubat subito librum dum uidit apertum;
Credens quod codex ex toto perditus esset;
At tamen inmittens undis corpus cum uertice summo;
Hoc euangelium profert de gurgite apertum;
O uirtus clara cunctis, O gloria magna;
Inuiolatus enim codex permansit ubique.
Exceptis foliis binis que cernis utrinque;
In quibus ex undis paret contractio quedam;
Que testantur opus Christi pro codice sancto;
Hoc opus ut nobis maius mirabile constet
De medio libri pannum lini abtulit unda;
Saluati semper sint rex reginaque sancta;
Quorum codex erat nuper saluatus ab undis.
Gloria magna Deo, librum qui saluat eundem;

Translation

O Christ, we all always give thanks to you
who make miracles known to us in our own time.
Certain folk who wanted to swear an oath among themselves,
took up this book, bare without a wrapper and not fastened.
A priest took it and placed it in the fold of his robe.

As he crossed the river, the codex plunged into the torrent.
The bearer was unaware that the book had sunk to the depths.
Much later, however, a certain soldier caught sight of it.
Straightaway he wanted to raise the submerged book out of the river;
but when he saw that the book was open, suddenly he hesitated
believing that the codex would be utterly ruined.
Nevertheless, he hurled himself head first into the waves
and bore the open gospel book out from the whirlpool.
What virtue clear to all, what a great glory!
For the codex survived entirely undamaged
except for the two folios which you see at either end
in which some cockling from the water is apparent
which proclaim the work of Christ on behalf of the sacred codex.
In order that this work should be manifested to us as even more miraculous,
the water washed away the sheet of linen from the middle of the book.
May the king and holy queen be safe for ever
whose codex was recently saved from the waves.
All glory be to God who saved the book in question!

Appendix 2

Distinctive Readings

The text was collated against *Biblia Sacra iuxta Vulgatam Versionem*, ed. R. Weber, 2 vols (Stuttgart, 1969). All departures from the principal text, except obvious errors, are listed below. The uncorrected errors are given in note 16.

Matthew
2:6 qui regat populum meum. 3:16 baptizatus autem ihs confestim. 4:9 haec omnia tibi dabo. 4:18 ambulans ihs iuxta. 26:5 non in die festo [om. dicebant]. 26:17 Prima autem die azymorum. 26:19 et fecerunt discipuli sicut constituit ihs [om. illis]. 26:46 Adpropinquabit. 26:47 missis a principibus sacerdotum. 26:71 uidit eum alia ancilla.

Mark
1:2 ante te. 1:7 veniet. 1:8 baptizabit. 6:17 misit Herodes. 6:24 quae cum exisset matri suae. 14:5 uenundari. 14:9 in uniuerso mundo. 14:21 tradetur. 14:24 effundetur. 14:49 impleantur. 14:51 eum. 15:39 summo. 15:41 hierosolyman. 16:14 Recumbentibus undecim discipulis apparuit ihs.

Luke
1:29 audisset. 2:16 puer. 2:22 matris ihu. 22:12 At ipse uobis ostendet cenaculum grande stratum. 22:20 qui pro uobis. 22:37 iniquis. 23:2 illum accusare. 23:8 erat enim ex multo tempore cupiens uidere eum. 23:19 ciuitatem. 23:27 lamentabantur. 23:44 horam nonam. 24:4 iuxta. 24:12 uidit.

John
14:23 dixit ihs discipulis suis. 14:23 mansionem. 18:9 eis. 18:28 ad caiphan. 18:36 ministri mei utique. 20:5 uidit linteamina posita. 20:9 oportuerat.

Notes to Chapter Nine

1. Printed as *Vita S. Margaretae Scotorum Reginae* in *Symeonis Dunelmensis Monachi Opera et Collectanea* i, ed. H.Hinde, Surtees Soc. 51 (1868), pp.234–54, following the passional, London, BL, MS Cotton Tiberius D. III, fols 179v–86r. Modern biographies include T.Ratcliffe Barnett, *Margaret of Scotland, Queen and Saint* (London, 1926), and A.J.Wilson, *St Margaret, Queen of Scotland* (Edinburgh, 1993). More incisive but narrowly focused is D.Baker, '"A Nursery of Saints": St Margaret of Scotland reconsidered', in *Medieval Women*, ed. D.Baker (Oxford, 1978), pp.119–41. For summaries of Malcolm's reign see A.A.M.Duncan, *Scotland: the Making of the Kingdom* (Edinburgh, 1975), pp.117–24, and G.W.S.Barrow, *Kingship and Unity: Scotland 1000–1306* (London, 1981), pp.25–31; *see also* V.Wall, 'Malcolm III and the Foundation of Durham Cathedral', in *Anglo-Norman Durham 1093–1193*, ed. D.Rollason, M.Harvey, and M.Prestwich (Woodbridge, 1994), pp.325–37.

2. *See* App. 1 below. Apart from the bleeding through the leaf of the colours on fol. 3, there is now little trace of water damage; however F.Madan, *Books in Manuscript* (London, 1893), p.124, recorded that 'a leaf at each end of the book shows unmistakable crinkling from immersion in water'.

3. Facsimile: *The Gospel Book of St Margaret*, ed. W.Forbes-Leith (Edinburgh, 1896). *See* further E.Temple, *Anglo-Saxon Manuscripts 900–1066* (London, 1976), cat. 91; A.G.Watson, *Catalogue of Dated and Datable Manuscripts c.435–1600 in Oxford Libraries* (2 vols., Oxford, 1984), i, no.549; ii, ill. 35; and J.Backhouse, D.H.Turner, and L.Webster (eds.), *The Golden Age of Anglo-Saxon Art* (London, 1984), no.69.

4. The volume was rebound in 1993 and now comprises: iv (modern flyleaves) + 38 (medieval leaves, of which 1 and 38 were originally pastedowns) + iv (modern endleaves, foliated as '39'–'42'). Collation: I (fols 1–2)^2; II–V^8 (first rectos: 3, 11, 19, and 27); VI (35–8) comprising a bifolium (36 + 38) the first half of which is flanked by two singletons (35 and 37). The parchment is arranged HF, FH throughout, except in the first bifolium (1–2), where the F side is outermost. The parchment is generally quite stout.

5. Prickings survive at the outer edge of a couple of leaves (33–4).

6. Cambridge, Pembroke Coll., MS 302 (197 x 102 mm): M.R.James, *A Descriptive Catalogue of the Manuscripts in Pembroke College, Cambridge* (Cambridge, 1905), pp.266–69; Temple, *Anglo-Saxon Manuscripts*, cat. 96. Warsaw, Biblioteka Narodowa, MS i. 3311 (155 x 99 mm): Temple, *Anglo-Saxon Manuscripts*, cat. 92. I have not seen this manuscript.

7. *See Gospel Book of St Margaret*, ed. Forbes Leith, p.6. Its later history seems to have been as follows: (14th cent.) ?Durham cathedral (by 1383); (16th cent.) Clayton Sudlaw; John Stowe; (17th cent.) Lord William Howard; Catherine Fane, mother of (18th cent.) Fane Edge (1716), who gave it to Brent Ely Library, (19th cent.) whence it was sold at Sotheby's in 1887, being bought by the Bodleian.

8. Needless to say, variations were possible here. I have followed W.H.Frere, *Studies in Early Roman Liturgy II: The Roman Lectionary* (Alcuin Club Collections 30, Oxford, 1934), pp.29–58 (the 'Standard Gospel Series') and 157–64 (an analysis of the series in five 11th-cent. Anglo-Saxon gospel books).

9. Two famous examples of the genre are Arras, Bibliothèque municipale (now 'Médiathèque'), MS 1045 (233) of the second half of the 9th cent. (J.Porcher, *Manuscrits à peintures du viie au xiie siècle* (Paris, 1954), no.61); and Trier, Stadtbibliothek, MS 24 of the last quarter of the 10th cent. (facsimile: *Codex Egberti der Stadtbibliothek Trier*, ed. H.Schiel (Trier, 1960); cf. G.Franz and F.J.Ronig, *Codex Egberti; Teilfaksimile-Ausgabe des* MS *24 der Stadtbibliothek Trier* (Wiesbaden, 1983)). A late Anglo-Saxon example is Florence, Biblioteca Medicea Laurenziana, MS Plut. XVII. 20 (Temple, *Anglo-Saxon Manuscripts*, cat. 69, with D.N.Dumville, *English Caroline Script and Monastic History* (Woodbridge, 1993), pl. XII).

10. Cambridge, Pembroke, Coll., MS 302; Florence, Biblioteca Medicea Laurenziana, MS Plut. XVII. 20; and Warsaw, Biblioteka Narodowa, MS i. 3311. Fragments survive of two others: London, College of Arms, MS Arundel 22, fols 84–5; and the enigmatic Malibu, J.P. Getty Museum, MS 9.

11. NY, Pierpont Morgan, MS M 708; Montecassino, Archivio della Badia, MS BB. 437. *See* now P.McGurk [and J.Rosenthal], 'The Anglo-Saxon Gospel Books of Judith, Countess of Flanders', *Anglo-Saxon England*, 24 (1995), pp.251–308. I am very grateful to Patrick McGurk for providing me with information on the text of these volumes before the publication of his seminal study.

12   *See* James, *Catalogue … Pembroke*, pp.267–8.

13   Cambridge, Univ. Library, MS Ll. 1. 10: *The Prayer Book of Aedelvald the Bishop Commonly Called the Book of Cerne*, ed. A.B.Kuypers (Cambridge, 1902); J.J.G.Alexander, *Insular Manuscripts 6th to 9th Century* (London, 1978), cat. 66; L.Webster and J.Backhouse (eds.), *The Making of England: Anglo-Saxon Art and Culture AD 600–900* (London, 1991), no.165. London, BL, MS Harley 2965: *An Ancient Manuscript of the Eighth or Ninth Century Formerly Belonging to St Mary's Abbey or Nunnaminster, Winchester*, ed. W.de Gray Birch, Hampshire Record Society (London and Winchester, 1889); Alexander, *Insular Manuscripts*, cat. 41; Webster and Backhouse (eds.), *Making of England*, no.164.

14   In Ottonian pericopes books such as Munich, Bay. Staatsbibl., MS Clm 4452, and Trier, Stadtbibliothek, MS 24, by contrast, the four evangelists are depicted one after the other at the start of the manuscript.

15   The fundamental guide to the textual content of late Anglo-Saxon gospel books is P.McGurk, 'The Text' in *The York Gospels*, ed. N.Barker, Roxburghe Club (London, 1986), pp.43–63. Unfortunately, however, none of the passages with distinctive readings in Margaret's book corresponds to the extracts presented in McGurk's table of comparative readings (pp.56–63). Equally unfortunately, only ten of the passages in question correspond to extracts included in Bonifatius Fischer's monumental collection of collations, *Die Lateinischen Evangelien bis zum 10. Jahrhundert* (4 vols., Freiburg-im-Breisgau, 1988–91). Of these ten, the readings of four are very common indeed; two are cases where the witnesses as a whole are divided into two nearly equal groups; while the remaining four are extremely rare. There is no basis here for perceiving a particular trend.

16   **Matthew** 27: 26 om. 'eis ut crucifigeretur'. **Mark** 14: 29 om. 'ait'. **Luke** 22: 5 om. 'sunt' after 'pactis'. 22: 5 'icit' for 'dicit' [lacks gold initial]. 22: 45 om. 'dormientes'. 23: 8 om. 'uidere' after 'aliquid'. 23: 9 'ciuitatem'. 24: 6 'surrixit' [corrected from 'surruxit']. 24: 9 'uddecim'. **John** 17: 5 om. 'tu' after 'me'. 18: 11 'alicem' (for 'calicem') [lacks gold initial]. 18: 36 'i' (for 'si') [lacks gold initial].

17   The minims are 2+ mm high and between 1 and 3 mm wide. The space between the ruled lines is 4–5 mm.

18   Other characteristics of the hand are that the downstrokes of the minims tend to curve to the right or to terminate in pronounced feet, while ascenders thicken to triangular or blob-like terminals. Neums were added to the first reading (4r–5r/9) at an early date.

19   The display scripts (discussed below) are compatible with this date range, and do not permit us to refine it.

20   For A, C, D, E, F, G, H, I, L, M, P, R and T. More expansive, hybrid forms were used for N, O, Q, S, and U.

21   These uncials have projecting ascenders and descenders. The letters have a tendency to rectilinearity.

22   Rustic capitals were also used for the tituli in the portraits.

23   Like the lection initials, the monumental gold capitals have undulating contours and pronounced serifs.

24   In the case of Matthew, Mark, and John, the remainder of the first sentence was written in golden minuscule.

25   The complete absence of foliage from the letter is archaic in 11th-cent. manuscript art.

26   The dimensions of the frames follow those of the textblock rulings. When, as in Luke, the frames for portrait and initial are different sizes, this is because the dimensions of the ruling on the pages in question were different.

27   Cf. R.G.Gameson, *The Role of Art in the late Anglo-Saxon Church* (Oxford, 1995), pp.192–95.

28   The surface of John was lightly painted. In each case, the whiteness of the ground behind the evangelist was accentuated by painting the parchment outside the frames a light red. Other Anglo-Saxon illuminated manuscripts with plain grounds include: Cambridge, Pembroke Coll., MS 301; Cambridge, Trinity Coll., MS B. 10. 4; London, BL, Add. MS 34890; Oxford, Bodleian Library, MS Douce 296; NY, Pierpont Morgan, MS 708; and 709: Temple, *Anglo-Saxon Manuscripts*, cats. 73, 65, 68, 79, 93–94.

29   It is likely that the colours were originally more intense.

30   Stains are visible where the gold was burnished. In some cases the rubbing strayed over the adjacent text, which is consequently damaged: this can be seen, for example, in the 'cu' of *secundum* in the rubric to Luke's gospel.

31 The basic figure types in late Anglo-Saxon gospel books are classified by J.J.G.Alexander, 'The Illumination of the Gospels' in *The York Gospels*, ed. Barker, pp.65–76.

32 And, of course, by the rubric and incipit on the facing pages. Each figure is defined as 'evangelista' as well as being named in his titulus.

33 Similarly, while Matthew has a green robe, a blue under-robe, and sits on a red cloth, Mark has a red robe, a gold under-robe, and sits on a blue cloth, Luke has a green robe, a red under-robe, and sits on a red cloth, while John has a blue robe, a green under-robe, and sits on a red-backed throne.

34 It is as significant as the circumstance that Luke has blue hair, while that of the other three evangelists is red! Given that the overwhelming majority of depicted scribes are portrayed as right-handed, it is extremely interesting to note that Hugo Pictor showed himself to be left-handed in his self-portrait in Oxford, Bodleian Library, MS Bodley 717, fol. 287v (on which *see further*, O.Pächt, 'Hugo Pictor', *Bodleian Library Record*, 3 (1950), pp.96–103).

35 NY, Pierpont Morgan, MS 708 and 709; Montecassino, Archivio della Badia, MS BB. 437.

36 Reims, Bibliothèque municipale, MS 9: Temple, *Anglo-Saxon Manuscripts*, cat. 105; M.de Lemps and R.Laslier, *Trésors de la Bibliothèque municipale de Reims* (Reims, 1978), no.16; W.Hinkle, 'The Gift of an Anglo-Saxon Gospel Book to the Abbey of Saint-Remi, Reims', *Journal of the British Archaeological Association*, 3rd ser., 33 (1970), pp.21–35.

37 She also seems to have owned a *textus argenteus*: *Reginaldi monachi dunelmensis libellus de admirandis beati Cuthberti virtutibus*, c.93: Surtees Society, 1 (London, 1838), p.218.

38 Munich, Bay. Staatsbibl., MS 30111: K.Görich and E.Clemm, *Gebetbuch Ottos III* (Munich, 1995). The manuscripts with more opulent decoration are Clm 4453: *Das Evangeliar Ottos III*, ed. F.Dressler, F.Mütherich, and H.Beumann (Frankfurt am Main, 1978); and Aachen, Domschatz, s.n.: E.G.Grimme, *Das Evangeliar Kaiser Ottos III. im Domschatz zu Aachen* (Freiburg, 1984).

39 *S. Anselmi Cantuariensis Archiepiscopi Opera Omnia*, ed. F.Schmitt, 6 vols. (Edinburgh, 1946–61), iii, ep.10 (pp.113–14).

40 *Vita Margaretae*, prologus, ed. Hinde, p.234. The text and its problems are discussed by L.L.Huneycutt, 'The Idea of the Perfect Princess: The *Life of St Margaret* in the Reign of Matilda II (1100–1118)', *Anglo-Norman Studies*, 12 (1990), pp. 81–97, superseding Baker, 'Margaret Reconsidered', pp.129–32. Huneycutt offers useful observations on the function and form of the work as a whole.

41 *Vita Margaretae*, c.6, ed. Hinde, pp.240–41.

42 *Conlationes* xiv, 10, ed. M.Petschenig (Vienna, 1886), pp.410–11.

43 Ep.21, s.3: *Sancti Caesarii Episcopi Arlatensis Opera Omnia*, ed. D. G. Morin (2 vols., Maredsous, 1937–42), ii, pp.134–44 at 136.

44 Isidore, *Sententiarum Libri Tres* iii, 8 (*PL* 83:679); Smaragdus, *Diadema monachorum*: *PL* 102:594.

45 *The Vita Wulfstani of William of Malmesbury*, iii, 9, ed. R.R.Darlington, Camden Soc. 40 (London, 1928), p.50. Cf. R.G.Gameson, 'St Wulfstan, The Library of Worcester, and the Spirituality of the Medieval Book', *St Wulfstan, Bishop of Worcester*, ed. J.Barrow and N.Brooks (London, forthcoming).

46 As quoted in the popular anthology *Liber scintillarum*: *Defensor's Liber Scintillarum with an interlinear Anglo-Saxon Version*, ed. E.W.Rhodes, EETS o.s.93 (Oxford, 1889), p.218. The concept that familiarity with scripture was the foundation of wisdom was regularly enunciated, e.g. by Hrabanus Maurus, *De clericorum institutione*, iii, 2 and 28: *PL* 107:379 and 407.

47 *Vita Maoli* ii, 3: *PL* 137:755.

48 *Vita Margaretae*, c.6, ed. Hinde, p.241.

49 A rare example is the dedication image in the San Paolo Bible (*c*.870), where Charles the Bald's consort appears at his side (plus attendant): Rome, San Paolo fuori le mura, MS s.n., fol. 334v: H.L.Kessler, *The Illustrated Bibles from Tours* (Princeton, 1977), pl. 197, with general comment at pp.135–38.

50 The volume is lost: the image is known from a copy made in 1842. The broad context for the image is that Matilda's husband, Duke Frederick of Lotharingia, was trying to find allies to counterbalance the power of the Emperor Conrad II; while Mieszko was attempting to establish the independence of his kingdom from Germany. *See* further F.Mütherich, 'Epistola Mathildis Sueviae. Zu einer verschollenen Handschrift

51   Lille, Bibliothèque de l'Institut catholique, MS s.n.: *Patrimoine des bibliothèques de France II: Nord, Pas-de-Calais, Picardie* (Paris, 1995), pp.128–9.

52   Madrid, El Escorial, MS Vitr. 17, fol. 3r: A.Boeckler, *Das Goldene Evangelienbuch Heinrich III* (Berlin, 1933), pl. 7; A.Goldschmidt, *German Illumination II: Ottonian Period* (Florence, 1928), pl. 58. The inscription around the frame reads: 'O Regina poli me regem spernere noli/me tibi commendo praesentia dona ferendo/ patrem cum matre quin iunctam prolis amore/ut sis adiutrix et in omni tempore fautrix' ('O Queen of Heaven, do not despise me, the King/I commend to you by offering the present gifts, myself,/my father with my mother, and indeed she who is joined by love of their offspring [i.e. Agnes]/so that you may be their helper and patron at all times').

53   Uppsala, Univ. Library, MS C. 93, fols 3v–4r: facsimile: *Codex Caesarius Upsaliensis*, ed. C.Nordenfalk (Uppsala, 1971).

54   Henry is stressed by his more opulent clothing and by the fact that he is at Christ's right hand.

55   Sinai, MS gr. 172 + Saint Petersburg, Public Library, MS gr. 291 (the image is on fols 2v–3r of the section in Saint Petersburg): I.Spatharakis, *Corpus of Dated Illuminated Greek Manuscripts to the Year 1453* (Leiden, 1981), nos. 81–2.

56   Santiago de Compostela, Biblioteca Universitaria, MS Rs. 1: J.P.O'Neill (ed.), *The Art of Medieval Spain AD 500–1200* (New York, 1993), no.144. Incidentally, in the inscription at the foot of the cross that was given to San Isidore, León, in 1063 by the same rulers, 'Fredinandus Rex' comes before and above 'Sancia Regina' (*Ibid.*, no.111).

57   P.Lasko, *Ars Sacra* (Harmondsworth, 1972), p.93, pl. 85. The emperor is named in the inscription on which they kneel; Theophanu holds the young Otto III.

58   J.-P.Caillet, *L'antiquité classique, le haut moyen âge et Byzance au Musée de Cluny* (Paris, 1985), no.163.

59   Munich, Bay. Staatsbibl., MS 4452. Facsimile: *Das Perikopenbuch Heinrichs II, Clm 4452 der Bayerischen Staatsbibliothek München*, ed. F.Mütherich and K.Dachs (Frankfurt am Main, 1994). More accessible is H.Fillitz, R.Kahsnitz and U.Kuder, *Zierde für ewige Zeit: Das Perikopenbuch Heinrichs II* (Munich, 1994).

60   London, BL, MS Stowe 944: Temple, *Anglo-Saxon Manuscripts*, cat. 78; cf. Gameson, *Role of Art*, pp.73–74.

61   One apparent exception which deserves brief comment is the mid 11th-cent. manuscript of the *Encomium Emmae Reginae*, London, BL, Add. MS 33241: Backhouse *et al.*, *Golden Age*, no.148; for the text *see Encomium Emmae Reginae*, ed. A.Campbell (Camden Soc. 3rd ser. 72, London, 1949). The prefatory image (fol. 1v) shows the scribe presenting the manuscript to an enthroned Emma, while Harthacnut and Edward look on from the side. However, this text was actually dedicated to Emma and 'devoted to her praise'; furthermore, Emma was the mother of Harthacnut and Edward, not their spouse. Nevertheless, it is notable that the leading male (presumably Harthacnut) joins Emma in receiving the book and has one hand on it. The image is, incidentally, concordant with the view that the ultimate function of the work was to promote Harthacnut's right to the English throne and Edward's position as his successor: *see* F.Lifshitz, 'The *Encomium Emmae Reginae*: a Political Pamphlet of the Eleventh Century', *The Haskins Society Journal*, 1 (1989), pp. 39–50.

62   Compare the description of his splendid reception of Edgar *Cild* in the *Anglo-Saxon Chronicle* (D) *sub anno* 1075 (*recte* 1074): *English Historical Documents ii, 1042–1189*, ed. D.C.Douglas and G.W.Greenaway (2nd edn., London, 1981), p.161.

63   Hildesheim, Dom und Diözesanmuseum, Inv. Nr. DS 18, fols 16v–17r: M.Brandt (ed.), *Das Kostbare Evangeliar des Heiligen Bernward* (Munich, 1993), pls.5 and 6.

64   *Vita Margaretae*, c.11, ed. Hinde, p.250.

65   See App. 1.

66   Symeon, *Historia Dunelmensis Ecclesiae*, cc.26–7: *Symeonis Monachi Opera Omnia*, (2 vols., RS, London, 1882–5), i, pp.64, and 67–68. Cf. the discussion in T.Kendrick *et al.*, *Codex Lindisfarnensis* (2 vols, Olten and Lausanne, 1956–60), ii, pp.21–23, where it is pointed out that Symeon, writing at Durham between 1104 and 1107/9, will certainly have known the story of Margaret's book, which was being recorded at Durham at the same time.

67 Muirchu, *Vita Sancti Patricii*, c.20: *St Patrick, his writings and Muirchu's Life*, ed. A.B.E.Hood (Chichester, 1978), p.71. For comment on the work in general *see* L.Bieler, 'Muirchu's Life of St Patrick', *Medium Ævum*, 43 (1974), pp. 219–33.

68 *Adomnan's Life of Columba* ii, 8–9, ed. A.O. and M.A.Anderson (Edinburgh and London, 1961), pp.342–43. In the first instance, a satchel containing several books is dropped into the water, and they are entirely spoiled except for the single page which had been written by Columba. In the second, a book of hymns written by Columba emerged undamaged after 3 months in a river.

69 *See* n. 37.

70 *The Letters of Lanfranc, Archbishop of Canterbury*, ed. H.Clover and M.Gibson (Oxford, 1979), ep.50.

71 The essays in *The Uses of Literacy in Early Medieval Europe*, ed. R.McKitterick (Cambridge, 1990) represent a spectrum of recent, balanced, empirical approaches.

72 *Gregorii I Papae, Registrum Epistolarum*, ep.xiv, 12, ed. P.Ewald and L.M. Hartmann (2 vols., MGH, Epistolae 1–2, Hannover, 1887–99), ii, p.431. Paul the Deacon, *Historia Langobardorum* IV, 5, ed. G.Waitz (MGH, Scriptores Rerum Langobardicarum et Italicarum, Hannover, 1878), p.117. For a good colour reproduction of the splendid Theodelinda gospel book covers *see* J.Hubert, J.Porcher, and W.F.Volbach, *Europe in the Dark Ages* (London, 1969), ill. 241.

73 Fulda, Landesbibliothek, MS Bonifatianus 2 (Isidore, *Synonyma*): E. A. Lowe, *Codices Latini Antiquiores*, 11 vols. and *Supplement* (Oxford, 1934–71), viii, no.1197; C.Jakobi-Mirwald and H.Köllner, *Die illuminierten Handschriften der Hessischen Landesbibliothek Fulda I: 6–13 Jahrhunderts* (2 vols., Stuttgart, 1976–93), i, cat. 2; ii, ills 4–6; and *Der Ragyndrudis Codex der Hl. Bonifatius*, ed. L.E.von Padberg and H.-W.Stork (Paderborn and Fulda, 1994).

74 P.E.Schramm and F.Mütherich, *Denkmale der deutschen Könige und Kaiser*, i (2nd edn., Munich, 1981), pp.93–94; with P.Riché, 'Les bibliothèques de trois aristocrates laïcs carolingiens', *Le Moyen Age*, 69 (1963), pp.87–104.

75 *Recueil des chartes de l'abbaye de Saint-Benoît-sur-Loire*, ed. M.Prou and A.Vidier (2 vols., Paris, 1900–7), i, pp.65–66; with E.Bishop, *Liturgica Historica* (Oxford, 1918), pp.362–69.

76 Ekkehard IV, *Casus Sancti Galli*, ed. G.Meyer von Knonau (Saint Gallen, 1877), pp.344 ff. [the new edition by H.F.Haefele was not available to me].

77 *Anglo-Saxon Wills*, ed. D.Whitelock (Cambridge, 1930), no.III, at p.14.

78 Emma (d. 1052): London, BL, Add. MS 33241 (Backhouse *et al.*, *Golden Age*, no. 148). Judith (d. 1094): Fulda, Landesbibliothek, MS Aa. 21 (J.Stiennon and R.Lejeune (eds), *Rhin-Meuse: Art et civilisation 800–1400* (2 vols., Brussels and Cologne, 1972), i, no. F.25; Jakobi-Mirwald and Köllner, *Die illuminierten Handschriften in Fulda*, i, cat. 22; ii, ills. 177–96) and, more controversially, NY, Pierpont Morgan, MS 709 (Temple, *Anglo-Saxon Manuscripts*, ill. 289). Matilda (d. 1115): Vatican City, Bibliotheca Apostolica Vaticana, MS Vat. lat. 4922 (A.M.C.Stickler and L.E.Boyle, *The Vatican Library* (Florence, 1985), pls. 39–41).

79 Cf. A.Petrucci, 'The Christian Conception of the Book in the Sixth and Seventh Centuries' in his *Writers and Readers in Medieval Italy: Studies in the History of Written Culture* (New Haven and London, 1995), pp.19–42, for the reorientation in attitude to books between Cassiodorus and Gregory the Great (d. 604).

CHAPTER TEN

From Eve to Bathsheba and Beyond: Motherhood in the Queen Mary Psalter

ANNE RUDLOFF STANTON

THE QUEEN MARY PSALTER is a densely-illustrated manuscript that was made for an unknown patron between 1310 and 1320, and gained its name after its presentation to Queen Mary Tudor in 1553.[1] Its fame rests largely on the delicate, courtly painting style of the artist who drew or painted all of its figural decoration; indeed, the style of this artist was so influential in the fourteenth century that over twenty manuscripts reflecting the Queen Mary Psalter style have survived.[2] The position of the Psalter as the primary example of this elegant style has guaranteed its continued familiarity to art historians.

The very familiarity of this Psalter's style has served to obscure many of its most unusual facets, for it tends to be treated almost as a portfolio of pretty pictures. Indeed, the scope of the Psalter can be overwhelming, since its figural decoration comprises over 800 images, nearly all of which are narrative. Its Latin psalms are prefaced by a unique cycle of 223 Old Testament scenes executed in tinted drawings, which are explained by an Anglo-Norman text. This series of images begins with the Fall of the Rebel Angels and the Creation of the Earth, and ends with the Death of King Solomon; it deviates considerably from its biblical source and from contemporary manuscript cycles. The Psalms themselves are accompanied by three different levels of decoration. First, historiated initials mark the main divisions of the Psalms and contain for the most part a cycle of David imagery seen in other contemporary psalters. In addition to these primary markers, pairs of large framed illuminations depict the life of Christ from the Annunciation to the Last Judgement at each division, and delicate marginal drawings echoing the subtle presentation of the prefatory scenes float at the bottom of every page. These drawings, of which there are over 400, fall into six sequences, ranging from a complete bestiary to the lives of the martyred saints. In fact, the codex is an intricately designed and encyclopaedic masterpiece, presenting largely visual stories that span the courtly world as well as biblical history.

The overwhelming number of narratives in the Queen Mary Psalter are knit together by several broad themes, including a focus on the correct actions of leaders, the importance of kinship, and the crucial nature of women's actions. In particular, a large number of mothers, ranging from Eve and Bathsheba to Mary and the mother of Thomas Becket, actively protect and champion their children. In this essay I shall first explore the mothers of the

FROM EVE TO BATHSHEBA AND BEYOND

FIG. 73 Expulsion from Paradise. Queen Mary Psalter. London, BL, MS Royal 2 B. VII, fol. 4r.

Queen Mary Psalter through a survey of selected scenes from the manuscript. Then I shall discuss both the possibility that they indicate a particular female audience for the Psalter, and their readability as role-models for such an audience.

From Eve to Bathsheba: Old Testament Mothers

The majority of these characters is found in the narrative Old Testament preface, in which the scenes are accompanied by chatty captions that usually refer to the drawings by beginning with the words *ici* or *coment*. While the women in these stories are all biblical characters, their inclusion, as well as the manner of their visual or verbal representation, is often very unusual.

The representation of the Expulsion of Adam and Eve from Paradise provides the first clue to the importance of women's actions in the Queen Mary Psalter. The Fall is depicted on fol. 3v, where the caption begins 'Here Eve makes Adam sin' ('*Ici fet Eve Adam peccher.*') At the top of fol. 4r, an angel lifts a sword as Adam and Eve walk away from the Tree of Knowledge, while the Serpent has slithered away so that only its tail is visible in the drawing (FIG. 73). A contrite Adam looks back toward the Angel, but Eve looks ahead with a jaunty air as if she is not entirely sorry that her curiosity and disobedience has traded her safe, eternal future for something more uncertain and mysterious.

FIG. 74 Abraham and Sarah. Queen Mary Psalter. London, BL, MS Royal 2 B. VII, fol. 8v.

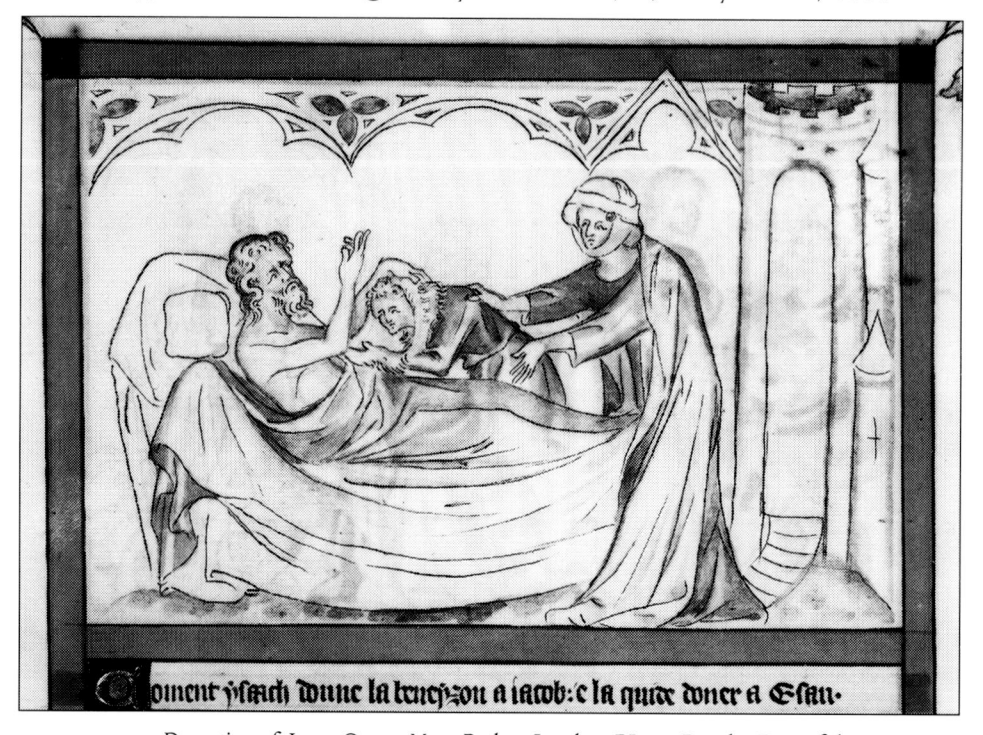

FIG. 75 Deception of Isaac. Queen Mary Psalter. London, BL, MS Royal 2 B. VII, fol. 13v.

This admittedly subjective interpretation of the scene is reinforced by the strong female characters who pervade the rest of the manuscript. The story of Eve highlights the weaknesses of women and the ease with which the devil can lead them astray, but at the same time it emphasizes the importance of their actions. The majority of female characters in the Queen Mary Psalter are just as crucial to the narrative, whether they can be construed as negative or positive characters. The most positive characters are almost always mothers.

The role Abraham's women play in his story as told in the Queen Mary Psalter exemplifies the importance of women in this manuscript. After a few scenes representing his youth and his repudiation of his idol-making father, he marries Sarah 'by law, and puts a ring on her finger' (FIG. 74). Sarah, represented during her marriage to Abraham, stands with hand raised and finger pointed in the rhetorical gesture used for speech throughout the Psalter and in other Gothic manuscripts. Is this just an example of the courtly, graceful liveliness favoured by the Queen Mary artist, or is Sarah intended to be taking an active part in the ceremony? She certainly appears more frequently here than in any other version, kneeling beside Abraham at his first altar, and arguing with him, again with her finger raised, about her inability to have children.

On fol. 9v Abraham is depicted with his arm around a very small woman who is identified in the text as the handmaid Hagar with whom Abraham, by the counsel of Sarah his wife, will have children (PLATE 5). Hagar appears in three scenes, a number only exceeded in one other contemporary manuscript, the Psalter of Isabella (now in Munich), where Abraham's relationship with Hagar occupies five scenes.[3] At any rate, in the Queen Mary Psalter Hagar is given to Abraham; she becomes pregnant and is cast out with her son Ishmael after arguing with Sarah, and is comforted in the desert by a curiously tender angel. It is interesting to compare the scene showing the patriarch's marriage to Sarah with that showing his meeting with the younger woman: Sarah as the legal wife is privileged by her size and by the formality of the gesture, in comparison with Abraham's intimate embrace of Hagar.

The inclusion of the Hagar story is extremely rare in Gothic manuscripts. The Queen Mary Psalter sequence also excludes one of the most typical Abraham scenes, that of his meeting with Melchisedek which often prefigured priestly activities. Contemporary Abraham cycles, such as those in the English Tickhill Psalter in New York and the French Psalter of St Louis in Paris, all emphasize the typological elements of Abraham's story, as well as the more warlike imagery.[4] The seven scenes in the St Louis Psalter focus on Abraham as a warrior, and ignore the story of Hagar. By comparison, the Queen Mary Psalter story deals almost exclusively with Abraham's immediate family and ignores his relationships with other leaders.

The story of Abraham in the Queen Mary Psalter ends when he commissions a search for a wife for his son Isaac, which culminates with the meeting of his seneschal with Rebecca at the well. Rebecca appears on every folio containing the stories of the adult Isaac and their twin sons Jacob and Esau. She appears at the well, rides behind the seneschal on his camel, meets and marries Isaac, and then gives birth to her twin sons in the first of seven childbed scenes in the Psalter. Next she shows her favourite son Jacob how to deceive her

FIG. 76 Jacob, Joseph, and Rachel. Queen Mary Psalter. London, BL, MS Royal 2 B. VII, fol. 20r.

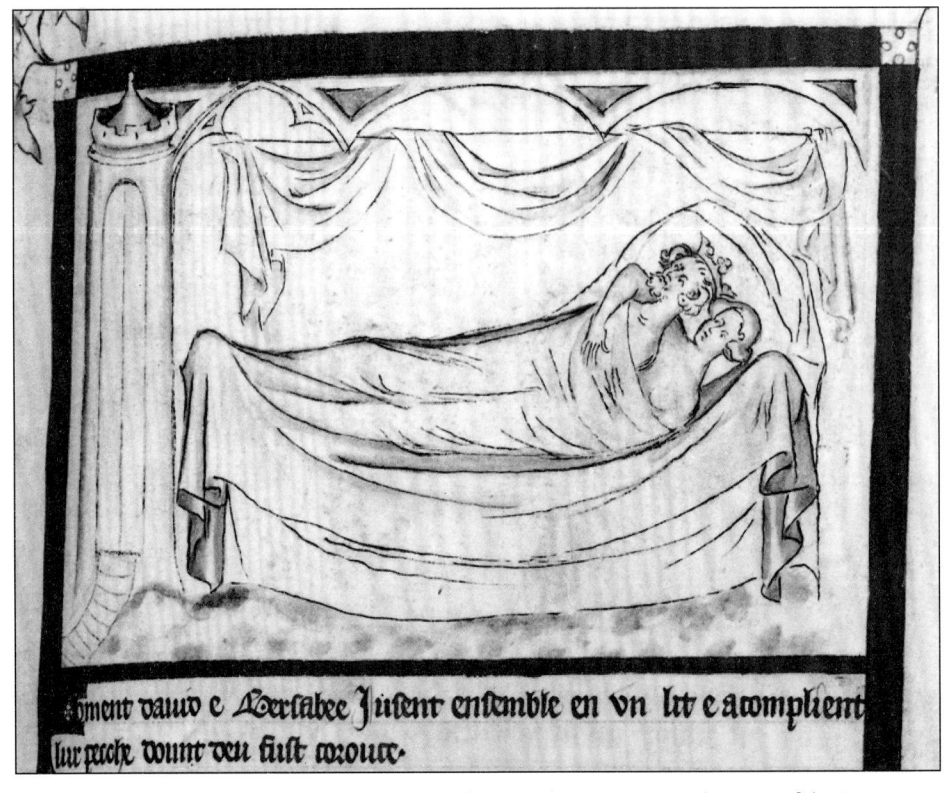

FIG. 77 Birth of Samuel. Queen Mary Psalter. London, BL, MS Royal 2 B. VII, fol. 48r.

elderly husband, and then on fol. 13v pushes him, disguised, toward Isaac (FIG. 75). The story of Jacob and Esau ends here, with the deception of their father in which Jacob receives the blessing that should have been given to Esau. The focus on Rebecca in this narrative, which in other cycles continues on to the adult lives of Jacob and Esau, emphasizes the pivotal nature of her actions in shaping Christian history.[5] She is the first character presented as a strong mother in the Queen Mary Psalter. Her dishonest actions in promoting Jacob are redeemed by the success of his son, Joseph.

Towards the end of the Joseph story, at the end of Genesis, another unusual twist to the scriptures is found as Rachel survives her scriptural death, to ride with Jacob to Egypt, and to meet the Pharaoh. She is never named, but is clearly Joseph's mother. The text underlines her appearance in the images as it notes that she accompanies her husband: Jacob and 'his wife' travel, and Joseph introduces 'his father and his mother and his brothers' to Pharaoh.

The end of the Joseph story as depicted in this period usually coincides with the death of Jacob and his burial in Canaan. In the Queen Mary Psalter, both Rachel and Jacob survive to return to their homeland (FIG. 76). This scene is captioned by the text, 'How Joseph conducts his father and his mother to Canaan.' This scene ensures that the first book of the Bible is capped by an energetic female character, who in fact leads her family, with her riding whip held aloft.

Thus, throughout this version of the book of Genesis, women play a very strong role. Eve, Sarah and Hagar, and Rebecca are pivotal characters in a narrative which revolves more around issues of family continuity and security than the political needs of the Hebrews. The book of Genesis indeed tends to focus on family matters, but the designer of the Queen Mary Psalter preface took extra care to emphasize the actions of women wherever possible. Furthermore, the appearance of strong female characters continues throughout the preface narratives. Miriam disbelieves her brother Moses and is stricken with leprosy as a result (fol. 27v), and Delilah's duplicity is a crucial part of the story of Samson.[6] These characters are balanced by the strong mothers of Moses, Samuel, and Solomon.

There are four childbirth scenes in the preface alone, including those of Jacob and Esau, and of Moses, Samson, and Samuel (FIG. 77). Their mothers all take action to ensure their survival and success: Rebecca champions Jacob, as mentioned above, and Moses' mother gives him up to a surrogate mother, the Pharaoh's daughter, who also champions his cause.

The story of Samuel provides ample opportunity for the Psalter's creator to emphasize the power of motherhood. In biblical and exegetical source material, Samuel's father has two wives, Hannah and Phennenah; in other lengthy Old Testament sequences from this period, like the Isabella Psalter in Munich, these two wives are both included. In the Queen Mary Psalter, however, only Hannah is mentioned, suggesting an interest in promoting monogamy. The only polygamist remaining in this Old Testament is Solomon, whose multiple marriages and tolerance for his wives' religions cause his downfall and the ruin of the kingdom of Israel.

The coverage of the Book of Kings in the Queen Mary Psalter begins on fol. 48, where Samuel's parents are shown speaking to the priest Eli in the temple above and the birth of

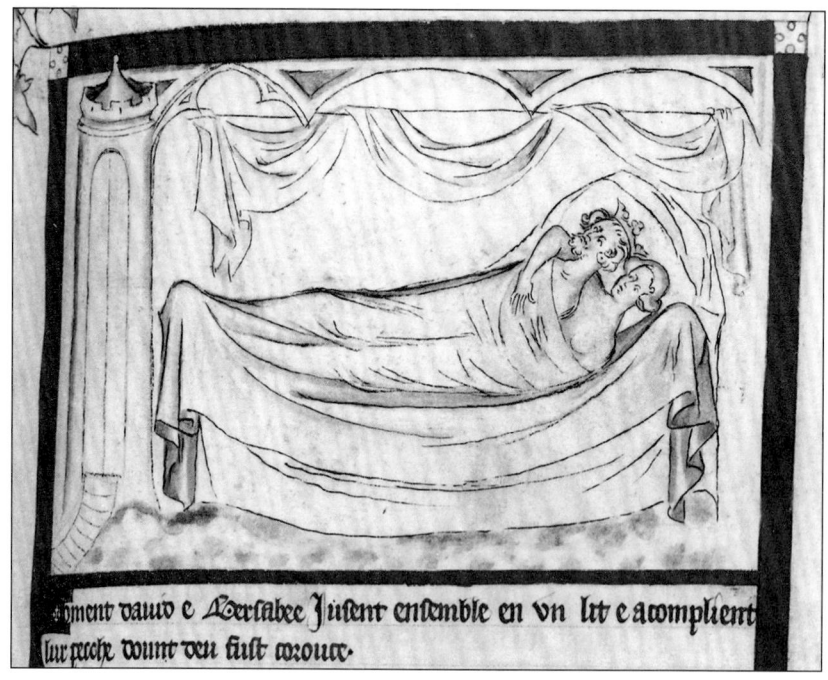

FIG. 78 Bathsheba and David. Queen Mary Psalter, London, BL, MS Royal 2 B. VII, fol. 57r.

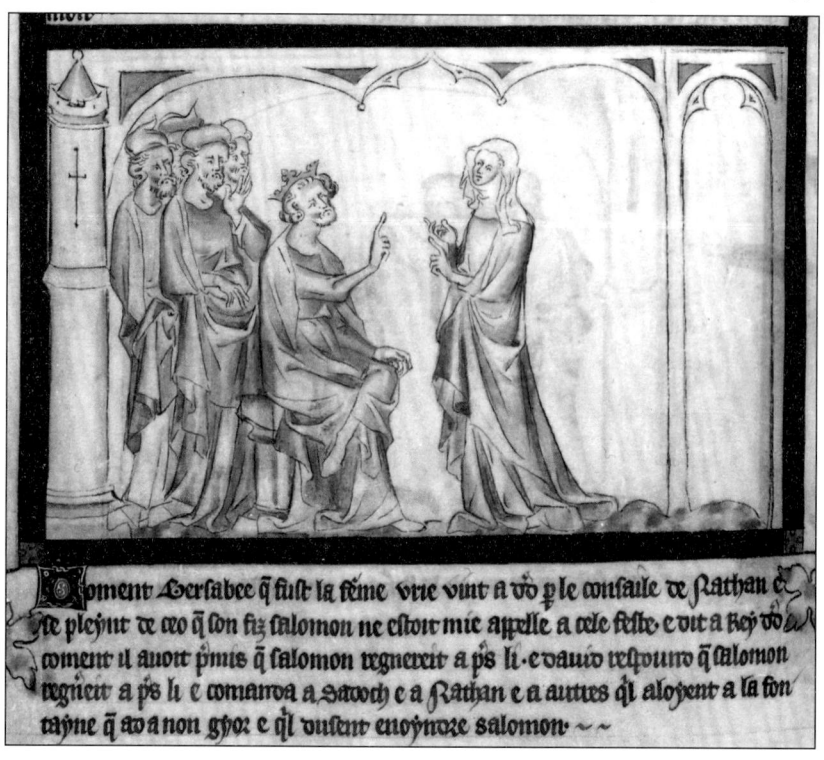

FIG. 79 Bathsheba reminds David of Solomon. Queen Mary Psalter. London, BL, MS Royal 2 B. VII, fol. 63v.

Samuel is shown below (FIG. 77). Hannah, like Sarah, is too old to have children, and her barrenness is mentioned in the captions to both images. The miraculous nature of Samuel's birth – and of Hannah's maternal state – is thus emphasized, and like that of Isaac and Samson it prefigures the miraculous birth of Christ. Hannah's gesture in the top drawing on the next folio (PLATE 6), as she pushes Samuel toward the priest Eli in the temple at Shiloh, also prefigures the gesture of Mary in the Christological paintings of the psalter proper, where she presents her own son to the scholars in the temple at Jerusalem (PLATE 7).

Bathsheba is an important character; her seductiveness causes the death of her first husband, Uriah, and great calamities for her second, King David. While David is presented as a responsible leader throughout fifty-two scenes (nearly one-quarter of the drawings in the preface), the text makes clear that many of his choices are necessitated by his early, signal sin with Bathsheba. They see each other on fol. 56v. David stands at the top of his castle, holding out his hand toward the fully-clothed Bathsheba, who does the same from atop her own residence; she is not represented as the passive recipient of his gaze. The next scene shows the two lying together naked in bed, and once again Bathsheba's active role is emphasized by the placement of her arm around David's shoulder (FIG. 78). David's murder of her husband Uriah leads directly into the incestuous rape of his own daughter, Tamar, by his son Amnon on fol. 58r, and the caption of this image emphasizes that the rape is the beginning of the punishment of David for his sin with Bathsheba, a punishment that will finally involve almost all of David's immediate family. Thus Bathsheba, like Eve, lures a man into a sin that will echo through his lineage.

Bathsheba redeems herself as a mother through her support of her son Solomon, for it is she who reminds David of his promise that the young Solomon, rather than his surviving older sons, shall be his successor. At the bottom of fol. 63v she stands before an enthroned David, her hands in a rhetorical gesture of explanation (FIG. 79). While this is her final appearance in the Queen Mary Psalter, her interference influences the rest of the story, for David commands that Solomon be anointed twice and then instructs the child in the intricacies of kingship.[7]

Thus mothers are key figures in the Old Testament preface of the Queen Mary Psalter. Their actions direct the lives of their sons and in some cases redeem them from their own sins. Because of the narrative nature and story-book quality of the preface, the vernacular language in which its text was written, and its wealth of fully developed female characters, I suggest that these characters were intended to be very important to the audience of the manuscript. The remaining narratives of the Psalter, however, continue to emphasize strong mothers through depictions of the Virgin and of the mothers of various saints in the psalter proper; they are even emphasized in the transition between the two sections of the manuscript.

Mothers in the New Testament and Beyond

After the end of the preface with the death of King Solomon and the division of Israel, a blank, unruled opening firmly announces a different section of the manuscript. Upon turning

FIG. 80A Genealogical charts. Queen Mary Psalter.
London, BL, MS Royal 2 B. VI, fol. 67v.

the page once again, the reader is presented with a pair of brilliantly coloured and gilded full-page paintings that encapsulate the genealogy of Christ and bridge the gap between the Old Testament history and the Christological imagery that will decorate the psalms (FIG. 80). On fols 67v–68r, a Tree of Jesse faces a chart that depicts the Holy Kinship, which delineates the kinship between Christ and some of the apostles. Although I have discussed these images in more detail elsewhere, I should note here that while the Tree of Jesse frequently decorates English Gothic psalters, the Holy Kinship is a much rarer image.[8]

FIG. 80B Genealogical charts. Queen Mary Psalter.
London, BL, MS Royal 2 B. VI, fol. 68r.

It focuses on St Anne, the mother of the Virgin, and her three marriages (the *Trinubium Annae*). Each marriage produces one daughter, each named Mary, and these daughters in turn bear Christ and five of his apostles.[9] Thus the immediate family of Christ, and the first group affected by his ministry, is formed by a genealogy traced not through fathers, but through mothers.

In the Queen Mary Psalter version of this image, which is unlike any of the other Holy Kinships I have found, the figures are presented in a registrated format that is designed to be

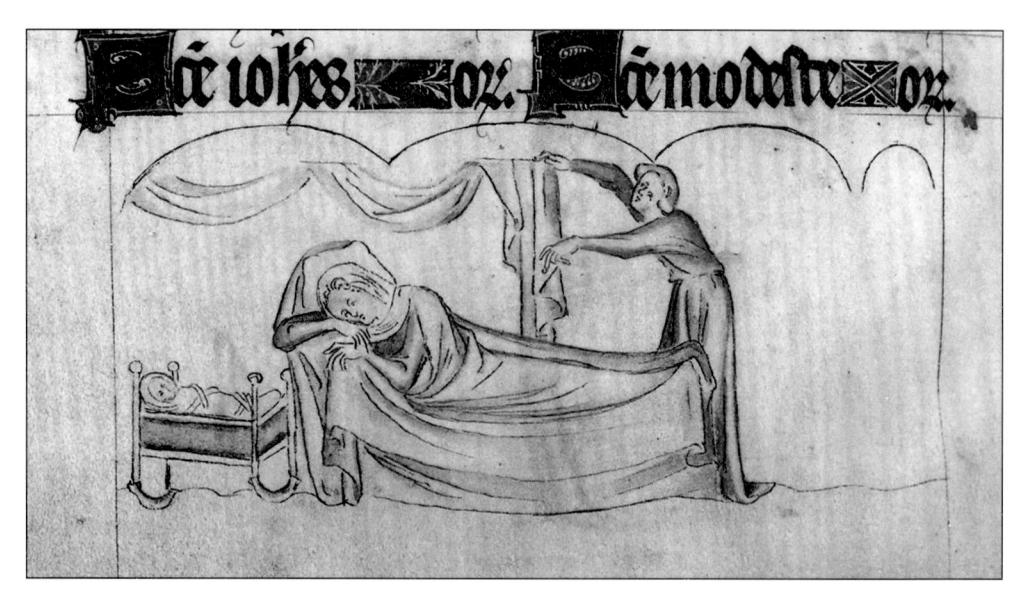

FIG. 81 Birth of Nicholas of Myra. Queen Mary Psalter. London, BL, MS Royal 2 B. VII, fol. 314v.

read from the bottom up, and is accompanied by a short Anglo-Norman caption that explains the relationships. This unusual orientation contrasts the active, standing, gesturing figure of St Anne, repeated three times at the bottom of the chart, and the supine figure of the patriarch Jesse on the facing page. The chart is manifestly different from the more common, organic, tree-form of the Jesse image, although the two paintings are both executed in brilliant colours and gold leaf. I suggest that the registrated format and vernacular text of the Holy Kinship painting was intended to provide a link between the Old Testament images, which are also presented in registers with a vernacular text, and the brilliantly coloured New Testament illuminations that accompany the Psalms. If so, the matriarchal Holy Kinship emphasizes the connection between the Old Testament mothers and the actions of the most important of all biblical mothers, Mary, whose presence accompanies the main divisions of the Psalms and hovers in many of their margins.

As noted above, the Psalms are decorated with three levels of figural imagery. The primary level, dividing them into ten major sections and common in psalters of this period and provenance, is a sequence of historiated initials containing word-pictures of the Psalm incipits that usually centre on David as their author. Each incipit is also marked by a pair of framed illuminations that depict scenes from the life of Christ. The Psalms of the Queen Mary Psalter are in fact divided into more than the ten divisions normal for English Gothic psalters, so opportunities for these scenes abound.[10]

The Annunciation and Visitation begin the Christological sequence, which includes episodes from the Infancy of Christ and an unusually long series of Ministry scenes; more than half of the illuminations treat the Passion of Christ. Several of these illuminations focus on the actions of the Virgin; for instance, the scene of Christ disputing with the learned scholars in the temple is preceded by a painting of the Virgin presenting him to the

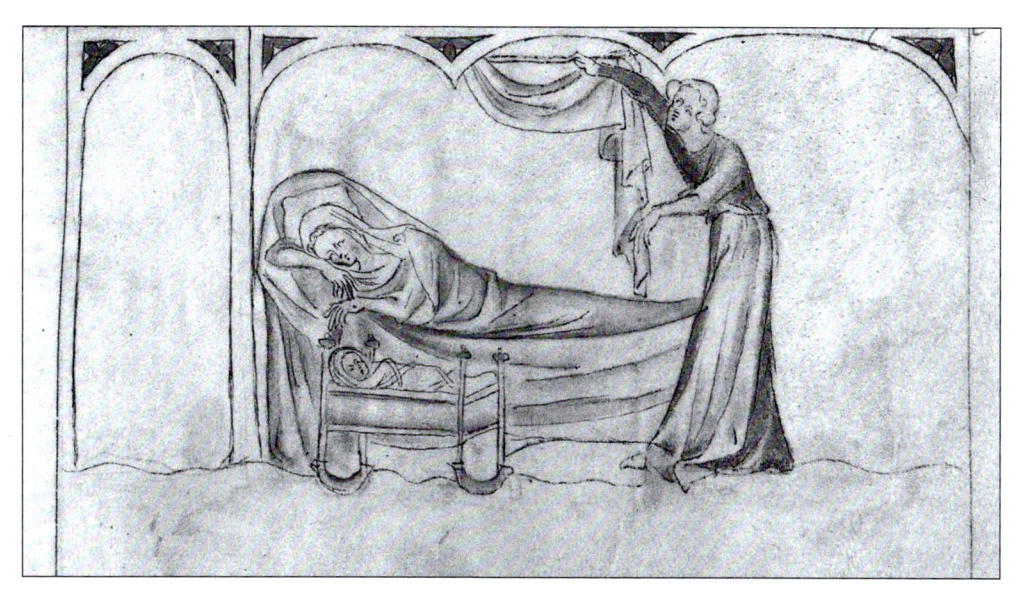

FIG. 82 Birth of Thomas Becket. Queen Mary Psalter. London, BL, MS Royal 2 B. VII, fol. 290r.

scholars. This illumination emphasizes her by isolating her on one side of the miniature as she seems to push the child toward the massed figures on the other side (PLATE 7). Mary's gesture echoes that of Hannah as she presents Samuel to Eli in the temple on fol. 48v (PLATE 6). The Virgin is also prominent in the Passion sequence, appearing, for instance, seated at the right hand of Christ in the Last Judgement scene on fol. 302v. Here she bares her breast in an image of mercy and intercession that is echoed very quickly on fol. 303v by a more iconic image of the *Virgo lactans*.[11]

These images of the Virgin fall, for the most part, within common iconographic trends of the period. When they are considered within the larger context of mother-images in the Queen Mary Psalter, however, they provide more evidence of a maternal focus throughout the overall iconographic thrust of the manuscript; and some scenes from the six cycles of marginalia at the bottom of each page of the psalter proper continue this focus.

One of the sequences focuses on the Miracles of the Virgin. Source material for the Miracles of the Virgin is ample, and representations of the miracles appear in several contemporary manuscripts. The Queen Mary Psalter contains the largest collection of marginal miracles I have found, with fifty-six scenes depicting thirty-seven separate Miracles. Indeed, twenty-three of these seem to be unique representations.[12] Many of the Miracles were of a contemporary nature, such as that of the knight who became a Cistercian monk (fols 221v–22r). This particular sequence accompanies the illuminations depicting the Ministry of Christ, so that the activities of the son seem to be echoed and continued into the present by the activities of his mother.

Mothers are also important in the lives of some of the saints in the Queen Mary Psalter. The final sequence narrates the lives of six saints in some detail.[13] Three of these are women: Catherine of Alexandria, Mary Magdalene, and Margaret of Antioch, who was the patron saint of childbirth. The inclusion of Nicholas of Myra is also interesting, given his importance as a children's saint and the inclusion of two scenes of his mother. She is depicted twice: first giving birth to her son (FIG. 81), and second as he refuses her breast during Lent.

Thomas Becket is given the most prominence in this sequence, as his life is narrated in a series of twenty-two scenes that form the longest extant pictorial *vita* of the saint.[14] These drawings begin with a focus on his mother's actions. Here, Becket's mother is a Saracen princess whose father had imprisoned Gilbert Becket when he was on Crusade.[15] After he escapes from his prison she runs away to London to find him, and there she is baptized, marries Gilbert, and gives birth to Thomas (fols 288v–90r; FIG. 82). Her action of leaving home and kin, which parallels that of the Old Testament Ruth on fols 46v–47v, is necessary to the formation of the story of Thomas.

The link between the marginal sequences and the Old Testament narratives is underlined by the artist's use of a similar pastel palette for both types of images. Furthermore, the Old Testament mothers and the post-biblical saints could have been more reachable for their audience than the Virgin, exalted as Queen of Heaven. The presence of mothers in prefatory and marginal drawings and in the illuminations, and the importance of their actions, may have provided constant reminders of the power of women to the audience of the Queen Mary Psalter.

Implications of the Imagery

Authorities spanning the medieval period instructed women to look to the Bible for female models to follow or anti-models to avoid. St Jerome, writing to Paula about her daughter's education, not only suggested that she make alphabet blocks for the child and teach her to read the Psalter at first, but also instructed that the child's model should be the Virgin.[16] At the other end of the period, the late-fourteenth-century Parisian known only as the Householder of Paris wrote to his young wife that she should follow the chaste examples of Sarah, Rebecca, and Rachel.[17]

Several questions should be asked whenever we agree to read literary or visual characters as models. Who commissioned or composed the work? Who was the intended audience? Were the characters intended to transmit very specific values or lessons to this audience? These questions cannot be answered definitively in the case of the Queen Mary Psalter, for its patronage has long been a subject of debate. The codex lacks the usual clues, such as obituaries or heraldry, that indicate patrons or recipients of some contemporary manuscripts, and its provenance before the sixteenth century is unknown.

Iconography provides some evidence, however. The emphasis on strong women throughout the Queen Mary Psalter suggests that the stories were moulded to catch the interest of a woman. The women's actions are crucial to the shape of the narratives throughout the manuscript, from the Old Testament to the lives of the saints. Other manuscripts with firmer connections to female owners display a similar focus on female characters. The Isabella Psalter, which provides many iconographic parallels to the Old Testament stories in the Queen Mary Psalter, is a primary case in point.[18] Some manuscripts with unknown patrons also emphasize female characters, which has led scholars to suggest female audiences for them. The Munich Psalter, which is one of the few Gothic manuscripts other than the Queen Mary Psalter to include the story of Ruth, is one example, and the Imola Psalter, which is the only manuscript other than London, BL ms Royal 2 B.vii to juxtapose a Jesse Tree with a Holy Kinship, is another.[19]

The most important female characters in the Queen Mary Psalter are mothers, which may suggest that it was intended either for the use of a mother, or to emphasize the primary role of motherhood in the life of a woman.[20] Can these stories be read as lessons, with the characters as role models?[21] On the whole the stories tend to underline traditional roles for women while granting a great deal of importance to their actions, providing the potential for lessons that would seem useful either to a male or female patron if the aim were education about proper female behaviour. The stories are not subtle, especially in the Old Testament preface, where the narrative is fairly straightforward and is explained in the short vernacular text beneath each scene. Women who are disobedient, curious, or doubtful are punished, like Eve, but Bathsheba's great sin of adultery, in which her active participation is emphasized (FIG. 79), is later redeemed by her championship of her son. Above all, these women are necessary, whether the stories follow a biblical or historical source or have been reshaped in terms of narrative or image. Without Rebecca's deceit, Jacob would not have been an important character; without the courageous act of Becket's mother in leaving her homeland, the saint would never have been born. Even the visual prominence given to Rachel as the mother of Joseph on fol. 20r (FIG. 76) underlines the potential power of women's actions, and particularly those of mothers. The choices of these mothers, from Eve to Bathsheba to Becket's mother, have a great impact upon the lives of their sons and thus upon history.

Many aspects of the Psalter support a royal patronage context. For instance, its well-established luxury status suggests a wealthy patron; the sheer number of illustrations done by the hand of one influential master, the quality of materials and of script, all indicate a great deal of expense. The careful planning and intricate organization evident in every aspect of the manuscript is another sign of its costliness.[22] Furthermore, localization of better-documented members of the Queen Mary group may indicate a patron from the London area, which was a centre for royal patronage in the thirteenth and fourteenth centuries.[23] One of these manuscripts was made for a royal woman, probably Queen Philippa, who married Edward III in 1328.[24] Kathryn Smith has examined the use of the dove-topped rod in the Joseph narrative in the Queen Mary Psalter as telling evidence of royal patronage, and suggests Queen Isabella, wife of Edward II and mother of Edward III, as the 'most logical target' of a lesson against infidelity inherent in the story of Joseph and Potiphar's wife.[25]

Isabella is indeed the most intriguing possibility, although space permits only a brief discussion of the evidence. Not only did she receive books as gifts, but she also borrowed and commissioned them.[26] Furthermore, manuscripts already connected with Isabella and Edward display some similarity to the Queen Mary Psalter in iconography, style, and sometimes layout. For instance, the Isabella Psalter in Munich and the psalter connected with Edward III's queen, Philippa, have been mentioned already as having iconographic or stylistic similarities to the Psalter.[27] The iconography of the Queen Mary Psalter provides some of the most persuasive evidence, emphasizing as it does both the actions of female characters and the consequences of those actions in shaping history. Isabella, as a daughter of the Capetian king, Philip IV, would have grown up with a clear sense of her own importance. As Queen of England she negotiated for her politically incompetent husband with his own magnates as well as with Scotland and France. She did not neglect her role as mother, bearing four children, beginning with the birth of Edward III in 1312. Isabella would later take drastic action in the interests of her son, just as had the Old Testament mothers in the Queen Mary Psalter, when she invaded England in 1327 with her lover, deposed her husband in the name of her son, and ruled for three years as regent.[28] The relationship between Isabella and the Psalter is strengthened by certain themes not discussed in this article, for instance an emphasis on the need for rulers to consider their decisions carefully with the help of good counsel.[29] The contemporaries of Edward II considered his lack of judgement and vulnerability to bad advice to be one of his greatest shortcomings.[30]

In all likelihood we will never know the precise identity of either the patron or the audience of the Queen Mary Psalter, and the intention of the narrative emphases will remain open to debate. However, given a careful exploration of its imagery we can suggest that the inclusion of and emphasis on female characters throughout its narrative would have been of greatest interest to a female audience. If we can accept the suggestion of Isabella as the audience, we can trace connections between the narratives of the Psalter and Isabella's actions that seem quite pointed. If the stories in the Psalter were to have been continued into the first half of the fourteenth century, Isabella herself would have joined the ranks of the strong mothers of the Queen Mary Psalter, who may have sinned but who redeemed themselves through their children.

Notes to Chapter Ten

1. London, BL, MS Royal 2 B. vii. G.Warner, *Queen Mary's Psalter* (London, 1912), provides a near-facsimile of the codex. See L.Freeman Sandler, *Gothic Manuscripts 1285–1385*, Survey of Manuscripts Illuminated in the British Isles V (2 vols., London, 1985), ii, p.66, for bibliography, with the addition of K.A.Smith, 'History, Typology and Homily: The Joseph Cycle in the Queen Mary Psalter', *Gesta*, 32/2 (1993), pp.147–59; Stanton, 'Notes on the Codicology of the Queen Mary Psalter', *Scriptorium*, 49/2 (1995) pp.250–62 and plates; Stanton, '*La genealogye comence*: Kinship and Difference in the Queen Mary Psalter', *Studies in Iconography*, 17 (1996), pp.1–18 and plates.

2. For a detailed discussion of these manuscripts, *see* Sandler, *Gothic Manuscripts* ii, pp.65 ff.; L.Dennison, 'An Illuminator of the Queen Mary Group: the Ancient 6 Master', *Antiquaries' Journal*, 66 (1986), pp.287–314; and M.A.Michael, 'Oxford, Cambridge and London: Towards a Theory for 'Grouping' Gothic Manuscripts', *Burlington Magazine*, 130 (1988), pp.107–15.

3. Munich, Bay. Staatsbibl., MS gall. 16, fols 26v, 28v. See Sandler, *Gothic Manuscripts* ii, pp.33–34; D.D.Egbert, *The Tickhill Psalter and Related Manuscripts* (New York, 1940).

4. For the Tickhill Psalter (New York, New York Public Library, MS Spencer 26), *see* Egbert as above. For the Psalter of St Louis (Paris, BN, MS lat. 10525), *see* M.Thomas, *Der Psalter Ludwigs des Heiligen* (Graz, 1985), for a facsimile of the preface. Also *see* H.Stahl, 'Old Testament Illustration during the Reign of St. Louis', *Il medio Oriente e l'Occidente nell'Arte del XIII Seccolo*, ed. H.Belting (Bologna, 1982), pp.79–93, and W.C.Jordan, 'The Psalter of Saint-Louis (Bibliothèque Nationale, MS lat. 10525): The Program of the Seventy-Eight Full-Page Illustrations', *The High Middle Ages*, ACTA vii (1980), pp.65–91.

5. For instance, Jacob's dreams of struggling with the angel are depicted in both the Isabella Psalter in Munich, on fols 33v and 34v, and in the reliefs that decorate the interior of the chapter-house at Salisbury Cathedral. For the latter, *see* P.Blum, 'The Middle English Romance "Iacob and Iosep" and the Joseph Cycle of the Salisbury Chapter House', *Gesta*, 8 (1969), pp.18–34.

6. The tale of Samson (fols 41v–46v) often includes several women, as it did in the scriptural source material, but in the Queen Mary Psalter all of these women are conflated into the beautiful and duplicitous Delilah (Dalidah in the Queen Mary Psalter), whom Samson woos, marries, and loses after she spoils his riddle; afterwards Samson gives a kid to her father to get her back.

7. The biblical Solomon is only anointed once, at the well of Gihon, and receives a few instructions only as David lies on his deathbed. The double anointing and education of Solomon are also depicted in the lengthy David narrative in the margins of the Tickhill Psalter.

8. In Stanton, '*La genealogye comence*', I explore the importance of genealogy throughout the narratives of the Queen Mary Psalter, and examine the Holy Kinship image as the crux of that theme. I have only identified four other Gothic Holy Kinship manuscript illuminations.

9. For a summary of the development of this image, *see* K.Ashley and P.Sheingorn's Introduction to *Interpreting Cultural Symbols: Saint Anne in Late Medieval Society*, ed. K.Ashley and P.Sheingorn (Athens Ga., 1991), pp.10–17, and W.Esser, 'Die Heilige Sippe: Studien zu einem spätmittelalterlichen Bildthema in Deutschland und den Niederlanden' (Univ. of Bonn, unpubl. Ph.D.diss., 1986). P.Sheingorn's 'Appropriating the Holy Kinship: Gender and Family History', *Interpreting Cultural Symbols*, pp.171–73, includes a discussion of the Queen Mary Psalter images.

10. In addition to the common divisions at Psalms 1, 26, 38, 51, 52, 68, 80, 97, 101, and 109, the long Psalm 118, which was often intended to be read at the Little Hours on Sunday afternoons, is also divided into four parts. Each of these has its own set of initials and illuminations, all of which illustrate scenes from the Passion. The Canticles receive a similar emphasis. For the use of Psalm 118, *see* A.Hughes, *Medieval Manuscripts for Mass and Office: A Guide to their Organization and Terminology* (Toronto, 1982), p.277.

11. For a discussion of this motif in Gothic England *see* N.Morgan, 'Texts and Images of Marian Devotion in Thirteenth-Century England', *England in the Thirteenth Century: Proceedings of the 1989 Harlaxton Symposium*, Harlaxton Medieval Studies 1, ed.W.M.Ormrod (Stamford, 1991), pp.69–104, *esp.* pp.95–97.

12 For manuscript collections of Virgin miracles, see H.L.D. Ward, *Catalogue of Romances in the British Museum* ii (London, 1893). L.M.C.Randall catalogued Gothic marginalia in *Images in the Margins of Gothic Manuscripts* (Berkeley, 1966), pp.223–24.

13 These seem to have been among the more popular saints in England during this period, receiving special attention in psalters and in books of hours connected with female patronage. For instance, Thomas, Nicholas, Catherine, Margaret, and Mary Magdalene appear in the margins of the Taymouth Hours, in which the prominent appearance of crowned women suggests a royal female owner (c.1325–35: London, BL, MS Yates Thompson 13, fols 85v–87r); see Sandler, *Gothic Manuscripts* ii, pp.107–9, and L.Brownrigg, 'The Taymouth Hours and the Romance of *Beves of Hampton*', *English Manuscript Studies 1100–1700* i, ed. P.Beal and J.Griffiths (New York, 1988), pp.222–41. Catherine and Margaret are depicted in a full-page miniature that faces a painting of the female patron in prayer in the Hours of Alice de Reydon (c.1320–24; Cambridge, Univ. Library, MS Dd. 4. 17, fols 1v–2r); see Sandler, *Gothic Manuscripts* ii, pp.75–76.

14 Randall, *Images in the Margins*, p.210; J.Backhouse and C.de Hamel, *The Becket Leaves* (London, 1988), p.12.

15 P.A.Brown, 'The Development of the Legend of Thomas Becket' (Univ. of Pennsylvania, unpubl. Ph.D diss., 1930), explores the sources, analogues, and descendants of this story.

16 S.Groag Bell, 'Medieval Women Book Owners: Arbiters of Lay Piety and Ambassadors of Culture', *Sisters and Workers in the Middle Ages*, ed. J.M.Bennett *et al.* (Chicago, 1989), pp.135–61, provides this and many other examples.

17 *Le Menagier de Paris*, ed. G.E.Brereton and J.M.Ferrier (New York, 1981), pp.56–67.

18 As noted above, the Isabella Psalter is the only other Gothic manuscript that includes the story of Hagar. It also prominently depicts Michal, Bathsheba, and Abishag in the historiated initials that mark the division of the Psalms with scenes from the life of David, and includes five marriage scenes and four births within the sequence of Old Testament scenes decorating the margins of its Latin Psalms. I am currently studying the relationship of the iconography of this psalter to the life of Queen Isabella.

19 The Munich Psalter is Munich, Bay. Staatsbibl., MS 835, c.1200–10. See N.Morgan, *Early Gothic Manuscripts 1190–1250*, Survey of Manuscripts Illuminated in the British Isles 4 (London, 1982), pp.68–72. The Imola Psalter is in Imola, Biblioteca comunale, MS 100, post-1204. See Morgan, *Early Gothic Manuscripts*, pp.74–75, and Sheingorn, 'Appropriating the Holy Kinship', pp.171–73. Sheingorn also suggests here that the Queen Mary Psalter was made for a female audience, on the basis of its pairing of these images.

20 C.W.Atkinson, in *The Oldest Vocation: Christian Motherhood in the Middle Ages* (Ithaca, NY, 1991), explores aspects of mothers and motherhood in medieval society.

21 Iconographic 'lessons' have been examined by many scholars in many contexts; two recent studies are M.H.Caviness, 'Patron or Matron? A Capetian Bride and a Vade Mecum for Her Marriage Bed', *Speculum*, 28 (1993), pp.333–62, and J.A.Holladay, 'The Education of Jeanne d'Evreux: Personal Piety and Dynastic Salvation in her Book of Hours in the Cloisters', *Art History*, 17/4 (1994), pp.585–611.

22 Stanton, 'Codicology of the Queen Mary Psalter'.

23 Sandler, *Gothic Manuscripts* i, pp.30–32.

24 London, Dr Williams's Library, MS Ancient 6. See Sandler, *Gothic Manuscripts* i, p.31, and ii, pp.81–82, and Dennison, 'Ancient 6 Master.'

25 In 'History, Typology and Homily', pp.154–55. In my 1992 dissertation 'The Queen Mary Psalter: Narrative and Devotion in Gothic England' (Univ. of Texas at Austin), I suggested tentatively that the intended audience of this manuscript was Queen Isabella of England; Smith's argument in conjunction with my subsequent work has strengthened that suggestion.

26 *See* S.H. Cavanaugh, 'A Study of Books Privately Owned in England: 1300–1450' (Univ. of Pennsylvania, unpubl. Ph.D. diss., 1980), pp.456–60, for lists of borrowed books, payments related to book production (i.e. 'to Richard Painter, for azure for illuminating the Queen's books'), and books in her possession at her death in 1358.

27 It is also interesting to note that one of the few other psalters to echo the peculiar *mise-en-page* of the Psalms in the Queen Mary Psalter, combining illumination, historiated initial, and text on the same page,

has been connected with Edward III (Oxford, Bodleian Library, MS Douce 131; *see esp.* fol. 1r). J.J.G.Alexander, 'Painting and Manuscript Illumination for Royal Patrons in the Later Middle Ages', *English Court Culture in the Later Middle Ages*, ed. V.J.Scattergood and J.W.Sherborne (New York, 1983), p.142.

28 S.Menache, 'Isabella of France, Queen of England – A Reconsideration', *Journal of Medieval History*, 10 (1984), p.108. Isabella's activities from birth to 1330, when she was forcibly retired from her regency by Edward III, are examined in detail in P.C.Doherty, 'Isabella of France, Queen of England 1296–1330' (Oxford University, unpubl. D.Phil.diss., 1977).

29 Certain scenes in the stories of Moses, Samuel, and David in particular point up this thematic emphasis. See Stanton, 'Queen Mary Psalter', pp.71–108, 190–91.

30 In the *Vita Edwardi Secundi*, for example, Edward is castigated for ignoring good advice, accepting instead 'the counsels of wicked men.' See *The Life of Edward the Second*, ed. Noel Denholm-Young (New York, 1957), pp.3, 39.

CHAPTER ELEVEN

Fables for the Court: Illustrations of Marie de France's Fables *in Paris* BN, MS *Arsenal 3142*

SUSAN L. WARD

WOMEN, ESPECIALLY those of the Capetian house, have long been cited by scholars as one of the principal influences in the establishment of court culture in medieval France.[1] One definition of court culture is given by Robert Fawtier, who suggests that it consisted of a 'circle of lords and ladies in permanent attendance on the king and queen leading a leisured and largely frivolous life'.[2] This life together consisted of a variety of activities which cemented the group together, including hunting, hawking, playing chess, and the oral recitation of poetry in the vernacular, frequently to the accompaniment of a musical instrument. From the early twelfth century and increasingly in the course of the thirteenth century these poems were written down. Initially committing the poems to writing was presumably to facilitate recitation;[3] however, the act of reading poetry from *de luxe* illuminated manuscripts, an act which included looking at the images, also came to be seen as an appropriate courtly activity, especially for women. By examining the miniatures accompanying the *Fables* of Marie de France, a text by a woman author in a manuscript (Paris, BN, MS Arsenal 3142), which was dedicated to Marie of Brabant, the second wife of King Philip III of France, we will see how the illuminations themselves could augment this courtly act of reading and particularize it to the interests and needs of an individual patron.

The illustrated *Fables* contained in the Arsenal manuscript are the work of Marie de France, one of the early authors of courtly literature, who was active in the second half of the twelfth century. Although Marie is most famous for her *Lais*, she also wrote a collection of animal fables. In the Prologue to her *Fables* Marie clearly identifies herself with Æsop, the source of about half her fables who, according to Marie and popular tradition of the time, translated the fables from Greek to Latin at the behest of his patron, Romulus. Marie, too, is a translator working for a noble patron identified in the prologue by his chivalric character: 'Thus he commissioned me, however – /That one, the flower of chivalry,/Gentility and courtesy'.[4] The text which follows contains 102 fables, about half based on the tradition of Æsop. The remaining fables, perhaps not previously collected together, come from a welter of sources. These fable sources, first catalogued by Karl Warnke at the end of the nineteenth century, range from high literary works to oral folk tales.[5] In the Epilogue

Marie again emphasizes her own authorship of the translation, in the famous line, 'Marie is my name, I am from France', a statement made necessary, Marie says, to protect herself from clerks who might want to claim her work.[6] She re-emphasizes the nobility of her patron, here identified by name as Count William.[7] She also suggests that her literary sources have a similar noble pedigree, for in the Epilogue she tells the reader that she is translating the fables into French verse from an English version translated by King Alfred the Great, who also liked them.[8]

Marie de France's selection and retelling of the fables has suggested a particular voice to many scholars.[9] Aspects of Marie's *Fables* frequently noted include greater sensibility to female figures on the part of the author than is usual in the Æsopic tradition, and a certain sympathetic identification with the poor and downtrodden, especially when they are victims of a capricious nobility. Yet overall, Marie's *Fables* indicate a basic support of the values of the upper classes, especially when they behaved in what she considered a reasonable way. This general tone, coupled with an emphasis on noble patrons and sources, made the *Fables* a desirable text for the upper classes to read and as such the *Fables* were copied frequently in the succeeding centuries.[10]

One of the early illustrated versions of the text is Paris, BN, Arsenal 3142, an illuminated manuscript probably made in Paris around 1300.[11] In this manuscript Marie's *Fables* are included with a miscellany of French poetry from the twelfth and thirteenth centuries. The poems range from the fabulous to the didactic, and include romances by Adenet le Roi, a court poet from Brabant, the *Livre de philosophie et de moralité* of Alard de Cambrai, religious writings by the Reclus de Moliens, a *Misere* and a *Dit de la charité*, Jean Bodel's *Congé* and *Chanson des Saisnes*, a series of *dits* by Baudoin de Condé, and the Proverbs of Seneca translated into French rhyming couplets. It is rather a rare compilation in which to find Marie's *Fables*, which are usually found in illuminated manuscripts containing what we would call scientific and didactic works rather than the courtly literature of Arsenal 3142.[12]

The illustration programme of the manuscript is lavish, as befits a courtly manuscript, and the physical presentation of the *Fables* is generally consistent with the other poems in the volume. The *Fables* are written in three columns of Gothic cursive hand with forty-four lines per column. While the number of lines on each folio corresponds to the layout of the other poems in the manuscript, many of the other poems are written in two rather than three columns. Each poem in the Arsenal manuscript is headed by a prefatory miniature and contains illuminated letters in red, blue, and gold heading the sections of the text. The *Fables* are preceded by a rectangular miniature of column width showing Marie seated and writing her book (FIG. 83). Marie's text is closed by a second, smaller image of Marie with a completed book, seated within the letter A. Each fable is preceded by a historiated letter of half-column width and eight text lines in height, illustrating the subject of the fable on a painted background. A small ornamented letter, two lines high, marks the beginning of the moral of each fable. This visual decoration both relates the *Fables* to the other parts of the manuscript, and also suggests that they merit particular attention, as the historiated initials make them one of the most highly illuminated portions of the manuscript.

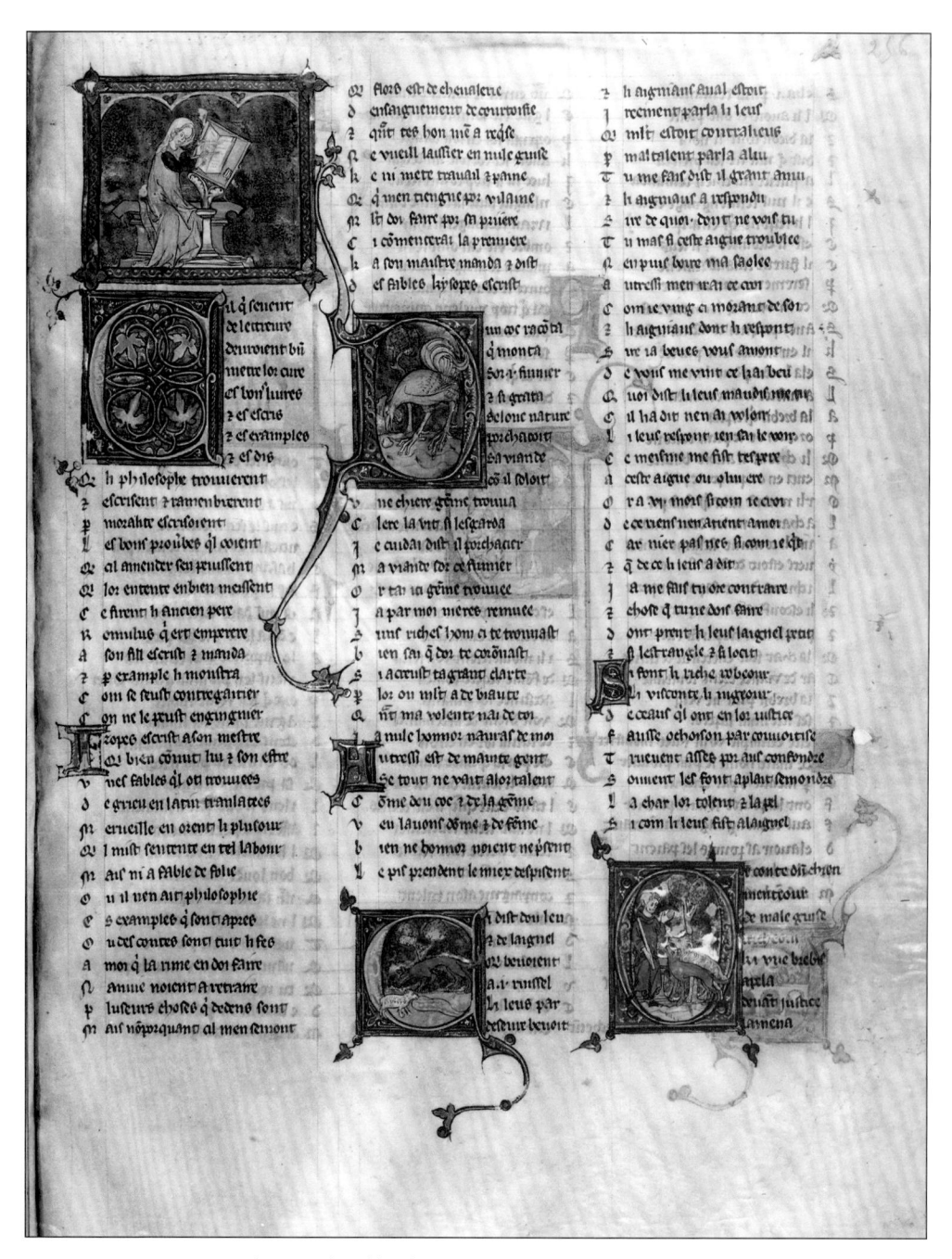

FIG. 83 Marie de France's *Fables*, frontispiece. Paris, BN, MS Arsenal 3142, fol. 256r.

FABLES FOR THE COURT

The style of the illuminations and the page layout found in Arsenal 3142 are representative of Parisian manuscripts of the last quarter of the thirteenth century. Several scholars have suggested connections between the Arsenal manuscript and works associated with the shop of the so-called Master Honoré.[13] The decorative vocabulary of the Arsenal manuscript, with its cusped ivy leaves and scrolls, as can be seen in the letter C beneath the portrait of Marie, is especially suggestive of Honoré's shop; and the dragons which appear in some of the initials of the Arsenal manuscript are also similar to devices found in his works.[14] While the figure style found in the Arsenal manuscript is generally similar to that of Parisian work in the late thirteenth century, the drapery is rather simply rendered and does not show the nascent interest in use of colour gradations to depict three-dimensional drapery which is a hallmark of the products attributed to Honoré's hand. These factors suggest a Parisian provenance and close association with the Honoré shop for the Arsenal manuscript, but not illustration by the so-called Master Honoré himself.

The gambolling beasts and rustics found in the letters which illuminate Marie's *Fables* are similar to the cast of characters found in the margins of Gothic manuscripts. In the centre of the page inside a letter C, fol. 266v (Fig. 84) several animals face a tree with two large clusters of foliage. They are illustrating the 'Fable of the Wolf and the Beetle' (number 65), a tale recounting how a wolf, incensed by a beetle crawling up his anus, summons other animals to fight the insects who are rallied by the insulted beetle. Before the fight the animals first all put on derrière bands to protect themselves from similar insulting assaults. The wasps are among the primary warriors of the insect band, and the deer is stung by one. His protective band drops off and the now-defenceless animals abandon their attack. The moral, in Harriet Spiegel's modern English verse translation, is:

> This example shows the way
> that some hate lesser folk than they.
> They rail at them so wickedly,
> They're shamed in an emergency.
> The lesser know best how, indeed,
> To aid themselves in times of need.[15]

The initial seems a curiously static representation of the vibrant and funny conflict described in the text. The image represents the moment mid-way in the drama where the animals and insects, fully arrayed, meet in battle, and the insect in front of the deer is probably meant to represent the wasp who stings him, resulting in the end of the battle. The animals represented in this fable initial are closer to the mainstays of marginalia than they are to the usual subject for illuminations. Even the mildly scatological subject of this fable seems similar to many marginal images. But although one of the characteristics of marginalia seems to be an exuberant life of forms actively interacting and even transforming from one thing to another, such action and reaction seem oddly absent from this fable initial. This can be clearly seen by comparing it to a marginal image of animals in battle from the Metz Pontifical, Cambridge, Fitzwilliam Museum MS 298, fol. 41r (Fig. 85), showing rabbits attacking a castle. Although the derrière bands which figure so importantly in the tale are clearly visible on the deer, and the randomly scattered wasps indicate the conflict recounted in the fable, the animals in the Arsenal initial are arrayed in static, parade-ground poses on the same ground line at the left of the tree. Only the wolf seems to react by looking up. Without reading the story the viewer would have little visual indication that a weird battle is taking place. These postures seem especially static when compared to the dynamism of the atextual rabbits. A rabbit with his bow drawn rears on his hind legs to fire an arrow which can be seen flying through the air, another rabbit lies supine with a rock on its stomach, while a third clambers up the scaling ladder to the castle. In spite of the absence of painted background here, the action is so vivid that the viewer is tempted to make up his or her own story to explain what is going on. Visually this marginal presentation is quite distinct from the Wolf and Beetle Battle initial. Clearly, the animal battle imagery in the Arsenal initials occupies a curious mid-ground between the decorous visual presentation customary for historiated initials and the rather earthy subject matter primarily associated with marginalia.

FIG. 84 Letter C (detail). Paris, BN, MS Arsenal 3142, fol. 266v.

The meaning of marginalia has recently been hotly debated in scholarly work by Michael Camille, extensively reviewed by Jeffrey Hamburger, and in an article by Madeline Caviness.[16] The traditional view of marginalia as a province for the 'creative' aspects of the artist has recently been displaced by a view which integrates the margins into a more complex whole including the more privileged image. Central to this new conception of the manuscript margins is the theory of carnival, a period of prescribed relief and laughter contained within an essentially monolithic system, which was formulated by the Russian structuralist, Mikhail Bakhtin. This thesis was originally developed by Bakhtin as a part of his study of the writings of Rabelais, and is applied by Camille, Hamburger, and Caviness to the marginalia found in medieval art.[17] Caviness has extended this new conception of the peripheral imagery in manuscripts to examine this marginal humour from a feminist perspective. She suggests that the margins reinforce the male dominance of the primary images by 'claiming the margins ... for the expression of male fantasy, leading to the private exchange of men's jokes, or a metaphorical locker room', which may, she says, overlook the reading of the imagery by women.[18] Caviness goes on to suggest that in specific instances, such as the Hours of Jeanne d'Evreux, the margins may be manipulated to effect a particular female reader.

In the initials of the Marie de France *Fables*, marginal-type subject matter becomes dependent on rules for the central image as it is positioned within the letter.[19] This change and

FABLES FOR THE COURT

FIG. 85 Marginalia showing a Battle of Rabbits (detail).
Cambridge, Fitzwilliam Mus., MS 298, fol. 41r.

addition of the more regular rules of the main image to the animal subject matter has two significant effects.[20] First, the visual treatment of the initials may have a textual parallel: Marie's formal octosyllables were probably perceived by her courtly audience as a foil for her folkloric subject.[21] The illuminator seems to have understood Marie's concept of gratifying the audience through juxtapositions, since the gambolling beasts and rustics, similar to those found in the margins of Gothic manuscripts, are here transformed to the more stable participants of the initial. In the same way both the text and initials took something associated by the audience with one artistic form and clad it in another. Certainly this functions as a sophisticated entertainment for the literate, visually astute reader. But by enlarging the subject matter permissible for historiated initials and changing the appearance of what was heretofore associated with the margins, visual categories shift, and it is also possible that in a book made to be looked at by another woman the regularizing of the animal imagery might be seen as an especially desirable feature, a sort of civilizing of the locker room.

The illuminations of Marie's *Fables* also include two images of Marie as an author. The *Fables* are begun by a column-width miniature of Marie seated, wearing a blue dress, sleeveless over-dress, and veil, with a horn in one hand and a pen in the other, writing in a codex which is resting on a slanted desk (FIG. 86). On the edge of the desk an inkwell is inserted. At the termination of the *Fables* a second image, now contained within a letter A, displays Marie seated and holding her book, now clearly inscribed with text (FIG. 87). Marie appears to be reading the book, which is now complete. Next to her is an open trunk containing additional volumes.

Most illuminated copies of Marie's *Fables* begin with a portrait not of Marie but of Æsop.[22] These versions usually conclude with a portrait of Marie, indicating visually the relationship between source and redactor suggested by Marie herself in the prologue of the

FIG. 86 Left: Marie de France (detail). Paris, BN, MS Arsenal 3142, fol. 256r.

FIG. 87 Above: Marie de France (detail). Paris, BN, MS Arsenal 3142, fol. 273r.

text. The appearance of two miniatures of Marie, first writing, then holding the apparently completed book, are unique to the Arsenal manuscript. This combination of two miniatures suggests the passage of time, indicating that while the reader has been reading, the book itself is being written, and the illuminations have implicated the author and the reader together in the action of reading and writing. The consistent emphasis on the intertwined process of the creation and reception of the book is not limited to the illustrations of Marie's *Fables* but is one of the themes of the illumination programme of the whole Arsenal MS, since almost all the authors are represented at the beginning of their selections. The images of Marie suggest that women as well as men participate actively in this process as writers, in addition to their more usual function as readers.

This special implication of the female reader is most likely directly related to the probable original patron of the Arsenal manuscript, Queen Marie of Brabant, second wife of King Philip III of France. Although the manuscript is not specifically listed in any medieval inventory or will of which I am aware, it has been associated with Marie of Brabant because of the presentation miniature at the beginning of the manuscript and because her name is uniquely emphasized in the text of the first poem, Adenet le Roi's *Cléomadès*.[23] Adenet le Roi was a court poet from Brabant who spent much of his career in the service of Marie of Brabant's relatives. His *Cléomadès* is the story of a Spanish prince and his fabulous horse, telling of magic, adventures, and love, and including a great deal of emphasis on the courtly life of the participants. The poem interweaves the behaviour of the fictitious nobility with that of living people, Adenet's noble patrons, whom he salutes directly in the text.

FIG. 88 Frontispiece. Paris, BN, MS Arsenal 3142, fol. 1r.

Cléomadès is dedicated to Marie of Brabant and her sister-in-law, Blanche of France, daughter of Louis IX and sister of Marie's husband, Philip III. In lines 21 and 22 Adenet relates that he got the tale from two ladies who are the flower of sense, beauty, and valour. A textual acrostic spells out the names of these two women, 'La Roinne de France Marie' and 'Madame Blanche Anne.'[24] Other noble patrons are also mentioned in the text. He offers prayers for Marie's father, Duke Henry of Brabant, who was both his first patron and teacher; Henry's two sons Jehan, the next duke, and Godefroy; Adenet's current patron, Guy of Flanders; and finally, in an envoi, the book is dedicated to Robert, Count of Artois.[25] The featuring of Adenet's work and its direct address to Marie of Brabant have led some scholars to suggest that he was the original compiler of the anthology, although this remains uncertain.[26] If this were indeed so, however, he would have been the person who selected Marie de France's *Fables* for inclusion in the book.

This relationship between text, physical book, and receptor is emphasized throughout the illumination programme, as we have already seen, in the miniatures of Marie de France's

Fables; however, it receives especially clear presentation in the frontispiece. This miniature shows Marie of Brabant as patroness, crowned, reclining on a couch, and holding a flower (FIG. 88). Marie wears a dress laterally divided, with the gold fleur-de-lis on an azure field of France on her right side and the gold lions rampant on a sable field of Brabant on her left side. Smaller than Marie, but also crowned, is Blanche, Marie's sister-in-law, who appears to be reciting. Blanche's garments heraldically identify her as well. They show the gold castles on a red ground of Castille, the fief of her deceased husband, Ferdinand de la Cerda, on the left side of her garment, and the golden French fleur-de-lis on azure on her right side. A crowned youth appears seated on a cushion at the centre of the bed wearing a sable gown decorated with the lions rampant of Brabant overlaid with the red label of cadency sketched on his shoulders. These heraldic devices indicate that this is Jean II of Brabant, Marie's brother and son of Adenet's original patron.[27] At the foot of the bed is Adenet le Roi himself, crowned and holding a musical instrument. In the initial beneath we see Adenet with two objects which probably represent a wax tablet, the notebook of the Middle Ages.

Certainly here we see Marie of Brabant in her role as patroness of the collection of poetry. But what specifically is the illumination expressing? Are these women merely commissioning the text from Adenet, as Sylvia Huot has suggested?[28] Or might something more substantive be occurring? The text explains that the story of Cléomadès is from Spain. Blanche was the widow of Ferdinand de La Cerda of Castille and had spent much time in Spain, which has caused Albert Henry and Henry Martin to conclude that the miniature shows her as the original source of the story, reciting it orally to the minstrel.[29] Supporting this thesis are her hand gestures, palm up in the standard rhetorical gesture for recitation, and Adenet's positioning with the musical instrument. Given the special role of the reader/viewer in the illuminations of Marie de France's *Fables*, this second interpretation of the miniature seems likely. We are again visually experiencing the process of literary creation at the same time as we read the product. The illumination shows a courtly woman as the source of an oral poem, but that oral poem must be recorded and transformed by the writer, in this case Adenet le Roi. A miniature near the end of *Cléomadès* (fol. 72r) shows Adenet handing a closed book to a knight holding a shield with the arms of Artois, undoubtedly Count Robert mentioned in the text. To make a book of poetry the writer must start with an idea or, in this case, an orally received source; then it must be recorded on a scratch pad, his wax tablets, and finally written as a finished volume. Social courtly activity is involved in both the creation of literature and its reception. As Michael Clanchy suggests, reading strategies for women were varied and potentially included:

> hearing the text read aloud while looking at the lettering and images on the pages; repeating the texts aloud with one or more companions until it was learned by heart; construing the grammar and vocabulary of the text silently in private; transposing the text, aloud or silently into Latin, French, or English; examining the pictures and their captions together with the illuminated letters, as a preparation for reading the imagery.[30]

The miniature program in Arsenal 3142 seems especially developed for Marie de Brabant, since it not only emphasizes her importance in the creation of literature, but represents her political interests as well. After the death of Philip's first wife, Isabelle of Aragon, on crusade in 1270–1, he married the young Marie of Brabant. Part of Marie's appeal for Philip may have been her direct twentieth-generation descent from Charlemagne. As Elizabeth Brown has pointed out, Philip displayed Charlemagne's sword Joyeuse at his coronation, and seemed especially anxious to bolster the Capetians' shaky relationship to this famous former monarch.[31] Marie was crowned at the Sainte-Chapelle on 24 June 1275 amid a splendid panoply emphasizing her descent. For her own part, Marie seems to have at least been aware of Brabantine propaganda which said that the Duke of Brabant rather than the Capetian king should rule France.[32] An illustration at the beginning of the *Chanson des Saisnes*, a *chanson de geste* by Jean Bodel, represents the coronation of Charlemagne by four angels, emphasizing divine intervention in his coronation rather than his connections to the French monarchy which were emphasized in the contemporary illustrations of his coronation which appeared in the *Grandes Chroniques de France*, made for the Capetians.[33] The rare type of Charlemagne's coronation appearing in Arsenal 3142 may be a further indication of Adenet le Roi's relationship with the manuscript's compilation and illumination, since Adenet was aware of his patron's connection to Charlemagne and was himself associated with the creation of the coat of arms of Charlemagne in about 1270.[34]

Although we have here concentrated on only part of the illustration programme of Arsenal 3142, the *Fables* and the frontispiece, it seems clear that the images in this manuscript were designed to impress the viewer, especially Marie of Brabant, in a particular way. Recent studies by Joan Holladay and Madeline Caviness have emphasized how men of the Capetian house commissioned manuscripts and other objects to be presented to young queens and which would reflect what men prescribe in the behaviour of those women.[35] The illumination programmme we have examined emphasizes not Marie's dependence on men or the French monarchy, but her independence both as an active reader and as a courtly patroness. The style of the Arsenal manuscript may be Parisian, but the message suggested by the illuminations emphasizes Marie's autonomy and her Brabantine origins. Although Blanche of France appears in the initial miniature, Marie's relatives and ancestors from Brabant are depicted more prominently, including her brother Jean of Brabant and Charlemagne, her most famous ancestor. This independence from Capetian control was heightened during her widowhood, as she pursued the interests of her own children during the reign of their stepbrother, Philip IV. Although Philip IV allowed Marie to continue in possession of her dowry, and in 1298 gave her a house in St Germain des Prés, their relationship, not surprisingly, remained cool and her attempts to become involved in politics were rebuffed.[36] This left Marie in a politically peripheral position, although she continued to enjoy a position of cultural importance which had begun in the court she had established as queen. In the later parts of her life Marie retained a court in Paris which was noted for literary patronage.[37] She also maintained close connections with other noble ladies who were important patrons, such as Mahaut d'Artois.[38] It is in such a courtly environment that we can imagine the *Fables* of Marie de France being perused.

The illuminations we have examined carry a complex message about women and literature. It has been suggested that Marie of Brabant was instrumental in establishing a non-peripatetic court culture with stable literary and artistic patronage, a role especially important after her husband's death.[39] The illuminations of the Arsenal manuscript may reflect this larger phenomenon, celebrating her role as a courtly patroness. The process of women creating, writing, and reading has become visually concrete in a unique way, perhaps analogous to the formalization of court culture under Marie of Brabant's aegis, and the illuminations themselves exalt the idea of literature by representing the physical process of making books. The oral source is indicated at the beginning of the volume by the reciting Blanche, the necessary patron is suggested by the larger-than-life Marie, but the role of the compiler is also presented in the image of Adenet Le Roi and his wax tablets. On subsequent folios other male authors are also illustrated writing their books. The inclusion of illustrations of Marie de France suggests that women too participate, not only in the recitation and patronage of literature but also in the actual writing of poetry. An awareness of the patroness's interests may be expressed more substantively in the illustration programme of the *Fables* than simply by an awareness of the role of women in poetry composition. The civilized depiction of animals in the *Fables* illustrations moves visual information, previously peripheralized, onto the main stage, possibly representing both a sophisticated courtly *jeu* and a deeper attempt to respond to the sensibilities of a female patron. The illuminated text of Marie de France's *Fables* suggests that poetry itself was to be crystallized in luxury manuscripts. Reading the *Fables* of Marie de France and looking at the initials was a way for Marie de Brabant and her followers to inaugurate a new type of court life, in a new community of interpretation.

Notes to Chapter Eleven

1 For some of the numerous works which consider these issues *see* the bibliography in J.Bumke, *Courtly Culture: Literature and Society in the High Middle Ages*, transl. I.Dunlop (Berkeley, 1991), pp.734–38.

2 R.Fawtier, *The Capetian Kings of France*, transl. L.Butler and R.J. Adam (London, 1960), p.205.

3 M.T.Clanchy, *From Memory to Written Record: England 1066–1307* (Oxford, 1993), p.216.

4 'Mes nepuruc cil me sumunt,/Ki flurs est de chevalerie,/D'enseignement, de curteisie.' Marie de France, *Fables*, ed. and transl. H.Spiegel (Toronto, 1987), p.30, ll. 30–32. The English translation is Spiegel's.

5 The classic analysis of the sources of Marie de France's fables is found in the work of Karl Warnke. His edition of the *Fables, Die Fabeln der Marie de France, mit Benutzung des von Ed. Mall hinterlassenen Materials* (Halle, 1898) contains discussion of the fable sources in addition to their text. He also examines the sources of the fables in his essay *Die Quellen des Esope der Marie de France* (Halle, 1900).

6 'Marie ai num, si sui de France', *Fables*, ed. Spiegel, p.256, Epilogue, l. 4.

7 *Fables*, ed. Spiegel, p.256, Epilogue, l. 10. The specific identification of Count William has been the subject of considerable scholarly interest. Leading contenders for Marie's count have included William Longsword, William Marshall, and Guillaume de Dampierre. As early as 1883 William Longsword was proposed by L.Hervieux, *Les Fabulistes latins depuis le siècle d'Auguste jusqu'à la fin du moyen âge* (5 vols, Paris, 1883), i, p.731. More recently M.Soudée, 'Le Dédicataire des Ysopets de Marie de France', *Les Lettres Romanes*, 35 (1981), pp.183–98, proposed William Marshall, and H.Gumbrecht, *Marie de France: Äsop, eingeleitet, fommentiert und übersetzt* (Munich, 1973) supported Guillaume de Dampierre, as Marie's Count William.

8 *Fables*, ed. Spiegel, p.258, ll. 16–18. There is no evidence that the King Alfred translation of Æsop ever existed. Warnke, in *Die Quellen des Esope der Marie de France*, suggested that an early 12th-century compilation of Fables by a man named Alfred, later conflated with the English king of the same name, was used as a source by Marie. Other scholars have believed Marie's Alfred to be a literary conceit; *see* E.Mickel, *Marie de France* (New York, 1974), p.40 for a discussion of Marie as a translator.

9 While most scholars who study Marie's *Fables* comment on her authorial voice, specific discussions of her bias and orientation can be found in the following works: O.Breivega, '*Vos* et *tu* dans les Fables de Marie de France', in *Actes du 6e Congrès des Romanistes Scandinaves, Upsall 11–15 août 1975*, ed. L.Carlsson, *Acta Universatatis Upsaliensis, Studia Romanica Upsaliensia*, 18 (Upsala, 1977), pp.31–40; C.Bruckner, 'La Conception du récit dans la fable ésopique en langue vulgaire: de Marie de France à Steinhöwel' *Le Récit bref au moyen âge: Actes du Colleque des 27, 28 et 29 avril 1979*, ed. Danielle Buschinger (Amiens and Paris, 1980), pp.389–406; and A.Henderson, '"Of Heigh or Lough Estat": Medieval Fabulists as Social Critics', *Viator*, 9 (1978), pp.270–71. See also K.Jambeck, 'Reclaiming the Woman in the Book: Marie de France and the *Fables*', in *Women, the Book and the Worldly: Selected Proceedings of the St Hilda's Conference, 1993*, ed. L.Smith and J.H.M.Taylor (Woodbridge, 1995), pp.119–37.

10 Ringger deduces the extraordinary popularity of Marie's *Fables* by analyzing the number of extant manuscripts of each of Marie's compositions in 'Prolégomènes à l'iconographie des œuvres de Marie de France', *Orbis Mediaevalis: Mélanges de langue et de littérature médiévales offerts à Reto Raduolf Bezzola à l'occasion de son quatre-vingtième anniversaire* (Berne, 1978), pp.329–42.

11 The bibliography for Paris, BN, MS Arsenal 3142, includes: Ottawa, National Gallery of Canada, *Art and The Courts: France and England from 1259–1328*, exhibition catalogue by P.Verdier and P.Brieger (Ottawa, 1975), pp.79–80, no.7; E.Millar, *The Parisian Miniaturist Honoré* (London, 1959), p.14; A.Henry, *Les Œuvres d'Adenet le Roi*, vol. i, *Biographie d'Adenet* (Brussels, 1951), pp.96–98, pls I–II; R.Freyhan, 'English Influences on Parisian Painting of About 1300', *Burlington Magazine*, 54 (1929), pp.320–30; H.Martin and P.Lauer, *Les Principaux manuscrits à peinture de la Bibliothèque de l'Arsenal à Paris* (Paris, 1929), pp.21–22, plate XIX; H.Martin, *La Miniature française du XIIIe au XVe siècle* (Paris and Brussels, 1924), pp.17, 18, 87–88, plate 13; G.Vitzthum, *Die Pariser Miniaturemalerei von der Zeit des hl. Ludwig bis zu Philipp von Valois und ihr Verhaltnis zur Malerei in Nordwest-europa* (Leipzig, 1907) p.55, plate 10; H.Martin, 'Cinq portraits du XIIIe siècle', in *Société nationale des Antiquaires de France: Centenaire 1804–1904* (Paris, 1904), pp.269–79; H.Martin, *Histoire de la Bibliothèque*

WOMEN AND THE BOOK

      de l'Arsenal (Paris, 1900), pp.158, 163, 177; H.Martin, *Catalogue des manuscrits de la Bibliothèque de l'Arsenal* (Paris, 1887), iii, pp.256–64.

12. Other examples where the *Fables* of Marie de France are included in compilations with 'scientific' material include two 13th-century examples, Paris, BN, MS fr. 24428 and BN, MS fr. 2173.

13. *Art and the Courts*, p.80; Millar, p.14. For a recent discussion and bibliography of Master Honoré and Parisian manuscript making in the beginning of the 14th century *see* C.Sterling, *La Peinture médiévale à Paris, 1300–1500* (Paris, *ca*.1987), i, pp.27–53.

14. Such a dragon may be seen beneath the image of Charlemagne on fol. 229r of Arsenal 3142.

15. 'Cest essamle nus dit de ceus/Que despisent les menurs de eus./Tant les avilent de lur diz/Que al grant busuin sunt honiz./E meuz se seivent cil eider/La u il unt greinur mester.' *Fables*, ed. Spiegel, p.176, ll. 55–60.

16. Camille, *Image on the Edge: The Margins of Medieval Art* (Cambridge, Mass., 1992), reviewed by J.Hamburger, 'Review of Michael Camille, *Image on the Edge: The Margins of Medieval Art*', *Art Bulletin*, 75/2 (June, 1993), pp.319–27; M.Caviness, 'Patron or Matron? A Capetian Bride and a Vade Mecum for Her Marriage Bed', *Speculum*, 68 (1993), pp.333–62.

17. Bakhtin, *Rabelais and His World*, transl. H.Iswolsky (Cambridge, Mass., 1968); Camille, *Image*, pp.12, 143–45; Hamburger, 'Review', p.320; Caviness, 'Capetian Bride', pp.359–60.

18. Caviness, 'Capetian Bride', p.358.

19. There are several other illuminated examples of the *Fables* of Marie de France including Paris, BN, MS fr. 24428 and Paris, BN, MS fr. 2173. The comparison of the different illumination programmes is beyond the scope of this study, although the historiated initial format is rare in other examples. The comparative study of the illumination of Marie's *Fables* is currently being undertaken by S.Hindman and was the subject of a paper: 'Æsop's Cock and Marie's Hen', 28th International Congress on Medieval Studies, Kalamazoo, Mich., May, 1993; now published in the present volume.

20. This point is also made by Hindman above.

21. For a discussion of the Fable text and Marie's audience, *see* Bruckner, 'Conception', pp.389–406.

22. For an author portrait of Æsop beginning Marie's *Fables, see* Paris, BN, MS fr. 2173, fol. 58r.

23. In the 17th and 18th centuries the manuscript was in the collections of the Duc de la Vallière, Guyon de Sardière, Gaignat, finally belonging to M. de Paulmy before it entered the collections of the Bibliothèque de l'Arsenal. *See* Martin and Lauer, 'Principaux manuscrits', p.21. Georg Vitzthum suggested that the presentation miniature represented Mahaut d'Artois: this has not been generally accepted. The book is not listed in the inventory of Mahaut d'Artois and the heraldry and text clearly represent Marie of Brabant: Vitzthum, 'Pariser Miniaturemalerei', p.55.

24. The first letters in ll. 18541–62 spell out 'La Roinne de France Marie'; in the succeeding lines the first letters spell out 'Mme Blanche Anne'.

25. The contents of the Arsenal manuscript include: Adenet le Roi's *Cléomadès, Enfance Ogier* and *Berthe aus grans piés*; Alard de Cambrai's *Livre de philosphie et de moralité*; Adenet le Roi's *Beuves de Commarchi*; the Reclus de Moliens's *Miserere* and *Dit de la charité*; Jean Bodel's *Congé* and *Chanson des Saisnes*; Marie de France, *Fables; Les Proverbes au vilain*; *dits* by Baudoin de Condé and others and the *Proverbes Seneke le philosphe*.

26. Sylvia Huot, *From Song to Book: the Poetics of Writing in Old French Lyric and Lyrical Narrative Poetry* (Ithaca, NY, 1987), p.40.

27. This identification was made by Martin in *La Miniature française*, p.88 and Henry, *Les Œuvres*, p.96. The red label of cadency is difficult to see in reproductions but can be clearly seen in the actual manuscript.

28. Huot, *From Song to Book*, p.42.

29. Martin, *La miniature française*, p.88 and Henry, *Les Œuvres*, pp.96–97.

30. M.T.Clanchy, *From Memory*, p.195.

31. Recent discussions of Philip III and his use of Charlemage as a family symbol include E.Brown, 'The Prince is Father of the King: The Character and Childhood of Philip the Fair of France', in *The Monarchy*

of Capetian France and Royal Ceremonial (Hampshire, England and Brookfield, Vt., 1991), pp.282–334; A.D.Hedeman, *The Royal Image: Illustrations of the 'Grandes Chroniques de France', 1274–1422* (Berkeley, 1991), p.20; A.Lewis, *Royal Succession in Capetian France: Studies on Familial Order and the State* (Cambridge, Mass., 1981), pp.188–89.

32 For a discussion of Marie's relationship to her Brabantine origins *see* Brown, 'The Prince', p.321. This interest in Charlemagne's descendants ruling France may have been more than theoretical, for in 1276 two of Marie's stepsons, Louis (the eldest) and Robert (the third) died in mysterious circumstances. Rumours were circulated that Marie poisoned them, especially when her own first-born son was named Louis, the name of his dead half-brother, the heir apparent. While Philip in the midst of personal political problems was unwilling to prosecute his wife, the charges were extensively circulated, and Marie was widely viewed as the villainess in the matter. M.Labarge, *A Small Sound of the Trumpet: Women in Medieval Life* (Boston, 1986), p.119, recounts that a beguine of Nivelle had a vision of Marie's innocence in the poisoning case which partially convinced Philip III. In thanks to the beguine Marie endowed a hospital for the poor beguines at Nivelles. Exemplifying a popular public sentiment of the time, Dante's *Divine Comedy* warns that she will go to the Inferno: Dante, *Divine Comedy*, Purgatorio, Canto VI, ll. 22–27.

33 Hedeman, *Royal Image*, pp.19–20.

34 Lillich, 'Early Heraldry: How to Crack the Code', *Gesta*, 30 (1991), p.45 and Lewis, *Royal Succession*, p.190.

35 Caviness, 'Capetian Bride', pp.338–55; J.Holladay, 'The Education of Jeanne d'Evreux: Role Models and Behavioral Prescriptions in her Book of Hours at the Cloisters', in *Art History*, 17 (1994), pp.585–611.

36 Brown, 'The Prince', p.303.

37 Fawtier, *Capetian Kings*, p.217, discusses Marie de Brabant's role in the formation of a permanent court with important literary patronage.

38 On Marie's friendship with Mahaut d'Artois *see* A.Henry, *Les Œuvres d'Adenet Le Roi*, i, p.46. On the patronage of Mahaut d'Artois herself, *see* J.M.Richard, *Une Petite-nièce de Saint Louis, Mahaut comtesse d'Artois et de Bourgogne (1302–1329): Étude sur la vie privée, les arts, et l'industrie en Artois et à Paris au commencement du XIVe siècle* (Paris, 1887).

39 Fawtier, *Capetian Kings*, p.217.

CHAPTER TWELVE

The Wound in Christ's side and the Instruments of the Passion: Gendered Experience and Response

FLORA LEWIS

THE *arma christi* and the wounds of Christ are among the most characteristic and pervasive elements of late-medieval imagery of the Passion. They are closely connected: both form important elements of Last-Judgement images, since both are signs of Christ's authority to judge; and more importantly, in their constant fragmentation and reassembling of the Passion narrative and the body of Christ, they epitomize the desire to encompass and anatomize the Passion, which is a key element of the late-medieval *memoria passionis*. Although in the majority of the images the five wounds are shown centred on the wounded heart, the earliest images combine the *arma christi* not with these, but with a single wound: that in Christ's side.[1] Women, particularly nuns, played an important part in the creation of these early images, but the aspect I wish to concentrate on here is the part played by gender in the viewer's response to the imagery. The wound in Christ's side could be seen as female and yet explored by men, as a site of union between *sponsus* and *sponsa*, and also of parturition.[2] Conversely, the *arma christi* were interpreted as Christ's weapons in the battle for the soul, but these weapons could also be wielded by women in their own defence. Nevertheless, though female imagery could be used by men and male imagery by women, this does not mean that their responses were identical. They were also manipulated: how women could use weapons was of particular concern to men. A key element in this manipulation of response was preaching: several of the manuscripts I shall be discussing are linked with the Dominicans, and the words with which Christ spoke to his viewers in the miniatures were provided by preaching verses. The *arma christi* were also closely associated with the allegory of Christ the knight, battling with the devil to save his *sponsa*, the human soul. This allegory is familiar from the version in the *Ancrene Wisse*, but it would have been most well-known to medieval listeners through preaching, where it was a widespread sermon exemplum.[3]

Two of the earliest images of the *arma christi* and the life-size wound are found in one of the most famous Bohemian manuscripts, a devotional collection written in the early fourteenth century for Kunigunde, abbess of St George's Benedictine nunnery in Prague castle, by Benes, a canon of St George's, who may also have been the illuminator.[4] The texts were composed for Kunigunde by the Dominican friar Kolda. The main text, *De strenuo milite*, is

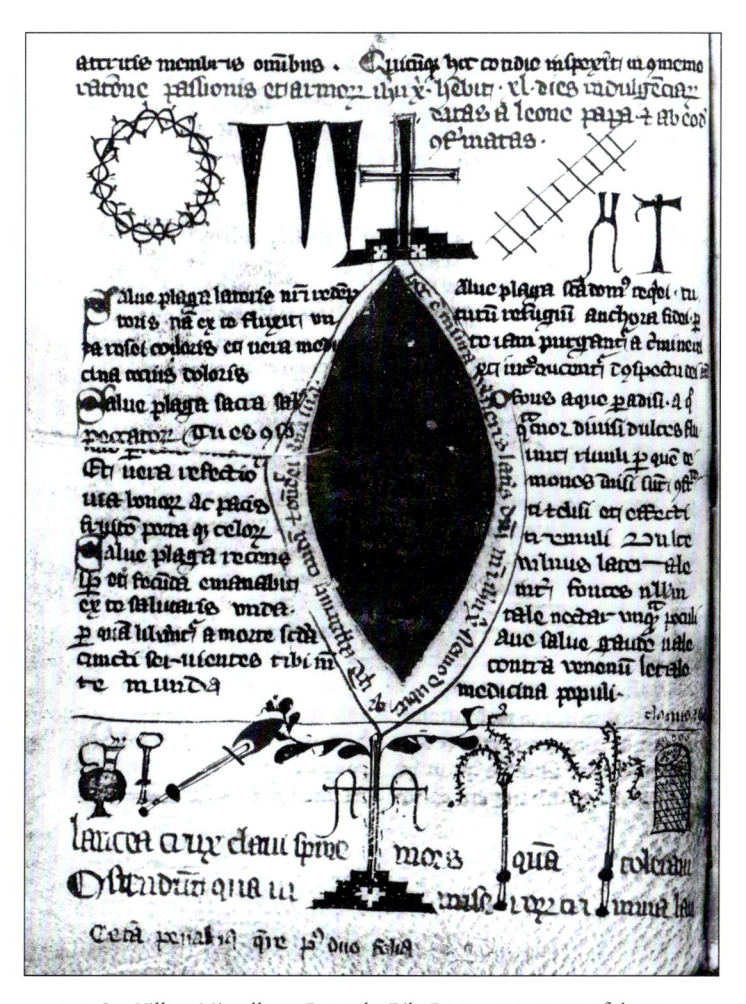

FIG. 89 Villers Miscellany, Brussels, Bib. Roy., MS 4459–70, fol. 150r.

based on this story of Christ the knight, which Kolda expands to provide an illustrated meditation on the Passion, seen in terms of the *arma christi*. It is clear from his text that devotion to the instruments had the support of the papacy, and that Kolda was adapting the pre-existing exemplum to promote this devotion. The preachers manipulated the basic story to emphasize certain parts of the allegory, and Kolda does the same. Here the *sponsa* is raped and imprisoned by a *latro degener*. Her betrothed, a noble knight of royal lineage (good breeding is very important to Kolda's version) sets out to a far country to rescue her, living in exile for 32 years, and fighting in many battles for his love:

> Moreover, in the wars and encounters he used various kinds of weapons in order that he, burning for his beloved, might the more forcefully set her free, and might fight the more gloriously.[5]

At length he finds the dungeon where his beloved is imprisoned, frees her, and restores her to his kingdom. The *parabola* is accompanied by a sequence of six images, showing the couple's betrothal, followed by the parallel gift-giving of the *sponsa*'s seduction. She is then pushed, crouched and blindfolded, into the narrow prison's burning doorway, where her crown falls from her head. The knight spears the lowborn thief through the neck, before leading her from her prison and restoring her crown. Although the illustration shows a single victorious encounter, Kolda's version of the parable describes a far more diffuse struggle, emphasizing the many conflicts and many weapons. His purpose here is to stress the way the Passion was composed of many torments inflicted in many ways; that is, to focus on the *arma christi*, a focus repeated in two full-page miniatures. Immediately after the prologue on fol. 3v is the heraldic shield, headed '*Titulus*: This is the shield, arms and insignia of the invincible soldier called *victor*, with the five wounds, supported with a spear and adorned with a crown'.[6] A later miniature shows Christ as the Man of Sorrows surrounded by the instruments, including the life-size wound.

The wound has much greater prominence in a miscellany compiled in 1320 by John of St Trond, a monk of Villers in Brabant, which includes two drawings of the *arma christi* (FIG. 89). These crude 'home-made' drawings appear very different from the Kunigunde's de luxe manuscript; but this distinction is more apparent than real. The context for both manuscripts is the care of nuns, since John of St Trond had the manuscript made when he was confessor to the nunnery of Parc-les-Dames (Vrouwenpark), near Louvain.[7] The wound and *arma christi*, this time surrounding the crucified Christ, occur together in another contemporary Cistercian document, a parchment leaf given by Wiegand, abbot of Marienstätt, to celebrate the dedication of the abbey church in 1324. It is one of a pair: the other leaf shows the founders of the abbey with Mary (who appeared to the first abbot in a dream and told him to found the monastery).[8]

The first images of the wound in manuscripts belonging to the laity are found in France, and the earliest of these also dates from the 1320s. This is the miniature at the end of a fine, copiously illustrated, Parisian copy of the *Image du Monde*, which was made for Guillaume Flotte, at that time one of the rising young councillors of Philip the Fair, who became Chancellor in 1339.[9] A later image is found in a manuscript for an even more aristocratic patron: the mid-fourteenth century Psalter and Hours produced by Jean le Noir and his daughter for Bonne of Luxembourg, wife of Jean, duke of Normandy, the son and heir of Philip VI, and mother of Charles V and the dukes of Anjou, Burgundy, and Berry (FIG. 90). But Kunigunde's manuscript is also a royal work: she was the sister of Wenceslas II, and although she was brought up among the Poor Clares, she left to marry, only re-entering religion as a Benedictine late in life. She was also Bonne's great-aunt, while Kolda was an important figure in the Dominican order in Bohemia, and frequented the courts of both Wenceslas and of Bonne's father, John of Luxembourg.[10] Among these three court manuscripts the Villers miscellany seems out of place, but the Cistercian nunneries also recruited from the upper strata of society.[11] These drawings are indeed crude and totally amateur, with no pretensions to skill or beauty, and in this they suggest associations with 'popular' or 'low' art; but this is misleading: as spiritual images their connotations are far from being 'popular' or 'low', any more than was their readership.

Just as the divisions between lay and religious, male and female are often blurred in

FIG. 90 Psalter of Bonne of Luxembourg,
New York, Cloisters Museum, MS 69.86, fol. 331r.

practice or challenged by other ties, so authority and status in these manuscripts can pull in different directions. It is likely that Kolda first devised the text for his own community, as he frequently addresses *fratres mei*, and given the story's roots in sermon exempla it may well be that Kunigunde first heard an oral version. He voices anxieties about the criticism that he may bring upon himself by teaching a woman, but in practice it is clear he had little choice: Kolda may be instructing Kunigunde, yet he defers to her royal birth, which he refers to constantly. He conventionally pleads that the burden placed on him by Kunigunde's request is too great, but he has done what she commanded since it is wrong to deny anything which originates from such excellent royal blood.[12] While he offers her the *arma christi* shield, he in turn asks for her protection 'with the shields of holy prayers against the darts of adversaries';[13] and the presentation frontispiece (though it may have been added after Kunigunde's death, as the angels hold a crown above her head) is a classic statement of the relative status of author, scribe and patron.

Visions and Sermons

Devotion to the *arma* had the backing of Pope Innocent IV, cited by Kolda in his prologue, who describes how Christ 'instituted the arms to be venerated by the devotion of the faithful, which also the ordinance of the pope approved at the Council of Lyons. Now we display these arms and confirm them by the testimony of scripture.'[14] Similarly, the second Villers drawing incorporates indulgences for the *arma christi* granted by Innocent, while the text which accompanies Guillaume Flotte's miniature is part of a hymn and prayer to the passion relics of the Sainte-Chapelle.[15] This was also a matter of power: the forces of the Church and the French royal house joined in the promotion of devotion to the relics, and also the image of the *arma christi* shared in the power of the actual relics, expressed in promises of indulgence and protection.

It is possible that relics of the holy blood (which the Sainte-Chapelle also possessed) also played a part in fostering people's awareness of the wound in Christ's side, though it must be remembered that a devotion to the wounds could focus purely on the crucifix, and indeed first did so.[16] In later manuscripts the hymn *Salve plaga lateris* (which forms part of the Villers drawing) carries an indulgence,[17] but the image also owes its power to forces which were certainly less official and also less exclusively masculine. In all except Kunigunde's manuscript the wound dominates the *arma*, but its size is not just for visual effect. The embodiment of the wound also has its source in another long-standing desire: that of the transference of power through the reproduction of the image. As the inscriptions in the two monastic manuscripts make clear, this is a life-size image, the true measure of the wound, and the equation of measurement is also the equation of power.[18] Here the wound is one among a number of late-medieval 'true measures', which included the height of Christ and the Virgin and the length of their feet. By far the oldest of these measures is that of the length of Christ, known from the eleventh century, whose sources lie in measurements brought back from the holy places, and which formed the model for the other measurements.[19] This is also reproduced among the *arma christi* in the Passional, though it has no place in the text.

However, the measurement of the wound was authenticated not from pilgrimage souvenirs, but from revelation, as is made clear by the inscription around the wound in the Villers drawing (FIG. 89): 'Hec est mensura vulneris lateris domini nostri ihesu christi. Nemo dubitet quia ipse apparuit cuidam et ostendit ei vulnera sua.'[20] By similar revelations (which concentrated on the person of Christ and his wounds rather than on the instruments) people knew how many wounds Christ had suffered, and stories of such visions helped foster devotion to the wound in the side and the heart of Christ.[21] The contents of the Villers miscellany reflect John's duties at Parc-les-Dames: they include hagiography, works on the religious life, sermons, exempla, and letters written by a monk of Villers to his sister in Parc-les-Dames. Many of the religious figures come from Villers itself and the surrounding region. This accords with what is known of Villers and its importance in the fostering of the spiritual life of the religious houses in the area.[22] It was a two-way process: the monks admired the nuns and beguines and their spiritual achievements, recorded their visions, and asked their advice; John included many women among his saints' lives, as well as narrating a revelation made to a local beguine. The manuscript's double emphasis on local religious life and the spiritual achievements of women may suggest that the drawings also refer to an event in the spiritual life of one of the *mulieres sacrae* of Limburg or Brabant.

The long-standing devotion to the wounds was clearly shifting to the concrete and visual, and visions, images, and bodies all demonstrate this desire to *see* Christ's wounds. In the twelfth-century Winchester Psalter the inscription for the Last Judgement reads 'Here God appears in his majesty and shows the wound of his side'.[23] Christ is indeed shown with hands upraised and with parted robes, but the wound in his side is a minimal dot, and no wounds at all appear in his hands and feet. During the thirteenth century the visual emphasis on all of Christ's wounds, both in Last Judgements and Crucifixions, became much greater. Crucifixions especially emphasised the quantities of blood that flowed from the wounds, a characteristic which is even more marked during the fourteenth century. This can be paralleled in the increasing importance of stigmata and the fascination with their actual appearance.[24] Despite Francis's efforts to hide his stigmata, Bonaventure reports how one of his brother friars was led by curiosity as to the size of the wound in his side to trick him into removing his tunic: 'watching closely he saw the wound, and he even quickly touched it with three of his fingers determining the size of the wound by both sight and touch'.[25] The desire to know the true size of the wound which led to this macabre parody of the scene of the incredulity of Thomas extended to the original wound in the side of Christ.

But the narratives of visions were not only important for the visionaries who experienced them. Much medieval devotion centred on the telling of stories of meetings with Christ and the Virgin. One strand was the rewriting and revisualization of the Christian narrative, most famously in the *Meditations on the Life and Passion of Christ*, where the reader is encouraged to insert herself as observer and actor in the scene, and to speak to the protagonists. She may receive an answer or a blessing in return, and this reciprocal possibility is an important part of the meditative process which links this more accessible practice with the experience of visionaries.[26] It is clear that much visionary experience was based on devotional practices whose popularity the subsequent visions helped to reinforce, and which also used images as a starting-point.[27] Most guides to meditation were written by men, while reports of visions can show us what use individual women made of them: a shared devotion experienced in different ways. Stories of visions, in turn, formed an important element of the preaching repertoire. The animating power of the imagination allowed great freedom in many areas of later medieval devotion, which is one reason for the creative force of religion in this period: displayed in the interrelated forms of devotional practice, visions, and preaching, and also, of course, in the creation of new images. The visionary element in all these stories was one means of establishing the authority of the message (and the messenger), but it also expressed a desire for a personal encounter between the human and divine.

As well as the explicit reference to the vision of the wound, the structure of the images themselves also draws on the conventions of vision and meditation. The readers and view-

FIG. 91 Psalter of Bonne of Luxembourg,
New York, Cloisters Museum, MS 69. 86, fol. 329r.

ers address their devotions to Christ, and he in turn responds to them in implied dialogue and gesture. Although there are no figures in the Villers drawings they are embedded separately within the well-known hymn, *Salve mundi salutare*, often ascribed to Bernard, but here said to be by Arnulf of Louvain, fifteenth abbot of Villers. The hymn is addressed to the feet, knees, hands, side, breast, heart, and face of the crucified Christ.[28] The wound is flanked by two further hymns in its honour, and the whole section can thus be read as a devotion to the elements of the body of the crucified Christ, who is both present and absent.[29] But among this collection of prayers addressed to Christ, we also hear his voice: 'Lancea, crux, clavi, spinee, mors, quam toleravi'. This was a widespread preaching verse:

> Spere and cros, nail, det[y] and þorn
> Schewen hou I bouthte man þat was forlorn.[30]

In the Passional Christ is portrayed freed from the Cross, and speaking to the viewer, as if

FIG. 92 Passional of Abbess Kunigunde, Prague,
National and University Library, MS XIV A 17, fol. 7v.

a crucifix has come to life. His appeal to Kunigunde is a variant of the first line of another common preaching couplet:

> In cruce sum pro te; qui peccas, desine pro me.
> Desine, do veniam, dic culpam, retraho penam.[31]

The emendment '*Sic* homo sto pro te' calls attention to the image itself, urging us to respond to the sight of His suffering.

The final part of Bonne's prayerbook contains two illustrated French poems which together form a coherent devotional exercise, moving from the wounded Christ to a close-up focus on the wound itself. The first miniature shows Christ on the Cross, adored by angels, pointing with one free hand to the wound in his side, like Christ in Kunigunde's manuscript (FIG. 91). This illustrates the *Complainte du crucifix*, based on the early thirteenth-century verses by Philip the Chancellor (often attributed to Bernard of Clairvaux), *Homo, vide quae pro te patior*, which were again familiar from sermons. In Bonne's version the *Homo* of the original has been expanded to *homme et femme*, and a couple representing Bonne and her husband kneel before Christ, whose gaze and gesture are directed to them. The text which accompanies the wound (which was written to accompany a life-size image), 'Beaulx tres doulx Jhesu Crist', could be used by Bonne as her response to Christ's appeal, just as the wound could represent how her gaze has followed Christ's pointing finger (FIG. 90).[32] In Guillaume Flotte's miniature Christ is still present, though he does not speak or move, but this is a less personal vision. The figures in prayer before the Crucifixion, wound, and relics are a mitred saint and a religious. The former is probably identifiable as St Denis, whose abbey owned several important Passion relics, including a nail of the Crucifixion. The accompanying text similarly is not a personal appeal but instead is associated with the cult of the relics of the Sainte-Chapelle.[33]

The closest visionary encounter is in one of the images accompanying Kolda's long exposition of the *parabola*, Here he relates the story of the Passion as seen through the roles of the various instruments. Each, when it appears first in the text, is rubricated for emphasis. The narrative is illustrated with miniatures of the events referred to, but it is only in the image which illustrates the wounds and the spear that Kunigunde herself is shown, stressing the importance of these elements (FIG. 92). She kneels close to Christ, who offers her his wound, in a grouping deliberately reminiscent of the incredulity of St Thomas. As throughout the text, inscriptions (written and perhaps composed by Benes) form part of the illustration. Here they form a dialogue. Christ says to Kunigunde 'Behold the grievous wounds and lashes which I have suffered', while she replies, 'O Christ, son of God, have mercy on me.' A further inscription could be asked by either: 'I beseech you, give yourself wholly to me, lest I be separated from you'.[34] Thus Kunigunde's devotion is presented in terms of a meeting with Christ who shows his wounds and pleads with her: an encounter typical of the visions of twelfth- and thirteenth-century nuns, of sermon exempla and verses, and of meditation on the Passion.

The sponsa *and the wound*

The language of vision is also central to an earlier manuscript with which the Passional has often been compared: the Rothschild Canticles, which has likewise been ascribed to a Dominican adviser and a female religious patron.[35] Both include important examples of the Man of Sorrows and *arma christi*, in both the relationship between Christ and the soul is that of the *sponsus* and the *sponsa*, and deeply evocative images are constructed around women, the spear, and the wounded Christ (FIG. 93). But these similarities also serve to point up the differences between the manuscripts. While the entire *sponsa* section of the Rothschild Canticles is a meditation on the *Song of Songs*, Kolda scarcely uses this text, though he constantly refers to the *sponsus* and *sponsa* of the parable. As Jeffrey Hamburger points out, the Man of Sorrows in the Rothschild Canticles is an image of triumph rather than suffering, and even though bound to the Cross and tied to the pillar, he is an active, upright, figure, gazing at the *sponsa*. His nakedness, marked only by the flower-like forms of the five wounds,

FIG. 93 Rothschild Canticles, New Haven, Beinecke Rare Book and Manuscript Library, MS 404, fols 18v–19r.

shows his humanity (as the text makes clear); but the image speaks far more clearly of beauty than of suffering. This is a very different Man of Sorrows from Kunigunde's: entirely covered with the wounds of the flagellation, freed from the cross only to carry the rods which caused them, and to appeal to the viewer to look at his suffering and refrain from sin. Similarly, the image of Kunigunde and Christ speaks of the fear of separation rather than the joy of union.[36]

Whereas Kunigunde meets with a clothed, resurrected Christ, and the blood-tipped spear plays no part in the action, the *sponsa* in the Rothschild Canticles wields her spear. There is a deliberate ambivalence in the action here, which encompasses both the wound of Longinus and the wound of love, as the accompanying verse from the *Song of Songs* 4:9 makes clear: 'Thou hast wounded my heart, my sister, my spouse'.[37] Christ has already been wounded, and yet his *ostentatio* gesture both displays the wound to the viewer, and points the way for the *sponsa*'s spear. The openness of the image to interpretation is a characteristic of meditative writing. Later in the manuscript the parallel wounding of the unicorn by the spear is enacted in an atmosphere of ecstatic exhilaration, the naked dancing virgin echoing Christ's pose: a pose designed for modesty, but which also blends the forms of these male and female bodies. In a manuscript where association plays such an important role, and the meditation moves forward by an allusive process of verbal echoes, these visual echoes also carry the inarticulate power of things almost stated. This Marian allegory (based ultimately

213

on a fable with a strong sexual content) is thus, like the previous miniature, also a image of penetration, blood and virginity, nakedness and wounding.[38]

There is extremely little internal evidence for the ownership of the Rothschild Canticles, and a great deal of weight has been placed on the *sponsa* imagery and its relationship to the *Brautmystik* of thirteenth-century nuns.[39] The inference of female religious ownership may well be correct, given the popularity of the *Song of Songs* in nunneries. But despite the brilliance of Hamburger's analysis of the manuscript's milieu and the undoubted suitability of the manuscript for female devotion, is the imagery necessarily alien to a male owner? Men could use the theme of the female soul, the *anima*, to explore the metaphor of sexual union with a male God.[40] How does this affect the use of the imagery by Hamburger's suggested Dominican adviser? It may be that, as Hamburger argues, nuptial imagery is commonly used by female rather than by male visionaries, but although these are extraordinary images of meditation, they do not necessarily represent visions (though there is clearly overlap between the two). Rather, like both visions and meditations, they use biblical metaphor as a spring-board to develop a series of freely associative images.[41] If we look not just at visions but at a far more widespread and accessible guide to meditation, the late-thirteenth- and early-fourteenth-century *Stimulus Amoris*, which had a wide diffusion, frequently in the company of works of pastoral care, we see a willingness to use metaphors of physical union which are gendered but fluid.[42]

The central image of meditative union is that of entering the wound. The reader is told to 'strive as far as you are able to share in Christ's Passion', for compassion on his sufferings and meditation on the Passion is the way into Christ's side and thus to the heart: 'O happy heart, which is so sweetly tied to Christ's heart, whose left hand is under his head and whose right hand embraces him (*Song of Songs* 2:6) because then is the bridegroom rightly joined in marriage with his spouse and they are united in the bedchamber'. The writer deals with the masculine/feminine divide of soul as female spouse by addressing his soul as both self and other, a device which is both distancing and enabling, by which he can encourage and advise the reader in the process of meditation, while at the same time offering him or her a preview of its fruits in the form of a commentary on the state of the rapt soul:

> But tell me, I implore you, most virtuous soul, the sweetness which you feel; do not hide the delights with which you overflow. But, as I well see, you do not hear, because your heart is absorbed in sweetness. Already you have forgotten your interpreter who remains in prison. For I see that you are so exceedingly taken with delight that neither voice nor sense can go further.[43]

Similar experiences are held out for the reader, who is told to concentrate solely on God, to be rewarded with sweet kisses and embraces, and thus 'you will be absorbed in exceeding sweetness'. This is a process which has already overcome the soul, who meets the author's appeals with silence: 'O my soul filled with delight ... But as I see, you will not speak to us, because you are ravished by your beloved.'[44]

Whoever was the original owner of the Rothschild Canticles, it is clear that the spousal imagery could be used in meditation by male or female. The compiler may well have used this manuscript in the care of nuns, but there is nothing in the *sponsa* imagery to suggest that it would not have been equally suitable for his own use.⁴⁵ Indeed, if we again consider the similarity of the bodies of the naked virgin and Christ, and the *sponsa* holding her spear, it is clear that the image enables a male viewer to imagine himself as a penetrating *sponsa*, piercing the naked and sexually indeterminate body of Christ. The author of the *Stimulus Amoris* similarly imagined himself as the spear, to rest in Christ's side for ever.⁴⁶ Although none of the *arma christi* images show the spear in the wound, it is emphasized both visually and in the texts, ready for manipulation by the viewer.

The description of union with Christ in the vocabulary associated with bodily union and sexuality caused some contemporary and a great deal of later anxiety, and this distrust and distaste of sexuality – dangerous as a metaphor and unacceptable when religious union was experienced by the body as a sexual phenomenon – is also part of the history of the imagery of the life-size wound. These large red forms, with their vertical axis (which is rare in representations of the wound on Christ's body), often shown bleeding, have a powerful sexuality, noted unwillingly by the seventeenth-century reformer Jean-Baptiste Thiers, who warned that certain scoundrels who publicly professed atheism and impiety 'ont voulu faire passer l'Image … pour une chose que la pudeur ne permet pas de nommer'.⁴⁷ Modern distaste for such imagery has been overtly based on their 'superstitious' nature, which has meant that they have been constantly labelled as part of 'popular' religion. Similarly, writers on mysticism have endeavoured to distinguish a true mysticism free from too much sexuality. Such attempts to construct a purified version of religion have often resulted in women ending on the wrong side of the divide.

Conversely, our own rediscovery of these images cannot be disassociated from present-day use of female genital imagery, for example in the central-core imagery of Judy Chicago and Miriam Schapiro. The sexual connotations of these images has led to an unwillingness to engage with or even reproduce them until recently. But would these connotations have been recognized by their original viewers, and how would they have dealt with them? We have seen how spousal imagery made the wound an entrance pierced by the spear to uncover the bedchamber of the heart. Caroline Bynum emphasized in her fundamental article the maternal associations of the crucified Christ: the wound was above all a breast at which to suckle, but also a place of rest and safety, sometimes explicitly seen as a return to the womb.⁴⁸ This wound/birth connection is reflected in representations of the Visitation in which the two unborn children are visible within their mothers' wombs. The womb shapes in such images vary, but the most common version is a pointed oval, often with a border running round it.⁴⁹ Since the creation of Eve paralleled the birth of the Church from Christ's side, she is also sometimes shown drawn out from a large red pointed oval on Adam's side.⁵⁰

The wound was a place of parturition for the individual soul, and in the later thirteenth and fourteenth centuries there was an emphasis, most importantly in Julian of Norwich, on the anguish of Christ giving birth to the world in His crucifixion.⁵¹ But if we return to the widespread *Stimulus Amoris*, we find a far more intimate treatment of the theme. The author resolves to enter and live in Christ's wounds, to move alternately from the Passion to the

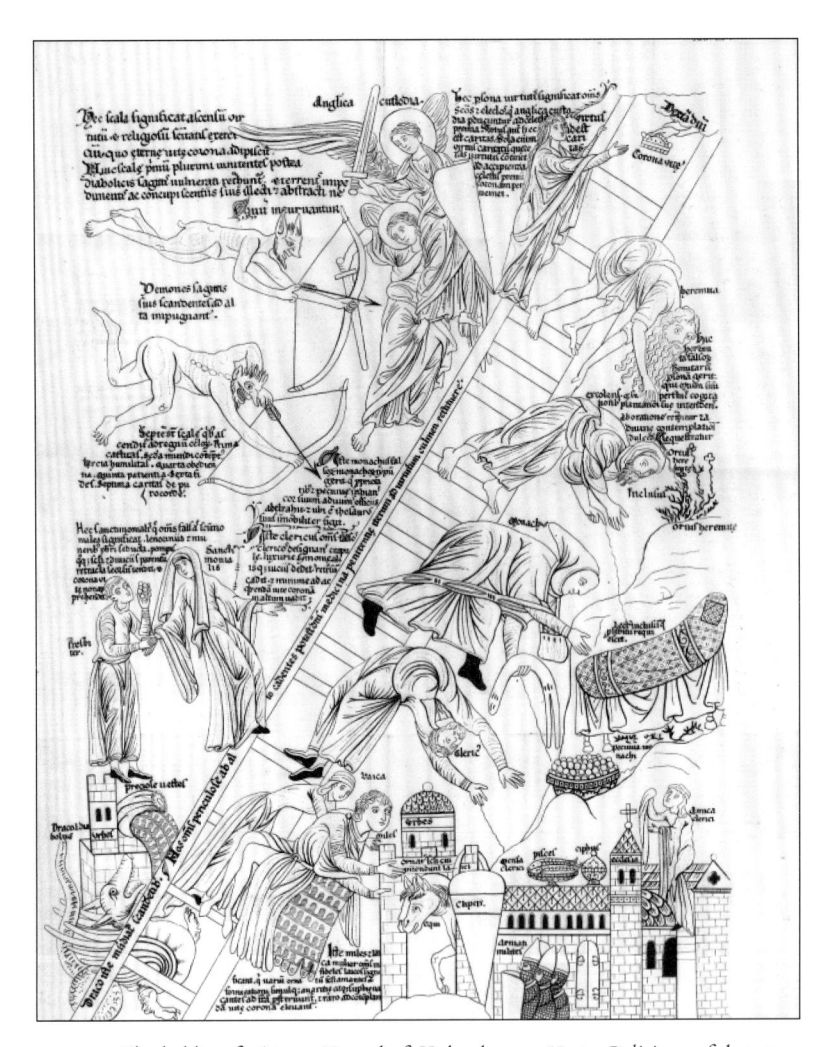

FIG. 94 The ladder of virtues. Herrad of Hohenbourg, *Hortus Deliciarum*, fol. 215v.

Nativity and suckle along with the infant Jesus, drinking mingled blood and milk. He enters the wounds, and blinded with blood, gropes with his hands further and further 'ad intima viscera caritatis sue' so that he cannot return. Here he dwells in Christ's bowels as the Virgin carried Christ in her womb, fearing only the time of childbirth. But this too brings its own delights: if Christ gives birth to him, he must then as a mother suckle, carry, and kiss him. Even after birth, he knows he can return again and again, till they are no longer separated.[52] This eroticized fantasy of an endless return to the womb is also an exploration of the bliss of union: before as union of lovers, here as ultimate dream of return to the mother. Again, Caroline Bynum points out how such maternal imagery could be used by men to express erotic play, and this passage does seem a very male view of childbirth, focused on the infant.[53]

It was a very different experience of childbirth which made Aude Fauré in the early fourteenth century doubt the eucharist because at the elevation she kept thinking about the filthiness of the placenta.[54] Aude's horrified focus on the blood and mess of childbirth is part of a well-documented medieval fear and disgust with the leaking orifices of a body which was 'nou[y]t elles/But of Muk bretful a sekke', where the liquefaction of dissolution was the ultimate insult to its wholeness.[55] The obverse of the fatally contaminated bodily fluids was the flow of holy oil from saints' tombs, of milk from the Virgin, and especially of water and blood from Christ. Similarly, Bridget of Sweden's description of her vision of the Nativity reveals and exorcizes her own anxieties about human birth, in a very different fantasy from the *Stimulus Amoris*. Mary gives birth in an instant, within a blinding pure light that hides the actual birth; her swollen womb immediately retracts and the placenta appears already neatly wrapped up beside her; the baby is 'most clean of all filth and uncleaness', and when the umbilical cord is severed no liquid or blood flows out.[56] Corporeality is not the problem: the shepherds are uncertain of the sex of their Saviour, and the Virgin shows them the baby's genitals. But this is a birth utterly tidied and purified from all the leaking bodily fluids that Bridget invokes elsewhere.[57]

The female imagery of the life-size wound could be used to explore and express the desires for union, incorporation, and rebirth: building freely on human experience and fantasy of love, sex, and pregnancy, and the perennial problem of the separateness of human beings and the desire to overcome this. The fluidity of such imagery is achieved partly because its creators allowed themselves the freedom to go beyond their social experience. Nevertheless, childbirth for women meant dealing with issues of pain, messiness and fear. Christ could share in the pain and offer purified orifices and excretions, and Mary could present a perfect birth; but images of the life-size wound could also give more practical aid as a talisman against the ever-present danger of death in childbirth. This talismanic power was modelled (as was the life-size measurement itself) on the protective properties of the length of Christ, and is reflected in the wound's inclusion in birth girdles, but we can also trace it back to the earliest images. The promises of indulgence that accompany the Villers image state that it 'offers an excellent remedy for women in labour'.[58]

Knights, Women, and Weapons

I have concentrated on the image of the wound rather than the *arma christi* as a whole, but weapons were also borne not in order to inflict a wound of love, but as a protection against the devil. The exemplum of the lover-knight is related to the much earlier theme of spiritual battle, but it engages with this very differently. I want to examine here not the earliest psychomachia imagery, but related images of women, knights, and spiritual struggle. One of the most famous series of images of the battle for the soul enacted by the virtues and vices is found in another book made for (and this time, by) nuns, the *Hortus Deliciarum* of Herrad of Hohenbourg.[59] The main concern of the second half of the *Hortus* is the struggle for salvation: Herrad progresses through the themes of the battle of virtues and vices, the need for contempt of the world and the love of God, the Church on earth and the prospects of its members for salvation, to the last days as envisioned in *Revelations* and the rise and fall of Antichrist, the Judgement, heaven and hell. In the *psychomachia*, the female personifications in their helmets and mail and flowing gowns, armed with the Pauline swords of *verbum dei*, battle with relish against the spears of the vices, but this is not Herrad's only depiction of the spiritual struggle, and as she moves towards a conception which deals more with the individual soul within the world the presentation both of women and, especially, of knights becomes far more problematic. We have seen how men could interpret the image of the *sponsa*: here instead we have a nun's critique of knighthood.

The virtues and vices are succeeded by a section on Solomon and the Temple which ends with the images of Fortune turning her wheel and Solomon watching a puppet game of two fighting knights, the *ludus monstrorum* glossed as *vanitas vanitatum*. This is the first of a group of three images and associated texts urging the contempt of the world and the love of Christ, of which the most well-known is the ladder of virtues based, as Katzenellenbogen showed, on Byzantine images of the monk's ascent to Christ, aided and obstructed by virtues, vices, and devils.[60] Herrad's is a celestial game of snakes-and-ladders where the odds are heavily loaded against the contestants, and only *caritas* gains the top and holds her hand out for the crown of life, protected from the arrows of the attacking demons by her guardian angels. She signifies all the saints and elect, led by their guardian angels to the heavenly rewards, as well as charity, 'which includes all other virtues'. As with the older battle of the virtues and vices, her triumph is inevitable, inherent in her name. But in keeping with the theme of contempt of the world this is not a ladder of virtues and vices; instead it is the temptations of the world which are the downfall of the figures struggling up the ladder, and they, in turn, are not personifications, but types of people attempting to live the religious life in the world – hermit, anchorite, monk, cleric, and nun – yet failing and falling as, wounded by the devil's arrows, they succumb to temptation. The nun is the only one who still stands on the ladder from which the others have already fallen; but even she turns away, seduced by the priest's gifts.

Although this is primarily an image of the religious life, knights and ladies also play a part: but a very different one from the lover-knight exemplum. The *miles* and *laica* are the first to slip: their downfall is shown as the city with the horses and shield at the gate and armed soldiers, all carefully labelled, and summed up as the adornments of this world to which the laity direct their thoughts (*ornatus seculi cui intendunt laici*). In the early fourteenth century the Franciscan Nicholas Bozon used the shield and horse in his version of the story as metaphors for the protection of the soul:

> Leave my steed at the entrance of the gate,
> At the entrance of the chamber hang my shield,
> Fix my lance near your bed,
> And then you will have no fear of any adversity.[61]

Later in the fourteenth century we find the same idea of the *arma* placed as protection at the entrances to the house of the soul – and of the body – taken up by Henry of Lancaster in his *Livre de Seyntz Medicines*, who describes how he must have 'vos armes de la greve passion … si proprement purtraites sur mes portes': that is, on his ears, eyes, nose, mouth, hands, feet, and especially on the heart. With the entrances thus marked, the devil will not be brave enough to set foot inside.[62] Weapons carry no such positive connotations for Herrad: like the fighting knights of Solomon's *ludus monstrorum*, they are purely vanity. In the next section, dealing with the Church and its organisation, Herrad's choice of extracts from the *Elucidarium* of Honorius Augustodunensis dealing with the orders of society and their hope of salvation shows that, as on the ladder, their prospects are precarious. The answer to the question 'What is your opinion of knights?' is 'Little that is good; for they live by booty and clothe themselves with plunder (*rapina*).'[63] In the battle of the vices and virtues, Rapine, born from Avarice, is shown as a male armed knight tearing off another knight's helmet (the only male personification in the entire battle) while his followers strip others of their clothes.[64] This is not the whole story. Herrad recognizes that knights have a part to play in the world: the *laici* are included in the miniature of the House of God, and the young girls (a significant choice for an inclusive image) signify all the obedient members of the Church, including knights and all the laity, both men and women.[65] Nevertheless, at the multi-folio panorama of the Judgement, representations of each group balance each other among the saved and condemned: wise and foolish virgins, hermits and false hermits, faithful and unfaithful laity. This is where the false and unfaithful who fall from the ladder end. But the knights are shown nowhere: they appear instead in the miniature of hell's torments. There, although a monk with a purse full of coins is the latest entrant, the only other identified groups – burning equally in their cauldrons – are the Jews and the *armati milites*, still in full armour.[66]

Where Herrad thought little of the knights' chances of salvation, Kunigunde welcomed the metaphor of Christ as a knight. This was not just due to the change in the status of knighthood in the intervening century.[67] The heraldic aspect of the *arma christi* was of great importance here. Together with the shield of Christ in the Passional are the three shields of the presentation miniature, bearing the arms of the kingdom of Bohemia, the convent of St George (which show the saint as a mounted knight with bearing his shield emblazoned with a red cross, like the shield held by Christ in the parable illustration), and St Wenceslas, the patron saint of Bohemia.[68] Knighthood viewed as a matter of birth was accessible to aristocratic women: they too could bear a coat of arms. It was the armigerous of this world – religious and lay, women as well as men – who had an especial interest in Christ's arms.

Herrad's ladder is an image warning of the fate of the *falsi* and *infideles*, but it does bear the promise that all who fall from it 'the Lord can restore again to the height of virtues by the medicine of penitence'.[69] In the thirteenth century the allegory of penitence in the Lambeth Apocalypse deals with similar themes, but here a *laica* is at the centre of the spiritual struggle, attacked, like *caritas*, by a demon archer.[70] She is not, however, a personification of virtue but a penitent, and the miniature stresses her passivity, her dependence on outside help (both supernatural and of the Church), and the uncertainty of her situation. She is placed in the midst of frozen, conflicting action: the helpers and adversaries trample, entreat, reveal, expound, strive, disturb, disperse, fire; but the lady herself is seated, the only verb associated with her is *orant*. She bears no weapon, but holds out the shield of faith as her defence. The actions of defence are those of the angel and above all of the preacher, who is both present as the cock trampling on the tree of the world and advocating its contempt (as in the *Hortus Deliciarum*), and who also reveals the water of holy

FIG. 95 *Speculum humanae salvationis*, Chicago, Newberry Library, MS 40, fol. 30v.

scripture, expounded with the aid of the Holy Spirit, and preaches the gospel, in the form of the axe biting into the tree. While the guardian angel merely swats the flies of vain thoughts, the angel with the sword is in this case an ambiguous defender: the weapon signifies 'the anguish of divine judgement' held close to the lady's head. The Christ-knight figure similarly threatens the lady with a sword above her head in the *Ancrene Wisse* exemplum.

Michael Evans points out that this is one of three contemporary English images which show the shield of faith. In all three it is a defence against spiritual attack: the *Collectanea* of John of Wallingford shows the shield flanked by two demons who again wield bows, and in an illustrated copy of Peraldus' *Summa de vitiis* the shield is borne by a knight who faces the massed ranks of vices.[71] Both the Apocalypse and the *Summa* include images of their owners: Lady de Quincy with her prayer book kneeling before the Virgin and child, and the anonymous Dominican monk kneeling before Christ, whose scroll bears the message adapted from *Ecclesiasticus* 2:1 'Fili accedens ad servitutem dei … prepara te ad temptacionem'. Nigel Morgan notes the similarity of the penitent's costume to that of Lady de Quincy.[72] There is inevitably no similar correspondence between monk and knight, but the images nevertheless form a coherent sequence: the knight is the monk's model, ready to withstand temptation. Penitence and preaching are central to both manuscripts, but as the lady needs the preacher's support while the Dominican is the preacher, so the knight bears not only the shield of defence, but also weapons of attack. Like *caritas*, he is offered a crown, this time by an angel, but the angel is unarmed: the sword of *verbum dei* is in the knight's hand. The differences reflect the divide between lay and religious, but also that between female and male. The knightly model carries none of the criticism visible in the *Hortus*, and an aristocratic laywoman can be the protagonist in the struggle for the soul; nevertheless, women are not free to fight as did the virtues.[73]

The battle against the devil was also a theme invoked by Kolda in the prologue to his treatise, where he urged Kunigunde 'you who daily fight manfully in this battle, in putting a man's courage in your woman's breast … have recourse to the arms of the Lord's passion.'[74] The virile fighting nun was a favourite topos, but it is evident that the arms of the Passion are employed in Kunigunde's spiritual battle as a purely passive and defensive shield, like that held by Lady de Quincy, rather than as the active weapons of the Dominican. Kolda omits the last element of the exemplum of Christ the knight: the shield/weapons/bloody shirt left with the *sponsa*, as described in a late-thirteenth-century preaching miscellany:

> But that maiden took up his arms and tunic and placed them in her room; every day gazing at them she saturated them with tears. Many others asked for her hand in marriage and she always replied that she wanted to take brief counsel. Then she would enter the room and, gazing at the arms of her husband, who had fought faithfully for her and was dead and who loved her so much, immediately she would leave the room in tears and say to them that because of the love of her first husband she could accept no other. Thus she answered all.[75]

The protagonists are then identified in the moralization: the maiden as the faithful soul, and so on. The arms are equated with the remembrance of the Passion (*memoria passionis*); when placed in the conscience and the heart and regarded every day with tears (i.e. repentance), they keep those tempted to marry (i.e. to sin) free from capture by the devil. The emphasis on *arma ejus et vestes* (and on the arms alone in the moralization) corresponds to the place given to the metaphor of shield/crucifix in the *Ancrene Wisse*, but there it was a pendant to the main parable, while here it is welded into the events of the narrative. Other aspects which were important to the author of the *Ancrene Wisse*, such as the lady's disdainfulness and the efforts of the great king to win her love (Christ's ministry on earth) are not found here, and the lady's response is also very different. Instead of responding with the fire of love, her role is to weep with repentance and to remember the Passion. Although Kolda omits this, yet implicitly he enacts the final part, giving Kunigunde the full-page *arma christi* shield so she may meditate upon them in her chamber. It is clear that in Kolda's treatise the instruments draw on the concept of the *psychomachia*; they are weapons against the devil, but to wield these weapons is a devotional exercise: the *memoria passionis*:

> Memoria passionis tue o bone ihesu
> lacrimas tollit oculos effundit
> faciem humectat cor dulcorat
>
> The minde of þi passiun, suete ihesu
> þe teres it tollid,
> þe heine it bolled,
> þe neb it wetth,
> in herte sueteth.[76]

These thirteenth-century preaching verses express the effect for which the 'minde' of the Passion aimed: that which the lady of the exemplum experienced when she wept over the arms in her chamber. The tears of the maiden in the exemplum are not only a symbol of repentance: they lie at the heart of the *memoria passionis*. That this co-existed with the idea of both the *memoria passionis* and the instruments as protection against the devil is also shown in preaching verses:

> Behold þu, man, her myth þu se
> þe armes þat I bar for þe.
> On my passioun be þi mynde
> þat þin enemi[y]e þe idel ne fynde.[77]

Although it is only the Passional which combines the exemplum and the image, the message of the preachers expressed in exemplum and verse in turn affected the way viewers interpreted the images. *Memoria passionis* is a key concept for the form of the instruments and for later images of the five wounds. It depends on a simultaneous fragmentation of the Passion narrative to meditate on each individual instrument and action, and a parallel desire for totality – for experiencing the entire *passiones* of Christ (a practice which carried with it an inherent anti-semitism expressed in the later development of the caricatures of the spitting Jews). This is also a constant of prayers and meditative writing on the Passion, and of hymns adoring the individual elements of Christ's body, such as those incorporated in the Villers drawings. Such devotions both play an important part in the development of images of the five wounds, and also show us how viewers could approach images of the whole body.[78] As with the instruments, alongside this itemization of the image there is also a parallel desire for totality, as in the devotion whose aim was to worship every wound of Christ (which is also referred to in the Villers drawings). It can also be linked to a persistent belief in the power of naming all the parts of the body which goes back to the early medieval *loricae* prayers, enumerating each part in a plea for protection.[79] Miri Rubin points out how the fragmentation of the body was also experienced in judicial dismemberment; but it is important to recognize that images of the five wounds present an orderly display of body-pieces as relics: transforming them into roses, surrounding them with the clouds that signal visions. The obverse of these images of orderly dismemberment was the tearing of Christ into pieces through sin, particularly gambling and swearing by the elements of Christ's body.[80] Similarly images of the *arma christi* can be paralleled by the images which show Christ wounded by the tools of those who work on Sunday.

We see the same themes of the use of the *arma* as weapons against the devil and the necessity of gathering together all the torments of Christ in the *Speculum Humanae Salvationis*, again with a female role-model. Christ conquers the devil by his Cross and Passion, and Christians are also to use the same weapons in their own struggle against the devil, following the pattern provided by Mary's response to the Passion:

> Everything which Christ endured in the Passion
> Mary carried with her through maternal compassion …
> And as Christ overcame the devil by his Passion,
> So Mary overcame with him by her maternal compassion.
> Mary armed herself with the arms of Christ's Passion
> When she prepared herself for battle against the devil.[81]

THE WOUND IN CHRIST'S SIDE

In the description of the arming a few of the instruments keep their literal meaning, as when Mary dresses herself in the seamless tunic; but their quantity and variety prove too much for the author to deal with in this fashion, and he falls back on an image from the *Song of Songs* 1:12, where she collects Christ's sufferings and makes of them a bundle of myrrh as a shield between her breasts. The contents of the 'bundle of myrrh' are enumerated in a list similar to but larger than any miniature, which includes actual objects, the protagonists of the drama, and brief notations of all the events. Mary's weapons provide some difficulties for the illustrators of the *Speculum*. She cannot be represented literally holding all the sufferings before her, and yet the bundle of myrrh is scarcely a visually convincing defence. A solution frequently chosen in earlier images was for Mary to hold a selection of the more portable instruments as she tramples the devil underfoot and pins him down with the lance.[82] But the later illustration of the Virgin's battle again demonstrates a shift from active to passive, from fighting to meditation. Thus in Bodleian Library MS Douce fol. 4, (fol. 14r) her foot is on the devil's head, but otherwise she merely stands in prayer before the cross and *arma christi*. In other examples she is shown peacefully seated on a bench reading, with the instruments forming a background against the wall behind her (FIG. 95).[83] Here the image becomes self-referential: the reader is shown the value of the very process on which she has embarked.

We have seen how the female imagery of sexual union and childbirth could be appropriated by men, and how women could use Christ's weapons – but only as a passive defence. Images of the *arma christi* and the wounds are central to an understanding of devotion to the Passion in the later middle ages. They are both extraordinarily varied and fluid in form, and polyvalent in the response they evoked. In discussing here some of the themes with which they engaged, I have also attempted to signal the forces inside and outside the book which aimed to manipulate and guide the viewers' responses to the imagery.

Notes to Chapter Twelve

1. For the *arma christi* see R.Berliner, 'Arma Christi', *Münchener Jahrbuch der Bildenden Kunst*, ser.6,3 (1955), pp.35–152, and R.Suckale, 'Arma Christi', *Städel Jahrbuch*, 6 (1977), pp.177–208; for the life-size wound, see L.Gougaud, 'La Prière dite de Charlemagne et les pièces apocryphes apparentées', *Revue d'Histoire Ecclésiastique*, 20 (1924), pp.211–38. See also F.Lewis, *Devotional Images and their Dissemination in English Manuscripts c.1350–1470* (unpubl. Ph.D. thesis, Univ. of London, 1989), chs.3–4.

2. See the fundamental article by C.W.Bynum, '"And Woman His Humanity": Female Imagery in the Religious Writing of the Later Middle Ages', in *Fragmentation and Redemption: Essays on Gender and the Human Body in Medieval Religion* (NY, 1991), pp.151–79.

3. *Anchoritic Spirituality. Ancrene Wisse and Associated Works*, trans. A.Savage and N.Watson (NY, 1991) pp.190–92. See also C.Innes-Parker, '*Ancrene Wissse* and þe Wohunge of Ure Lauerd: the Thirteenth-Century Female Reader and the Lover-Knight', in *Women, the Book and the Godly* ed. L.Smith and J.Taylor (Woodbridge, 1995) pp.137–47. For the tradition of the textual allegory see R.Woolf, 'The Theme of Christ the Lover-Knight in Medieval English Literature', *Review of English Studies*, n. s.13 (1962), pp.1–16, and W.Gaffney, 'The Allegory of the Christ-Knight in Piers Plowman', *Proceedings of the Modern Language Association of America*, 46 (1931), pp.155–68.

4. Prague, National and University Library, MS XIV A.17, published in facsimile by K.Stejskal and E.Urbánková, *Pasionál Premyslovny Kunhuty* (Prague, 1975). See also K.Stejskal, 'Le Chanoine Benes, scribe et enlumineur du Passionaire de l'abbesse Cunégonde', *Scriptorium*, 23 (1969), pp.52–69, and A.Scherzer, 'Der Prager Lektor Fr. Kolda und seine mystischen Traktate', *Archivum Fratrum Praedicatorum*, 18 (1948), pp.337–96 (with an edition of the text). The MS was made in 2 stages (1314 and 1321), and the treatise belongs to the earlier date. Kolda had actually composed the work 2 years earlier.

5. 'In bellis autem et occursibus variis armorum instrumentis usus est, ut vigoriosius eriperet, pro cuius amore fervens, victoriosius decarteret' (ibid., p.366).

6. 'Hic est clipeus, arma et insignia invictissimi militis, qui cognominatus est Victor cum quinque vulneribus, fultus lancea decoratusque corona' (ibid., p.362). The emphasis on wounds and spear is notable.

7. Brussels, Bib. Roy. MS 4459–70. Parc-les-Dames was an Augustinian convent, founded c.1058, which became a Cistercian house in 1215.

8. Bonn, Rheinisches Landesmuseum Inv. no. 235.; see *Vor Stefan Lochner*, exhib. cat. (Cologne, 1974), no. 5, pp.70–71.

9. Paris, BN, MS fr. 574, fol. 140r. L.Freeman Sandler, 'Jean Pucelle and the Lost Miniatures of the Belleville Breviary', *Art Bulletin*, 66 (1984), pp.73–96, Fig.16.

10. Scherzer, 'Der Prager Lektor', pp.337–45; A.Matejcek, *Le Passionaire de l'abbesse Cunégonde* (Prague, 1922), p.11.

11. J.B.Freed, 'Urban Development and the *Cura Monialium* in 13th-Century Germany', *Viator*, 3 (1972), pp.311–27.

12. Scherzer, 'Der Prager Lektor', p.382.

13. 'Sanctarum oracionum clipeis contra adversariorum iacula' (ibid., p.362).

14. 'Que profecto arma devocio fidelium venerari instituit, quod eciam in Concilio Lugdunensi providencia Summi Pontificis approbavit.' (ibid., p.366).

15. For indulgences in the promotion of the *arma* see F.Lewis, 'Rewarding Devotion: The Role of Indulgences', in *The Church and the Arts*, ed. D.Wood, *Studies in Church History*, 28 (1992), pp.179–94.

16. For the use of the crucifix see L.Gougaud, *Devotional and Ascetic Practices in the Middle Ages* (London, 1927), pp.75–9, 85, and B.Raw, 'The Prayers and Devotions in the Ancrene Wisse', in *Chaucer and Middle English Studies in Honour of Rossel Hope Robbins*, ed. B.Rowland (London, 1974), pp.260–71.

17. Boulogne, Bibliothèque municipale, MS 90, fol. 7v promises 100 days from John XXII and 40 days from Leo, accompanying an image of Longinus piercing the heart. The MS also contains an image of the *arma*

christi with part of the Villers indulgence. This is one of a group of English MSS with images of the wound and *arma christi* which depend on the same tradition as the Villers MS (*see* Lewis, 'Devotional Images', *esp.* pp.213–17, 231–32).

18 The wound shown here does not agree with that in the Villers manuscript in either size or shape; like the length of Christ, the measurement varied, and the shape of the wound was also open to reformulation.

19 On measured images *see* L.Gougaud, 'La Prière dite de Charlemagne et les pièces apocryphes apparentées', *Revue d'Histoire Ecclésiastique*, 20 (1924), pp.211–38; D.A.Jacoby, 'Heilige Längenmasse', *Schweizerisches Archiv für Volkskunde*, 29 (1929), pp.1–17 and 181–216, and Lewis, 'Devotional Images', pp.72–97.

20 'This is the measure of the wound in the side of our lord Jeus Christ. Let no-one doubt that he appeared to a certain person and showed his wounds'. Richstätter mentions a 15th-century German image of a heart wounded by a spear with a Latin protective promise which says that the length, breadth, and size of the wound in the side of Christ was shown by God to a pious person, followed by *Summi regis cor aveto*. This is probably a late image (Richstätter does not reproduce or identify it) but it may represent an older tradition. See K.Richstätter, *Die Herz-Jesu-Verehrung des deutschen Mittelalters* (Regensburg, 1924), pp.249–50.

21 For nuns and visions, *see* the fundamental studies by C.W.Bynum, particularly *Holy Feast and Holy Fast* (Berkeley, 1986). For the revelation of the number of Christ's wounds *see* A.Breeze, 'The Number of Christ's Wounds', *Bulletin of the Board of Celtic Studies*, 32 (1985), pp.84–9. Visions of the wounded Christ, particularly those experienced by nuns, are discussed by P.Dinzelbacher, 'Das Christusbild der heiligen Lutgard von Tongeren in Rahmen der Passionsmystik und Bildkunst des 12 und 13 Jahrhunderts', *Ons Geestelijk Erf*, 56 (1982), pp.217–77. In the 13th cent. Caesarius of Heisterbach recorded a number of visions experienced by monks of Villers; *Caesarius of Heisterbach: the Dialogue of Miracles*, transl. H.van E.Scott and C.C.S.Bland, (2 vols.; London, 1929), i, pp.46–48, 229, 469–70, 487–88, and 517–18.

22 See S.Roisin, 'L'Efflorescence cistercienne et le courant féminin de piété au xiiie siècle', *Revue d'Histoire Ecclésiastique*, 39 (1943), pp.342–78, and B.M.Bolton, '*Vitae Matrum*: A Further Aspect of the *Frauenfrage*', in *Medieval Women*, ed. D.Baker, Studies in Church History: Subsidia i, (Oxford, 1978), pp.253–74.

23 F.Wormald, *The Winchester Psalter* (London, 1973), fig.38.

24 For stigmata, *see* G.Constable, *Three Studies in Medieval Religious and Social Thought* (Cambridge, 1995), pp.213–21.

25 *Bonaventure: The Soul's Journey into God, The Tree of Life, The Life of St. Francis*, transl. E.Cousins (London, 1978), p.311.

26 I.Ragusa and R.B.Green, *Meditations on the Life and Passion of Christ* (Princeton, 1961), e.g. pp.64, 78–79, 84.

27 *See* the important article by J.Hamburger, 'The Visual and the Visionary: The Image in Late Medieval Monastic Devotions', *Viator*, 20 (1989), pp.161–82.

28 Ascribed in the MS to Arnulf of Louvain, 15th abbot of Villers. 'Rhythmica oratio ad unum quodlibet membrorum Christi patientis et a cruce pendentis'; printed *Patrologia Cursus Completus, series latina* ed. J.P.Migne (221 vols., Paris, 1844–64), clxxxiv, 1319–24.

29 *Salve plaga lateris* and the verse to the wound in the side, from the hymn *Omnibus Consideratis*; printed *Analecta Hymnica Medii Aevi*, ed. C.Blume and M.Dreves (55 vols., Leipzig, 1886–92), xxxi, nos. 85 and 68.

30 H.Walther, *Lateinische Sprichwörter und Sentenzen des Mittelalters. Carmina Medii Aevi Posterioris Latina*, (5 vols., Göttingen, 1963–7), ii. no. 1343a; E.Wilson, *A Descriptive Index of the English Lyrics in John of Grimestone's Preaching Book*, Medium Ævum Monographs, n.s., ii, (Oxford, 1973), p.33, no. 158.

31 'I am on the Cross for you; you who sin, desist for my sake. Desist, I give pardon, acknowledge your guilt, I withdraw the punishment'. For the couplet and its Middle Engliish versions, see S.Wenzel, *Verses in Sermons. Fasciculus Morum and its Middle English Poems* (Cambridge, Mass., 1978), pp.119, 164–65.

32 'Ha homme et femme, voi combien sueffre pour toi, voy ma douleur'; J.Sonet, *Répertoire d'incipit de prières en ancien français*, Société de publications romanes et françaises 54 (Geneva, 1956), p.133; K.V.Sinclair, *French Devotional Texts of the Middle Ages* (London, 1979), p.71; P.Rézeau, *Répertoire d'incipits de prières françaises de la fin du moyen âge* (Geneva, 1986), p.58. Printed by P.Meyer, 'Prières et poésies religieuses tirées d'un manuscrit lorrain', *Bulletin de la Société des Anciens Textes Français*, 27 (1901), p.71. For its use in sermons *see* Wenzel, *Verses in Sermons*, pp.119, 122. Another copy in Metz, Bibliothèque municipale, MS 600,

fol. 138v begins 'Ha *fille*, voy que je soffre por toy' (Rézeau, *Répertoire*, p.58). The poem occurs in several books of hours close in date, accompanied by a range of Passion images. In the *Petites Heures*, another MS to which Le Noir contributed, the image is a pietà. Another copy in a mid-14th cent. hours of Metz use, Paris, BN, MS Arsenal 570, fol. 152v, shows a crucifixion, and the heading urges the reader to recite the verses with pity and great devotion before a crucifix. 'Beaulx tres doulx Jhesu Crist' (Sonet, p.212) is printed by Meyer, p.52. from Arsenal 570, where it is illustrated by a Man of Sorrows, although the hymn refers specifically to the wound 'of which this is the size' (*dont si est la longesce*).

33 For the text *see Analecta Hymnica* xviii, p.218. St Denis is also mentioned in the text accompanying a c.1300 miniature of the heraldic *arma*, Paris, BN, MS Arsenal 288, fol. 156r. The text describes both the shield and the destructions of nature caused by the crucifixion, when the earth trembled and the dead arose. These signs were observed by a foreign philosopher, who did not then know Christ, but who was later converted to Christianity by St Paul: 'on dit que se fut saint denis de france'. The preceding text is the *Complainte du crucifix*, with a space left for a miniature.

34 'Queso michi da te totum, ne digreger a te'; 'Aspice vulnera severaque verbera que toleravi'; 'Fili christe dei tu miserere mei'.

35 *See* Jeffrey Hamburger's magisterial study of the MS and its devotional context, *The Rothschild Canticles. Art and Mysticism in Flanders and the Rhineland circa 1300* (New Haven, 1990).

36 It is no coincidence that Kolda moves from the treatise immediately to the *Planctus Mariae*, and it is in this Marian passage that he alludes most frequently to the *Song of Songs*. Just as the sponsa in the *arma christi* treatise was the soul, and in the later text on the heavenly mansions she is identified as the Church, here implicitly she is identified with Mary, represented in the illustration as joined with Christ in a deeply emotional embrace (fol. 16v).

37 Hamburger points out the influence on the Rothschild Canticles of the image of Christ crucified by the virtues, with Caritas wielding the spear: the replacement of Caritas by the sponsa makes this image more accessible as a model for the viewer. Hamburger, *Rothschild Canticles*, p.72.

38 For the Marian allegory of the Rhenish text on which this image is based, *see* Hamburger, pp.99–100.

39 The owner has been identified as a woman kneeling before the virgin on fol. 142r (Hamburger, *Rothschild Canticles*, Fig.73 and p.30); however, the image and text 'Item non desperet peccatrix sed beatam virginem habeat in memorie et cito resiliet a peccato' comes at the end of a group of illustrated exempla and seems more probably to refer to the moral of an exempla of the virgin.

40 *See* C.W.Bynum, *Jesus as Mother*, p.161.

41 Although the *Song of Songs* is a very important part of the manuscript, the main emphasis is on the final section of the contemplation of the Trinity which, though not alien to nuns, is less obviously linked with female mysticism. The *Song of Songs* cycle has an extreme Marian emphasis, which again is not a particular characteristic of female mysticism.

42 The late 13th-cent. original text was expanded in the early 14th cent. The expanded version is printed by Peltier, *S. Bonaventurae... opera omnia* (Paris, 1868), xii. pp.631–703. For the MSS *see* J.Canal, 'El *Stimulus Amoris* de Santiago de Milan, y la *Meditatio in Salve Regina*', *Franciscan Studies*, 26, (1966), pp.174–88. I am grateful to Dr Teresa Webber for this reference.

43 'Sed optimum cor mihi narra, obsecro: dulcedinem quam tu sentis, quibus affluis deliciis, non occultes. Sed ut bene video, non audis, quia cor tuum absorptum est prae dulcore. Jam tu interpretis tui existentis in carcere oblitus es. Cerno enim sic te amoenitate nimia esse captum, ut jam non sint amplius neque vox, neque sensus.' (Peltier, *S. Bonaventurae*, p.677). This split between the soul and 'the interpreter remaining in prison' (*see* Genesis 40:23) also draws on the body/soul divide.

44 'o anima mea, jucunditate repleta ... Sed, ut video, nobis non loqueris, quia rapta es a dilecto' (ibid. 677–78).

45 The exempla and pastoral elements of the second, non-meditative part of the MS do not rule out a female owner. Nevertheless, the large number of men shown engaged in devotion, and the concern of the texts with preaching and confession, do suggest otherwise. An interpolation in the *Pharetra* on fol. 128v which Hamburger (*Rothschild Canticles*, p.29) interprets as extolling meditation as the art of arts, seems instead to emphasize the importance and responsibility of the pastoral care of souls: 'Item nulla ars doceri presumitur nisi prius intenta meditacione discatur. Ab imperitis ergo pastorale magisterium qua temeritate suscipitur. quoniam ars artium est regimen animarum'.

46 'O si fuissem loco illius lanceae, exire de Christi latere noluisse, sed dixissem: *Haec requies mea in saeculum saeculi* (Psalm 131: 14)'. This is part of the expanded version of the text (Peltier, *S. Bonaventurae*, p.634).

47 J-B.Thiers, *Traité des superstitions qui regardent les sacrements* (4 vols., Avignon, 1777), iv, p.123; cited Jacoby, 'Heilige Längenmasse', p.208.

48 As in the sermons of the 12th-cent. Cistercian Guerric of Igny; see C.W.Bynum, *Jesus as Mother*, pp.120–22.

49 See V.Lehmann, *Die Geburt in der Kunst* (Brunswick, 1978), p.53, Figs 38–40, and H.Speert, *Iconografia Gyniatrica. A Pictorial History of Gynaecology and Obstetrics* (Philadelphia, 1973), p.55, Fig.2–24; p.57, Fig.2–27; also Hamburger, *Rothschild Canticles*, Fig.185.

50 Oxford, Bodleian Library, MS Douce 204, *Speculum Humanae Salvationis*, ch.1; made for the bishop of Béziers, c.1430–50 (*see* O.Pächt and J.J.G.Alexander, *Illuminated Manuscripts in the Bodleian Library, Oxford* (3 vols., Oxford, 1966–73) i, no. 86). In the original, the red of the wound dominates the drawing.

51 For example in the writings of Marguerite d'Oingt; *see* Bynum, *Jesus as Mother*, pp.151–52, and also E.A.Petroff, *Body and Soul* (Oxford 1994), pp.216–17.

52 Peltier, *S. Bonaventurae*, p.634. The *vulva/vulnus* analogy in the *Stimulus Amoris* is noted by W.Riehle, *The Middle English Mystics* (London, 1981), p.46. For the openness of the wounds and the dissolution of the boundaries between the bodies of Christ and the devotee in this passage *see* S.Beckwith, *Christ's Body. Identity, Culture and Society in Late Medieval Writings* (London, 1993), pp.58–59. See also the stimulating discussion by T. Luongo, 'Catherine of Siena: Rewriting Female Holy Authority', in *Women, the Book and the Godly*, ed. L.Smith and J.Taylor (Woodbridge, 1995), pp.96–97 who interprets this passage as dealing with sexual union with a feminized Christ. Instead, I would argue that in this passage (which does not use sponsa imagery) Christ is feminized as a mother, whereas in the passages dealing with sexual union the author identifies with the female sponsa/anima, and it is here that Catherine follows the *Stimulus Amoris* in visualizing both Raymond and Niccolò as brides of Christ.

53 Bynum, *Jesus as Mother*, p.161.

54 Aude's experience is discussed by M.Rubin, 'The Person in the Form: Medieval Challenges to Bodily "Order"', in S.Kay and M.Rubin (eds.), *Framing Medieval Bodies* (Manchester, 1994), pp.100–22 at p.112. Her disgust may have focused on the eucharist through the practice of baking the placenta and feeding it to the mother.

55 Carl Horstmann (ed.), *The Minor Poems of the Vernon MS*, EETS, o.s. 98 (London, 1892), p.270.

56 *The Life and Selected Revelations of Bridget of Sweden*, ed. M.T.Harris, A.Kezel, and T.Nyberg (New York, 1990), pp.202–5. At the birth of Bridget's own son, Mary appeared and assisted as midwife and helped her to achieve a purified painless birth, and Christ also helped as a midwife at his death (pp.76, 119).

57 As when she describes how the carnally minded will be cast out like a miscarriage or a soiled menstrual napkin (Isaiah 30: 22, p.132), or visualizes Joanna of Naples as a woman in a shift spattered with sperm and mud. Like a parodic Man of Sorrows Joanna is also seen naked and crowned with thorns – but these twigs are covered with mud and human excrement (p.175).

58 'Item mulieribus in partu laborantibus prestat optimum remedium'. For birth girdles, *see* W.J.Dilling, 'Girdles: Their Origin and Development', *Caledonian Medical Journal*, 9 (1912–14), pp.337–57, 403–25, and Lewis, 'Devotional Images', ch.2.

59 *Hortus Deliciarum*, ed. R.Green *et al*, Studies of the Warburg Institute 36, (2 vols., London, 1979).

60 The third image (fol. 221r) is that of Ulysses and the sirens, inscribed 'Salemon et rota fortune et scala et syrene admonent nos de contemptu mundi et amore Christi'. *See Hortus Deliciarum*, i, pp.200, 202. For the ladder, *see* A.Katzenellenbogen, *Allegories of the Virtues and Vices in Mediaeval Art* (London, 1939), pp.22–26.

61 'Du roy ki avait un amye', ed. and transl. T.Wright, *Pierre de Langtoft's Chronicle* (2 vols., RS, London, 1868), App. II, p.437.

62 'Et, tresdouz Sires, mesqe les entreez de ma pour meson soient ensi merchez de vostre noble ensigne, jeo ne doute mye qe le diable soit si hardy de mettre einz le piee'; ed. E.J.Arnauld, *Henry of Lancaster: Le Livre de Seyntz Medicines*, (Anglo-Norman Texts II, Oxford, 1940), p.103.

63 'Quid sentis de militibus?' is 'Parvum boni. De preda enim vivunt, de rapina se vestiunt'; *Hortus Deliciarum*, ii, p.398 (text 807). For Herrad's use of Honorius, *see* i, pp.46–49.

64 'Hic exercetur rapina ex avaricia nata'; *Hortus Deliciarum*, ii, plate 111 (fol. 203r).

65 Ibid., i, p.204 (fol. 225v), ii, p.372 plate 128. The extracts from Honorius' sermon on the orders of society also expound the right conduct of the different groups, and here the *milites* are described as the arms of the church, so-called because they should defend it from enemies: 'Quos convenit oppressis subvenire, a rapina et fornicatione se custodire ... Tali milicia obtinebunt a summo Rege preclara beneficia' (*Hortus Deliciarum*, ii, p.376, text 782).

66 Ibid., ii, p.439 (plate 146, fol. 255r).

67 Herrad includes an analogous narrative, the first of Bernard of Clairvaux's *Parables: De pugna spirituali* (fol. 25r–v, printed *Hortus Deliciarum*, ii.41–43). This is also a story of imprisonment and liberation, but here the victim is male and his allies are both male and female, and it is the *psychomachia* rather than the redemption which is cast as a courtly narrative. A *puer delicatus*, the son of a great king, is led away from his tutors (the angels) by the devil. He is bound fast, sent him away to exile, and thrown into the prison of despair, whence he is rescued by the virtues (both female and male), who aid his escape on the horse of desire, equipped with the saddle-cloth of pious devotion, to the castle of wisdom. The castle comes under siege by temptations, but Prayer is sent on the horse of faith to get help from the king, who sends his consort, *caritas*. She restores peace, and the king and his son are reconciled.

68 Albert of Metz's version of the exemplum, also from the beginning of the 14th century, describes how at Christ's arming 'Il prist la cuiree blanche a la croix de geules'; printed in B.Hauréau, *Notices et extraits de quelques manuscrits latins de la Bibliothèque Nationale* (6 vols.; Paris, 1890–3), iv, p.25.

69 'Potest Dominus medicina penitentie iterum ad virtutem culmen restituere'.

70 *See* N.Morgan, *The Lambeth Apocalypse* (London, 1990), pp.59–65.

71 M.Evans, 'An Illustrated Fragment of Peraldus's *Summa* of Vice: Harleian MS 3244', *Journal of the Warburg and Courtauld Institutes*, 45 (1982), pp.14–68 (plate 5a and p.22).

72 For the owner images *see* Evans, 'An Illustrated Fragment', plate 1a and p.37, also Morgan, *Lambeth Apocalypse*, p.60.

73 Evans publishes an example of *anima* as a female knight engaged in spiritual battle, from the mid-14th-cent. Cistercian Abbot Ulrich of Lilienfeld's *Concordantiae Caritatis* (Lilienfeld, Stiftsbibliothek MS 151, fol. 253r; *see* Evans, 'An Illustrated Fragment', plate 7c and p.34). However, her gender requires her to ride demurely side-saddle, surrounded by female virtues, who hand her the shield and spear, put the helm on her head, hold the horse's bridle and so on; and even in this they are playing a role sanctioned for women by secular imagery, as in the well-known images of the Luttrell Psalter and the Codex Manasseh.

74 'Vos ergo, que femineo pectori virilem inserendo animum in in hac pugna quotidie viriliter confligitis, ad arma passionis dominice prudenti usa consilio convolatis' (Scherzer, 'Der Prager Lektor', p.361).

75 'Ipsa autem domicella accepit arma ejus et vestes et posuit in camera propria, et quotidie respiciens ea saturabat de lacrymis. Multi alii quaerebant eam in uxorem et ipsa semper respondebat quod libenter haberet consilium et breve. Ipsa intrabat cameram, et, respiciens arma sponsi sui qui ita fideliter, pugnaverat pro se et mortuus fuerat et tam dilexerat eam, statim exibat de camera cum lacrymis et dicebat eis quod amore prioris sponsi sui nullum alium acciperet. Sic respondebat omnibus.' The text and part of the moralization are printed from Paris, BN, MS lat. 16499 by B.Hauréau, *Notices et extraits*, v, p.152.

76 C.Brown (ed.), *English Lyrics of the Thirteenth Century*, (Oxford, 1932), no. 56A, pp.113, 211.

77 E.Wilson, *A Descriptive Index of the English Lyrics in John of Grimestone's Preaching Book*, Medium Ævum Monographs, ns. ii (Oxford, 1973), p.41, no. 195.

78 As the devotions to Christ were addressed to images, so similar devotions to the Virgin's limbs show us one way of looking at images of the Virgin, as in a set of *aves* in the Vernon manuscript includes verses to the Virgin's head, brain, forehead, brows, right ear, left ear, eyes, nose, cheeks, mouth, tongue, chin, face, neck, throat, shoulders, arms, hands, thumbs and fingers, breast, heart, womb, sides, back, 'Maydenhede', thighs, knees, shanks and shins, haunches and feet, toes, flesh, blood, skin and bones (*Minor Poems of the Vernon MS*, i, pp.125–31). Such a fetishizing treatment of the Virgin's unattainable and unshown body had its dangers: St Bridget (who also gives prayers to the limbs of Christ and the Virgin) describes a monk who came to her because he 'could never name Mary without sordid thoughts and blasphemy'; and such devotions were later prohibited (*Life and Selected Revelations*, p.91). See also S.Ringbom, *Icon to Narrative*,

(Åbo, 1965), pp.21, 49, and Jacoby, 'Heilige Längenmasse', pp.198–201.

79 *See* L.Gougaud, 'Etude sur les *loricae* celtiques et sur les prières qui s'en rapprochent', *Bulletin d'ancienne littérature et d'archéologie chrétiennes*, 1 (1911), pp.265–81, 2 (1912), pp.33–41 and 101–27. Similarly the *c*.900 Welsh *Leiden lorica* names the parts of a woman's body in order to enforce a love-spell upon her, and such enumeration forms a frequent part of late antique sexual magic; *see* Peter Dronke, 'Towards the Interpretation of the Leiden Love-Spell', *Cambridge Medieval Celtic Studies*, 16 (1988), pp.61–75.

80 L.Nochlin, *The Body in Pieces. The Fragment as a Metaphor of Modernity* (London, 1994), pp.16–17, contrasts Géricault's paintings of severed heads strewn on the horizontal plane, with those formally displayed on the vertical plane, retaining the dignity of subjecthood.

81 'Omnia, quae Christus in passione tolerabat,/Haec Maria per maternam compassionem secum portabat …/Et sicut Christus superavit diabolum per suam passionem/Ita etiam superavit cum eum Maria per maternum compassionem./Armis passionis Christi Maria se armavit,/Quando contra diabolum ad pugnam se praeperavit'; *Speculum Humanae Salvationis*, ed. J.Lutz and P.Perdrizet (2 vols., Mulhouse and Leipzig, 1907–9), i, p.62.

82 For example, Paris, BN, MS lat. 9584; *see* M.R.James, *Speculum Humanae Salvationis* (Oxford, 1926), ch.xxx, no. 1, and Oxford, Bodleian Library, MS Douce 204 ch.xxx. (*see above*, n. 50).

83 *See* A. and J.Wilson, *A Medieval Mirror, Speculum Humanae Salvationis 1324–1500* (Berkeley, 1984), plate III–11, and plate III–24.

CHAPTER THIRTEEN

The Cult of Angels in Late Fifteenth-Century England:
An Hours of the Guardian Angel presented to Queen Elizabeth Woodville

ANNE F. SUTTON AND LIVIA VISSER-FUCHS

ELIZABETH WOODVILLE, Queen of Edward IV from 1464, who was widowed in 1483 and died in 1492, has been associated with a small manuscript book containing the Hours of the Guardian Angel.[1] The association is based on the presentation scene showing a queen receiving a book from a female donor, the dedicatory poem in English to a 'lady sovereyn princes' which is an acrostic with the name ELISABETH, and the general style of the illumination which fits the period of her reign.[2] The book's unusual features are self-evident. Any book associated with the poorly documented cultural lives of the fifteenth-century queens of England is of interest, and Elizabeth Woodville herself can only be linked to a few texts, despite her participation in a court of undoubted magnificence. Secondly the volume's presentation to a queen by a woman, with a dedicatory poem by the donor herself, makes it a rare and intriguing object.[3] Lastly, the text of the Hours of the Guardian Angel[4] is also rare, an unusual survival of a largely unstudied fifteenth-century cult. The purpose of this paper is to look briefly at this cult, examine the book in detail, and see if more can be said about the donor, the Queen, and the circumstances of its presentation.

In the Christian tradition angels are the army, the council, and the court of God.[5] Their Nine Orders or Choirs – seraphim, cherubim, thrones, dominations, virtues, powers, principalities, archangels, and 'common' angels – perpetually sing God's praise, thereby helping man to realize God's greatness. The angels are also the messengers of God, conveying His will and His grace. The Church never officially defined the role and nature of angelic beings, but no medieval theologian denied their existence, and it was generally agreed that angels acted as protectors of nations, cities, and individuals.

There was considerable confusion concerning the identity and status of these protectors; St Michael, the most powerful of all, the commander of the heavenly armies, was the one most often invoked, and he was also the individual angel that represented the multitude.[6] All orders of angels played their part; each order protected the faithful against particular sins, or extended its care to a particular group of mortals.[7] After death man could be raised to the company of one of the orders according to the greatness and intensity of his faith.[8]

A detailed mythology of the Nine Orders developed. In England, as in the rest of Europe, the *Golden Legend* of Jacobus de Voragine (d. 1298), which collated much of the 'evidence' available in his time, became the best known source and probably the most influential. The *Golden Legend* carefully explained the orders, comparing them to the ranks of the servants of a king, each of which performs its own duties.[9] The whole system was largely based on the elaborate hierarchy attributed to Denys the Areopagite (fifth or sixth century).[10] In England the pseudo-Dionysian *Celestial Hierarchy* was known, directly and indirectly, in full and in paraphrase. It was, for example, translated by Robert Grossesteste.[11] Richard Rolle in his treatise on love, *Ego dormio* (1343), named all the Nine Orders, describing even the lowest order as 'seven times as bright as the sun'. The recipient of his treatise was encouraged to long for the fellowship of the angels: 'for thy seat is ordained for thee, full high and joyful before the face of God, among his holy angels'.[12]

The *Book of Special Grace* of the German mystic Mechtild of Hackeborn (1241–98), which was first translated into English in the early fifteenth century and was used by several of Elizabeth Woodville's relatives, describes many visions of the Nine Orders and how the author heard their music and their singing in praise of God.[13] At one time she saw the choir of her own church filled with angels all singing with:

> delycious mynstralsye... Botte whene hitt come to the course of tho two orders whiche as fyre brennys all in luffe, that es to saye cherubyne ande seraphyne, these twa orders sange that antymme with so grete swetnesse of myght that hitt myght nought be comparsonde to none erthely sowne.[14]

In the 1460s the author of the *Court of Sapience*, which may have been dedicated to Edward IV, called on each order by name as they lamented God's intention to punish mankind, ending:

> Now may ye wepe, and, jerarchys thre,
> Your ordres nyne may not restored be.[15]

There was, and still is, an official liturgy of angels; offices and prayers had existed since the time of Charlemagne.[16] The angels were usually venerated jointly with St Michael and any distinction between the archangel and the innumerable other angelic beings was blurred.[17] In England many parish churches – especially those in high places – were dedicated to St Michael and all angels; a few of these had fraternities that bore his name.[18]

De Voragine's *Golden Legend* did not describe the angels' outward appearance, and English artists in the fourteenth and fifteenth centuries had to turn for information to a version of the pseudo-Denys's work, for example the relevant section of the encyclopaedia of Bartholomew the Englishman,[19] or the Bible itself. None of these authorities was very helpful as they did not describe the dress and accoutrements of each order separately.[20] Widely different interpretations of the sources of symbolic images were possible, as is evident from the inconsistency with which the Nine Orders are depicted in churches all over England:[21] angels in stained-glass windows, carved in wood or stone and painted on rood-screens defy modern attempts at exact identification, however detailed they appear at first sight.[22] The presence of the angels and St Michael, particularly on rood-screens, was intentional and symbolic: in this position they stood in the doorway between the people in the nave and the sanctity of the altar, bridging the gap, mediating between God and mankind, between this world and the next, protecting men and women from the dangers of the other world.[23] People believed that it was the angels who had long ago been the first to kneel at God's feet and ask for mercy for mankind, which He was about to destroy for its sins. This story was known from the *Meditations on the Life of Christ* and its many versions; in England in the translation by Nicholas Love:

> alle that blessid companye of aungels gedered to gidre with one wille and souereyne deuocion fellen down prostrate to fore the throne of god.[24]

Since that first act of the angels as guardians and intercessors mankind had been under an obligation to all angels and owed them gratitude and worship.

On the individual guardians, who were simultaneously separate from and part of the company of angels, the *Golden Legend* was also the most definite and influential source. It stated that each human being had a bad angel 'to put him or her to the test'(*ad exercitium*) and a good angel 'to guard' (*ad custodiendum*). In Caxton's translation:

> To every man ben gyven two Aungels, one evylle for to styre hym to ylle, and one good to kepe hym.[25]

In the 1440s Osbern Bokenham in his *Life of St Agnes* had made the saint say to her tormentors:

> I wyl thou knowe …
> That a keper I have of my body,
> An aungel of god, wyche dylygently
> Me kepyth and helpyth in every nede
> And that me bold makyth the not to drede.[26]

Not all authors displayed the same certainty and it remained a matter for argument whether everyone had such a protector, regardless of individual merit, and whether everyone had one or several personal guardians.[27]

Countless prayers to the guardian angel were composed, in Latin and the vernaculars. They contain a number of recurrent themes: celebration of the virtues and God-given powers of the angel; supplication for its protection in all circumstances and at all times; and, particularly, confession of a failure to venerate it according to its deserts by committing sins in spite of its presence.[28] The earliest surviving prayers were made in the ninth century and their numbers reached their peak in the fifteenth and sixteenth centuries. Many books of hours used in England in the fifteeenth century had one or more prayers to the 'good angel' or 'proper angel', most of them very short and for everyday, *informal* use.[29] The sheer number of these devotions indicate that the cult was popular in England, but everything suggests that it was also very 'private'; most people believed and trusted in their angel but no official feast was instituted in this country.[30] All angels were honoured collectively, together with St Michael, on his main feast day, 29 September. On the Continent, especially in Spain, the guardians had their own holy day on various dates by the end of the fifteenth century, and protectors of individual towns and regions, who were more important than the guardian angels of the individual, had been honoured on set days from the beginning of the century.[31] Fraternities dedicated to St Michael and the angels, or to the guardians in particular, were founded in France, Spain, and Italy from the late fifteenth century on, and the cult gradually received official sanction. In 1670 Pope Clement X fixed the Feast of the Guardian Angels on 2 October, on which day it is still celebrated.[32]

Surviving visual representations of the individual good angel in fifteenth-century England are limited to miniatures accompanying prayers, and illustrations of events during which the good and the bad angel were assumed to be struggling for a man's soul. The sacrament of penance, represented by the confession, was such an occasion, and it was frequently depicted with the other sacraments on baptismal fonts, especially in East Anglia. The good or the bad angel, or both, are present; they may be carrying instruments of comfort or torment and sometimes they are engaged in actual physical combat.[33] Deathbed scenes could also include the guardian angel, fighting the devil, hovering ready to take the deceased's soul, or actually pulling or carrying him or her up to heaven.[34]

The cult of the guardian angel was an integral part of fifteenth-century English devotion. The numberless companions of St Michael enabled people to believe in personal protectors who guarded each man and woman against evil and temptation and carried up their prayers to God. The angels and their protective and mediating role may have been almost as important as the intercessory one of the Virgin Mary herself, but the guardians also had the attraction of being very 'personal' in an age when devotional experience was becoming more personal. This may explain why the widespread and popular cult remained unofficial: for the time being the devotion to the 'proper' angel was, as it were, 'hidden away' in the corners of people's private books of hours. This privateness may have made the cult particularly popular with pious women, both lay and religious. The more public and less specifically feminine face of the cult of angels tended to devote itself to St Michael and the Nine Orders. Evidence for both aspects of the devotion to angels can be found in the activities of the London milieu to which the manuscript of the Hours of the Guardian Angel can be linked.

There was one author who was to have a great influence on lay devotion in fifteenth-century England and to whom the existence and support of her own 'good angel' appears to have been so natural and obvious that neither she herself nor medieval and modern commentators have remarked upon it. St Bridget of Sweden (c.1303–73) was canonized in 1391, and the religious order she founded was firmly established in England by royal and aristocratic patronage in the 1420s.[35] Part of her writings were of angelic inspiration: the *Sermo angelicus*,[36] which later formed the lessons of the office said by Bridgettine nuns, was dictated to her by an angel who visited her every day. Whether this was her own guardian angel or a messenger deputed for this particular task is left unexplained.[37] In the best-known work of St Bridget, the *Revelations* or *Liber Celestis*, there are many intimate references to her 'good angel' who appears to be continually present. It is 'the angel that prays for her' and Christ compares it to 'the knight of a lorde, that put neuir awai his helme for irksomnes, ne for drede turnes neuir awai his eyn fro the bataile'.[38]

The angel itself remembers how it nourished St Bridget spiritually, and the Virgin Mary says of all angels:

> It is sothe that God hase set aungels to all men for to kepe thaim, and if thai take hede to mannes saule, nowthir for that are thai departed fro God, ne thai leve noght God, bot ai are in his sight and enflawmes and excites the saule to god…,

thus touching on the mystery of the angels' permanent adoration of God while at the same time guarding the faithful. Elsewhere the angel says: 'I ame assigned to kepe saules, and yet am I ever in presens of God'.[39]

The main purpose of the Bridgettine Order was the veneration of the Virgin Mary and all parts of the nuns' office were primarily concerned with her: 'from Sonday tyll Saterday dayly, wekely, and yerely ye are occupied with youre tongues in oure Ladyes servyce'.[40] The angels were always there, however: the nuns in the choir were to be as 'angels enclynynge togyder, rysynge togyder, knelyng togyder, stondynge, turnynge and syttynge togyder',[41] and the Monday office was dedicated to the Holy Angels with their foreknowledge of the birth of Mary.[42] Bridgettine nuns were unusual in using books of hours, which were essentially the laity's books of devotions, for private contemplation.[43] So many laypeople had prayers to the guardian angel in their hours that it is difficult to establish convincingly that the Bridgettine nuns were exceptional, but several of the surviving manuscripts – books of hours as well as others – that can be connected to Bridgettine nuns in the late fifteenth and early sixteenth centuries display a marked preference for the guardian angel and St Michael and all angels, often in texts that were added especially for their use.[44] Moreover, the only other surviving copy of the devotion here called the Hours of the Guardian Angel occurs in a manuscript with clear Bridgettine links: a psalter and hours of the Virgin made in Flanders for a northern English owner. Its contents include several prayers to and by St Bridget, two prayers and a complete little office (a *commemoratio*) to the guardian angel, as well as miniatures showing St Bridget (fol. 17v) and two guardian angels (fol. 6v).[45]

St Bridget's writings did not introduce the cult of the guardian angel into England; but the natural way in which she accepts the angel's role in her life and work may have literally 'sanctioned' its worship. The little book owned by Edward IV's Queen appears to contain the text that came closest to an official liturgy for this very popular but unorganized and private cult; it may have had Bridgettine origins.

When the donor handed over the book, the dedicatory poem was the first text to meet the eye of the new owner on folio 2:

Everlastinge welthe withe owte disconfeture	[adversity].
Lady sovereyne princes moste fortunate,	
In the cowrte of fame evermore to endure,	
Surmountinge [fol. 2v] in glory regestirde youre astate.	
After all lowly obeisauns ordinate	[due]
By havour of trowthe withe servyce unfenyd,	
Enterely I youre subiecte whiche [fol. 3r] promisid of late	
Theis boke of youre grace I troste not disdenyd	
Have me recommendid withe humbille subieccioun	

>   Ande of youre highthe bownte [fol. 3v] so pore a gifte to take,
>   To yow presentid of inwarde affeccioun,
>   I lowly beseke yow for youre suppleaunte sake,
>   My promise observyd I troste [fol. 4] that I did make,
>   Whiche shulde have bene moche mor illumynid withe plesure
>   Ande if I had tyme whos ioius I indirtake.
>   Welthe everlastinge withe owghte disconfetur.[46]

The poem does not give as much information as the modern reader would like, but it is a competent piece of verse. It makes clear that the recipient is a queen 'lady sovereyne *princes*', ensured of a place in the Court of Fame, and that the donor is her obedient 'subiecte' who had previously promised her this book – a promise which must have specifically concerned a copy of this rare and desirable text of the Hours of the Guardian Angel. The donor is conscious of the poorness of the gift[47] which 'I did make' and which should have been more 'illumined' and which she would have been both pleased and joyous to undertake 'if I had tyme' – presumably she had to have it ready by a certain date. This is an enigmatic statement which leaves us in doubt as to whether she means she in fact painted the decoration herself rather than merely composing the poem and commissioning the book; the remark also leads one to speculate whether she was the scribe of the text. The reader of the original book cannot immediately read the acrostic ELISABETH, made up from the first letters of the first nine lines of the poem, because there is room for only a few lines of script on each page (FIG. 96). The first letter of each line is emphasized by decoration: gold and blue letters alternate, with either red or blue pen flourishes; and the end of each line is completed by a blue and gold line-filler. The initial **E** and the final **H** of ELISABETH are additionally emphasized by flourishes in both red and blue, a detail that makes it certain that the remaining letters contain no message.[48]

Between the end of the poem – the last line ends neatly at the bottom of folio 4 – and the presentation scene, there are two blank pages (fol. 4v, fol. 5r). The presentation scene is on the last page (fol. 5v) of the first gathering of the book and is designed to face the opening page of the text of the hours.[49] The poem and the presentation scene, therefore, were made as an entirely separate unit, in their own gathering of six leaves, a fact that is important for the correct understanding of the circumstances of the commissioning of this book as a whole.

The presentation scene (PLATE 8) is a formal one, the donor kneeling before the Queen, the book poised at the moment of its transfer from one to the other. Nothing in the scene makes it unique when compared to other such scenes. Between the two women floats a scroll bearing the words 'with everlastyng ioy', almost a quotation, as will be seen, from the Hours of the Guardian Angel,[50] and an entirely appropriate expression of the donor's devotion and piety at the moment of presentation of this particular text, and undoubtedly chosen by her. Indeed, on close examination, the entire presentation scene, like the poem, has been carefully designed and thought out by a woman who was obviously familiar with books and their making. The picture as a whole is competently executed; the colour scheme is attractive, the faces of both figures are pleasant and well drawn.

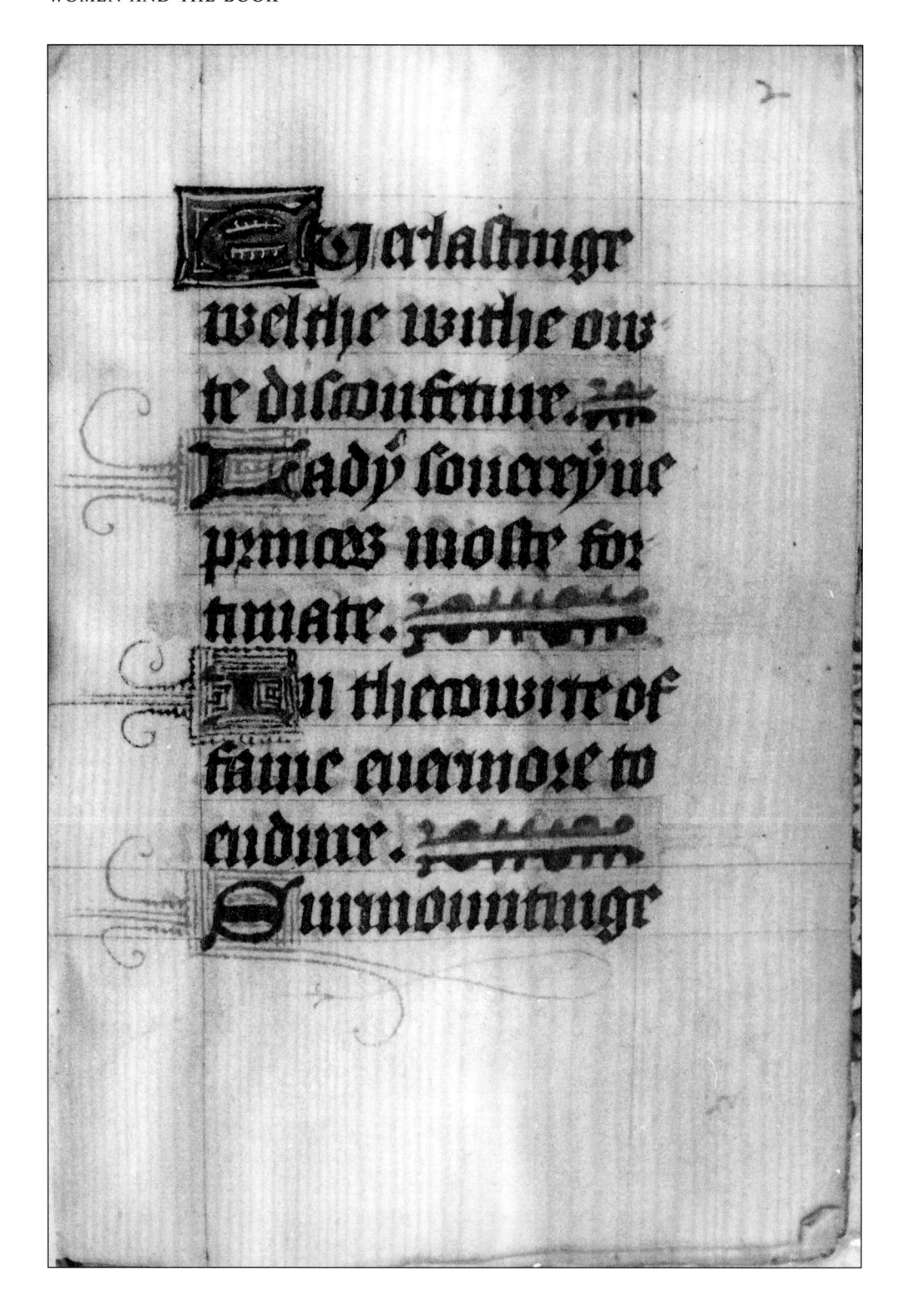

Everlastinge
welthe withe ow
te discontinue.
Lady soueryne
princes moste for
tunate.
In the wytte of
fame euermore to
endure.
Surmountinge

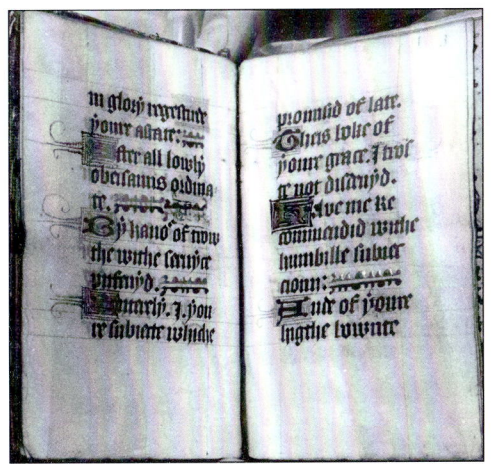

FIG. 96 *See opposite also*: Dedicatory poem to her 'lady sovereyn princes'. The beginning and end of the acrostic ELISABETH are clearly marked by the additional decoration of the first and last letters (all 5 pages of the text are shown). Liverpool, University Library, Liverpool Cathedral MS Radcliffe 6, fols. 2r–4r.

The donor is dressed in a plain blue gown, fitted to the waist with long tight sleeves, the cuffs modestly turned down to her knuckles, both cuffs and the high round neckline edged with a white line. The gown is both decorous and moderately fashionable, datable to the later 1470s and '80s. The headdress is equally carefully painted and appears to consist of a white cap or coif completely covered by a transparent linen veil looped up simply to the nape of the neck and then falling down the back to below the waist; a central fold (or folds) in the linen runs along the centre of the head. The veil covers the forehead to the eyebrows and covers the ears; there is an irregular row of dots along the veil across the forehead, presumably indicating that the underlying cap is decorated. The headdress is a modest one, perhaps especially suitable to a widow who preferred plain clothes to the more ostentatious trappings of widow's weeds and barb. The pinned-back veil enabled the wearer to work without being troubled by it, as did the simple lines of the dress. An English example of this type of headdress also worn with a comparatively simple dress can be found in the wall-painting of the 'Christ's Image as Hostage' on the north wall of Eton Chapel, executed within a few years of this presentation scene.[51]

One other striking comparison can be made: the donor's clothing is very reminiscent of the type of modest but fashionable white linen headdress and blue gown chosen for herself by Christine de Pizan, the French poet and moral adviser, who so carefully oversaw the illumination of the presentation copies of her works.[52] Fashion had changed only minor details over the 80-odd years between her time and that of the donor of the Hours of the Guardian Angel. Christine's works were popular in England, and copies including her chosen illustrations were not uncommon among the wealthier of our donor's contemporaries. For example, Elizabeth Woodville's mother and, later, her brother Anthony, Lord Rivers, owned one of the most elaborate of Christine's presentation copies of her works, made originally for Queen Isabel of France and coming to Anthony from his mother, Jacqueline,

237

dowager Duchess of Bedford. The last word on how a hard-working, pious woman of social and moral standing *should* be represented was therefore available for the study of a well-connected English lady in the third quarter of the fifteenth century who, like Christine, was planning to present a book to her Queen.[53]

The Queen is depicted entirely conventionally in her robe of estate (three garments), but this is done with a care that may indicate particular knowledge or interest. She has been given an abundant supply of red-gold hair beneath a pearl-decorated, open crown, long unbound hair being appropriate only to queens displaying their estate and to virgins.[54] Her sleeveless surcoat is the fourteenth-century garment that had become customary to indicate rank for a noble woman or queen by the late fifteenth century: it is crimson, with its body and broad hem of ermine. The Queen's kirtle, of which only the tight-fitting sleeves and part of the bodice show, is also crimson; the cuffs are worn down like the donor's. Her mantle is a rich, slightly purplish grey, lined with ermine and laced across the neck, with two buttons of gold and silk attaching the lace to the mantle. The edge of the mantle is outlined by a double white line, possibly a careful indication of the row of gold ribbon that bordered a queen's mantle of estate.[55]

She is seated on a wooden throne with a small dais, beneath a cloth of estate of crimson cloth of gold fringed or bordered with green. Both women are set against a backdrop of the same purplish grey as the Queen's mantle, patterned with gold, and a green tiled floor. The care accorded to the dress of both figures is mirrored in the depiction of the book itself: larger than life (or it would disappear entirely) and painted to imitate the crimson cloth of gold which fortunately still covers the book today.[56]

The entire presentation scene is surrounded by a bar of gold and another of blue and red. Fanciful flowers and acanthus foliage erupt from the bar in blue, red (both a maroon and the crimson of the Queen's surcoat), emerald and olive-green, with pink and a little yellow. Fine sprays with gold and green dots as finials fill in the space between. Both the two fanciful flowers have the strawberry-like centres so common in English borders of this period.

As has been said the text of the hours begins on a new gathering. Its first page (fol. 6r) has a crowded vignette and a four-line initial D of pink and blue overpainted with a white button-hole pattern. In this D is a stylized double five-petalled rose with a yellow centre, white inner petals and bright orange outer petals, against a gold background. There is no attempt by the artist to represent this as a 'real' flower, and it does not have sepals. All the border decoration of this manuscript (fols. 6r, 30r, 39r, 44r, 49r, 54r, 58v, and 68r) may be described as conventional work of the 'London' style of the 1470s or early '80s. All are demi-vignettes (except for fol. 6r) and all have their large blue and pink initials filled with a fanciful flower on a gold ground. The foliage is acanthus and flowers of the three-five-petalled type with sepals or trumpets, occasionally with prominent fruit-centres dotted or barred with yellow or white. Wiry black sprays ending in finials of gold and green dots fill in the spaces. There is little, but adequate, variety between the pages. The colour is bright with a lavish use of orange especially on fol. 6; blue predominates on other pages. Gold usually backs the inner part of the border, swelling out behind the corner foliage. Other colours are dark and light blue, pink, maroon red (never the crimson of the Queen's kirtle and surcoat), brown-red, green, some yellow, and twice a pale, clear grey (fols. 49r, 54r), not the purplish grey of the Queen's mantle.

It is safe to conclude that a skilled artist painted the presentation scene, and that the borders of the rest of the book were commissioned from a London workshop producing standard work of the time. As regards the involvement of the donor herself in the illumination so explicitly stated, it seems, in the poem: it is possible that she did the presentation scene and its border.

The identification of the Queen has to be made on the basis of the above evidence. Everything about the style of both portions of the book inclines us to agree with the opinion of J.J.G.Alexander[57] that she is Elizabeth Woodville and that the book should be dated *c.*1475–83. The evidence in favour of her daughter, Elizabeth of York, who married Henry VII in January 1486 and was crowned in November of the same year after the birth of Prince Arthur in September, is that of the orange and white rose on the first page of the text put forward by the makers of earlier book-sale catalogues who were not yet sufficiently competent to consider style.[58] Such formal two-coloured roses were not uncommon before and after the birth of the heir to the red and white roses of Lancaster and York, and more important, this is an *orange* and white rose. The palette of the artist of the border certainly included a maroon red which would have given a better Tudor rose if required. Far too little work has been done on the precise development of Yorkist and Tudor devices: the white York rose, with or without the sun's rays behind it, was an emblem of Edward IV's from the start of his reign. The regularly shaped five-petalled version is to be found in the books illuminated for him *c.*1478–83 and in many other sources directly or indirectly linked to him. What his children and his queen used in the way of rose devices is not known; it is possible that Elizabeth Woodville had her own version.[59] Whether this orange and white rose has any emblematic significance or not, the book might still have been presented to Elizabeth of York, but on the basis of the style and dress of the donor, this certainly took place no later than 1490. We have therefore a period of approximately 8 years, from 1475 to 1483, when the book could have gone to Elizabeth Woodville, and a period of perhaps 4 years, from 1486 to 1490, when it could have been presented to her daughter once the latter's position as mother of the heir of York and Lancaster was secure. The weight of years is still in favour of Elizabeth Woodville.

The text itself, the Hours of the Guardian Angel, is an almost unique survival, and even at the time it was written it must have been very rare. The only other copy is to be found in Aberdeen, University Library MS 25 which was produced *c.*1420 and is not identical to the manuscript discussed here.[60] In the Aberdeen manuscript the hours of the angel are added to the hours of the Virgin as a *commemoratio sancti angeli proprii custodis* ('a commemoration of the holy guardian angel'). The text given to Elizabeth Woodville is longer, and treats the Hours of the Guardian Angel as an independent devotion: the hours of the day have been put in their usual order, beginning with Matins – in the Aberdeen manuscript they start with Vespers – and include the *Te deum* as well as more prayers and other short devotional phrases, to make a full book of hours. All psalms and many of the texts are given in full and not merely abbreviated to their first lines.[61]

The overall scheme of the hours of the Guardian Angel is identical to that of the hours of the Virgin and has a few sections in common with it (*see* the analysis of the text, *below*). All other sections, however, are either connected with angels generally or, more often, addressed directly to the guardian itself.[62] They celebrate the titles and virtues of the guardian angel, expressing the adoration of the faithful in eloquent phrases which dispel any picture that the modern reader might have of rosy-cheeked cherubs hovering over the bed of a child. The angel is 'lord', 'glorious prince among the great princes of the heavenly kingdom', 'undefeated warrior', and 'shining star'. He protects the faithful against the 'darkness of the world' and the 'blandishments of the devil', and takes away the 'fear of the arrows of the night'. His status and powers are evidently considered on a par with those of St Michael the Archangel himself; here, as so often, the two have been confused.

The Latin of Elizabeth Woodville's copy is not flawless. When compared with the Aberdeen manuscript it is clear that the copyist's command of the language was not sufficient to avoid odd mistakes, or correct the errors of her exemplar. A major error, for instance, is the first word of the hymn in Matins: *Salus* instead of the correct *Laus*, which creates an unusual beginning for such a text and throws out the metre. The texts of the two manuscripts are not directly related and the weaknesses of the one cannot be blamed on the other; whatever the quality of the original composition, errors no doubt accumulated over the years, and they cannot all be laid at the scribe's door. In some cases, however, a better scholar could have improved the text on her or his own initiative. The imperfection of its Latin is the only corroborative evidence that the scribe of this manuscript was the donor. However familiar this woman was with her Latin devotions, as a female she would have been barred from a sophisticated Latin education. She was careful, however, to put in – or leave in – the female forms of the last prayer of Sext: *Omnipotens et misericors deus, respice me famul**am** tu**am** magiestati tue subiect**am*** ('Almighty and merciful God, look down on your handmaiden who bows before Your majesty'), which suited the gender of the future owner.

It is well known that there is little surviving evidence of women as scribes or illuminators in the later Middle Ages. Some women certainly did such work, but rarely in a professional capacity: Christine de Pizan often acted as her own scribe; a French husband and wife made a book of hours between them, she doing the illumination; and, most important of all, the so-called 'Lambeth Devotion' was written by one woman for another within the circle of Syon Abbey in the late 1400s or early 1500s. The manuscript discussed here, as well as a Bodleian book of devotions to be mentioned later, offer more equivocal evidence that women did write and that they could write well.[63]

The donor of the hours cannot be identified from the evidence of the book alone. Further investigation has to concentrate on the Queen, if the identification of her as Elizabeth Woodville is accepted. She was one of the many children of Jacquetta de Luxembourg, widow of John, Duke of Bedford, and Richard Woodville, esquire, later Earl Rivers, a marriage that scandalized their contemporaries. As a widow herself (of Sir John Grey) and the mother of two young sons, Elizabeth attracted the attentions of Edward IV, several years her junior; they were married secretly in 1464 and she was crowned on 26 May 1465. Her press, and that of her family, has always been bad. The men were depicted as greedy upstarts and the women as haughty at best and witches at worst, most effectively by the Earl of Warwick, whose plans for a French marriage for Edward IV had been upset by the secret marriage of 1464; and few chroniclers or historians have since challenged this point of view. There is certainly evidence that Elizabeth was not as bad as she has been painted, and also that she adopted the intercessory role expected of earthly queens in imitation of the merciful Queen of Heaven. As Mary was so often depicted in the robes of secular queenship, by the time of Elizabeth Woodville this identification was almost impossible to avoid. Elizabeth is known to have interceded successfully on behalf of several of her subjects in financial trouble, and during the readeption of Henry VI some of her London subjects responded with loyal affection, and gave succour to the pregnant Queen, then immured in sanctuary. Perhaps especially important in the present context, she is also known to have cared for the spiritual well-being of her subjects: she secured the King's licence for a fraternity of the Holy Trinity which aimed to support sixty priests; and she supplicated the Pope for full indulgences for her subjects to accompany the private recital of prayers in honour of the Visitation. Elizabeth, like the rest of her family and her household, was aware of the benefits of prayer and of being a member of fraternities which existed to support prayers: she became a sister of the fraternities of the Holy Trinity Luton, the Parish Clerks of London, and the Assumption of the Virgin of the London Skinners and of Christchurch Cathedral Canterbury. Nothing is known about her ownership of any religious texts beyond the one under discussion. If the comment in the dedicatory poem of the Hours of the Guardian Angel that the Queen requested that text is precise, then her tastes may have been both positive and sophisticated. In 1477 she received papal permission to attend divine service in Carthusian houses in England. Her last years spent in the religious seclusion of Bermondsey Abbey, her choice of a doctor of theology and a canon of St Paul's as her executors, with the prior of the Carthusian house of Sheen as one of their supervisors, and her low-key funeral procession and burial at Windsor may also reflect her piety. As Queen, her personal patronage included the customary pious and expensive projects. In gratitude for her safe survival of the events of 1470–1 she rebuilt the chapel of St Erasmus next to the Lady Chapel of Westminster Abbey and endowed a two-priest chantry there for the royal family. Like Margaret of Anjou before her, she adopted the role of benefactress to Queens' College, Cambridge. Most important in the present context, together with her husband she took an active interest in Syon Abbey, the house which had been one of the greatest expressions of devotion and patronage by the Lancastrian kings and which the Yorkists took over in a very deliberate way, finding in the writings of St Bridget another prophetical text to support Edward IV's claim to the English throne. In 1480 Elizabeth's last daughter was named after the foundress of the Bridgettine Order.[64]

Queens like Elizabeth would have known very well what they were expected to be like and how to fulfill the expectations of their husband and male public. Often their fortunes depended on it, and even then it did not ensure a comfortable old age, as the careers of almost all fifteenth-century English queens demonstrate. A request for a copy of the Hours of the Guardian Angel may have been just such a public-conscious and gracious act – as well as an expression of an awareness of how much a queen needed every assistance that such an angel could offer, especially a queen who experienced such fluctuations of fortune.

There is little more direct evidence to connect Elizabeth with the cult of All Angels or of the Guardian Angel in particular. Nevertheless, the cult was prevalent, and a well-known chapel with a fraternity and hospital dedicated to the Virgin Mary and All Angels near Syon Abbey, and across the river from the royal palace of Sheen, cannot have escaped her attention. It certainly attracted the attention of some of her servants: of officials of the duchy of Lancaster (from which her income was mainly derived), and of the Exchequer; of leading lawyers and citizens of the City of London, any of whom might have had a wife or mother who might have presented this Hours to the Queen. Precise evidence of a connection between the Queen herself and this chapel is lacking but a brief examination of this foundation is the only means by which we can place this unusual little book in a living context of people and the cult of angels in England. Although we cannot identify the donor of the Hours of the Guardian Angel, we can provide the name of a woman who was an important patron and devotee of the cult of angels, and who had links both with Queen Elizabeth Woodville and with an important literary and pious circle.

Between March 1443 and late 1446 Henry VI had laid the foundation-stone of a chapel to be dedicated to the Virgin Mary and the Nine Orders of Angels (All Angels) at the west end of the bridge across the River Brent, south of the main London road at Brentford, Middlesex, and just north of the Bridgettine Abbey of Syon in the abbey's lordship of Isleworth. This was the first dedication to the Nine Orders in England, and the King was conscious of it. In 1446 the foundation was extended by a hospital for nine poor old men near the chapel and a guild of brothers and sisters to be called 'of the nine orders of holy angels by Syon', with the usual officers, servants, and priest. From the 1440s to the early sixteenth century a list of over fifty names of putative and certain guildsmen and guildswomen can be compiled, an association sometimes supported by their wills and other evidence; neither a register or a bederoll (prayer-roll) of the brethren and sisters survives, however.[65]

The foundation (chapel, hospital, and guild) was the brain child of John Somerset, Henry VI's physician and Chancellor of the Exchequer, an ex-schoolmaster, a promoter of education and a book-collector.[66] He built the chapel, possibly almost beggaring himself in the process, and his very extensive lands in the neighbourhood were to support it, together with the almshouse, after his death.[67] Somerset's inspiration may have owed much to Reginald Pecock and John Colop, to take just two of his original feoffees: from 1431 to 1444 Pecock was master of the chantry college of priests and almshouse for old men recently established in London by Richard Whittington at St Michael Paternoster Royal, the period during which he wrote some of his first literary works; John Colop, possibly a friend of Whittington, was housed by Whittington's executors close by St Michael's, and was one of those appointed to distribute alms for Whittington's soul.[68] It has not proved possible to link Somerset's choice of dedication to the Virgin and the Nine Orders precisely to any of his known pursuits; but it is likely that he was at least partly inspired by the devotional preoccupations of the nuns of Syon, particularly their Monday office. The abbess of Syon was the 'lady' of the manors from whom he held his lands, and she and her officials would have dominated the immediate area tenurially.

As with all groups of feoffees, witnesses, and legal agents, a common background and specific business and family links between them can be readily established – in this case, to state the obvious, the earliest group had John Somerset in common. It was Somerset's extensive connections in the royal household, especially at the clerical and official level, and in the city of London, which set the dominant tone of the fraternity in so far as that can be recovered. There was also a persistent involvement of the local clergy and a certain number of people who lived locally, some from genuine local families and some who were Londoners and courtiers who had acquired land nearby. Conspicuous were a group of ironmongers in the 1460s and '70s, a sequence of leading lawyers and, most interesting, a group who had dwellings in or close connections with St Bartholomew's Hospital.

Over half a dozen persons can be directly linked to Elizabeth Woodville's household and that of her husband, among them Thomas Luyt, attorney for the Duchy of Lancaster and of Elizabeth Woodville from 1466, who played a major role in the history of the chapel alongside his wife, Joan.[69] The Luyts were both of prominent Shrewsbury families, as was Thomas Grafton, another key figure in the fraternity.[70] Grafton was a leading merchant of the Calais Staple, often employed by the Yorkist kings,[71] and his brother, Adam, was a chaplain of the household of the Prince of Wales in the Welsh March and a founder member of the Fraternity of St Winifred at Shrewsbury.[72]

Apart from the lawyers and royal officials associated with the guild of All Angels at Brentford, it is the group of persons distinguished by their dwelling in St Bartholomew's Hospital which stands out. The Hospital was one of the most important and best-loved centres of charity, piety, and education in London, and the dwelling-place of many men and women – notably John Shirley, the amateur scribe and 'publisher' – associated with the book-trade and several surviving manuscripts. The books of the inhabitants of the Hospital's Close show that they had wide literary and pious tastes; Shirley himself made translations and wrote verse, and to judge by the number of English and Latin verse epitaphs that survive for this group, this activity was not limited to him.[73] The impressive John Wakering, master of the Hospital 1423 to 1466, must have been one of the key figures. In his 40 years of office, Wakering built up the Hospital's reputation as a place of care and piety, commissioned books for it, and increased its endowments. Was he also responsible for attracting 'interesting' tenants to its Close?[74]

Several of his wealthy and pious tenants were aware of the cult of angels. A chapel in honour of the Virgin Mary and St Michael the Archangel was built in the cemetery of St Bartholomew's Hospital[75] by Richard Sturgeon, Clerk of the Crown from 1415 to 1449.[76]

His career as a royal official overlapped with that of John Somerset and they died within 2 years of each other, but whether they knew each other well has not been established. Others among Sturgeon's relatives and neighbours in the Close were involved in both his and Somerset's foundations: Sturgeon's son-in-law, Thomas Frowyk, steward of Syon Abbey's lordship of Isleworth by 1453 (until his death 1485) and a feoffee of All Angels;[77] Henry Ashborn, secondary of Bread Street Compter by 1486, who had a personal devotion to St Michael the Archangel;[78] Thomas Burgoyne, under-sheriff from the 1430s until his death in 1471,[79] who acted for both establishments and lived in the Hospital next door to John Shirley, the man who was certainly one of the most enthusiastic members of the Close's literary circle;[80] and Thomas Portaleyn who, like John Shirley, was a past official of Richard Beauchamp, Earl of Warwick,[81] and who owned a considerable estate near the chapel of All Angels.[82] Portaleyn had joined both the Brentford and St Bartholomew's communities after 1445 on his marriage to Alice, the wealthy widow of William Markeby and Richard Shipley.[83] Alice lived in Isleworth and St Bartholomew's from the 1430s to 1479 and may have been the kind of woman to give a book of hours to a queen, but unfortunately nothing is known of her interests or character except the glowing recommendation contained in her second husband's will.

At some date between 1456 and 1487 Thomas Luyt, attorney of Elizabeth Woodville from 1466, and Joan, his wife, joined the community of St Bartholomew's[84] and became involved in its affairs: Thomas lent the Hospital money, taking plate as security, he bequeathed it his brewhouse in St Botolph without Aldgate, and his sister became a working sister of the Hospital caring for the sick.[85] The Luyts had also joined the fraternity of All Angels Brentford by the early 1480s at the latest. How the connection was formed is not known: it could have been made through any of the many lawyers and royal officials who were associated with the guild and who worked with Thomas, or it could have originated in the pious interests of Joan. In 1484 Thomas headed a coalition which acquired the Chapel and the nearby properties that went with it from the existing feoffees.[86] It is difficult to assess precisely what was going on behind this transfer: was it just a normal transaction between members of the fraternity, or was it a takeover by four well-connected and powerful members who regarded themselves better qualified to run the chapel and almshouse and direct its fraternity? Certainly the chapel's subsequent history as an increasingly 'private' concern seems to suggest that the guild had become weak and susceptible to a takeover, however piously and beneficently intended.

In 1487–90 Joan Luyt, now a wealthy widow, took control of the chapel.[87] From her will of 1497, it is clear that she considered the chapel to be hers: she commuted between her houses at Isleworth and in St Bartholomew's Hospital; she kept possessions at the chapel, and she had her own chaplain, John Bromfeld, who may have been the chaplain of All Angels. Before her death she carefully arranged that the chapel and lands passed to 'my most well beloved friend', Edward Cheseman, lawyer of Gray's Inn, an officer of King's Bench and a future cofferer of Henry VII – a man whose career was very like that of her husband under Edward IV. Thirteen years later he still remembered his care for the health of the soul of 'Dame' Joan Luyt in his own will.[88] Joan Luyt's role as patroness of the chapel of All Angels and as pious widow is enough to make her interesting; it acquired her the title of 'dame' among some of her contemporaries.[89] It may well have been her piety, even more than her wealth and age, that allowed her to achieve such a position. Among her acquaintances at the end of her life was Dr John Chapman, whom she chose to be the supervisor of her will and whom she probably got to know while he was rector of All Hallows Honey Lane in London from 1479 to 1494. He was a famous preacher, preaching before Henry VII in 1496 and regularly at St Paul's between 1493 and 1505.[90] Joan's connection with Chapman endorses the impression we have of a woman whose piety was formed and nourished in a fairly select world of clever, well-educated laity and clergy, employed in the middle ranks of the royal household and administration.

Joan can also be suggested as the owner of a book of offices and devotions, Bodleian Library, MS Lat. liturg. e. 17.[91] The book dates from approximately the 1420s, the texts being in the usual masculine forms, but its main interest derives from the additional devotions written on its blank pages by at least two hands in the second half of the fifteenth century. These were made for a woman and are in Latin and English, and a 'Joan' is the subject of two of the Latin prayers. Several of the texts refer to the 'good angel', and on the last surviving flyleaf (fol. 108v) one of the persons who made some of the additions to the manuscript writes of having started a sequence of one hundred paternosters on All Hallows Eve, 1492,[92] followed on the next day by the 'servys' of the Nine Orders of Angels. It has been pointed out that the Joan who owned this book is likely to have been associated with a place dedicated to the Holy Cross and the Nine Orders.[93] Joan Luyt lived in St Bartholomew's Hospital, originally dedicated to the Holy Cross, where good works of 'good angels' were to be expected quite literally; and she 'owned' a chapel dedicated to the Nine Orders where the worship of the 'good angel' was most appropriate. Some of the additions to the book are probably in her hand, others possibly in the hand of her chaplain, of her husband, or of one of her successors who cared for the chapel.[94] One short English prayer from 'Joan's' book is particularly worth quoting here, because it seems to epitomize the cult of the good angels whose business it was to protect in an everlasting hierarchy from heaven to earth:

> O thow angell of God that keptyst owr lord Ihesu Crist yn hys manhode, and thu blessyd angell that keptist hys blessyd modur Mary, helpeth my good angell to kepe me that love pes and charite. Be betwene God and all the worlde and me.[95]

One more point needs to be mentioned: 'Joan's' book of devotions also contains, among its additions, three examples of English verse: a version of the prayer 'Almighty God, maker of heaven/Of earth, water and wind', some verses usually associated with Carthusian manuscripts of the *Mirror of Simple Souls*, and a rendering of the Ten Commandments.[96]

We may conclude that we have two manuscripts containing unusual devotions addressed to the good angel, both owned by women, both containing English verse of the second half of the fifteenth century, one poem being certainly by one of the women, and that both manuscripts testify to active commissioning and making of pious texts by women.

The background of the Hours of the Guardian Angel is elusive. Queen Elizabeth Woodville was involved with many fashionable fraternities and she must have been well aware of the Guild of All Angels; both the Guild and the Queen can be linked to the Bridgettine house at Syon, and to the literary and devout community at St Bartholomew's. Among the members of the guild there were several with an undoubted interest in devotional books, mainly in the vernacular, while some of them were active in the dissemination of the so-called 'common profit' books, texts meant to be circulated and copied among acquaintances, and usually left to someone who would in his or her turn encourage their circulation.[97] The scribal and literary activities of Syon, particularly in exchanges with the Carthusians at Sheen, together with those of some people living at St Bartholomew's, are becoming increasingly well known.

Somewhere in this network of often very personal relationships between people sharing a wealthy city background and an interest in devotional texts and their 'publication', there must have been a lady who told the Queen that she had access to a rare and desirable devotion to the guardian angel, and promised her a copy. She kept her promise in an exemplary way and she may have hoped for prayers at least, in return. She did not, however, request the Queen to have the book copied for or by others – as she might have done in the case of a friend – and the text remained unique.[98]

The evidence is in favour of the Bodleian book of prayers being owned by Joan Luyt of the Fraternity of All Angels, Brentford, by Syon, and inhabitant of St Bartholomew's Hospital Close. It could have been Joan Luyt who gave the Hours of the Guardian Angel to Queen Elizabeth Woodville, or perhaps to Elizabeth of York. Certainly the Hours of the Guardian Angel now in Liverpool was given by a woman from a similarly sophisticated, pious, and literary background to that of Joan Luyt, with money enough but of no more than gentry status; and above all, it was given by a woman who had achieved her own *personal* status through piety. Equally, there is no doubt that this little book can be added to the increasing number of books which are being associated with the Bridgettine nuns of Syon Abbey.

APPENDIX I

Description of the Manuscript and the Text of The Hours of the Guardian Angel, Liverpool University Library, Liverpool Cathedral. MS Radcliffe 6.

The Manuscript

The manuscript is written on vellum and still in its original binding of crimson cloth of gold – now very worn – over thin wooden boards; it has a single, central silver clasp. The book is very small, overall size 89 x 64 mm.; written space 50 x 30 mm, 10 lines to a page, rulings in the ink of the script, prickings near the edge. It has 78 folios and 2 flyleaves at the end (78+ii; 1^6, 2–10^8; 1^1 is unnumbered and pasted down; 1r, 4v, 5r, 77v and 78r are blank, the last flyleaf is pasted down). On fol. 1 it reads: 'Numb[er] 425', and: 'This MS was given to my Father in December 1828 by our old neighbour in Suffolk and pleasant acquaintance for many years Mrs Plumpton widow of the late elegant scholar and right worthy man the rector of Whatfield near Hadleigh. E W H Drummond Hay'.

The Text

Editorial Note: The spelling of the original has many errors; the more important of these are indicated by round brackets or given in the notes. Editorial additions are in square brackets. A minimum of capitals and punctuation has been added; **c**, **t**, and **s** have been rationalized, and abbreviations extended. Psalm numbers follow the Vulgate. For the sake of brevity, Latin quotations have not always been translated, but some translations have been included to give an impression of the text and its tone; others can be found in Bible editions. The text as a whole and especially the parts that could not be traced deserve further study in a more strictly liturgical context.

Matins (fols. 6r–30r): Matins – and each of the other hours – has the same opening sentences as the corresponding section of the better known Hours of the Virgin.[99] The invitatory *Assis ad custodiam angele psallenti, mentisque concordiam obsta de(x)trahenti*[100] has not been traced. It is repeated throughout, and at the end of, the first Psalm, 94 (fols. 7r–10r) *Venite, exsultemus domino*, which is the usual Psalm in this position as it contains a summons to worship God. It is followed by the first five stanzas (fols. 11r–12v) of an apparently unique hymn (*see below* for its text) which is divided over all the hours of the day.[101] These first stanzas praise the guardian angel, describing how it preserves the supplicant from temptation, helps him up when he falls, and dispels the fears of the night. The antiphon that rounds them off is used at the end of other sections of the hymn, in Prime (fol. 40r), Terce (fols. 49v–50r), None (fols. 54v–55r) and Compline (fol. 74r); it reads *Gloria tibi, domine, qui tali me munimine custodis a discrimine, in hac mundi caligine* ('Glory be to you, Lord, who guards me by such protection from danger in this darkness of the world'). This antiphon, like many of the antiphons, versicles, responses, and other short texts in the present manuscript has not been found elsewhere.

Psalm 8 (fols. 13r–15r), *Domine dominus noster quam admirabile*, follows, with the unidentified antiphon *Angele non despicis hominem minorem, trahens me ad gloriam tuam et honorem*, and the versicle *Stetit angelus iuxta aram templi* with the response *Habens thuribulum aureum in manu sua.*[102] The text of the last two (Apoc.8:3) was often used in the liturgy of angels and in full it occurred e.g. as the offertory of the Mass of the Angels in the Sarum Missal.[103] It is also used in Prime and Terce (fols. 43r, 47v–8r), and in full as capitulum in Sext (fols. 51v–52r), *below*.

Matins has no nocturns. The first lesson (fols. 16r–18v) begins, *Gloriose princeps inter magnos celestis regni principes humilis servi tui custos* ('Glorious prince among the great princes of the heavenly kingdom, guardian of your humble servant') and ends *meque fideli et solicita protectione custodis* ('and you guard me by loyal and careful protection'). This text contains many of the elements and concepts of traditional angelology, but its origin has not been established. It is followed by versicle, response, and benediction which have also not been identified: *Te cor meum doce diligere quem fecisti;*[104] *recolere, caritati grates rependere; Dignas laudes dona depromere et instinctus tuos perficere,* and *Angelica cura sit mors et vita secura.*

The second lesson of Matins (fols. 19r–21v) begins *Quoniam invisibiles adversarii rationem abducere per astutias* ('Because invisible enemies [strive] to take away reason by their malice') and ends *quamvis hoc spiritus mei non percipiat hebitudo* ('although the dullness of my mind does not perceive this'). This text leans heavily on the description of the guardian angel and its role by Jacobus de Voragine in the *Legenda aurea* (29 Sept.)[105] summarizing and borrowing words and phrases to such an extent that there can be no doubt about its inspiration. It is followed by versicle, response, and benediction that have not been traced: *O sincere mundeque spiritus, mundum fecit quem dei digitus, mundos motus immittas celitus, Ab immundis me munda penitus, ut a mundo sit [mundus]*[106] *obitus,* and *Angele mi custos, michi mores tolle vetustos.*

The third lesson of Matins (fols. 22r–24v) begins *Confiteor tamen, beate spiritus, quod nimis fui ingratus* ('I confess, blessed spirit, that I have been most ungrateful') and ends *sollicitudinem tuam ad felicem finem gaudens perducas* ('joyfully fulfill your care to a happy end'). This text is partly inspired by the twelfth of St Bernard's famous sermons on Psalm 90, *Qui habitat,*[107] and contains some Bible quotations, but has not been identified as a whole. The response and versicle that follow have also not been found elsewhere: *Mee mortis hora formidinis, turris michi sis fortitudinis, et levamen*[108] *confer solaminis, Per te cadat princeps caliginis, meque ducas ad locum luminis.*

Matins ends with the *Te deum* (fols. 25v–30r). The *Te deum* is found in the same position in the Hours of the Virgin, and contains references to all angels, *potestates, cherubyn* and *seraphyn.*[109]

Lauds (fols. 30r–38v): starts with the usual opening lines and the usual Psalm 92 (fols. 30v–32r), *Dominus regnavit,* with the antiphon *Tu*[110] *laudando iubilas creatorem tuum, adoptivus filius astrum matutinum,* followed by a capitulum (fols. 32v–33r): *Factum est prelium magnum in celo, Michael et angeli eius preliabantur cum dracone, et draco pugnavit et angeli eius; et non prevaluerunt neque locus inventus est eorum amplius in celo.* This passage from the Apocalypse (12:7–8) was and is frequently used in liturgical texts connected with St Michael. It is also the capitulum of Vespers in the present manuscript (*see below*).

The hymn continues with four stanzas (6–9, fols. 33r–34r) emphasizing the power of the guardian angel through images of light, and asking it to be a light to its charge even after death. The last line of stanza 7 wishes the angel everlasting joy, and may have inspired the donor of the book to use the words in the presentation scene.[111] The versicle rounding off this part of the hymn, *Angeli eorum semper vident faciem patris,*[112] is from the words spoken by Christ in the gospel of Matthew (18:10): 'Never despise one of these little ones; I tell you, they have their angels in heaven who look continually on the face of my Father'. This is one of the key texts concerning the existence and role of guardian angels,[113] and is also used as capitulum in None (fol. 57r–v), *see below.*

As in the Hours of the Virgin, there follows the Canticle of Zacharias, *Benedictus dominus deus Israel* (fols. 34v–37r), with the antiphon *Penitere me, custos, moneas, ut super me dolente gaudeas, digne deum orare doceas, et incensa precum adoleas.*

Next a short prayer: *Omnipotens sempiterne deus, qui inter hostiles insidias fragilitatis mee sanctum angelum tuum deputasti custodem, da michi queso sic sub eius custodia proficere et eo preducente ad te merear pervenire* ('Almighty, everlasting God, who has sent your holy angel as the protector of my weakness in the midst of the snares of the enemy, I pray you grant that I may thus prosper under his protection and under his guidance be allowed to finally come to you'). This prayer has not been found elsewhere,[114] but its antiphon *Angele qui meus es custos pietate superna, me tibi commissum serva, defende, guberna* ('Angel who are my guardian by divine mercy, keep me who has been entrusted to you, defend me and rule me') is the beginning of a well-known verse prayer;[115] in the present manuscript it also occurs on fols. 44r, 48v, 53v, 58v, 68r, and 76r at the end of the main prayer of each hour.

Prime (fols. 39–43v), after the usual opening, has the next two stanzas of the hymn (10–1, fols. 39v–40r), with their antiphon. The hymn here reminds the angel of his role in defending unworthy mankind against the anger of God. Psalm 120 (fols. 40r–42r), *Levavi oculos meos*, follows[116] with its antiphon *Valde bonam dominus lucem te videbat, ab aversis tenebris primo dividebat.*[117]

The capitulum that follows (fol. 42r–v), *Ecce ego mitto angelum meum qui precedat te et custodiat in via et introducat ad locum quem paravi* is from Exodus 23:20.[118] It is also used, for example, in the lesson of the modern Mass of the Guardian Angels. The versicles and responses that follow are Psalm 33:8, *Immittit angelus domini in circuitu timentium eum, Et eripiet eos*, and the text is from the Apocalypse, *Stetit angelus* (*see above*).[119]

The short final prayer of Prime (fol. 42r–v) is conventional, but has not been found elsewhere: *Concede queso, omnipotens deus, ut sanctum angelum apud tuam clementiam sentiam intercessorem quem ineffabilis gratia tua vite mee tribuit protectorem* ('Grant, I pray you, almighty God, that I may have as intercessor with your clemency the holy angel whom your ineffable mercy has given as protector of my life').

Terce (fols. 44r–48v) has the usual opening lines followed by stanzas 12 and 13 of the hymn (fols. 44v–45): 'You are my keeper when I sleep ... You take away the dangers of life'. Next Psalm 123 (fols. 45r–47r), *Nisi quia dominus*,[120] rounded off by the antiphon *Facit deus angelum spiritum insignem et ministrum inclitum exurentem ignem*, a paraphrase of Psalm 103:4. A capitulum follows (fol. 47r–v): *Observa angelum meum et exaudi vocem eius nec contempnendum putes [quia] nec dimittet te cum peccaveris et est nomen meum in illo*. This is Exodus 23: 21, also used in the modern breviary (2 Oct., first lesson of Matins) and in the modern Mass of the Guardian Angels. The versicles and responses that follow also occur earlier in the present text: *Stetit angelus* and *Qui facit angelos* (*see above*).[121] The prayer of Terce (fol. 48r–v) reads: *Omnipotens sempiterne deus, miserationis tue mihi presta subsidium cui et angelica prestitisti suffragia non deesse* ('Almighty everlasting God, of your mercy grant help to me, to whom you have also granted to enjoy angelic intercession'); this is a text known from the Mass asking for angelic protection in the Gregorian sacramentary,[122] and used in the *Missa de angelis* of the Sarum missal[123] and in the liturgy of Mont-Saint-Michel.[124]

Sext (fols. 49r–53v) has the usual opening, and stanzas 14 and 15 of the hymn (fols. 49r–50r): 'You sing the hymn of joy', 'you chase away the enemies of the church', followed by Psalm 124 (fols. 50r–51v), *Qui confidunt*, which occurs in the same position in the Hours of the Virgin.[125] Its antiphon, *Tibi sit meridies clara lux divina, matutina rutilans atque vespertina*, has not been identified; it uses images similar to those in the hymn of the present hours. The capitulum (fols. 51v–52r) is the fuller text of Apoc. 8:3 *Stetit angelus iuxta altare habens thuribulum aureum in manu sua et ascendit fumus aromatum de orationibus sanctorum de manu angeli coram deo*. Of the versicles and responses (fol. 52v) some occurred previously (*Qui facit angelos* etc.), others are from Psalm 102:20, *Benedicite dominum omnes angeli eius* and *Potentes virtute qui facitis verbum eius*. The latter also constituted the introit of the Mass of the Angels in the Sarum missal and are still used in the modern Mass of the Guardian Angels. The prayer of Sext reads (fol. 53r–v): *Omnipotens et misericors deus, respice me famulam tuam, magestati tue subiectam, et ne me furor sevientis mortis inveniat inermem preces meas angelico interveniente suffragio et placatus accipias et ad* *salutem meam pervenire concedas* ('Almighty and merciful God, regard me your servant/handmaiden, bowing to your majesty, and lest the fury of raging death finds me unprotected receive my prayers by the intercession of the angels and favourably and allow me to come to my salvation'). The second half of this prayer already occurred in the *secretum* of the Mass included in the Gregorian sacramentary, and was used in the *missa de angelis* of the Sarum missal.[126] In the present manuscript, its feminine forms appear to confirm the book's presentation to a female recipient.

None (fols. 54–58v) has the usual opening lines, and stanzas 16 and 17 of the hymn (fols. 54r–55r), which refer to Jacob's dream of the ladder to heaven and the intercessory role of the angels, going up and down between God and man. They are followed by Psalm 126 (fols. 55r–58v), *Nisi dominus aedificaverit*, with the antiphon *Beate custos spiritus, accensum ut divinitus fac ferveat cor meum, contempnam [sic] mundi prospera, fornacem carnis tempera, liges et amo deum [sic]*.[127] The capitulum (fol. 57r–v) is the full text of Matthew 18: 10, which was also used in Lauds (*see above*); the versicles and responses (fol. 57v) are partly the same as those used in Sext (fol. 52v, *see above*) *Benedicite* and *Potentes*.[128] The prayer of None reads (fol. 58r–v)[129]: *Concede michi queso, omnipotens et misericors deus, ut haec* [130] *que indigna tibi offero celestis spiritus michi prodesse sentiant auxilio* ('Grant me, I pray you, almighty and merciful God, that these which I offer you though they are unworthy may help me to prosper through the aid of the heavenly spirit'). It is partly found in the angels' Mass in the Gregorian sacramentary and in the *missa de angelis* of the Sarum missal.[131] The antiphon is the same as in the case of the other prayers (*see above*).[132]

Vespers (fols. 58v–67v) has the usual opening lines, followed by Psalm 137 (fols. 59r–61v), *Confiteor tibi domine*, which in other books of hours is used in Placebo (=Vespers) of the Vigil of the Dead.[133] The first five words of its antiphon are from the first verse of the same Psalm: *In conspectu angeli*[134] *psallam tibi deus qui laudator tuus est et protector meus*. The chapter (fol. 62r–v) is the same as that of Lauds (*see above*), *Factum est prelium*; it is followed by six stanzas of the hymn (18–23, fols. 62v–64): a long list of the virtues and powers of the guardian angel, rounded off by versicle and response, *Stetit angelus* and *Habens* (*see above*).[135] Next follows the Magnificat or the Canticle of the Virgin (fols. 64v–66v), which is found in the same position in the Hours of the Virgin. Its antiphon *In mundanis*[136] *nil te nobilius anime [?]*[137] *tu magnus filius factus tamen ministratorius peccatori quo nichil vilius* has not been found elsewhere.[138] The prayer of Vespers (fol. 67r–v) is better known than the preceding ones, occurring in books of hours and prayers from the twelfth century on;[139] it reads *Queso te et obsequenter rogo, sancte angele dei cui omnipotens deus dignatus es[t] committere cura[m] anime mee contra malignos angelos et iniquos viros, fer michi potenter auxilium ne me vel astutia circumveniant aut potentia frangant. Queso et viribus me fove et precibus, auxiliante domino nostro Ihesu Christe* ('I pray you and humbly beseech you, holy angel of God, to whom almighty God has designed to commit the care of my soul against malicious angels and evil men, give me strong support, that, with the help of our lord Jesus Christ, they may not defeat me by their malice or break me by their power').

Compline (fols. 68r–77r) has the usual opening lines followed by Psalm 90 (fols. 68v–72v), *Qui habitat*. This Psalm contains some of the essential biblical references to angels as guardians, and was the subject of a series of sermons by St Bernard.[140] His discussion of the verse *Quoniam angelis suis mandavit de te*, in which he preaches love, familiarity, and intense respect for one's angel, was officially embraced by the Church and became part of the office of 2 October in the Roman breviary.[141] The Psalm's antiphon found inspiration in its own lines: *Iuxta p[receptum?]*[142] *domini tu de me mandatum, me in viis omnibus pro[tegis?] ingratum*.[143]

The chapter *Omnes sunt administratorii* (fol. 73r) is from St Paul's letter to the Hebrews (1:14); it is followed by the last two stanzas of the hymn (fols. 73v–74r), its usual closing phrase, *Gloria tibi domine* (fol. 74r, *see above*) and the versicle and response from Psalm 90, *Angelis suis mandavit de te* and *Ut custodiant* (fol. 74r–v).[144] The antiphon *Custos mi non dormiens* occurs here and after the *Nunc dimittis* that follows on fols. 74v–75r.

The prayer of Compline reads: *Oblatam tibi, domine, orationem meam per sanctum custodem meum benignus assumas et effectum salutarem solicita ipsius meditatione concedas* ('Lord, graciously accept my prayer brought to you by your holy angel my guardian and grant my perfect salvation through his careful mediation').

The text ends on fol. 77r with the words *Sancti spiritus assit nobis gratia que corda nostra sibi faciat habitacula expulsis inde cunctis viliis spiritualibus. Gloria etc. Sicut etc.* Fols. 77v–80r are blank, fol. 80 is pasted down.

Appendix 2

The Hymn to the Guardian Angel.

1
Laus[145] tibi sit cum gaudio,
mi custos, et devotio;
quantum sub te proficio
referre non sufficio.

*Praise to you, with joy,
my guardian, and love;
I cannot say sufficiently
how good you are to me.*

2
Erremne per astutias
averter [sic][146] per blanditias[147]
premar per violentias[148]
repellis[149] has nequitias.

*For when I err through craftiness,
am led astray by flattery,
when I'm oppressed by violence,
you drive away such wickedness.*

3
Tu iuvas me non cadere,
si cadoque resurgere;
non tot nec tanta facere
ut hostis vult suggerere.

*You take care I do not fall,
and when I do you raise me up;
you help me not to do the things
the enemy tries to suggest.*

4
Non timeo supplicium
per te timoris noctium,
sagittam nec negotium
incursum aut demonium.

*Because of you I do not dread
the torture of the fear of night;
nor yet the arrow, or the harm
the devil or the world may do.*

5
Si preces in periculo
tuo suades parvulo
divino tu spectaculo
has donas in turribulo.

*When you tell your little one
to pray when I'm in danger,
you take these prayers up
to God's sight, in your censer.*

6
Clare sydus essentie,
refulgens naturaliter,
ex luce micans gratie
et glorie sublimiter.

*You are the star of perfect light,
you are by nature splendid,
shining sublimely with the light,
the light of grace and glory.*

7
Tibi semper meridies,
perpetuum solsticium,
laus ympnus atque requies
et sempiternum gaudium.

*To you it is forever noon,
the sun of summer always shines
and songs of praise and peace
and everlasting joy are yours.*

8
Solis non eget lumine
superna tua civitas,
de vite fructus flumine
dulcis tibi saturitas.

*Your lofty dwelling never lacks
the splendour of the sun;
the sweet fruit of the stream of life
always suffices you.*

9
Post huius cursum temporis,
prece precor assidua,
post mortem michi corporis
lux luceas perpetua.

*And I do pray assiduously
that when I finish this life's course,
and when my body is no more,
you will be my perpetual light.*

10
Cum rex olim superbie
cetus traxit nequitie,
te deo donum gratie
iunxit[150] et lumen glorie.

*When once the king of evil pride
dragged down with him the beast of sin,
the gift of grace and glory's light
joined you to God.*

11
Supra celum syderum
felix tenens imperium
orbem defendens luteum
contra regem aereum.[151]

*Above the heaven of the stars
you, happy one, hold sway,
shielding the vile and worthless earth
from the celestial king.*

12
Tu custos es cum dormio,
cum vigil malum facio
tua fervet dilectio
nec desinit[152] monitio.

*You are my keeper when I sleep;
if I do evil when awake,
you burn with love for me:
your warnings never cease.*

13
Vite tollis pericula,
hosti ponis obstacula,[153]
tu salvas habitacula
et ammones piacula.

*You take away the perils of my life
and keep the enemy at bay;
you protect my dwelling place
and warn me to act piously.*

14
Te voluptatis reficit
torrens nec sitis deficit,
quod habes tibi sufficit,
teque beatum afficit.

*The stream of joy refreshes you
and thirst does never weaken you;
what you have suffices you;
you know that you are blessed.*

15
Assistis trono glorie,
ympnum canis letitie,
celi decus militie
fugas hostes ecclesie.

*You stand near the throne of glory,
you sing the hymn of happiness,
defeat the church's enemies,
splendour of the heavens' host.*

WOMEN AND THE BOOK

16
Scandis scala prophetica,
consultas votum domini,
descendis ad extrinseca
pie ministras homini.

You climb the stairs of prophecy,
you ask the Lord for His commands;
descending to mankind on earth
you duly minister to them.

17
Horasque cum emitteris
intrinseca non deseris,
divino vultu frueris
sed ubicumque fueris.

Those hours that you are sent away,
you do not leave the blessed place:
you're still rejoicing in God's face
and yet are present everywhere.

18
Eya pusille, gaudeas
hostilem cernens aciem,
custos tuus ne pereas
paternam vidit faciem.

Come, little one, take pleasure when
you see the hostile battle lines:
your guard looks on the Father's face
and will not let you perish.

19
Divinis astat laudabilis
simplex intelligentia,
pollens in naturalibus,
purus in innocentia.

Worthy of praise and close to God,
you are pure intelligence,
you hold power over nature,
you are clean and innocent.

20
Vita perenni stabilis,
clarus, fortis et agilis,
liber et impeccabilis,
deo totus amabilis.

Secure in the eternal life,
bright and strong and quick of foot,
free and without blemish,
wholly lovable to God.

21
Amans fervoris ignei,
felix sublimis meriti,
altaris presul aurei,
legatus bene placiti.

You love the fiery zeal of faith,
you're happy with sublime good deeds;
you are the golden altar's priest,
the messenger of God's good will.

22
Adherens deo spiritus
et virtus invisibilis
est tutor meus inclitus,
demonibus terribilis.

A spirit that stays close to God,
a power that I cannot see,
you are my famous guardian,
whom all the devils fear.

23
Deo sit benedictio
cuius tam necessariam
magna fecit dilectio
mecum misericordiam.

May God be blessed
whose love so great
showed me the mercy
that I need so much.

24
In tenebrarum medio
lux lucis tue radio
sit lucis meditatio
et lucis operatio.

When I find myself in darkness
give me one ray of your light,
give me your light's intercession
and your light's beneficence.

25
Non demonis suggestio,
non hominis incursio,
nec mortis subitatio
quietis sit turbatio.

Let not the council of the devil,
nor the harm that man can do,
nor the suddenness of death
ever again disturb my rest.

Notes to Chapter Thirteen

1. Now in the ownership of the Dean and Chapter of Liverpool Cathedral, MS Radcliffe 6. The authors are most grateful to the Revd Canon David Hutton, Chancellor of Liverpool Cathedral, for his permission to publish this study and the illustrations; and for the assistance of Mr J.Clegg and his successor, Ms. K.Hooper, and her staff, at the Sydney Jones Library (Special Collections) of Liverpool University where the MS is now housed; and to Miss E. Danbury for facilitating our researches. We are also indebted to Dom Eligius Dekkers, OSB, Dr Ian Doyle, Prof. Ann Eljenholm Nichols and Mr Nicholas Rogers for their interest and generous help. Advice on specific points has been received from Prof. Mary Erler, Mrs Jo Mattingley and Dr Nicholas Watson.

2. The MS has been described: Bernard Quaritch, *Catalogue of Illuminated and Other Manuscripts* (London, 1931), pp.53–56, item 73 (ill.), and id., *Catalogue Number 532*, (London, 1937), p.124, item 403; J.J.G.Alexander et al., *Medieval and Early Renaissance Treasures in the North West. An Exhibition held at the Whitworth Art Gallery, Manchester, 15 January – 28 February 1976*, p.29, item 49; N.R.Ker, *Medieval Manuscripts in British Libraries*, 4 vols (Oxford, 1969–92), iii, pp.165–66, *Medieval Manuscripts on Merseyside*, catalogue of an exhibition held in the University Art Gallery, Liverpool, and the Courtauld Institute Galleries, London, 1993 (Liverpool, 1993), item 25 (ill.).

3. K.L.Scott, '*Caveat lector*: Ownership and Standardization in the Illustration of Fifteenth-Century English Manuscripts', *Manuscript Studies*, 1 (1989), p.28, on the uniqueness of this MS, given by one woman to another, for England in this period.

4. This title is a name of convenience (though also correct), and does not occur in the MS under discussion.

5. J.Duhr's entry *Anges* in *Dictionnaire de spiritualité ascétique et mystique. Doctrine et histoire*, ed. M.Viller (15 vols., Paris, 1932– [in progress]), i, cols. 580–626, exhaustively covers the history of the cult of angels and guardian angels. An important source is *Acta Sanctorum*, September VIII, used in most modern studies.

6. St Michael and All Angels were celebrated on 29 Sept. To this combination churches were dedicated and prayers addressed. Famous sermons about the angels were composed for this feast-day, e.g.: St Bonaventure, *Doctoris Seraphice S. Bonaventurae ... Opera Omnia...*, ed. studia et cura pp.collegii a S.Bonaventura (10 vols., Quaracchi, 1882–1902), ix, V Sermones de Sanctis Angelis, pp.609–31; Jean Gerson, *Oeuvres complètes*, ed. P.Glorieux (10 vols., Paris, 1961–73), vii, L'oeuvre française. Sermons et discours, pp.622–39, Pour la fête de S. Michel (Sermon des anges). On St Michael being the angel *par excellence* see e.g. *Iohannis Belethi Summa de Ecclesiasticis Officiis*, ed. H.Douteil, Corpus Christianorum Medievalis, vol. 41A (Turnhout, 1976), pp.294–96.

7. For example, St Bonaventure, *Doctoris Seraphice*, Sermon II; Jacobus de Voragine, 29 Sept., *De sancto Michaele archangelo*, in *Legenda Aurea*, ed. Th.Graesse (Dresden/Leipzig, 1846), pp.642–53; translation: G.Ryan and H.Ripperger, *The Golden Legend* (London, 1941, repr. Salem, 1987), pp.578–86.

8. Gerson, *Œuvres complètes*, pp.980–1. In the pseudo-Bonaventurian *Meditationes* and its derivative texts (*see* n.24 *below*) the angels complain that their ranks are depleted since the fall of Lucifer and that they have not been joined by the souls of men and women since the expulsion of Adam.

9. *See* n.7 *above*.

10. The author should strictly be called pseudo-Denys the Areopagite, but 'pseudo' is often omitted. Greek text with French translation and long introduction in Denys l'Aréopagite, *La Hiérarchie Céleste*, ed. M.Roques, G.Heil and M.de Gandillac, Sources chrétiennes 58 (Paris, 1958). English translation in Pseudo-Dionysius, *The Complete Works*, ed. and transl. C.Luibheid, P.Rorem, R.Roques et al. (London, 1987); modern commentary on the angels' hierarchy in A.Louth, *Denys the Areopagite* (London, 1989), pp.33–51. Pseudo-Denys used earlier Christian sources for all details but was the first to structure them elaborately. From the 9th to the 17th century pseudo-Denys was identified not only with Dionysius the Areopagite (Acts 17:34) but also with St Denis of Paris, the patron saint of France. The possible influence in England of the vast treatise on angels by the Catalan Franciscan Francesc Eiximenes (c.1340–1409) needs to be studied. The French translation, *Le Livre des Anges*, became known at the Burgundian court in the 1470s and was the first text to be printed at Geneva (1478).

11 *See* Duhr, *Anges.*

12 Spelling modernized. S.J.Ogilvy-Thomson, ed., *Richard Rolle: Prose and Verse* (EETS o.s. 293, 1988), pp.26–27.

13 When the Latin text of the *Liber Specialis Gratie* became known in England is not certain. The English translation was probably made in the second quarter of the 15th century. Two copies survive, of which one belonged to Elizabeth Woodville's brother in law, Richard of Gloucester, and his wife; her mother-in-law is known to have read the text. See T.A.Halligan (ed.), *The Booke of Gostlye Grace of Mechtild of Hackeborn*, Pontifical Institute of Mediaeval Studies. Studies and Texts 46 (Toronto, 1979); M.J.Finnigan, OP, *The Women of Helfta* (Athens, Ga/London, 1991). The *Liber* was also highly regarded by the Bridgettines. The library at Syon contained several copies of the Latin text: M.Bateson (ed.), *Catalogue of the Library of Syon Monastery, Isleworth* (Cambridge, 1898), M 22, 47, 59, 94, 98; London, BL, MS Sloane 982, which was probably a Syon MS, also includes Mechtild's work, *see* R.Ellis, 'Flores ad fabricandam ... coronam: An Investigation into the Uses of the Revelations of St Bridget of Sweden in Fifteenth-Century England', *Medium Aevum*, 51 (1982), pp.172, 176.

14 Halligan, *Booke of Gostlye Grace*, pp.138–39. Mechtild was a gifted singer and particularly interested in music and dance. On one occasion she had a vision in which the angels were not singing; Christ told her: '"Thowe schalte synge with aungells" Ande anone these holy aungells ande that blyssede maydene sange togyders.' (pp.148–49). Towards the end of the *Book* Mechtild's virtues are compared one by one to those of the Nine Orders, pp.608–10.

15 E.R.Harvey (ed.), *The Court of Sapience*, Toronto Medieval Texts and Translations 2 (Toronto, 1984), ll.442–55; quotation: ll.454–55.

16 There is a *missa ad postulanda angelica suffragia* among the supplements of the so-called Gregorian sacramentary, a collection of liturgical texts of the 9th century and earlier; *see* J.Deshusses, *Le Sacramentaire grégorien. Ses principales formes d'après les plus anciens manuscrits*, 3 vols., Specilegium Friburgense, vols. 16, 24, 28 (Fribourg, 1971–82), ii, no.14, pp.47–48; Duhr, *Anges*, col. 618.

17 *Millénaire Monastique du Mont Saint-Michel*, ed. J.Laporte et al. (4 vols., Paris, 1962–71) contains many contributions on the cult of St Michael; *see also* Dom J.Lemarié, 'Textes relatifs au culte de l'Archange et des Anges dans le Bréviaires Manuscrits du Mont-Saint-Michel' and 'Textes liturgiques concernant le culte de S. Michel', *Sacris Erudiri*, 13 (1962), pp.113–52, and 14 (1963), pp.277–85; id., 'Les formules de prières du manuscrit du Mont Saint-Michel, Avranches B.M. 213', *Studi medievali*, 13 (1972), pp.1015–42.

18 H.F.Westlake, *The Parish Gilds of Medieval England* (London, 1919), p.163 (Grantham), pp.204, 215 (Norwich). On St Michael *see also* the present authors' *The Hours of Richard III* (Stroud, 1990), p.73.

19 Bartholomaeus Anglicus probably wrote his *De proprietatibus rerum* between 1230 and 1250. It was translated into French by Jean Corbechon in 1372 and into English by John Trevisa in 1398, but it is unlikely that these translations were generally known. Basing himself on the pseudo-Denys, Bartholomew gives many details without connecting them to a specific Order; e.g. the angels are always clothed, but their feet are bare; they are dressed for war and wear golden girdles; and they carry sceptres, swords, spears, plummets, measures, phials, pens, inkhorns and other tools. See *On the Properties of Things. John Trevisa's translation of Bartholomaeus Anglicus De Proprietatibus Rerum*, ed. M.C.Seymour et al. (2 vols., Oxford, 1975), i, pp.64–65.

20 The Bible and the *Celestial Hierarchy* used heavily symbolic terms, avoiding accurate description and thus the danger of a too literal interpretation; Louth, *Denys*, p.46; Pseudo-Dionysius, *Works*, pp.182–91.

21 *See* e.g. E.Duffy, *The Stripping of the Altars* (New Haven/London, 1992), pp.270–71; C.Woodforde, *The Norwich School of Glass-Painting in the Fifteenth Century* (Oxford, 1950), ch.4, 'The Angels', pp.128–48; E.A.Gee, 'The Painted Glass of All Saints' Church, North Street, York', *Archaeologia*, 102 (1969), pp.151–202; P.B.Chatwin, 'The Decoration of Beauchamp Chapel', *Archaeologia*, 77 (1927), pp.313–33.

22 Identification appears to be further bedevilled by the fact that the odd number of the Orders was often depicted on objects requiring an even number of illustrations because of architectural symmetry.

23 *See* e.g. Duffy, *Stripping*, p.269.

24 For a discussion of the story and its popularity, see e.g. Harvey, *The Court of Sapience*, pp.xxvii–xxxii; Nicholas Love's translation of the pseudo-St Bonaventure's *Meditations of the Life of Christ, The Mirrour of the Blessed Life of Jesu Christ* (qu. from the ed. by L.F.Powell, [London etc., 1908], p.14) survives in more

than fifty MSS; *see* V.Gillespie, 'Vernacular books of religion', in *Book Production in Great Britain, 1375–1475*, ed. J.Griffiths and D.Pearsall (Cambridge, 1989), pp.323–24. *The Court of Sapience*, ll.610–700, has the story in full.

25 *The Golden Legend of Master William Caxton*, ed. F.S.Ellis (3 vols., Kelmscott Press, 1892), iii, p.874.

26 Thorn, yogh, and ampersand modernized. Osbern Bokenham, *Legendys of Hooly Wummen*, ed. M.S.Serjeantson, EETS o.s.206 (1938 for 1936), St Agnes, ll. 284–89.

27 Duhr, *Anges*, cols. 586–88.

28 The veneration of the guardian angel was particularly stimulated by St Bernard of Clairvaux in his seventeen sermons on Psalm 90, *Qui habitat* (*St Bernardi Opera Omnia*, iv, ed. J.Leclercq and J.Rochais, Rome, 1966, pp.457–63, esp. 459 ff.); a passage from sermon 12 came to be used in the angels' liturgy, and is now the third Lesson of Matins in the Office of the Guardian Angels (2 Oct.) in the Roman breviary.

29 A list of such prayers would be too long for the scope of this paper. The main source is still Dom A.Wilmart, *Auteurs spirituels et textes dévots du moyen âge latin* (Paris, 1932), ch.24, Prières à l'Ange Gardien, pp.537–58, and App. II, Prières aux saints anges, pp.578–82; Dom Wilmart noted the frequency of such prayers in England and the scarcity of them in France; whether this is merely a matter of survival he was not prepared to say. See also P.Rézeau, *Les Prières aux saints en français à la fin du Moyen Age. Prières à un saint en particulier et aux anges* (Geneva, 1983), pp.511–15, and references given there; W.Maskell, *Monumenta Ritualia Ecclesiae Anglicanae*, 3 vols (London, 1846–7), iii, pp.289–92. There are many prayers, hymns, *pia dictamina* and rhyming offices throughout *Analecta Hymnica Medii Aevi*, ed. C.Blume, G.M.Dreves, H.M.Bannister (55 vols., Leipzig, 1886–1922). Most modern catalogues of MS collections list prayers to the guardian angel in their indices. Texts to the guardian are also found with headings addressing them to St Michael. Among people close to Elizabeth Woodville, her brother-in-law Richard III owned a unique text of such a prayer in his book of hours (London, Lambeth Palace Library, MS 474, fol. 179r–v; *see The Hours of Richard III*, p.60); and his father, Richard, Duke of York, had two such prayers in the pages added for his use in his book of hours, Ushaw, St Cuthbert's College, MS 43, fols. 1r–2v.

30 On such feasts generally R.W.Pfaff, *New Liturgical Feasts in Later Medieval England* (Oxford, 1970), *passim*. With more encouragement a Feast of the Guardian Angels might have become official on the lines of the Feast of the Holy Name of Jesus, patronized by Margaret Beaufort, mother of Henry VII (*see* Duffy, *Stripping*, pp.113–16 and 284), and also by John Colet who re-founded a Fraternity of the Holy Name which had been established in St Paul's by a remembrancer of the Exchequer and clerks of the privy seal in 1459 (see Oxford, Bodleian Library, MS Tanner 221). Compare also the Feast of the Five Wounds, which failed to materialize in spite of an important cult: see Duffy, *Stripping*, pp.238–48 and 294. In his paraphrase of the *Celestial Hierarchy* John Colet (d.1519) was to recommend prayers to the guardian angels: every one has his own custodian angel and keeper ... All angels look after us, but those to whom we are 'entrusted especially provide for us with earnest care. Wherefore they act most rightly who daily worship and pray to their own guardian angel with some special prayer'. See *Two Treatises on the Hierarchies of Dionysius*, ed. and transl. J.H.Lupton (London, 1869), pp.45–46.

31 Duhr, *Anges*, cols 614–15; and e.g. G.Llompart, 'El Angel Custodio en la Corona de Aragón en la Baja Edad Media (fiesta, teatro, iconografía)', *Fiestas y Liturgia*, ed. A.Esteban and J.-P.Etienvre (Madrid, 1988), pp.249–69, and references given there. The popularity of angels in Spain was due to the work of Eiximenes; *see* n. 10, above.

32 Duhr, *Anges*, cols. 615–18; *Acta Sanctorum*, Sept.VIII.

33 A.E.Nichols, *Seeable Signs: The Iconography of the Seven Sacraments, 1350–1544* (Woodbridge 1994), pp.224–35.

34 Duffy, *Stripping*, pp.316–17, on the popularity of block-books with such scenes. Many tombs and their effigies include angels, often seated protectively at the head of the dead, sometimes carrying up the soul to heaven; *see* e.g. T.S.R.Boase, *Death in the Middle Ages* (London, 1972). See also Rézeau, *Les Prières*, p.507; R.Chartier, 'Les Arts de bien mourir, *Annales E.S.C.*, 31 (1976), pp.51–75.

35 The literature about St Bridget is vast. See e.g. A.Jefferies Collins, *The Bridgettine Breviary of Syon Abbey*, Henry Bradshaw Society 96 (Worcester, 1969), intro.; F.R.Johnston, 'The English Cult of St Bridget of Sweden', *Analecta Bollandiana*, 103 (1985), pp.75–93.

36 For the *Sermo angelicus de excellentia virginis*, see S.Eklund (ed.), *Sancta Birgitta Opera Omnia Minora II: Sermo*

Angelicus, Samlingar vtgivna av Svenska Fornskriftsällskapet, Ser. II, Latinska Skrifter 8/2 (Uppsala, 1972); and Collins, *Bridgettine Breviary*, intro.

37 The iconography of St Bridget may have encouraged the belief in the guardian angel, as she is often represented with her dictating angel at her shoulder in a composition similar to some miniatures of the supplicant with his or her angel accompanying prayers to the guardian. When complete, pilgrims' badges commemorating visits to Syon Abbey almost all showed a little angel speaking into St Bridget's ear; *see* B.Spencer, *Pilgrim Souvenirs and Secular Badges*, Salisbury Museum Catalogue, pt. 2 (Salisbury, 1990), pp.45–46.

38 The *Revelationes celestes* or *Liber celestis* was written by St Bridget in Swedish but soon translated into Latin and into English early in the 15th century. *See* Roger Ellis (ed.), *The Liber Celestis of St Bridget of Sweden*, EETS o.s. 291 (1987), i, Text; the same, 'Flores', pp.163–86.

39 Ellis, *Liber celestis*, pp.23, 63, 407, 17, and 345. Thorns and yoghs modernized. On this subject *see also* e.g. J.Daniélou, *Les Anges et leur mission d'après les Pères de l'Eglise* (Chevetogne, 1953), pp.106–7, and stanza 17 of the hymn to the guardian angel, *see* Appendix 2 to this chapter.

40 *See The Myroure of our Ladye*, ed. H.J.Blunt, EETS e.s. 19 (1873), the first prologue, p.5. The office of the Bridgettine nuns differed (and differs) from the usual office of Our Lady in that it does not vary with the seasons but with each day of the week: Sunday is dedicated to Mary and the Trinity; Monday to Mary and the Angels and their joy at her birth; Tuesday to Mary, the Creation and the Fall, and Adam's foreknowledge of Mary's birth, etc. (*Myroure*, pp.5 and 175–90). On the use of the Bridgettine office *see also* A.Hutchinson, 'Devotional Reading in the Monastery and in the Household', in *De cella in seculum*, ed. M.G.Sargeant (Cambridge, 1989), pp.219–23.

41 Quoted by Collins, *Bridgettine Breviary*, p.xvi.

42 The Monday was dedicated to the Angels throughout the church, but *see* n.40 *above*.

43 Sotheby's catalogue, 17 Dec.1991, pp.112–13, item 69. C.de Hamel, *Syon Abbey. The Library of the Bridgettine Nuns and their Peregrinations after the Reformation* (Roxburghe Club, 1991), pp.73–77.

44 Oxford, Bodleian Library, MS Bodl. 62, Sarum hours, late 14th c., with late 15th-c. Bridgettine additions, e.g. Sts Bridget and Katherine, her daughter, inserted high into the litany (conveniently at the bottom of the page) which already included Bridget. Additional prayers are to God and Christ (fols. 102r 106v), St Michael and All Angels (fols. 106v–108r) and the Guardian Angel (fol. 108r–v); this last text is almost identical with Aberdeen, University Library, MS 25, fol. 6v, *see below*. South Brent, Syon Abbey, MS 2, hours, mid 15th c., has a commemoration of the angels, memorials of Michael, Gabriel, Raphael and the guardian in prominent places, two other prayers to Michael, and four to the Guardian Angel; *see* Ker, *Medieval Manuscripts*, iv, pp.336–42; de Hamel, *Syon*, p.65. South Brent, Syon Abbey, MS 4, hours (1424?), has memorials of St Michael and the Guardian Angel; the latter has four collects; de Hamel, *Syon*, p.66. Formerly Bristol, Baptist College, MS Z.e.37, now London, Lambeth Palace MS 3600, private prayers, early 16th c., has three prayers to the Guardian Angel; *see* Ker, *Medieval Manuscripts*, ii, pp.198–200, and Sotheby's Catalogue, 17 Dec.1991, item 64. Oxford, Bodleian Library, MS Auct.D.4.7, Bridgettine breviary, 1425–30, owned by the nuns during their first exile at the house of James Yate, at Buckland, 1539–57 (*see* Collins, *Bridgettine Breviary*, p.v), contains a prayer inserted at the beginning asking first God for His protection of the order and the house *in hoc loco*, then asking for Him to send *sanctum angelum tuum de celo, qui nos protegat, visitet et defendat: ne patiamur detrimentum animarum nostrarum*; next the intercession is begged collectively of Sts Mary, Michael, both Johns, Peter, Paul, Augustine, Bridget, and Katherine.

45 Aberdeen, University Library, MS 25. We are grateful to Nicholas Rogers for bringing this MS to our attention and for the use of his microfilm. In his researches he has found no other copy of the text of the Hours. *See* M.R.James, *A Catalogue of the Medieval Manuscripts in the University Library, Aberdeen* (Cambridge, 1932), no. 25, pp.25–35, ill.; N.Rogers, 'About the 15 "O"s, The Brigittines and Syon Abbey', *St Ansgar's Bulletin*, 80 (1984), 29–30; id., 'Books of Hours produced in the Low Countries for the English market in the fifteenth century', unpubl. M.Litt.diss., Cambridge, 1982, pp.202–14, 217–18, and 346–47, pls 58–60.

46 Two blank flyleaves precede the verse, the first being pasted to the board; both are now covered with notes by later owners.

47 A royal book of hours did not have to be large or magnificent, particularly if it was for daily use. Compare London, BL, MS Add. 65100, a small and modest hours made for Queen Katherine de Valois,

widow of Henry V, or the hours used by Richard III while king, the present authors' *Hours of Richard III*, Figs. 9, 18 and *passim*.

48   Several cataloguers have attempted to explain the last letters as part of the acrostic: *see* n.2.

49   Scott, '*Caveat lector*', p.28, points out that it takes the place usually assigned to an Annunciation.

50   *See* stanza 7 of the hymn, Appendix 2.

51   M.R.James and E.W.Tristram, 'The Wall Paintings in Eton College Chapel', *Walpole Society*, 17 (1928–29), pl. XIX (VII); and compare pl. XIV (II). These paintings show a good range of women's headdresses. This headdress can also be seen in the 'Portrait of a Lady' by the Master of St Severin, National Trust, Polesden Lacey. The headdress of the donor in no way resembles the very distinctive one of the Bridgettine nuns.

52   S.L.Hindman, *Christine de Pizan's 'Epistre Othea'* (Toronto, 1986), ch. 2. Several types of modest headdress from Christine's time through the 15th century taken from copies of her works are illustrated in M.Quilligan, *The Allegory of Female Authority. Christine de Pizan's 'Cité des Dames'* (Ithaca, NY, 1991). Christine was very conscious of what was suitable dress for women of all ranks, as shown in her chosen illustrations and her *Treasure of the City of Ladies*, transl. S.Lawson (Harmondsworth, 1985), e.g. pp.64, 99, 159, and 163.

53   London, BL, MS Harl. 4431 (plates in Hindman, *Christine*).

54   Compare Elizabeth's 'portrait' in the Book of the Fraternity of the Assumption of Our Lady, in which she wears her hair loose beneath a closed imperial crown, a very similar crimson and ermine surcoat and kirtle, and a blue mantle edged with gold: J.J.Lambert, *Records of the Skinners of London* (London, 1933), p.82.

55   All terms used here to describe the queen's garments are the contemporary ones; her robe corresponds most closely to the two robes of crimson velvet and purple velvet (three garments in each) described by A.F.Sutton, 'The coronation robes of Richard III and Queen Anne Neville', *Costume*, 13 (1979), 12–15, Figs. 1, 2; and *see* A.F.Sutton and P.W.Hammond, *The Coronation of Richard III* (Gloucester, 1983), p.163, for the contemporary great wardrobe accounts' description.

56   The textile is now very worn, but the crimson is still bright, although the gold of the gold thread has largely been rubbed off its core thread of yellow silk. The contemporary sewn headband is of red and green silk. *See Coronation of Richard III*, p.111, for the frequent use of 'crimson' cloth of gold.

57   *See* n. 2 *above*.

58   Quaritch, *Catalogues* (1931 and 1937) says the rose is red and Tudor; Ker, *Medieval Manuscripts*, similarly says the rose is 'red' – which it most definitely is not – but accepts the pre-Tudor date of the MS given by Alexander et al. on stylistic grounds.

59   For the use of formalized roses in two colours before 1485 see J.H.Marrow et al., *The Golden Age of Dutch Manuscript Painting* (Utrecht, 1989), pp.251–2, pl. 89. E.Danbury, 'The Decoration and Illumination of Royal Charters in England, 1250–1509', in *England and her Neighbours, 1066–1453. Essays in honour of Pierre Chaplais*, ed. M.Jones and M.Vale (London, 1989), pp.175–76, deals briefly with the use of English royal badges as decoration.

60   *See* n.45 *above*.

61   As the hours of the angel in the MS discussed here are not preceded by any other texts, e.g. psalms, they had to be given in full.

62   Many capitula, antiphons, verses, and responses are inspired by Bible texts relating to angels, but it has not been possible to trace them all.

63   Hindman, *Christine*, pp.15–16, etc.; C.de Hamel, *A History of Illuminated Manuscripts* (Oxford, 1986), p.172 (Fig. 168). V.M.O'Mara, 'A Middle-English Text Written by a Female Scribe', *Notes and Queries*, 235 (1990), pp.396–98. *See also* J.J.G.Alexander, *Medieval Illuminators and their Methods of Work* (New Haven, 1993), Fig. 204 (Paris, BN, MS fr.25526, fol. 77v).

64   For the preceding paragraphs *see* the present authors' 'A "Most Benevolent Queen": Queen Elizabeth Woodville's Reputation, her Piety and her Books', *The Ricardian*, 9 (1995), pp.214–45. For illustrations of the Virgin Mary in secular royal robes *see* e.g. E.Danbury, 'English and French Artistic Propaganda during the period of the Hundred Years War: Some Evidence of Royal Charters', in *Power, Culture and Religion in France c.1350–1550*, ed. C.T.Allmand (Woodbridge, 1989), pp.75–97.

65 *Calendar of Patent Rolls 1446–52*, p.29. The main sources used for the following account are: S.Reynolds (ed.), *Victoria County History: Middlesex*, iii (London, 1962), p.109 and in particular the Ancient Deeds cited there; G.J.Aungier, *The History of the Antiquities of Syon Monastery* (London, 1840), pp.215–22, 459–78. The court rolls of Isleworth, 1440s–90s, Greater London Record Office, (GLRO) Acc.1379/9–13, virtually complete, add some details not elsewhere, and to these rolls Ms. Jo Mattingley kindly provided an introduction and answered many questions; she also generously allowed access to pages of her thesis. Despite this apparent abundance of records the precise mechanics of the endowment and how and why certain individuals were able to gain such dominant positions as regards the chapel is not entirely clear. Although the guild was certainly still in existence in 1479, it is not known how long it lasted after that. It is hoped to publish a detailed study of the chapel and its fraternity. For the full text of the licence to found the chapel, *see* W.Scase, *Reginald Pecock* (Aldershot, 1996), pp.125–27.

66 Emden, *Oxford*, and *Dict. of Nat. Biog.*, under Somerset. C.H.Talbot and E.A.Hammond, *The Medical Practitioners in Medieval England. A Biographical Register* (London, 1965), pp.184–85. C.P.Christianson, *A Directory of London Stationers and Book Artisans 1300–1500* (New York, 1990), p.80. His will does not survive.

67 He died before 16 May 1454, Isleworth court rolls, GLRO, Acc. 1379/9, m. 97v. Probably in April, as Syon Abbey recorded his obit in April (he gave £10 to the House), Syon Martiloge, London, BL, Add. MS 22285, fols. 6v, 70v.

68 Whittington's rebuilding of the church dedicated to the Archangel may have occasioned a new interest in angels and their worship and representation. Emden, *Oxford*, under Pecock. V.H.H.Green, *Bishop Reginald Pecock* (Cambridge, 1945), pp.18–20 and 46, n.1, has nothing on the relationship between Pecock and Somerset. J.Imray, *The Charity of Richard Whittington. A History of the Trust administered by the Mercers' Company 1424–1966* (London, 1966), pp.14–15, 20–21, 30–31 and 39, n.1. Pecock was appointed while John Carpenter, the leading executor and another man of considerable literary interests, was in charge of the College of Priests. One of the other executors, John White, was the master of St Bartholomew's Hospital. *See also* M.G.Sargent, 'Walter Hilton's *Scale of Perfection*: The London Manuscript Group Reconsidered', *Medium Aevum*, 52 (1983), pp.206–8, and W.Scase, 'Reginald Pecock, John Carpenter and John Colop's 'Common-Profit' Books: Aspects of Book Ownership and Circulation in Fifteenth-Century London', *Medium Aevum*, 56 (1992), pp.261–74, *passim*, for Colop and the London book-trade, for 'common profit books' and the influence of Pecock and Carpenter over the dissemination of devotional literature. (Somerset is not pursued by the latter.)

69 Feoffee 1484. J.C.Wedgwood, *History of Parliament*, i: *Biographies 1439–1509* (London, 1936), pp.547–48; A.R.Myers, 'The Household of Elizabeth Woodville, 1466–7', *Bulletin of the John Rylands Library*, 1 (1967–8), p.298 (the identifications are more certain than Myers implies); R.Somerville, *History of the Duchy of Lancaster*, i, *1265–1603*, (London, 1953), p.457, and J.H.Baker, 'The Attorneys and Officers of the Common Law in 1480', *Journal of Legal History*, 1 (1980), p.197. Under-sheriff of Middlesex in 1450s, N.Ramsay, 'The English Legal Profession c.1340–c.1350' (unpubl. Ph.D thesis, Cambridge 1985), App. 8. He appears for the first time in the Isleworth court rolls as a landowner in 1483, GLRO, Acc. 1379/11, m.3. He died 1487 and bequeathed one of his funeral torches to the chapel of All Angels; his executors and overseers show the extent of his royal official and legal network (PCC 7 Milles) PRO, PROB 11/8, fols. 53v–54v.

70 Wedgwood, *Biographies*, pp.547–48. J.Morris, 'The Provosts and Bailiffs of Shrewsbury', *Shropshire Archaeological and Natural History Society Transactions*, ser.3, 2 (1903), pp.283–86; 3 (190), pp.363, 373, and 379. Joan's maiden name was Whitcombe.

71 Grafton was also a local landowner, holding the manor of Norwood with others by 1484, *VCH* Middlesex, iv, p.44. He also traded with Italy: M.E.Mallett, 'Anglo-Florentine commercial relations', *Economic History Review*, 15 (1962–3), pp.260, 262. For his trade and shipping, e.g. *CCR 1476–85*, no. 1145; *CPR 1476–85*, p.240; PRO, C1/64/517; *British Library Harleian Manuscript 433*, ed. R.Horrox and P.W.Hammond (4 vols., London and Upminster, 1979–83), i, pp.260, 262; ii, pp.14, 53; iii, pp.32–34. (The will of 1504, PCC 15 Holgrave, is unlikely to be his).

72 Emden, *Oxford*, under Adam Grafton. His career was eminent and mostly in Shropshire; his precise position must have been much as described in the text, although his funeral brass 'elevates' him to chaplain to Edward V and Prince Arthur.

73 A.I.Doyle, 'More light on John Shirley', *Medium Aevum*, 30 (1961), pp.93–101. Kerling, *Cartulary*, pp.153–54 (the one surviving rental of 1456; others living there in 1456 included William Cleve, clerk of the

king's works, 1444–51, and Joan Astley, nurse of Henry VI). The priory church attracted the burials of some exchequer officials: J.Stow, *Survey of London*, ed. C.L.Kingsford (Oxford, 1918), i, pp.27–28, and pp.23–24 for other people buried in the Hospital and Shirley's English verse epitaph. N.Moore, *History of St Bartholomew's Hospital* (London, 1918), i, pp.18–44, for the Latin verse epitaphs of Richard Shipley and Sturgeon's wife Joan. And *see below* for the verse content of Oxford, Bodleian Library, MS Lat.liturg.e.17.

74 Kerling, *Cartulary*, pp.6, 8, and 9. Stow, *Survey*, i, p.23, on Wakering's gift to his house of the 'fayrest Bible, that I have seene'; it had an addition by Wakering's clerk and renter, John Cok, when he was 68, and is now Wolfenbüttel, Herzog August Bibliothek MS Extrav.25.1 (*ex inf.* Dr Ian Doyle).

75 St Bartholomew's Hospital Archives, HC1/1010 (indenture of 1464 sets out all the services, etc., of the chantry) and HC1/1482. *See also* Kerling, *Cartulary*, pp.110, nos. 1113–23. Thanks are due to Mr Geoffrey Yeo, the Archivist.

76 Emden, *Oxford*. PRO, PROB 11/4, fol. 65r–v; proved 1 June 1457: to be buried in the chapel of the Virgin in the church of the Holy Cross of St Bartholomew's Hospital; no reference to his chapel in his will; Margaret Cok was his servant, possibly a relative of the Hospital's renter, John Cok; his wife was dead and his daughter married to Thomas Frowyk; his brother, John, overseer of his will, was almost certainly the mercer and chamberlain (1450–53), *Cal. Letter Book K, passim*; Richard bought membership of the Mercers' Company, 1447–8, Mercers' Company, Wardens' Accounts 1347, 1390–1463.

77 J.C.Wedgwood, *History of Parliament* (2 vols., London, 1936–8), i: *Biographies*, pp.358–59. S.L.Thrupp, *The Merchant Class of Medieval London, 1300–1500* (Chicago, 1948), p.343. Isleworth court rolls, GLRO, Acc. 1379/9, m. 89 (1453). Died 1485, one of his executors being John Ward, whom he describes as steward of Syon Abbey, perhaps junior to himself, (PCC 18 Logge) PRO, PROB 11/7, fols. 137v–38v. For more details on Frowyk and his family, *see* A.F.Sutton and L.Visser-Fuchs, 'The Making of a Minor London Chronicle in the Household of Sir Thomas Frowyk (d.1485)', *The Ricardian*, 10 (1994), pp.86–103. Dr.I.Doyle has reminded us that John Ward's name occurs in London, Lambeth Palace Library, MS 546, written for (and by?) Syon nuns (*see also* O'Mara, 'A Middle-English Text').

78 Acting in one deed of 1462 and the scribe of another; d.1496. It might be argued he was not a 'lawyer' in the full sense, but a scrivener; his work was, however, largely legal: an active 'writer of the court letter' in London, e.g. in the 1450s, St Bartholomew's Hospital, Deeds HC1/839, 1012, 1504 (not in *Cartulary*); N.Ramsay, 'English Legal Profession', p.135, and App. 7. His will specified burial before the altar of St Michael in Blackfriars, a torch to St Michael Highgate, and masses to be celebrated for his soul at places including the Charterhouses and Syon (PCC 31 Vox) PRO, PROB 11/10, fols. 247v–48r.

79 Feoffee 1463. *Cal. Letter Book K*, p.359. N.J.M.Kerling, *Cartulary of St Bartholomew's Hospital* (London, 1973) p.154 (26) and *passim*, and *see below* for his involvement in the chapel of St Michael there. Of Cambridgeshire; Burgoyne family still living in St Bartholomew's in the 16th century, E.A.Webb, *The Records of St Bartholomew's Priory and of the Church of St Bartholomew the Great, West Smithfield* (2 vols., London, 1921), i, wills. Died 1471; hoped to be buried before Holy Cross in St Bartholomew's, (PCC 1 Wattys) PRO, PROB 11/6, fols. 4v–5v. Associated with John Pye, stationer: Christianson, *Directory*, pp.142, 147.

80 Kerling, *Cartulary*, p.154 (25, 26), and nos.1144–50 for Burgoyne's and Sturgeon's work for the Hospital.

81 Doyle, 'More light on John Shirley', pp.94–95. Portaleyn was in Beauchamp service certainly from the 1430s, and Shirley retired in the '30s (and died 1456). We are indebted for details of his Beauchamp employment to Dr Alix Sinclair. *See also* Wedgwood, *Biographies*, which is inaccurate e.g. over his date of death.

82 Isleworth court rolls, GLRO, Acc. 1379/9, 10, *passim*. Alice, his widow, sold it all immediately after his death in 1471, *ibid.*, 1379/10, m. 21(2,3).

83 Alice *née* Domenyk was an heiress in her own right; William Markeby died 1439, leaving her his houses in Isleworth and St Bartholomew's (next door to Richard Sturgeon), PRO, PROB 11/3, fols. 204r–205r. Shipley, d.1445, PROB 11/3, fols. 253v–54r; before his death Shipley improved their house in St Bart's; Portaleyn also leased another tenement and a stable from the Hospital, Kerling, *Cartulary*, pp.154 (43), and 156 (73, 77). Portaleyn died 1470–1, and Alice 1479, GL. MS 9171, fols. 282v–83r.

84 This is based on their wills, Thomas, 1487, PCC 7 Milles PRO, PROB 11/8, fols. 53v–54v, and Joan 1497, proved 1498, PCC 28 Horne, PROB 11/11, fol. 226r–v: both asked to be buried in the church of Holy Cross and Alice was nursed in her last illness by her 'sister', Agnes, a sister of the Hospital, presumably Agnes, the sister of Thomas.

85 St Bartholomew's Hospital Deeds, HC1/1464, an indenture of 27 Feb. 1487 returning the plate upon repayment. See n.98.

86 Isleworth court rolls, GLRO, Acc. 1379/11, mm.5v–6; this included Thomas Grafton. Were these Shrewsbury families of Luyt and Grafton also the promotors of Caxton's *Life of St Winifred* in this same year of 1484? Thomas Grafton was a mercer like Caxton, and his brother was to be a founder member of the Fraternity of St Winifred in Shrewsbury, where the Luyts also maintained close links. The main feature of Caxton's edition of the text is its deliberate emphasis on the saint's connection to Shrewsbury. The 1484 date for *St Winifred* is derived from the paper of the edition, cited M. Lowry, 'Caxton, St Winifred and the lady Margaret Beaufort', *Library*, 6th ser., 5 (1983), p.116 (*pace* Lowry's theory that *St Winifred* was linked to Margaret Beaufort, mother of Henry VII, and politically inspired).

87 PRO, CP 25/1/152/100/23 (fine), by which she bought out the interest of Thomas Grafton and his wife Agnes for 100 marks.

88 For her will *see* n.84, *above*. Cheseman was also her executor; he was possibly married to Alianore Luyt, cousin of Thomas; his younger son was called Michael. For Cheseman, *see* Baker, 'Attornies', p.161; like the Luyts, he had connections with Shropshire, and extensive lands, his main manor being Southall, acquired 1496, *VCH* Middlesex, iv, p.44. PCC 33 Bennett, PRO, PROB 11/16, fol. 260r–v, his will shows concern for All Angels and the obit there for Joan Luyt, but makes no reference to the chapel lands.

89 Cheseman's will, *see* preceding note.

90 A.B.Emden, *A Biographical Register of the University of Cambridge to 1500* (Cambridge, 1963) under Chapman. He owned London, BL, MS Harley 2344, a book of sermons or ideas for them. His date of death is unknown and he left no surviving will.

91 A.I.Doyle, 'A Text Attributed to Ruusbroec Circulating in England', in *Dr. L. Reypens-Album ... 26 februari 1964*, ed. A.Ampe (Antwerp, 1964), p.158.

92 In this context reference must be made to a text that has been called 'The Revelation of the Hundred Pater Nosters', ed. F.Wormald, Laudate, 14 (1936), pp.165–82, which occurs in London, BL, MS Lansdowne 379, fols. 41r–54r, together with a number of conventional prayers. According to the MS the text was sent from the Charterhouse in London to the house of the same order at Mount Grace; it is an intense meditation on the physical aspects of Christ's passion and includes mention of St Bridget. The story of the text's efficacy and its multiple copying refers to a prayer of 'saint Mawde'; *see also* Duffy, *Stripping*, p.295. In the editions of the 'Revelation' by Wynkyn de Worde, 1500? (STC 14546) and 1509 (STC 14572), the text ends with prayers to each of the Nine Orders; in the MS, which is a copy from a (different) printed version, no such text appears at the end. We are grateful to Dr Veronica O'Mara for her interest and information.

93 Doyle, 'A text', 158.

94 Oxford, Bodleian Library, MS Lat.liturg.e.17 also contains an English translation of the 'revelations' of Christ to 'Albert of Cologne' (fols. 54r–55r; probably in the same hand as the note on fol. 108v made in 1492, Doyle, 'A Text', p.158 and n.26). This text occurs in many versions under many names: *see A Manual of Writings in Middle English 1050–1500*, gen. eds. J. Burke Severs and A.E.Hartung (9 vols., New Haven, 1967–93), vii, XX [p.157].

95 Oxford, Bodleian Library, MS Lat.liturg.e.17, fol. 72v. Punctuation and *th* modernized; abbreviatons extended. The 'mistakes' in the text suggest it was composed straight on to the page.

96 Oxford, Bodleian Library, MS Lat.liturg.e.17, fols. 51r–55r. C.Brown and R.H.Robbins, *The Index of Middle English Verse* (New York, 1943), and R.H.Robbins and J.L.Cutler, *Supplement to the Index of Middle English Verse* (Lexington, 1965), items 253 and 3102. Doyle, 'A Text', p.158.

97 V.Gillespie, 'Vernacular Books of Religion', in *Book Production*, pp.319–20; Sargent, 'Walter Hilton's *Scale of Perfection*', pp.205–6; Scase, 'Reginald Pecock', *passim*.

98 *See* Doyle, 'Publication', in *Book Production*, pp.116–17, on the fact that such dedications to aristocrats often proved 'abortive for circulation' but compare the request of the Bridgettine scribe Simon Wynter to Margaret, Duchess of Clarence, to 'rede hit and to doo copye hit for youre self and syth to latte other red hit and copy hit whoso wyl', quoted *ibid.*; and *see* G.Keiser, 'Patronage and Piety in Fifteenth-Century England: Margaret, Duchess of Clarence, Symon Wynter and Beinecke MS 317', *Yale University Library Gazette*, 60 (1985), pp.32–46.

99   Throughout the MS the opening initial of each hour is a three-line capital; lessons, psalms, chapters and sections of the hymn are marked by two-line initials (*see also* the description of the illumination *above*). For the usual contents of books of hours see e.g. R.S.Wieck, *The Book of Hours in Medieval Art and Life* (London, 1988).

100 Aberdeen, University Library, MS 25 reads *distrahenti*.

101 The text appears to be a unity, but each stanza could stand on its own.

102 Aberdeen 25 (*see above* and n.45): *Versus. Lux que me ducis. Responsorium. Facies lucet tibi lucis. Benedictio. Laudes exiles celestis suscipe.*

103 Ed. J.Wickham Legge, *The Sarum Missal* (Oxford, 1916), p.459.

104 Aberdeen 25: *que fecisti michi*.

105 Ed. Th. Graesse (*see* n.7, *above*), pp.649–50.

106 *mundus* supplied from Aberdeen 25.

107 *See* n.28, *above*.

108 Supplied from Aberdeen 25; the Liverpool MS had *laudamen*!

109 The *Te deum* is not included in Aberdeen 25.

110 *Tu* supplied from Aberdeen 25; the Liverpool MS has *Te*.

111 *See above*, and n.50.

112 Aberdeen 25: *Versus. Ante deum gaudes. Responsorium. Non cessans psallere laudes.*

113 *See A Critical Commentary on the Gospel According to Saint Matthew*, ii, W.D.Davies and D.C.Allison, Jr. (Edinburgh, 1991), pp.769–72.

114 Except in Aberdeen 25, where it is also the prayer in Terce, Sext, None and Vespers.

115 Wilmart, *Auteurs*, pp.556–57.

116 Aberdeen 25 here has Ps.53, *Deus in nomine tuo*.

117 Compare Gen. 1: 4. The present MS has *devidebat*; Aberdeen 25 has *quam et dividebat*.

118 Compare Malachi 3: 1; Matt.11: 10; Mark 1: 2.

119 Aberdeen 25: *Versus. Empirei sydus. Responsorium. Comes esto tu michi fidus.*

120 Aberdeen 25 here has Ps.120, *Levavi oculos meos*, but the same antiphon.

121 Aberdeen 25: *Versus. Spiritus exoras. Responsorium. Dum benedicis adoras.*

122 *See* n.16 *above*.

123 Ed. Wickham Legge (*see* n.103), p.459.

124 Lemarié, 'Textes', pp.118 and 151; id., 'L'Office des fêtes de saint Michel dans les Bréviaires du Mont', in *Millénaire Monastique*, pp.473–87, esp. p.483.

125 Aberdeen 25 here has Ps.123, *Nisi quia*, but the same antiphon.

126 *See* nn.16 and 103 *above*.

127 Aberdeen 25: *asmodeum*.

128 Aberdeen 25 here has *Versus. Angele sis scutum. Responsorium. Sit mortis iter michi tutum.*

129 Aberdeen 25 here has the same prayer as in Lauds of the present MS: *Omnipotens sempiterne deus qui inter hostiles insidias.*

130 Reading *haec* for abbreviated *h*; this prayer does not occur in Aberdeen 25.

131 *See* nn.16 and 103 *above*.

132 Aberdeen 25: *Versus. Angele sis scutum. Responsorium. Sit mortis iter michi tutum.*

133 *See* e.g. Wieck, *The Book of Hours*.

134 Supplied from Aberdeen 25; the Liverpool MS has the original but here less likely *angelorum*.
135 Aberdeen 25: *Versus. Angele carnalem. Responsorium. Facias me spiritualem.*
136 The text has *Immundanis*.
137 Both the Liverpool MS and Aberdeen 25 have *aname* [?].
138 Compare Paul's letter to the Hebrews 1, *passim*.
139 Wilmart, *Auteurs*, pp.551–52, 581.
140 Duhr ('Anges'), cols. 600–1.
141 *Ibid.*, col. 600.
142 *preceptum* is conjectural; the MS has no abbreviation mark, but offers a confusion of minims, perhaps *prum*.
143 Supplied from Aberdeen 25; the Liverpool MS has *promgratum*.
144 Aberdeen 25: *Versus. Angelicis pennis. Responsorium. Me vis defende perhennis.*
145 Supplied from Aberdeen 25; the Liverpool MS has *salus*.
146 Should it read *avertar*? Aberdeen 25 has *seducat* [sic], which should perhaps be *seducar*.
147 The Liverpool MS has *blanducias*.
148 Supplied from Aberdeen 25; the Liverpool MS has *deprime ne sinas*.
149 From *ibid.*; the Liverpool MS has *repellas*.
150 From *ibid.*; the Liverpool MS has *vinxit* [sic].
151 From *ibid.*; the Liverpool MS has *areum*.
152 From *ibid.*; the Liverpool MS has *desit*.
153 From *ibid.*; the Liverpool MS has *ostacula*.

CHAPTER FOURTEEN

Women and Books of Hours

SANDRA PENKETH

P ROBABLY THE BEST KNOWN image of a woman reading a book of hours is that of Mary of Burgundy in the Hours of Mary of Burgundy[1] (FIG. 97), in which she is sitting before the window of an oratory. The book is carefully supported on a lavish green cloth, and Mary delicately follows the words of the text with a single finger whilst apparently reading in silence.[2] The text she reads may be that of the *Obsecro te* ('I beseech you'), as suggested by the capital 'O', a prayer specifically addressed to the Virgin as intercessor with God. The oratory in which Mary sits is filled with a number of symbolic and significant emblems: a dog, the common symbol of faithfulness (for example, see Jan van Eyck's *Portrait of the Arnolfini* in the National Gallery, London), sits quietly on her lap, on the window-sill behind is an iris, a flower normally present to identify the purity of the Virgin Mary, and carnations, symbolic of betrothal. Also on the sill is a rosary which, like the book of hours, is an aid to private prayer. In front of her there is a purse, presumably intended to carry her book. Looking through the window of the oratory we see the interior of a Gothic church and before its altar the Virgin and Child. A decorative carpet which is marked at each corner by an angel carrying a candle designates the ground as holy. To the left of the group we again see Mary of Burgundy, this time as she kneels in prayer, carrying beneath her right arm a small red prayer-book.

The image shows a woman in possession of a book and using it for private devotion; the very fact that she is shown to be using it rather than simply carrying it suggests at least a rudimentary literacy or some basic understanding of its contents. The image also tells us something about the way in which private devotion may have been carried out in the later Middle Ages. The book of hours itself is depicted as a precious object which is treasured and treated with care and respect. The scene in the interior of the church shows what at first may be interpreted as a vision granted to the blessed devotee, Mary of Burgundy; in fact it is a visualization of the prayer she reads, an attempt to create – by some empathetic turn of the imagination – an exact replica of the intent of the words she looks at. The occurrence of the iris in Mary's chapel implies the presence of the Virgin there also. The presence of Mary of Burgundy, the Virgin (symbolic and real), and the act of devotion in both front and interior scenes makes the two parallel compositions: the content of both is devotion to the Virgin.

FIG. 97 Mary of Burgundy reading her book of hours. Hours of Mary of Burgundy. Vienna, ON, MS 1857, fol. 14v.

FIG. 98 Mary Magdalene reading. Rogier van der Weyden.
London, National Gallery, 654.

The image raises a number of questions. First, if a woman is shown to possess a book of hours does this mean she could actually use it or was it simply a fashionable accessory? Second, were women more likely to own books of hours than men and, if so, what special messages, spiritual or earthly, could the text or illustrations hold for them? Could, indeed, the fact that the intended owner of the book was female influence the type of illustration contained in it?

There exist numerous visual representations of medieval women reading apart from those which occur in books of hours. A small panel painting in London's National Gallery by Rogier van der Weyden, dating from about 1440 or 1450, shows Mary Magdalene reading (FIG. 98). The dress of Mary Magdalene and the setting show that the aim of the artist was to transpose a religious phenomenon into a contemporary setting; and the argument follows that Mary Magdalene is involved in a contemporary practice, that of a woman reading. It implies that laywomen were commonly involved in religious devotion through the study of books.[3] Mary actually seems to read the book instead of simply holding it, suggesting that she could use it rather than just treasure it as a sacred object. It is worth noting that this panel was most probably part of a larger altarpiece with the Virgin and Child as its subject, and therefore there are good grounds for supposing that she is reading a book of hours. However, the appearance of the text does not provide any conclusive evidence as to the book's type.[4]

Such images of women with books, and in particular with books of hours, suggests their use by those women. To what degree is this assumption correct? If we take the commonly held view that large sections of medieval society were illiterate, especially illiterate in Latin which, on the whole, is the language of a book of hours, then it is difficult to believe that these were used extensively. Since it is also generally assumed that women were much less likely to be educated than men, it becomes an even more difficult task. The pleas of Christine de Pizan (died *c.*1431) for the education of women in spite of male objections, in her treatise on women's education, *Le Livre des Trois Vertus*,[5] might appear to confirm the view that the number of educated women was few. Some medieval writers imply that books of hours were quite simply a status symbol and, for women, nothing more than a fashion accessory. Eustache Deschamps (1346–1406), the French court poet, satirized women's desire for books of hours, claiming that they could not even bear to be seen in church without one:

> A book of hours, too, must be mine,
> Where subtle workmanship will shine,
> Of gold and azure, rich and smart,
> Arranged and painted with great art,
> Covered with fine brocade of gold;
> And there must be, so as to hold
> The pages closed, two golden clasps.[6]

Although medieval piety undoubtedly incorporated a substantial element of public display,[7] it is perhaps too cynical to say that the possession of these books served no practical purpose other than adornment. There are accounts of women storing away books of hours with their most precious jewels and objects which might suggest they were not used frequently and were simply treated as *objets d'art*. However, it was common for a woman to own more than one copy of a book of hours, one to be used on special occasions, the other for daily use, which may explain why they are described so often as treasured.

The women whose portraits appear in books of hours are all relatively wealthy, as exemplified by their dress and relative learning. They are women of royalty, aristocracy, the new bourgeois and religious orders: women at the highest levels of medieval society. Some can be identified, others are unknown. Some are shown holding an open book, others are in prayer before the Virgin. Contrary to the often-held opinion that these women would have no knowledge of Latin, it is more than likely that they had at least a basic knowledge, certainly enough to use and read the text of a book of hours, if only partially. Royalty, of course, had the best access to education of all laypeople because of their wealth and significance. Often they would be tutored by the clergy, which in itself might imply a Latin education. By the thirteenth century all children of the nobility, whether male or female, were taught a small amount of formal Latin.[8] The bourgeois classes were much more likely to be acquainted with reading and writing in the vernacular, a necessity of business; but it is probable that they gained a rudimentary knowledge of Latin simply from attending Mass regularly. Members of religious orders would acquire a basic understanding of Latin in the same way. The argument that the high visual content of many books of hours must mean that their readers, often women, were illiterate holds little sway, since many books of hours have minimal illustrative material, or none at all.

Books of hours were designed to be read eight times a day at the canonical hours. They were read either in privacy at home, or in family or personal chapels, and they were taken into church, where they might be used as Mass was being said, as is perhaps suggested by the reverse of a panel from the Crucifixion altarpiece by the Master of the Aachen Altarpiece (Liverpool, Walker Art Gallery, No. 1226). Indeed, some sections of the text in books of hours directly echo the words of the Mass. This opportunity to follow along the text with the priest, and the frequency of acquaintanceship with it, must have guaranteed at least some basic understanding and perception of the content of a book of hours by its owner. As Clanchy observes, using the example of St Godric in the late eleventh and early twelfth century, a knowledge of Latin could depend primarily on hearing and memorizing.[9] One other piece of evidence that may suggest that a greater number of women than is normally assumed were to some degree literate, in late medieval society, is that they often acted as teachers to their children. It was often the mother who taught her child the basics of reading and writing and, in fact, books of hours were frequently employed as 'first reading books'. Some even contain the laboured 'As' and 'Bs' of someone learning to write. Taking this into account, the representation of St Anne teaching the Virgin to read becomes all the more understandable and touching.

This paper is concerned to look at those books of hours produced for women and owned by them, but of course it would be ridiculous to imply that men did not own such books, especially since many male owner-portraits do exist. However, it would seem that a special association existed between women and books of hours. Many were commissioned for women on the occasion of their marriage, often by their future husbands. Famous examples include the Grey-FitzPayn Hours (Cambridge, Fitzwilliam Museum, MS 242) and the Hours of Jeanne d'Evreux (New York, Metropolitan Museum of Art, the Cloisters Collection, MS 54.1.2). Even the derogatory proclamations by Deschamps propound a connection between women and books of hours. A doctoral dissertation by Susan Cavanaugh[10] lists private owners of books in England in the fourteenth and fifteenth centuries using surviving wills as evidence. Approximately 1,000 owners are listed; of these just over fifty are women. Of the many male book owners included in the thesis, approximately twenty-eight are listed as owning a book of hours. However, of the fifty-three women mentioned, thirty are noted to have possessed one. Cavanaugh states that the thesis only looks at a small sample of wills, and that far fewer books are mentioned in wills than were actually owned; but she also notes that the sample is meant to be representative, and that the books least likely to be left out of wills are devotional books such as books of hours.[11] Examining the documents themselves, we find frequently that the legatee of a female owner will be her daughter or another woman. For example, Elizabeth FitzHugh, Lady of Ravensworth, who died in 1425, bequeathed to 'my daughter a primer covered in red, and my daughter Maude Eure a primer covered in blue'.[12] If a book of hours was not left to the daughter, or there was no daughter, then the daughter-in-law was often chosen as the recipient, as in the case of Isabella Wyleby, who left her primer to Isabella, 'the wife of my son'.[13] Occasionally, inscriptions recording such bequests can be found in the book; for example a manuscript from the Hart collection, Blackburn (Blackburn, Museum and Art Gallery, MS Hart 21040, fol. 7r) states that the volume was a gift of Elizabeth Hull, abbess of Malling, to her godchild Margaret Neville.

If, then, it is possible to establish a close relationship between books of hours and a female readership, how might this affect the interpretation and choice of illustrations and text in a book of hours, and its spiritual significance for a woman? By looking at where female owner-portraits are likely to occur in books of hours, and by considering the significance of the text they accompany, it may be possible to begin to answer this question.

The majority of owner-portraits, whether male or female, in books of hours are situated at the beginning of the Little Office of the Blessed Virgin Mary. This office, which makes up the central core of such a book, contains a series of psalms, prayers, gospel extracts, and hymns taken from the Breviary. The text is divided into eight sections, to be read at the canonical hours, and each section may be introduced by a miniature. Owner-portraits usually occur at Matins, the first hour, which is most often prefaced by a depiction of the Annunciation or of a Virgin and Child in Glory. In the Hours of Catherine of Cleves, a Netherlandish manuscript of about 1440 (New York, Pierpont Morgan Library, MS M 917 and New York, Guennol Collection), Catherine, Duchess of Guelders, is shown kneeling in prayer outside a chapel before the Virgin and Child. She holds an open book and in front of her is a banner inscribed, 'O mater dei, memento mei' ('O mother of God, remember me'). Catherine's own identification, her individuality, and her historic identity are emphasized by the heraldic shields which refer both to herself and her ancestors. We are not conscious of the two figures existing in compatible time and space. Not only the dominant scale of the Virgin, but also the exterior positioning of the devotee and the minimal interaction between them serve to promote the idea of distance between the two groups. If the manifestation of the Virgin and Child were a vision given to a blessed believer, that is, to Catherine, we would perhaps not be unjustified in expecting a greater show of communication, a

FIG. 99 a and b: A female worshipper is encouraged in her devotions by the Angel Gabriel; opposite, the Annunciation. Buves Hours. Baltimore, Walters Art Gallery, MS 267, fols 13v, 14r.

possible reaction to and explanation of the occurrence. What in fact we do see here is a visualization of Catherine's prayer.

The Buves Hours (Baltimore, Walters Art Gallery, MS 267, fols 13v–14r) also includes the portrait of a female owner at Matins (FIGS. 99a and 99b). The worshipper kneels before an altar on which is placed her open book of hours. The Angel Gabriel gently encourages the worshipper in her devotions. On the opposite page is a standard Annunciation scene, the Virgin before an altar, her arms crossed in a pose of quiet submission. On the altar sits an open book, presumably the Bible. At first glance the portrait of the owner would appear to be a simple one, a scene of encouragement, but in fact we see here a worshipper visualizing herself present at the most intimate and important moment in the life of the Virgin. The extreme empathetic nature of this visualization creates an atmosphere of the utmost intimacy, an intimacy necessary to facilitate true and effective dialogue between the devotee and the Virgin.[14] Here, unlike in the Hours of Catherine of Cleves, the figure of the owner and that of the Virgin are on the same scale and juxtaposed in the same space; this equality of composition helps to promote the sense of intimacy, the feeling of actually being present at the event. Depictions of the Virgin reading before the altar might be interpreted as exemplars of pious devotion, especially where the devotee's position before an altar parallels that of the Virgin; but we must not forget that the Virgin is divine, and that the book she reads is not a book of hours but the Bible. It is interesting to note also that her book lies on an altar, the exact position traditionally given to the sacramental host and wine. The book contains the message of the Word, and the wine and host symbolize (at the very least) the Word made manifest.

The text of Matins opens with a general request to the Lord for assistance with prayer, 'Lord open my lips' ('Domine labia mea aperies'). This is followed by a greeting to the Virgin, the words of the Annunciation, and Psalm 94. It is here that the connection between text and image occurs: 'Come let us worship and bow down before the Lord: let us kneel in person before the Lord who made us' ('Venite adoremus et procidamus ante Deum: ploremus coram Domino qui fecit nos'). The text explains the supplicant position of the worshipper in these images, encouraging a close and intimate devotion on the part of the devotee. The idea of visualization of the Holy Mother whilst at prayer, and the desire for a close and intimate relationship with her, was expounded by Thomas à Kempis in the fifteenth century in his 'Sermons to the Novices Regular':

> But especially before the altar of God and in presence of the image of the blessed Virgin bare your heads and bow: humbly bend the knee, as if you saw Mary present in the body speaking with the angel, or holding her Son in her bosom: and then lifting up yours eyes with good hope of the salvation for which we look, most lovingly implore the help of Mercy from the Mother of Mercy.[15]

The idea of visualization of prayer is obviously integral to medieval prayer.

Besides the Hours of the Virgin, it is also common to find owner-portraits before prayers specifically addressed to the Virgin. The most popular of these are the 'I beseech you' ('Obsecro te') and the 'O immaculate virgin' ('O intemerata'), (cf. Oxford, Bodleian Library, MS Rawl. liturg. e. 20., fol. 19r and Oxford, Bodleian Library, MS Canon. liturg. 147., fol. 53r). The content of these prayers emphasizes the purity, humility, and especially the motherhood of the Virgin. The reader of the prayers addresses the Virgin directly; in the *Obsecro te* ('I beseech you, Mary, holy lady, mother of God'),[16] and similarly in the *O intemerata* ('O immaculate virgin ... be kind to me a sinner').[17] Each entreaty not only sets up an intimate correspondence between the worshipper and the Virgin, but also reminds the devotee of the nature of the Virgin's motherhood. She is 'the most glorious mother, mother of orphans, consolation of the desolate' and has a unique character as 'fountain of pity, fountain of salvation and grace, fountain of piety and joy'.[18]

Another popular prayer to the Virgin is the Fifteen Joys of the Virgin. Harthan claims it is rare to find depictions of an owner before the Joys,[19] but in French manuscripts this appears to be a popular location. The Joys recounts the joyous and significant moments in the Virgin's life with Christ, and is frequently illustrated by a depiction of the Virgin and her Son, thus asserting the love of motherhood. A Parisian manuscript of *c.*1420–30 (Oxford, Bodleian Library, MS Lat. liturg. 100, fol. 144r) and a Rouen manuscript of *c.*1440 (Liverpool, Walker Art Gallery, MS Mayer 12024, p.245) both have owner-portraits before the text of the Joys, although the nature of these compositions is very different. The first introduces the prayer with a resplendent coronation scene. On the right, the female owner of the book is presented by St John the Baptist, presumably her patron saint. In the second

FIG. 100 Virgin and Child and female worshipper before vernacular prayer.
Book of Hours. Oxford, Bodleian Library, MS Buchanan e 3. fol. 74r.

miniature, instead of a victorious image of the mother, there is a visual account of her grief after the Crucifixion. It displays motherly love for the Son, but also the redemptive quality of Christ's wounds. At the right the female owner of the book kneels in prayer.

There are, in fact, numerous prayers to the Virgin to be found in books of hours; some are hymns (cf. Blackburn, Museum and Art Gallery, MS Hart 20084, fol. 180v), some are prayers in the vernacular (cf. Oxford, Bodleian Library, MS Buchanan e 3., fol. 74r, FIG. 100), but all of them proffer appropriate locations for owners' portraits.

All these images of devoted prayer promote the idea of intimate communication before the Virgin, and consequently God. The ability of the devotee to imagine with such power and vigour a manifestation of their prayer, to visualize in such effective terms the content of the texts, sets up an atmosphere of intense emotion. The very nature of these images infers the desire for an intimate dialogue between the believer and the divine in the late Middle Ages. Such intimate portraits occur for male as well as female devotees; however, in view of the emphasis of some of the text which accompanies owner-portraits, and observing the content of the illustrations, it should be considered that for women readers these pages may have had a special significance. The qualities of motherhood and of humility to which the illustrations and text draw attention are the very qualities to which for centuries the Church had encouraged women to aspire. Above all, they were expected to be servile. As Marina Warner points out, 'In Christian theology Mary's consent to the Incarnation, her *Fiat*, exemplifies the most sublime fusion of man's free will in the divine plan ... but this lofty view of Mary's act of acceptance came to epitomize a restricted moral notion quite unworthy of the term: that of feminine submissiveness.'[20] Ready-made phrases such as the Pauline dictum, 'wives submit yourselves unto your husbands as unto the Lord' (Eph. 5: 22) only served to further the Church's argument for the superiority of man.

At this point it is worth remembering that many books of hours were given to women on the occasion of their marriage, and that many female owners were of the bourgeois class, women who, because of the new-found wealth of their husbands, for the first time could lead completely domestic lives. The religious ideal of woman as obedient, humble, and devoted conveniently came to be projected onto a family ideal. Contemporary secular accounts confirm the notion of 'perfect behaviour' in the home for women. In the *Livre du Chevalier de la Tour Landry* written *c.*1372 by a father for his daughters, submissiveness to one's husband is encouraged.[21] In *Le Menagier de Paris* (1392–94), an old, rich husband teaches his bride her daily tasks; amongst these she is to be humble, obedient, and patient. He quotes approvingly the story of Griselda with its theme of total obedience. She is also to show her husband animal-like devotion.[22] It would be too obtuse to claim that books of hours were bought by men to give to their future wives as 'code books of behaviour'; they were, after all, religious devotional texts. However, the very figure of the Virgin as the main emphasis of the book, and the attempts at identification with her through intimate prayer, must have made any underlying messages concerning female character and behaviour all the more clear.

The presence of 'instructive' visual messages compounded the idealistic perception of the Virgin's behaviour and the need for men and women to aspire to her example. However, the qualities they emphasize, obedience, humbleness, and purity, were, on the whole, perceived as female characteristics. Images of the Holy Family in a domestic setting started to appear in the fifteenth century. In the Hours of Catherine of Cleves (p.151) there is an image of the Holy Family at supper. As the Virgin nurses Christ, Joseph ladles soup from a bowl. Emile Mâle suggested that such scenes of the Holy Family's domestic life were derived from medieval theatre where, for dramatic reasons, it was necessary to give Joseph 'something to do' whilst focal attention centred on the Virgin and Child.[23] From the end of the fourteenth century Joseph becomes more and more prominent in representations of the Nativity and infancy of Christ. Such depictions of domestic bliss supported the theory of the perfect household.

Messages of moral behaviour can also be found in books of hours. The Annunciation page of the Walker Art Gallery's Rouen manuscript (p.51) contains two instructive marginal illustrations (FIG. 101). At the top left, two monkeys carry a man upside-down to display his genitals. In medieval art, monkeys were traditional symbols of lust, and were also frequently employed to mimic and mock the behaviour of humans. At the centre of the bottom margin a siren combs her hair and admires herself in a mirror. In the medieval period sirens were believed to distract sailors with their lascivious behaviour and subsequently cause the wreck of ships. Both scenes represent lust, in contrast to the purity of the Virgin depicted in the miniature of the same page.

Other representations of women in books of hours, which may have been chosen by the owner herself, support the idea of piety and purity. Sometimes women are actually shown in the role of pious benefactor. In her Hours, Catherine of Cleves has been depicted as a personification of charity (p.65). The illustration prefaces the Hours of the Holy Ghost at Vespers: above the beggars is a banner inscribed with the phrase 'Give alms and all things are clean unto you'. In the bottom border there is a parallel scene: a woman gives food to Christ through the bars of his prison window. In the same manuscript a depiction of a female pilgrim appears, in the Suffrages, on the same page as an illustration of St James the Great. In the border the weeping woman is comforted by a cleric. This female figure seems to be the same as that of a woman who previously appeared at a deathbed scene (p.41). The iconographic intent of the page is of a widow about to set out on pilgrimage. The figure again appears, this time *en route*, on the page of St Thomas the Apostle.

Other female characters which predominantly appear in books of hours are, of course, female saints. The most popular female saints of the medieval period – Catherine of Alexandria, Barbara, Margaret, Agatha – like the Virgin, extol the virtues of virginity and humbleness. The Hours of Margaret de Foix (London, Victoria and Albert Museum, Salting Collection, MS 1222) contains several illustrations of female saints undergoing their legendary tortures to safeguard their virginity. In the Middle Ages many saints were viewed in terms of their medicinal properties as well as personifying purity and devotion. For example, St Margaret, who by prayer to God escaped the belly of a dragon unhurt, was the patron saint of childbirth. St Agatha, who vowed her virginity to Christ and suffered the torture of having her breasts cut off by the brothel-keeper Aphrodisia, was often invoked against diseases of the breast (cf. Blackburn, Museum and Art Gallery, MS Hart 20844. fol. 202v) (FIG. 102). Images of female saints occur in many books of hours, owned by male or female readers, but their particular inclusion in those belonging to women might be expected; this is especially true when the saint has some obvious connection to a female condition. However, it must also be remembered that these saints were some of the most popular of the Middle Ages and therefore their choice was at times obvious. Occasionally, the inclusion of a female saint may be a clue to the name of the owner of a book. The inclusion of St Margaret in a Flemish book of hours of the third quarter of the fifteenth century, made for Carmelite use and showing a Carmelite nun at prayer before St Francis (Liverpool, Walker Art Gallery, MS Mayer 12020, pp.282–83), surely cannot have been to protect the devotee in childbirth (unless this was a particularly liberal nunnery), and may well refer to the name of the devotee.

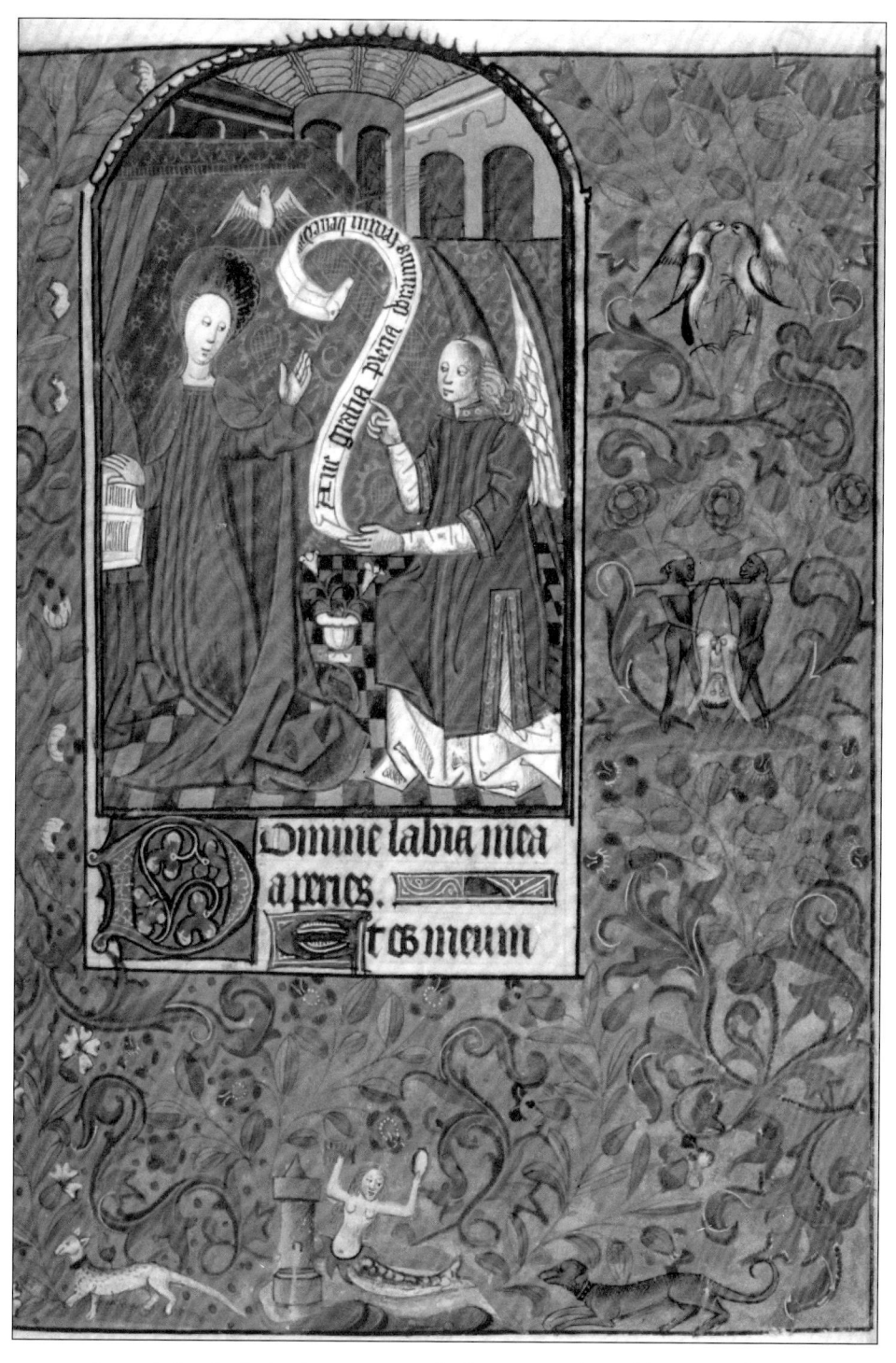

FIG. 101 Annunciation. In the borders are two symbolic representations of lust; top right two monkeys display a man's genitals, lower a siren admires herself in a mirror.
Book of Hours. Rouen. Liverpool, Walker Art Gallery, MS Mayer 12024, p.151.

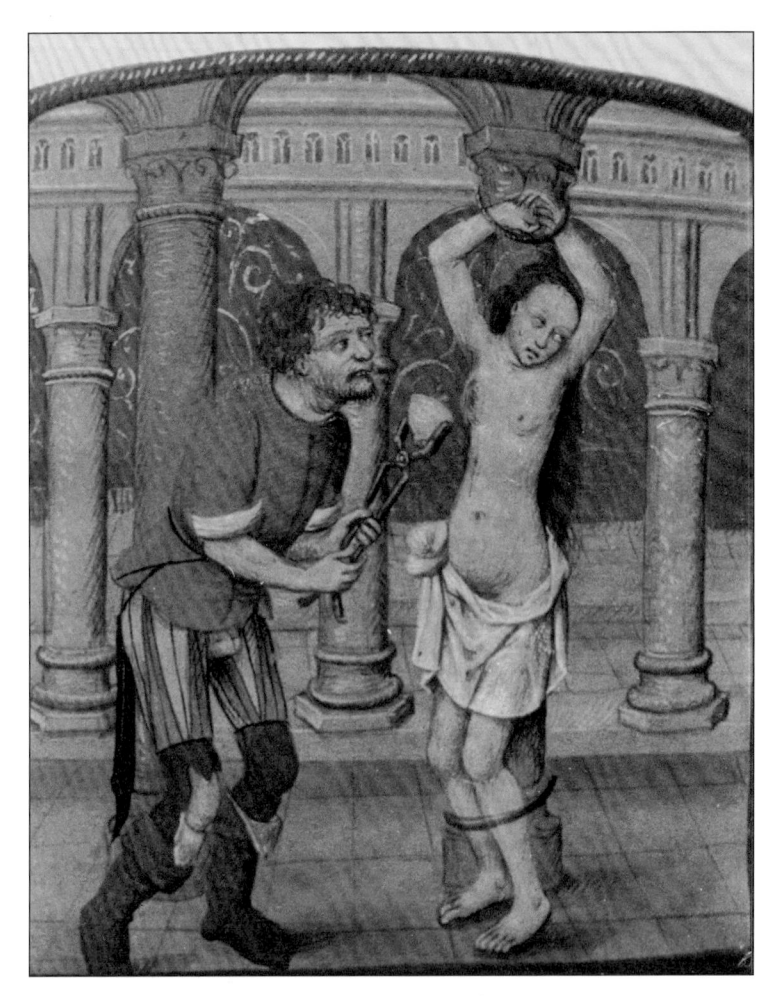

FIG. 102 St Agatha. Book of Hours.
Blackburn, Museum and Art Gallery, Hart Coll. MS 20844, fol. 202v.

Some illustrations in books of hours which belonged to women appear to have no connection to the textual content whatsoever. The Taymouth Hours, an English book of the early fourteenth century (London, British Library, MS Yates Thompson 13), contains at Lauds in the Hours of the Virgin thirty hunting scenes in which all the participants are women. These hunt scenes, introduced by the phrase 'here begins the sport of ladies' ('cy commence jeu de dames') might represent the world inverted, a revolutionary exchange of roles, but it is more likely that they in fact represent women chasing men and that the illustrations act as a guide to courtship.[24] A hunting scene in a book of hours given to Anne of Bohemia (Oxford, Bodleian Library, MS Lat. liturg. fol. 3, fol. 71r) depicts the capture of a stag by a dog (FIG. 103). The stag hunt, representative of the male pursuit of woman, had erotic connotations in the medieval period, which explains the often gleeful expression of the stag about to be run down. Depictions in the borders of Anne's manuscript of other small mammals are also equally mystifying; for example, a squirrel in a cage appears in the border

FIG. 103 Crucifixion. In the border a dog captures a stag. Hours of Anne of Bohemia. Oxford, Bodleian Library, MS Lat. liturg. fol. 3, fol. 71r.

of fol. 74r, whose implications can only be suggested. It could be the innocent depiction of a pet squirrel or a more lewd reference (it is worth bearing in mind, as Michael Camille points out, that small furry mammals were often euphemisms for the sexual organs).[25] The books of hours in which such illustrations occur were made or bought for the nobility, for a class who read and followed the principles of 'courtly love'. Scenes of love-games and seduction were not unusual in art patronized by them.

In conclusion, it is fair to say that women owners of books of hours were most likely to have at least some basic understanding of their content, and their possession of them was not merely a useless status symbol. It would also seem that there is a significant connection between women and books of hours, something which made them the more likely recipients of such volumes. The illustrations of the books extol ideals of purity, humility and obedience, virtues particularly associated with the female sex. Only a few illustrations seem to fall outside this category, and here the women are interested in a code of behaviour other than religious. Above all, books of hours with female owner portraits provide us with evidence not only of a strong female patronage but also of an active participation in personal worship on the part of their owners.

Notes to Chapter Fourteen

1. Vienna, ÖN, MS 1857, fol. 14v.

2. For a discussion of the way books of hours were read *see* P.Saenger, 'Books of Hours and the Reading Habits of the Later Middle Ages', in *Scrittura and Civiltà,* 9 (1985), pp.239–69.

3. For a consideration of the ownership and use of books for worship by women in the later Middle Ages, *see* S.G.Bell, 'Medieval Women Book Owners: Arbiters of Lay Piety and Ambassadors of Culture', in *Sisters and Workers in the Middle Ages,* ed. J.M. Bennett *et al.* (Chicago, 1989), pp.135–61.

4. J.Dunkerton *et al., Giotto to Dürer: Early Netherlandish Painting in the National Gallery* (London, 1991), pp.270–73. In a letter dated 6 Oct. 1993, Susan Foister (National Gallery) commented that she and Lorne Campbell (Courtauld Institute of Art, London) could not be certain about the type of the book which appears in the Weyden painting. They think it unlikely that it is a book of hours or a Bible and suggest that it may be some other devotional volume. The text of the book is illegible even when observed under a microscope. In fact the artist has painted the lines so that they will appear as text even when they are not. Only the initials **A** and **D** are identifiable. It seems justifiable to suggest that the book is not meant to represent any actual known text but is a symbolic representation of the Word.

5. Christine de Pizan, *Le Livre des Trois Vertus,* ed. E.Hicks and C.C.Willard (Paris, 1989).

6. E.Panofsky, *Early Netherlandish Painting* (Cambridge, Mass., 1953), i, p.68.

7. J.Harthan, *Books of Hours and their Owners* (London, 1977), p.32.

8. M.T.Clanchy, *From Memory to Written Record. England 1066–1307* (London, 1979), p.196.

9. *Ibid.,* p.191.

10. S.H.Cavanaugh, *A Study of Books Privately Owned in England 1300–1450,* (unpubl. Ph.D. thesis, Univ. of Pennsylvania, 1980).

11. *Ibid.,* pp.3–10.

12. *Ibid.,* p.347.

13. *Ibid.,* p.934.

14. R.S.Wieck, *The Book of Hours in Medieval Art and Life* (London, 1988), p.44.

15. V.Scully, transl., *Thomas à Kempis: 'Sermons to the Novices Regular'* (London, 1907), p.194.

16. Wieck, *Book of Hours,* p.163.

17. *Ibid.,* p.164.

18. *Ibid.,* p.163.

19. Harthan, *Books of Hours,* p.112.

20. M.Warner, *Alone of All Her Sex. The Myth and Cult of the Virgin Mary* (London, 1976), p.177.

21. W.Caxton, transl., *The Book of the Knight of the Tower* (Oxford, 1971), pp.35–37.

22. E.Power, transl., *The Goodman of Paris (Le Ménagier de Paris)* (London, 1928), pp.110–70.

23. E.Mâle, *L'Art Religieux de la fin du moyen âge en France* (Paris, 1908), p.36.

24. V.Sekules, 'Women and Art in England in the Thirteenth and Fourteenth Centuries', in *Age of Chivalry: Art in Plantagenet England 1200–1400,* ed. J.J.G.Alexander and P.Binski (London, 1987), pp.47–48.

25. M.Camille, *Image on the Edge: The Margins of Medieval Art* (London, 1992), p.38.

INDEX
OF MANUSCRIPTS CITED

Aachen, private collection: 32, 33, 39
Aachen, Domschatz
  MS s.n.: 169
Aarau, Kantonsbibliothek
  MS Wett fol. 1 (MS 7): 40
Aberdeen, University Library
  MS 25: 239–40, 259, 264–5
Aberystwyth, National Library of Wales
  MS 5667: 30–1, 43
Arras, Bibliothèque Municipale
  MS 1045(233): 167

Baltimore, Walters Art Gallery
  MS 26: 117
  MS 148: 110–12, 121
  MS 267: 272–3
  MS 759: 110, 119
  MS 760: 110, 120
Berlin, Staatliche Museen
  MS K6156: 122
Blackburn (Lancs.) Museum
  Hart MS 20844: 274, 276, 278
  Hart MS 21040: 271
Bonn, Rheinisches Landesmuseum
  Inv. no. 235: 224
Bonn, Universitätsbibliothek
  MS 384: 118
Bornem, Abdij Sint Bernardus
  MS 1: 107, 117
Boulogne, Bibliothèque Municipale
  MS 90: 224
Brussels, Bibliothèque Royale
  MS 4459–70: 205, 206, 224
  MS 8895–6: 117
  MS 9009–11: 91
  MS 9236: 91
  MS 9508: 39, 42
  MS 10309: 39, 42
  MS 10366: 39, 42

Cambridge, Corpus Christi College
  MS 2: 120
Cambridge, Fitzwilliam Museum
  MS 159: 75, 77
  MS 242: 270
  MS 298: 194
Cambridge, Pembroke College
  MS 301: 168
  MS 302: 167
Cambridge, Trinity College
  MS B.10.4: 168
  MS B.11.22: 32, 33, 39, 43
  MS R.17.1: 42
Cambridge, University Library
  MS Dd.4.17: 188
  MS Ll.1.10: 152, 168
Chicago, Newberry Library

MS 40: 220
Cologne, Diözesanbibliothek
  MS 1B: 118
Cologne, Wallraf-Richartz Museum, Graphische Sammlury
  Inv. Nrs 67–71: 118

Darmstadt, Hessisches Bibliothek
  MS 2777: 120

Eibingen, Bibliothek der Abtei St Hildegard
  MS s.n.: 39, 41

Ferrara, Biblioteca Comunale Ariostea Statuti
  MS 47: 22, 40
Florence, Archivio di Stato
  Conventi Soppressi 78, tilza 1: 145
  Conventi Soppressi 79, tilza 80:146
Florence, Biblioteca Nazionale
  MS II II 509: 144, 145, 146
Florence, Laurenziana
  MS Plut. XVII. 20: 167
  MS 5. Marco 190: 39, 40
Frankfurt, Stadt und Universitätsbibliothek
  MS Barth 42: 29, 30, 43, 121
Fulda, Landesbibliothek
  MS Aa.21: 171
  MS Bonifatianus 2: 170

Geneva, Bibliothèque Publique et Universitaire
  MS FR/T.1: 80, 81

Hague, The, Koninklijke Bibliotheek
  MS 78 D 42: 39, 42
Heidelberg, Universitätsbibliothek
  MS Germ.848 (*Codex Manesse*): 33, 39, 43, 228
Hildesheim, Dom und Diözesanmuseum
  MS Inv. Nr. DS 18: 170

Imola, Biblioteca Comunale
  MS 100: 188

Liège, Eglise Sainte–Croix
  MS 1–2: 120
Lilienfeld, Stiftsbibliothek
  MS 151: 228
Lille, Bibliothèque de l'Institut Catholique
  MS s.n.: 170
Liverpool, National Museums and Galleries on Merseyside
  MS M.12004: 40
Liverpool, University Library
  Cathedral MS Radcliffe 6: 230, 234–51, 256
Liverpool, Walker Art Gallery
  MS Mayer 12020: 276
  MS Mayer 12024: 273–4, 275–7
London, British Library
  Add. MS 21114: 107, 117
  Add. MS 22285: 261
  Add. MS 33241: 170, 171
  Add. MS 34890: 168
  Add. MS 60629: 107, 108, 112, 116, 118
  Add. MS 65100: 259
  Harley MS 2965: 152, 168
  Harley MS 2344: 263
  Harley MS 3244: 228
  Harley MS 4431: 14, 39, 42, 91, 260
  Lansdowne MS 379: 263
  Royal MS 1E.IV: 33, 43
  Royal MS 2B.VII (Queen Mary Psalter): 16, 172–86
  Sloane MS 982: 257
  Stowe MS 944: 170
  Yates Thompson MS 13: 188, 278
London, College of Arms
  Arundel MS 22: 167
London, Dr William's Library
  MS Ancient 6: 188
London, Lambeth Palace
  MS 474: 258
  MS 546: 262
  MS 3600: 259
London, Victoria and Albert Museum
  Salting MS 1222: 276
Lucca, Biblioteca Statale
  MS lat. 1942: 39, 41

Madrid, El Escorial
  MS Vitr. 17: 170
Malibu, J. P. Getty Museum
  MS 9: 167
Metz, Bibliothèque Municipale
  MS 600: 225
Montecassino, Archivio della Badia
  MS BB.437: 169
Montecassino, Monastery
  MS 132: 39, 40
Munich, Bayerische Staatsbibliothek
  MS 835: 185, 188
  MS 4452: 170
  MS 30111: 169
  MS Cgm. 6396: 130
  MS Clm. 4452: 168
  MS Clm. 23046: 29, 30, 43

INDEX OF MANUSCRIPTS CITED

MS gall. 11: 39, 42
MS gall. 16: 187

New Haven, Beinecke Rare Book Library
  MS 404 (Rothschild Canticles): 212–15
New York, Cloisters Museum
  MS 69.86: 207, 208–9, 210
New York, Metropolitan Museum, Cloisters Coll.
  MS 54.1.2: 270
New York, Pierpont Morgan Library
  MS 52: 85, 87
  MS 399 (Da Costa Hours): 79–80, 86
  MS 451: 86, 92
  MS 498: 26, 27, 39, 41, 42
  MS 708: 167, 168, 169
  MS 709: 168, 169, 171
  MS 917 (Hours of Catherine of Cleves): 88, 89, 271–2, 275, 276
New York, Public Library
  Spencer MS 26 (Tickhill Psalter): 187
  Spencer MS 33: 39
Nuremberg, Stadtbibliothek
  MS Cod. Cent. III, 40: 131
  MS III, 41: 131
  MS III, 86: 132
  MS III, 87: 132
  MS IV, 17: 131
  MS IV, 20: 131
  MS IV, 37: 131
  MS V, 10a: 132
  MS V, App.: 132
  MS VI, 43f: 132
  MS VI, 43g: 132
  MS VI, 46g: 131
  MS VII, 11b: 132
  MS VII, 14: 131
  MS VII, 15: 131
  MS VII, 30: 131
  MS VII, 33: 131
  MS VII, 37: 131
  MS VII, 63: 131
  MS VII, 88: 132
  MS VII, 100: 132
  MS VIII, 18: 132

Osnabrück, Gymnasium Carolinum
  Codex Gisle: 108–9, 111, 112–14, 119, 120
Oxford, Bodleian Library
  MS 4: 223
  MS 270b: 34
  MS 717: 42, 169
  Auct. MS D.4.7: 259
  Bodl. MS 62: 259
  Bodl. MS 451: 41
  Bodl. MS 717: 42, 169
  Bodl. MS 270b: 43

Buchanan MS e.3: 274
MS Canon. liturg. 147: 273
Douce MS 131: 188–9
Douce MS 204: 215, 216, 227, 229
Douce MS 296: 168
MS Lat. liturg. e.17: 245–6, 262–3
MS Lat. liturg. fol.3: 278–80
MS Lat. liturg. fol.5: 148–66
MS Lat. liturg. 100: 273–4
Laud. MS Misc. 570: 91
Rawlinson MS liturg. e.20: 273
Tanner MS 221: 258
Oxford, Keble College
  MS 40: 40
Oxford, Queen's College
  MS 305: 41

Palermo, Biblioteca Nazionale
  MS IV.G.2: 26, 39, 41
Paris, Bibliothèque Nationale
  Arsenal MS 288: 226
  Arsenal MS 570: 226
  Arsenal MS fr.2681: 39, 42
  Arsenal MS 3142: 31, 39, 43, 49–52, 190–203
  Arsenal MS 5196: 84
  MS fr.574: 224
  MS fr.598: 39, 43
  MS fr.599: 78–9
  MS fr.603: 39, 42, 91
  MS fr.606: 37, 38, 39, 43
  MS fr.607: 13
  MS fr.794: 52, 53
  MS fr.835: 39, 42
  MS fr.836: 39, 42
  MS fr.1171: 15
  MS fr.1174: 81, 82
  MS fr.1176: 39, 42
  MS fr.1178: 91
  MS fr.1433: 51, 52
  MS fr.1610: 53, 56
  MS fr.2173: 46–8, 202
  MS fr.9140: 80
  MS fr.12420: 36, 37–8, 39, 44
  MS fr.24428: 202
  MS fr.25526: 260
  MS lat. 9471 (Rohan Hours): 20, 22, 40
  MS lat. 9474 (Grandes Heures): 89
  MS lat. 9584: 229
  MS lat. 10525: 187
  MS lat. 16499: 228
  MS lat. 17323: 133–46
Paris, Bibliothèque Sainte-Geneviève
  MS 1126: 81, 82
Paris, Musée Jacquemart-André
  MS 2: 22, 40
Poitiers, Bibliothèque Municipale
  MS 250: 30, 31, 39, 43
Prague, National & University Library
  MS XIV A 17: 211, 212, 224
Prague, Universitätsbibliothek
  MS Kap.A.xxi: 42

Reims, Bibliothèque Municipale
  MS 9: 169
Rome, San Paolo Fuori le Mura
  MS *s.n.*: 169

St Petersburg, Public Library
  MS gr.291: 170
Santiago de Compostela, Biblioteca Universitaria
  MS Rs.1: 170
Sinai
  MS gr.l72: 170
Stockholm, Ericsberg Castle
  MS *Liber celestis*: 26, 27, 28, 39, 41, 42
Stockholm, Kungliga Biblioteket
  MS A.172: 108, 119
Strasbourg, Bibliothèque du Grand Séminaire
  MS 37: 118
Stuttgart, Landesbibliothek
  MS Hist. fol. 411: 39, 40
Syon Abbey (South Brent)
  MS 2: 259
  MS 4: 259

Trier, Stadtbibliothek
  MS 24: 167, 168
Tübingen, Universitätsbibliothek
  MS Theol. Lat. Nordenfalk: 39, 42

Uppsala, University Library
  MS C.93: 170
Ushaw, St Cuthbert's College
  MS 43: 258

Vatican City, Biblioteca Apostolica Vaticana
  MS Vat. lat. 4922: 171
Vienna, Österreichische Nationalbibliothek
  MS 1857: 266, 267, 281
  MS 2549: 83–4
  MS 2759: 85

Warsaw, Biblioteka Narodowa
  MS i.3311: 167
Wiesbaden, Hessische Landesbibliothek
  MS 1 (*Liber Scivias*): 39, 41
  MS 2 (*Riesen Kodex*): 105
Wil
  MS *Schwesternbuch*: 130, 131
Wolfenbüttel, Herzog August Bibliothek
  MS Extrav. 25.1: 262

283

INDEX

Aachen, Altarpiece, Master of, 270
Abraham, 174, 175
Adelaide, Princess, 156
Adelhaid (nun), 29, 30
Adenet le Roi, 52, 191, 196–7, 198, 200
   Cléomadès, 52, 196–7, 198
Adomnan, 161
Ælfgar, Ealdorman of Mercia, 156
Ælfgifu, 159
Æthelflæd, 162
Æsop, 45, 47–8, 190, 195
Agatha of Hungary, 149
Agatha, St, 276, 278
Ages of Man, 64
Agnes, St, 115, 116, 134, 232
Alart de Cambrai, 50, 51, 191
Alcuin, 29
Alexandria, 86
Alfred, King, 191
Alphonso de Vadaterra, 26
Altenhohenau, convent, 124–5
Amalthea, 36, 37–8, 39
Amboise, castle, 79
Ambrose, St, 34
Anastasia (illuminator), 17, 110
Ancrene Wisse, 204, 220, 221
Andrew, St, 128, 152
Anne, St, 22, 86, 89, 180, 182
Anne of Bohemia, 278–80
Anne of Brittany, 79, 89–90
Anne of Burgundy, 86
Anselm, St, 156
Aquinas, St Thomas, 127
Aristotle, 35, 51
Arnulf of Louvain, 210
Arthurian romance, 52, 53
Ashbery, John, 76
Ashborn, Henry, 244
Athanasius, 33
Athelflæd, 162
Atre perilleux, 52
Attavanti, Attavente, 137, 141–2
Augustine, St, 15, 26, 34, 35, 111
Augustodunensis, Honorius, 100, 219
authorship, 45–54, 97–103, 190–1, 233

Baden, 84–5, 92
Bamberg, 107, 118
Barbara, St, 85, 86, 87, 276
Bartholomeus Anglicus, 80, 231, 257
   De proprietatibus rerum, 80
Basle Altar, 159
Bathsheba, 178, 179, 185, 188
Baudoin de Condé, 191
Baudouin de Molin, 110
Baudonivia, 30, 31, 39

Beatrice of Nazareth, 106
Beaupré Antiphonal, 110, 119
Becket, St Thomas, 183, 184, 185
Benedict, St, 23
Benedictines, 35, 114, 118, 133, 135, 143, 204, 206
Bening, Simon, of Bruges, 86
Benoît de St-Maure
   Roman de Troie, 53
Bérard, St, 133
Bermondsey Abbey, 241
Bernard of Clairvaux, St, 71, 127, 210, 211, 228, 248, 250, 258
Bernward, bishop of Hildesheim, 160
Berry, Duc de, 14
Bible, 33, 34, 126, 127–8, 152, 231, 272, 272–3
Bible moralisée, 34
Blanche of France (daughter of Louis IX), 52, 197, 198, 199, 200
Boccaccio, 38, 78–9, 80, 81
   De claris mulieribus, 38, 39, 78–9, 81
Bodel, Jean, 191
   Chanson des Saisnes, 199
Boethius, 51
Bokenham, Osbern, 232
Bonaventure, St, 133
Boniface, St, 25, 112
Bonne of Luxembourg, 206, 211–12
Bourdichon, Jean, 89
Bozon, Nicholas, 218
Brabant, 209
Brentford, Guild of All Angels, 242–3, 244, 246
Bridget of Sweden, St, 26, 28, 31, 39, 79, 141, 217, 228, 233–4, 241, 258, 259
   Liber celestis revelationum, 26, 233
   Sermo angelicus, 233
Bridgettines, 79, 233, 234, 241, 246, 259, 260
Bristol Cathedral, 67, 74
Bromfeld, John, 244
Bruges, 86, 87
Bucga, abbess of Withington (Kent), 25
Buildwas Abbey, 41
Burgoyne, Thomas, 244
Buves Hours, 272

Cadmus and Scylla bowls, 68
Caedmon, 97
Caesarius of Arles, 157
Calogrenant, 52
Cambridge, Queens' College, 241
Campin, Robert, Master of Flemalle, 76, 87

Canterbury Cathedral, 241
Carducci, Battista, 17, 133, 134, 137, 139, 143
Carmelites, 276
Carpenter, John, 261
Cassian, John, 157
Catherine, St, of Alexandria, 86, 87, 125, 128, 183, 188, 276
Catherine, St, of Siena, 26, 31, 79
Catherine, Duchess of Guelders, 271–2
Catherine of Cleves, 88, 89, 272, 275, 276
Caxton, William, 79, 91, 263
Cecilia, St, 152
   Celestial Hierarchy, 231
Cerne, Book of, 152, 168
Chapman, John, 245
Charlemagne, 199, 202, 231
Chartres, 53
Chaucer, Geoffrey, 85
   The Canterbury Tales, 85
Chelles, 25, 30, 41
Cheseman, Edward, 244–5, 263
Chevalier aus deux epees, 52
Chrétien de Troyes, 52
   Yvain, 52
Christ, 20, 22, 77, 86, 98, 99, 103, 112, 126, 128, 154, 159, 172, 180, 182–3, 204–23 passim, 275, 276
   Crucifixion, 128, 139, 209, 270, 274, 279
   Nativity, 115, 126, 216, 217
   Passion, 182–3, 204–23 passim
   Resurrection, 109, 111, 112, 121, 126, 128
Christine, St, 14
Christine de Pizan, 13–15, 17, 26–7, 37, 38, 39, 78, 79, 80, 83, 91, 110, 237–8, 240, 269
   Book of the Three Virtues, 83, 269
   Cité des Dames, 13–14, 17, 38, 39, 82
   Epistre d'Othéa, 38, 39
   Moral Proverbs, 79
Christmas, 112, 113, 121
Cicero, 51
Cistercians, 33, 108, 110, 114, 118, 206
Clara, Keyperin, 125
Clares, Poor, 107–8, 118, 119, 206
Claude, Princess, 75, 77
Clere, Sir William, 61
Cnut, 159
Colet, John, 258
Cologne, 108
Colop, John, 242–3
Columba, St, 160

284

INDEX

Comestor, Peter, 100
Court of Sapience, 231
Cunigunde, 159
Cuthbert, St, 160–1
Cuthswith (abbess), 34

Dares and Dictys, 53
David, 172, 178, 179, 182, 188
Deborah, 34–5
Denys the Areopagite, 231, 256, 257
d'Evreux, Jeanne, 270
Dialectica, 67–9
Diana (goddess), 65, 68, 74
Dominicans, 106, 123–9, 214, 220
Douze Dames de Rhetorique, Les, 81, 82
Dufour, Antoine, 79
 La Vie des Femmes Célèbres, 79
Durandus, Wilhelm, 124, 130
Dürer, Albrecht, 65
Durham, 161

Eadburg, abbess of Thanet, 25, 112
Eadwine, 29–30
Easter, 121, 133, 134
Eberhard of Friuli, Duke, 162, 163
Eccard of Mâcon, 162
Edward the Confessor, King, 160
Edward IV, King, 230, 231, 239, 241
Edward of Ætheling, 149
Eibingen monastery, 101
Eirene, 159
Eleanor, Queen of Portugal, 87
Elizabeth, St, 22, 86
Elizabeth (Woodville), Queen, 230–46 *passim*
Elizabeth of York, 239, 246
Ely Cathedral, 61, 62, 63–4, 65, 72
Emma of Normandy, 162
Engelberg, 106
Erithraea, 38
Euclid, 98
Eurythrea, 39
Eustache, Deschamps, 269
Eustochium, 34
Eve, 173, 175, 185, 215, 216

fables, 45–54, 190–200
Fauré, Aude, 216–17
Ferdinand of Castile, 52
Ferdinand de la Cerda, 198
Fernando of Leon, 159
Firenze, Andrea di Paolo di Giovanni da, 137
FitzHugh, Elizabeth, 271
Florence, 136, 139, 141
 Le Murate convent, 133–7, 139–43
 Sant' Ambrogio convent, 141
 San Francesco convent, 137
Flotte, Guillaume, 206, 208, 212
Forster, Johannes, 127
Fortunatus, Venantius, 30, 31
Fouquet, Louis, 137
Francis, St, 209, 276
Frauenaurach, convent, 124
Freiburg convent, 119
Frowyk, Thomas, 244

Gabras, Eirene & Theodore, 159
Gabriel (angel), 22, 75, 86, 272
Gautier de Metz, 46
Georgius Agricola, 81–2
 De re metallica, 81–2
Gerarduccius of Padua, 120
Gertrude, abbess of Helfta, 25, 114–16, 121
 The Herald of Divine Love, 114
Gertrude the Great, 25
Gewichtmacherin, Barbara, 128–9
Giles, St, 63–4, 73
Giovanna (nun), 137
Giovanni, Gherardo & Monte di, 137, 142
Gisle de Kerzenbroeck, 108–20, *passim*
Glossa ordinaria, 34
God, 96, 99, 100, 103, 112, 126, 128, 214, 217, 230
Godric, St, 270
Golden Legend, The, 86
Goodman of Paris, 23, 34
Goslar Gospels, 159
gospels, 149–57
Grafton, Thomas, 243, 261, 263
Gratian, 35
 Decretum, 35
Greek, 98, 103
Gregory the Great, Pope, 162
Grey-FitzPayn Hours, 270
Grimani Breviary, 79, 86
Griselda, 275
Grosseteste, Robert, 231
Guda (nun), 29, 30, 110, 121
Guiars des Moulins, 80, 81
 Bible Historiale, 80, 81
Guido, Maddalena di Luigi di, 137
Guta (nun), 118
Guy of Flanders, 197

Hagar, 175
Hallerin, Kunigund, 125
Hannah (mother of Samuel), 176, 177, 183
Hedwig of Sweden, 162
Helena, St, 89
Helfta, 25–6, 41, 114, 121
Héloïse, 31
Henry I, 157
Henry III, Emperor, 159
Henry VI, King, 241, 242
Henry of Brabant, 197
Henry of Lancaster, 218
Hereford gospel lectionary, 151, 156
Herrad of Hohenbourg/Landsberg, 96, 97–101, 103, 217–19
 Hortus deliciarum, 96, 97, 98–101, 216, 217
Hilda of Whitby, 97
Hildebertus, 29
Hildegard of Bingen, 24–5, 26, 29, 36, 39, 41, 97, 101–3
 Liber compositae medicine, 103
 Liber divinorum operum, 24, 102
 Liber simplicis medicine, 103

Liber vitae meritorium, 102
 Ordo virtutum, 102–3, 105
 Scivias, 24, 97, 102
Hohenbourg, 97
Honoré, Master, 193
Horace, 162
Hortus deliciarum, see Herrad of Hohenbourg/Landsberg
hours, books of, 16, 17, 22, 33, 79–89 *passim*, 206, 230, 259, 266–80
Hours of the Guardian Angel, 230, 234–56
Hroswitha of Gandersheim, 97
Hugo, pictor, 29, 30
Hull, Elizabeth, 271
Humbert of Romans, 127

Ida of Leau, 107, 117
illumination, 106–14 *passim*, 127–9, 137, 140, 142, 154–6, 172–200 *passim*, 235–9, 240
Image du Monde, 206
Imhoff, Margareta, 128
Imola Psalter, 185, 188
Io, 37, 38, 39
Irene, 38
Irmengarde, 159
Isaac, 174, 175–7
Isabeau de Bavière, 14
 Isabel, Queen of France, 237
Isabella, Queen, 185, 186, 188
Isabella Psalter, 175, 177, 184, 185–6
Isaiah, 29–30, 86
Isidore of Seville, 98, 158

Jacob, 174, 175–7, 185, 187
Jacobus de Voragine, 230–1
 Golden Legend, 230–1, 232
Jacques, St, abbey, 110
Jacquetta de Luxembourg, 240–1
James, St, 276
Jean de Meun, 14
Jean II, Duke of Brabant, 52
Jean le Noir, 206
Jeanne de Montbaston, 17
Jerome, St, 29, 33, 34, 158, 184
Jews, 33–4, 58, 60
Joan, St, 79
John, St, 68, 150, 154, 156, 166, 169
John the Baptist, St, 22, 121, 273
John of St Trond, 206, 208
John of Wallingford, 220
Joubert, Guillaume, 46
Jude, St, 159
Judith of Flanders, 151, 156, 162
Julius II, Pope, 133, 141
Justice, Dame, 13

Knight of the Tour Landry, 34, 275
knights, 51, 52, 64, 204–6, 217–21
Kolda (friar), 204–12 *passim*, 221, 226
Kunigunde (abbess), 204–13 *passim*, 219, 221

La Ramée, convent, 106–7, 117
Lambeth Devotion, 240
Lancelot, 52

285

Lanfranc, archbishop of Canterbury, 162
Lapidoth, 35
Latin, 23, 48, 86, 98, 103, 124, 126, 190, 240, 270
Leo X, Pope, 135–7, 138
Leviathan, 96, 99, 100
Liège, 106, 110
Liège Psalter, 107
Lier, 106
Lincoln Cathedral, 64, 66
Lindisfarne Gospels, 160
Lioba, abbess of Bischofsheim, 25
liturgy, 124, 126, 128, 133–4, 141
Leogaire, 161
Lombard, Peter, 35, 100
London, 238, 239, 241, 242, 243
St Bartholomew's Hospital, 243–4, 246, 262
Loppa de Speculo, 108, 109, 110, 113, 119
Louvain
Parc-les-Dames nunnery, 206, 208, 224
Lübeck, 82
Luke, St, 154
Luton, Holy Trinity, 241
Luxuria, 66
Luyt, Joan & Thomas, 243, 244–5, 246, 263

Maagdendaal convent, 1–6
Mahaut d'Artois, 199
Maiolus of Cluny, St, 158
Malcolm III, King of Scotland, 149, 158–61, 163
Marcia, 38
Margaret, St, Queen of Scotland, 149, 156–62, 163, 276
Margaret of Antioch, St, 183–4, 188
Marguerite de Foix, 276
Margareta, Karthäuserin, 125, 128
Marie of Brabant, 46, 52, 190, 196–7, 198–9, 200
Marie de France, 15, 31, 45–56, 190–203 passim
Fables, 45–51, 53, 54, 190–202 passim
Lais, 45–6, 54
Marienboem, Revelatus of, 36
Mark, St, 154
Mary, the Virgin, 13–23 passim, 66–75 passim, 86, 111–26 passim, 159, 160, 172, 179, 180, 182–3, 184, 206, 208, 209, 228, 233, 234, 241, 266–75 passim
Annunciation, 15, 22, 86, 107, 172, 182, 271–7 passim
Assumption, 260
Coronation, 108, 116
Visitation, 241
Mary Magdalene, St, 31, 75, 119, 128, 188, 269
Mary, Queen, 172
Mary of Burgundy, 266–8
Massys, Quentin, 89, 90, 93
Matheolus, 14

Matilda, Queen, 157
Matilda of Lotharingia, 159
Matilda of Tuscany, 162
Matthew, St, 154
Mechthild of Hackeborn, 25, 114–16, 121, 231, 257
  Book of Special Grace, 231, 257
Mechthild of Magdeburg, 25–6, 121
Medici, Lorenzo de', 136, 141
Meditations on the Life and Passion of Christ, 209, 232
Merode altarpiece, 75, 76, 87
Metz Pontifical, 194
Meyer, Johannes, 124
Michael, St, 230–59 *passim*
Mieszko II, King, of Poland, 159
Mirror of Simple Souls, 245
misericords, 57–74
Mont-Saint-Michel, 249
Montaillou, 84
Montecatino, Antonio da, 136
Moore, Marianne, 90
Muirchu, *Life of St Patrick*, 161
Munich Psalter, 185, 188

Nantwich, St Mary's Church, 66–7
Nazareth Antiphonal, 107
Nazareth convent, 106–7
Neville, Margaret, 271
New Minster Liber Vitae, 159
Nicciolini, Giustina, 135, 139, 142
Nicholas of Lyra, 34–5, 184
Niklasin, Kunigunde, 125, 126
  nonnenbucher, 107–16
Norwich Cathedral, 61, 74
Nunnaminster, Book of, 152, 168
Nuremberg, 82
  St Catherine's convent, 123–9, 130, 131

Odile, St, monastery, 99, 101
Origen, 34
d'Orléans, Duc, 14
Otto, St, 133
Otto I, 162
Otto II, 159
Otto III, Emperor, 156
Ovid, 64–5

Paris, 110, 191, 193, 273
  Sainte-Chapelle, 208
Patrick, St, 161
Paul, St, 34
Pecock, Reginald, 242, 261
Pepwell, 38
Pericopes Book of Henry II, 159
Peter Lombard, 35
Peter the Venerable, 29
Phaedrus, 48
Philip III, King of France, 46, 52, 190, 199, 202
Philip of Navarre, 34
Philip the Chancellor, 211
Philippa, Queen, 185
Philosophia, 68
Plato, 68
Poggio Bracciolini, 84–5, 92

Poitiers, 31
Portaleyn, Alice & Thomas, 244, 262
Prague, St George's nunnery, 204
Priscion, 54
Proba, 38
psalters, 106, 107, 112, 126, 163, 172–86

Queen Mary Psalter, 172–89
Quincy, Lady de, 220, 221

Rabelais, 59, 60, 195
Rachel, 177, 184
Radegund, St, 31
Ragyndrudis, 162
Rashi, Rabbi, 34
reading, 22–3, 49, 75, 78–9, 86–90, 114, 161–4, 198, 266–9, 270, 271
Rebecca, 174, 175–7, 184, 185
Reclus de Moliens, 191
Reinmar von Zweter, 34
Relindis, abbess of Hohenbourg, 98
Rheims, 156
Remi, St, 156
Rhenish Psalter, 107, 108, 112
Ripelin, Hugo, 126
Robert of Artois, Count, 197, 198
Robert of Boron, 53
Rolle, Richard, 231
  Ego dormio, 231
Roman de la Rose, 81, 82
Roman des Girart von Roussillon, 83–4
Romulus, 45
Romulus Nilantii, 48
Rondinelli, Scolastica, 140–1
Rothschild Canticles, 212–13, 214–15, 226
Rüdesheim, 101
Rulle convent, 108, 109, 119, 120
Rupert of Deutz, 100
Rupert, St, monastery, 101, 103
Ruth, 185

St Gall, St Catherine's convent, 124, 125
Saint-Mihiel, pericopes books of, 158, 159
Samuel, 176, 177, 179
Sancha of Leon, 159
Sappho, 38
Sarah, wife of Abraham, 174, 175, 184
Sarum Missal, 247, 249, 250
Savonarola, Girolamo, 143
Scholastica, St, 31
Schönensteinbach, 123, 125
Scotland, 156
scribes: *see* writing
scriptoria, 37, 38, 108
Seneca, 51, 191
Sheen, 242, 246
Sherman, Cindy, 77–8
Shirley, John, 243, 244
Shrewsbury, 243, 263
Siena, Santa Maria Maddalena

INDEX

convent, 137
Simon of Goslar, St, 159
Simon of Tongres, 110
Sintram (monk), 118
Smaragdus of Saint-Mihiel, 158
Socrates, 51, 68
Solomon, 51, 53, 86, 172, 177, 179, 187, 218, 219
Somerset, John, 242, 243–4
Southwark, 85
Speculum humanae salvationis, 215, 216, 220, 222
Speyer Gospels, 159
Stagl, Elsbeth, 129
Stimulus Amoris, 214, 215–16, 217
Stratford-upon-Avon, 66
Sturgeon, Richard, 243–4
Swine Priory, Yorks., 71–2
Symeon of Durham, 160
Syon Abbey, 79, 241, 242, 244, 246, 259, 262

Talmud, the, 34
Tamar, 38
Tauler, Johannes, 124, 130
Taymouth Hours, 278
Texery, Bartholomäus, 124
Theodore Gabras, 159
Theodoret, 34
Theophanu, 159
Theudelinde, Princess, 162
Thiers, Jean-Baptiste, 215
Thomas, St, 209

Thomas à Kempis, 273
Toledo, 98
Torelli, Filippo di Matteo, 140
Töss, convent, 129
Trebizond, 159
Trent, Council of, 134, 143
Trinity, the, 13
Tristan, 30
Tristan, prose, 30
Tucherin, Katherina, 124
Turgot, Prior of Durham, 149, 157, 160, 161, 163, 164

Urban V, Pope, 26
Urban VI, Pope, 26
Ursula, St, 89, 125

Valerius Maximus, 84
  Des Faits des Romains, 84
Van Damme, Antonius, 86
Van dem Uorst, Gertrude, 108
Van der Weyden, Rogier, 75, 268, 269
Vecchio, Boccardino, 142
Venice, 146
Villers Miscellany, 205–25 *passim*
Virgil, 162
Virtues, the three, 14, 15
von Sweter, R., 33
von Valkenburg, Johannes, 108, 109, 113

Wakering, John, 243, 262
Warwick, Earl of, 241, 244, 262

Wenceslas, St, 219
Wenceslaus Bible, 85
Werner, 159
Westminster Abbey, 67, 74, 241
Whalley, St Mary's Church, 65–6, 74
Whittington, Richard, 242–3, 261
Wichingham, Denise, 61
Wiegand, abbot of Marienstätt, 206
Wienheusen convent, 115, 116
William I, King, 156
William, abbot of St Thierry, 71
William, Count, (patron of Marie de France), 45, 191
William of Conches, 51
  Moralités des philosophes, 51
William of Gembloux, 101
Winchester Cathedral, 65
  Nunnaminster, Book of, 152, 168
  nunnery, 25
  Psalter, 209
Worcester Cathedral, 67–70
writing, 21–2, 23–34, 49, 52, 67, 79, 98–103, 106–7, 114, 125–7, 128, 142–3, 153–4, 162, 163–4, 191, 234–5, 239–40
Wulfstan, St, bishop of Worcester, 158
Wyleby, Isabella, 271
Wynflæd, 162

Yseult, 30
Yvain, 51, 52, 64